Patriots and Tyrants

Patriots and Tyrants

Ten Asian Leaders

Ross Marlay
and
Clark Neher

ROWMAN & LITTLEFIELD PUBLISHERS, INC.
Lanham • Boulder • New York • Oxford

ROWMAN & LITTLEFIELD PUBLISHERS, INC.

Published in the United States of America
by Rowman & Littlefield Publishers, Inc.
4720 Boston Way, Lanham, Maryland 20706

12 Hid's Copse Road
Cumnor Hill, Oxford OX2 9JJ, England

British Library Cataloguing in Publication Information Available

Library of Congress Cataloging-in-Publication Data

Marlay, Ross.
    Patriots and tyrants : ten Asian leaders / Ross Marlay and Clark
Neher.
        p. cm.
    Includes bibliographical references and index.
    ISBN: 978-0-8476-8442-7

    1. Asia—History—20th century—Biography.   2. Asia—Politics and
government—20th century.   3. Heads of state—Asia—Biography.
4. Nationalists—Asia—Biography.   I. Neher, Clark D.   II. Title.
DS35.M342 1999
950.4'092'2—dc21
[B]   98-52020
                                                                        CIP

Printed in the United States of America

♾ ™ The paper used in this publication meets the minimum requirements of
American National Standard for Information Sciences—Permanence of Paper for
Printed Library Materials, ANSI Z39.48–1992.

To Matthew and Daniel.

*To the people of Asia who gave their lives in
the struggle for freedom and independence.*

Contents

List of Illustrations   ix

Preface   x

1. Introduction   1

    For Further Reading   11

Part I. China   13

    Map of China   14
    China Timeline   15
    The Chinese Setting   19

2. Mao Zedong: The Utopian Warrior   25

3. Deng Xiaoping: The Leninist Capitalist   47

    For Further Reading   71

Part II. Vietnam

    Map of Vietnam   74
    Vietnam Timeline   75
    The Vietnamese Setting   79

4. Ho Chi Minh: The Communist Patriot   89

5. Ngo Dinh Diem: The Conservative Nationalist   115

    For Further Reading   137

Part III. Cambodia   139

    Map of Cambodia   140

Cambodia Timeline 141
The Cambodian Setting 143

6. Norodom Sihanouk: The Populist Prince 151

7. Pol Pot: The Architect of Autogenocide 175

For Further Reading 201

Part IV. Indonesia 203

Map of Indonesia 204
Indonesian Timeline 205
The Indonesian Setting 207

8. Sukarno: The Fiery Emancipator 215

9. Suharto: The Impassive Administrator 239

For Further Reading 259

Part V. India 261

Map of India 262
India Timeline 263
The Indian Setting 265

10. Mohandas Gandhi: The Spiritual Nationalist 271

11. Indira Nehru Gandhi: The Autocratic Democrat 297

For Further Reading 325

Conclusion 327

Glossary 339

Appendix 341

Index 343

About the Authors 355

Illustrations

PHOTOGRAPHS

Mao Zedong, 1925   26
Mao Zedong with Richard Nixon, 1972   26
Deng Xiaoping with Mao Zedong, no date   48
Deng Xiaoping, 1978   48
Ho Chi Minh, no date   90
Ho Chi Minh with Nikita Khrushchev and Mao Zedong, 1959   90
Ngo Dinh Diem with family, 1963   116
Ngo Dinh Diem with Henry Cabot Lodge, 1963   116
Norodom Sihanouk, 1941   152
Norodom Sihanouk, no date   152
Pol Pot, no date   176
Pol Pot, no date   176
Sukarno, no date   216
Sukarno, 1965   216
Suharto with his family, no date   240
Suharto, 1966   240
Mohandas Gandhi, 1895   272
Mohandas Gandhi with Herbert Hoover, 1946   272
Indira Gandhi with Jawaharlal Nehru, 1938   298
Indira Gandhi with her son, Sanjay Gandhi, 1980   298

MAPS

China   14
Vietnam   74
Cambodia   140
Indonesia   204
India   262

CHART

The Nehru–Gandhi Dynasty   324

Preface

This book was inspired by our lifelong fascination with Asia and our desire to understand and explain why modern Asian history and politics has been so tumultuous, and why Asian national leaders have been such forceful personalities. As university teachers, we often have wished for a book that presents the lives of the famous (and infamous) leaders of modern Asia in the light of their national cultures and histories. We intend *Patriots and Tyrants: Ten Asian Leaders* to be that book. Our approach is to juxtapose the personal characteristics of these ten leaders—their beliefs, goals, strategies, styles, tactics, even their gimmicks—with the political cultures of the nations that they led to triumph or to catastrophe. We have made comparisons and offered judgments—how could we do otherwise when considering the legacies of leaders so different as Mohandas Gandhi and Pol Pot? Nevertheless, we encourage readers to look at the facts and reach their own conclusions.

We were fortunate to have received encouragement from friends such as Jane Gates and M. Ladd Thomas. We would especially like to thank, for their generous contributions of knowledge and time, colleagues who read portions of the manuscript: Richard Cooler, David England, Ben Kiernan, Afak Haydar, Dwight King, Judy Ledgerwood, Suzanne Marlay, Patric McCormick, Vijayan Pillai, Susan Russell, William Topich, Paul van der Veur, Brantly Womack, and Qidong Zhang. These scholars offered many constructive suggestions. Of course we, not they, are responsible for any errors that may remain.

For help with bibliographic research we thank Mai Kyi Win, director of the Donn V. Hart Collection of the Founders Library at Northern Illinois University (NIU); Nancy Schuneman and Robert Vore of NIU's Center for Southeast Asian Studies; and Jeff Bailey, Willis Brenner, Margaret McDaniels, and Patsy Spurlock of the Dean B. Ellis Library at Arkansas State University. Many others helped us uncover background information on Asian leaders: Robert Dayley, I Ketut Putra Erawan, Yoshinori Kaseda, Ajaz Ali Khan, Jeffrey Lattimer, Chartchai Norasethaporn, David Oldfield, Bryan Ulmer, and Warner Winborne.

We would especially like to thank Jody Berman for reading our manuscript with a fine eye. To Susan McEachern, our editor extraordinaire at Rowman & Littlefield, who encouraged and guided us at every stage of this endeavor, our sincere appreciation.

1

Introduction

> Life can only be understood backwards; but it must be lived forwards.
>
> Søren Kierkegaard

LEADERSHIP

Political scientists and sociologists have found the concept of leadership to be elusive. Yet it is hard to treat the subject dispassionately because leadership carries an enormous potential for good or evil. Because of great differences from one culture to another, patterns may be difficult to see. Leadership may be fleeting, based on temporary circumstances, or it may become nearly permanent. It may be limited to a specific sphere of human activity (a religious leader in a secular polity, for example) or expanded to embrace nearly everything in society (as when Josef Stalin claimed to be a genius of literature, science, and military strategy). No one has yet formulated a satisfactorily rigorous or universal definition of leadership, but as a starting point we posit five basic elements in political leadership: the leader, his ideas, his organization, the followers, and the situation.

Political leadership can only be understood within its cultural and historical context. There are no leaders without followers, and common people have their own hopes, dreams, and fears. Their values and prejudices can be molded, but not ignored, by those who would lead them. National cultures may be related—we may validly speak of Southern Asian civilization, for example, or East Asian civilization, but each country also has its own unique culture. By focusing on two different leaders from each country we demonstrate that there is no single type of leader that fits each culture. In some cases the two leaders' goals are similar, but their means differ.

NATIONALISM

We live in the age of the nation-state. The Latin root of the word *nation* is the same as that of *native: nasci*, to be born. Thus, one's nation is a primordial identity. But until modern times most people derived their psychological identity from their clan, village, occupation, or religion. Only in the past two hundred years, since the French Revolution, has the claim of the nation-state superseded all others.

Nationalism spread across Asia as a consequence of Western imperialism. The colonial powers paved the way for their own expulsion by bringing Asians into contact with European ideas of national sovereignty while at the same time denying Asian countries that sovereignty. The temporary eclipse of European power in Asia during World War II encouraged Asian nationalists to believe they might become independent after the war. Asian nationalist leaders did not seek to restore the old precolonial order; rather they sought to shape a new society on the model of Western nations.

Because all national identities are synthetic but must be made to seem natural, "fragile identifications with the new national entities are nurtured by mass loyalty to the leader," who must personify the new national values.[1] In the following chapters, we show how our ten Asian leaders defined patriotism, how they molded their images to fit the preexisting culture, and how they set out to transform that culture, to take what they thought was the best of the old and adapt it to the modern age.

THE BIOGRAPHICAL APPROACH

Men and women—not vague forces, trends, or movements—make history. People make choices; often they are torn between what they think is right and what seems necessary. History and politics are riveting precisely because they are suffused with moral drama. The biographical approach brings history to life. Because life must be lived forward, and causes must precede effects, history unfolds chronologically and so do our chapters.

We have blended biography with political analysis. For example, we propose reasons why Mao Zedong's dream of human equality produced the nightmarish Great Proletarian Cultural Revolution, why Ngo Dinh Diem's government in South Vietnam fell despite almost unlimited money and advice from the United States, why Mohandas Gandhi's program of righteous living could not be achieved, and why there is such terrible fury in Cambodian politics. Certainly, there can be no single reason why 1.7 million Cambodians died under Pol Pot. We have tried at all times to avoid the temptation of unicausal explanation.

THE "GREAT MAN" DEBATE

The reader is invited to try to answer the question, Who makes history, the "great man" or "the masses"? Thomas Carlyle wrote that "the history of what man has accomplished in this world is at bottom the history of the Great Men who have worked here."[2] The other side of this long-standing intellectual debate was forthrightly stated by Friedrich Nietzsche, who wrote that "eleven out of twelve great men of history were only agents of a great cause."[3]

To understand history and politics as more than random happenings, people devise categories. Yet if we carry this too far we risk falling into the Marxian fallacy that a great tide of events sweeps everyone along, and that individuals cannot make much of a difference. Ironically, the history of communism is the story of enormously powerful individuals such as Vladimir Lenin, Stalin, Mao, Ho Chi Minh, Fidel Castro, and Pol Pot. It is hard to believe that the world would be the same if these men had never been born.

The English philosopher Herbert Spencer points to a way out of this impasse: "If it be a fact that the great man may modify his nation in its structure and actions, it is also a fact that there must have been those antecedent modifications constituting national progress before he could be evolved. Before he can re-make his society, his society must make him."[4]

GENDER AND LEADERSHIP

In none of our five countries—China, Vietnam, Cambodia, Indonesia, and India—do women have political status, access, or influence equal to that of men. These countries are patriarchal societies in which women have traditionally been subordinate to men, especially in public. With rare exceptions, men have also held all the major positions of leadership. In Asia, sexual inequality is still the norm.

However, there are clear signs of change. A prominent feature of Chinese communism is a policy of reducing gender differences and promoting equality. Mao's regime put an end to child marriage, foot-binding, concubinage, and female infanticide, and gave women the right to divorce and to receive inheritances. Nevertheless, Chinese women have been excluded from most positions of political leadership.

In India women have enjoyed improved access to schools and universities, and prejudice against them in their professions has lessened, but Indira Gandhi's strong leadership did not reflect a new view about women.

In Vietnam the Communist Party proclaimed equality between the sexes, but virtually the entire communist leadership has been male. Few women are to be found in the bureaucracy. Men also dominate Vietnamese industry. The Vietnamese family remains patriarchal and authoritarian. Despite the affirmation of women's equality in the Vietnamese constitution, most women still perform household chores and unskilled labor.

A surprising number of Asian countries have been led by women in recent years. Without exception, these female leaders inherited power as wives, widows, or daughters of famous men. President Corazon Aquino of the Philippines was the widow of Senator Benigno Aquino, a martyr of the anti-Marcos movement. Prime Minister Benazir Bhutto of Pakistan was the daughter of Prime Minister Zulfikar Ali Bhutto, who was executed by the general who overthrew him. The Burmese opposition leader Aung San Suu Kyi is the daughter of independence movement hero General Aung San. Indian Prime Minister Indira Gandhi was groomed for leadership by her father, Prime Minister Jawaharlal Nehru. A leader of opponents of Indonesia's President Suharto was Megawati Sukarnoputri, daughter of President Sukarno. These determined, courageous women were accepted as political leaders because of their family background.

CONTEMPORARY ASIA

The twentieth century brought profound changes to Asia. In 1900 most Asian countries were colonies or semicolonies. Although by the end of the century, all were independent, not all were free. The popular appeal of radicalism has diminished. In China, Cambodia, and Vietnam charismatic leaders have been replaced by pragmatists. Vietnam now welcomes investors and tourists.

Economics is in command throughout Asia. Following the advice of experts from the World Bank and the International Monetary Fund (IMF) and used to pursue an export-oriented development strategy, Asia has become the most rapidly developing part of the world. The new wealth is not always equitably distributed, though, and is accompanied by significant social pathologies.

Today's Asian leaders face new challenges, quite unlike the revolutions and independence struggles waged by Mao Zedong of China, Sukarno of Indonesia, Mohandas Gandhi of India, Prince Norodom Sihanouk and Pol Pot of Cambodia, and Ho Chi Minh of Vietnam. Today's leaders grapple with the IMF and the international trading environment. Their followers are different, too—less likely to want charisma from their national leaders, more interested in maintaining and improving their standards of living. Today's Asians receive information from a wide variety of sources. Moreover, they are healthier and better educated than any previous generation.

Mass involvement in politics is a new phenomenon in the countries of Asia, at odds with traditional hierarchical social patterns. Leaders must now take popular opinion into account.

PURPOSES OF THIS BOOK

This book has three goals: (1) to present biographies of ten giants of twentieth-century Asian political history—men and women who, for better or worse, transformed their countries; (2) to interpret the histories, cultures, and politics of five Asian countries using a human-centered approach; and (3) to stimulate the reader to think about the relationship between political leadership and nationalism.

Here are the lives of ten great Asian leaders who, by their ideas and their political zeal, changed history. Some recast their countries by force of arms, others by the power of their thought. One was hailed as a saint; another was universally condemned as a moral monster. Some of these leaders were born into poverty, others into privilege. Some were democrats, some were autocrats, and some were communists. But however great their differences, each can claim to be an authentic nationalist.

The ten biographical chapters focus on Mao Zedong and Deng Xiaoping of China, Mohandas Gandhi and Indira Gandhi of India, Ho Chi Minh and Ngo Dinh Diem of Vietnam, Norodom Sihanouk and Pol Pot of Cambodia, and Sukarno and Suharto of Indonesia. These patriots and tyrants exhibit radically different personalities and leadership styles. Three countries (India, China, and Indonesia) were chosen for their intrinsic importance. The other two (Vietnam and Cambodia) were chosen because of their special interest to American readers. Asia's three broad regions are represented: East Asia (China), Southeast Asia (Vietnam, Cambodia, and Indonesia), and southern Asia (India).

Many other Asian patriots have led equally dramatic lives—for example, Chiang Kai-shek of China, Kim Il Sung and Kim Dae Jung of Korea, Aung San Suu Kyi of Burma, Phumipol Adunyadej of Thailand, Lee Kuan Yew of Singapore, and Ferdinand Marcos and Corazon Aquino of the Philippines. We hope that this volume will encourage other scholars to employ the biographical method to illuminate the political histories of other countries in Asia and elsewhere.

The book is divided into five parts, one for each Asian country. We begin each part with a description of the country's setting—its geography, demography, culture, and history. In all five countries glorious kingdoms and empires rose and fell for centuries, even millennia, before Europeans arrived to colonize and "civilize" Asians. Indeed, the fundamental insight required to understand Asian nationalism is the depth of Asian history and the intricacy of Asian culture. Asians had good reason to feel shocked, humiliated, and angry at the apparent ease with which the Western powers subjugated them. Colonialism disrupted traditional economies, undermined native elite classes, upset village life, and created "new men" who were not accepted as equals by Europeans but who could not return to their villages, either.

In the biographical chapters we present details of the future leader's background and childhood, his or her formative influences, education, personal attributes, early political activities, and entry into national politics. In some cases (especially for Mohandas Gandhi, who compulsively recorded nearly every thought that entered his mind) we drew on a wealth of information, but in other cases (Diem, Pol Pot, and Suharto) these leaders never revealed details of their youth. In all cases the actions of each leader, once in power, are well recorded, although when dealing with communist disinformation (in China, Vietnam, and Cambodia) we must be cautious in interpreting official accounts.

We have tried to show how Asian leaders used modern means of mass communication (newspapers, radio, film, television, posters) to shape their images to appeal to the masses and how, once in power, they created national institutions, distributed patronage, and manipulated foreigners to maintain and deepen their hold on power. We also draw attention to what happens to men and women who accumulate too much power. This is the eternal dilemma of politics: Rulers must have enough power to accomplish national goals, but then the power often goes to their heads and warps their judgment. In Lord Acton's famous observation, "Power corrupts and absolute power corrupts absolutely." At least four of our leaders—Mao, Ho, Sihanouk, and Sukarno—constructed or tolerated a personality cult. Most felt divine guidance at some point in their careers. Some even began to believe themselves infallible. With Asian family ties being very strong, these leaders relied on kinship networks for support. Some relied heavily on their siblings and spouses for honest advice. Some even tried to pass power down to their children. Many fell into what Westerners call nepotism.

We end each chapter with an evaluation of the leader's accomplishments and failures and also provide a short list of selected readings for those who want to dig deeper.

THE LEADERS

Mao Zedong, the utopian Chinese communist ideologue, was equally at home on the battlefield and in his study. He was a warrior and a revolutionary leader and, more than anyone else, was responsible for designing the communist system his party imposed on one-fifth of humankind. A master of mass persuasion, Mao stamped his personality on modern China. During his lifetime, the national goal was perfect equality of all Chinese. But Mao's grandiose dreams, his neglect of details, his ruthlessness, and his rejection of compromise brought catastrophe to tens of millions of people, especially during his two sweeping mobilization campaigns, the Great Leap Forward and the Great Proletarian Cultural Revolution. Mao must be placed alongside Adolf Hitler and Joseph Stalin to form a trinity of twentieth-century totalitarian leaders, but Mao is still widely admired whereas the other two are reviled.

Deng Xiaoping, Mao's disciple and successor, was in most ways his absolute opposite. Deng was a pragmatist who jettisoned ideological orthodoxy. That is why we call him a Leninist capitalist. Deng reversed nearly all Mao's policies. His goal was to release the competitive spirit he knew the Chinese still possessed, even after decades of state socialism. Deng propelled China into a new era of prosperity. His greatest achievement was to open China's windows to the rest of the world, but he rejected democracy as understood in the West. It was Deng who ordered the suppression of student demonstrators at Tiananmen Square in 1989.

Ho Chi Minh was a revolutionary communist and a Vietnamese patriot. Marx and Lenin considered patriotism to be a fetish. The interests of the world's workers, they said, transcend national borders. Ho showed that the most compelling brand of communism was national (patriotic) Marxism. Surprisingly, Ho Chi Minh's remarkable life story is little known to most Americans, even though he dealt them their first defeat in war. Ho is an elusive quarry for the biographer, who must try to pluck facts from the many myths that surround him. On the run for half of his long life, Ho used many aliases and definitely enjoyed creating an aura of mystery about himself. Ho Chi Minh was both patriot and tyrant, liberator and imprisoner of his people. His lifelong goal was to win Vietnamese independence and to unite the country under his communist leadership.

Ngo Dinh Diem was a conservative nationalist, no less patriotic than Ho Chi Minh but ideologically pointed in the opposite direction. By striking contrast with Ho the populist, Diem was an isolated mandarin. The Catholic president of a Buddhist country, Diem was completely unable to—indeed, did not see any reason to—gain the admiration of his people. Although possessing many traits that Vietnamese expected of a mandarin, Diem proved unable to create a nation, or even sustain the half-nation called South Vietnam. Lyndon Johnson compared Diem to Winston Churchill, but to many Vietnamese he seemed little more than a lackey of foreigners. That was untrue—had Diem been a lackey, the United States ambassador would not have schemed to have him assassinated.

Norodom Sihanouk was sui generis—a populist monarch. His entire life was a bundle of contradictions and paradoxes. Who could have foreseen that the callow youth whom the French picked to be their Cambodian puppet prince would evolve into a fiery nationalist, then make common cause with the communists? Sihanouk was either a supreme genius or a supreme fool—or perhaps a little of both. He was a seeker of pleasure who collaborated with fanatic ascetics. Sihanouk's lifelong goal was a free, neutral Cambodia, but his people paid the price for his inability to imagine how savage the Khmer Rouge (Cambodian communists) could be.

Pol Pot was the architect of Cambodia's autogenocide. The ominous, faceless leader of the Khmer Rouge, Pol Pot sought to retain complete anonymity while revolutionizing Cambodian society. When Phnom Penh fell to his soldiers in the spring of 1975, few people inside or outside Cambodia even knew his real name, Saloth Sar. Over the next three years the truth trickled out: Pol Pot was a maniacal communist whose goal was wholly to re-create society. This entailed the murder of about one-fourth of Cambodia's population. At the end of his life, when he was tried by his comrades, who were no less bloodthirsty than he, the world got its first televised look at Pol Pot. He looked like a bland, ordinary grandfather.

Sukarno was the father of modern Indonesia. Endowed with an extraordinary ability to project his lively personality to crowds, Sukarno forged a nation. He was the unquestioned leader of Indonesia's independence movement and became its first president. Sukarno was not ruthless or overly ideological. He always had to balance the many opposing forces around him. Sometimes he leaned toward his conservative army officers and the even more conservative Islamists; other times he favored the Indonesian Communist Party and its peasant followers. He loved to deliver passionate, almost hypnotic speeches, but he hated the mundane details of government administration. Political discord turned to turmoil and then to chaos, until Sukarno was deposed by his own army. Decades after his death, his name still evokes nostalgia among his people.

Suharto, the army general who forced Sukarno into retirement, surrounded himself with Western-oriented technocrats who transformed Indonesia's dysfunctional socialist system into a moderately productive capitalist economy. Suharto projected himself as the antithesis of Sukarno. His "New Order" regime was considered a model for economic development in the Third World, at least until the Asian currency crisis of 1997–98, but there was a dark side to Suharto's rule, as the people of East Timor—and anyone else who publicly opposed him—learned.

Mohandas Gandhi was a spiritual nationalist. Gandhi believed in the equality of human souls and regarded the existing division of humankind into separate nations as a great deceit, but he struggled with the reality that Indians were unjustly dominated by Englishmen. Gandhi was a deep and original thinker who merged Christianity and Hinduism into a harmonious body of religious thought and social practice. His achievement of Indian independence without revolution puts him in a class by himself. His doctrine of nonviolent political action has universal and enduring relevance.

Indira Gandhi (no relation to Mohandas Gandhi) was a pragmatic prime minister of India during a time of tension. We call her an autocratic democrat to highlight the contradictions in her nature and her actions. Indira Gandhi's political agenda included socialism and a kind of personal authoritarianism. She flirted with dictatorship but ultimately bowed to adverse judgments of the courts. She was a modernizer who repudiated Mohandas Gandhi's fixation on the past, yet her patriotism was every bit as ardent as his. Mrs. Gandhi could be arrogant and haughty, though many people believed that India needed just such a forceful leader. Like Mohandas Gandhi, she died at the hands of vengeful religious assassins.

QUESTIONS ABOUT ASIAN LEADERSHIP

We ask the reader to keep these questions in mind:

1. Are there certain personality traits that all leaders possess?
2. What personal satisfaction does a leader seek? For example, is he compensating for perceived inadequacy or trying to please a long-dead father?
3. Is there such a thing as "Asian leadership"?
4. Is there a distinct category of revolutionary leaders? Revolutionaries are visionaries who succeed when they can transmit their vision to others. They seize power violently and may then try to overturn the entire social order. Can we analyze revolutionary leaders using the same categories we would use to analyze a nonrevolutionary leader?
5. Are there particular characteristics of political leadership in developing countries?
6. Does leadership in communist systems differ fundamentally from leadership in noncommunist systems? Is it always bloodier?
7. Do leaders inevitably succumb to the corruption of power?
8. Is nationalism such a dominant force in the present world that all leaders must be nationalists?
9. Does leadership inevitably become oligarchic or can a single dictator maintain control indefinitely?
10. Do the masses actually want to participate in politics or would they rather be led?

ACKNOWLEDGMENT OF SUBJECTIVITY

Pupul Jayakar, in her fine biography of Indira Gandhi, writes that a serious biography is "a dialogue between the author and the unfolding personality of the person portrayed."[5] We have strived to conduct such a dialogue in the following pages. We acknowledge, but do not apologize for, our own preferences for civil liberties, human rights, and political democracy. At the same time, we have always tried to bear in mind the profound differences between Asian and Western civilizations.

NOTES

1. Lester G. Seligman, "Political Aspects of Leadership," in *International Encyclopedia of the Social Sciences,* ed. David L. Sills (New York: Free Press, 1979), p. 107.

2. Thomas Carlyle, "The Leader As Hero," in *Political Leadership: A Source Book,* ed. Barbara Kellerman (Pittsburgh: University of Pittsburgh Press, 1986), p. 5.

3. Rudolf Flesch, ed., *The New Book of Unusual Quotations* (New York: Harper & Row, 1966) p. 147.

4. Herbert Spencer, "The Great Man Theory Breaks Down," in *Political Leadership,* pp. 13–14.

5. Pupul Jayakar, *Indira Gandhi: A Biography* (New Delhi: Penguin Books India, 1992), p. ix.

For Further Reading

Anderson, Benedict. *Imagined Communities: Reflections on the Origin and Spread of Nationalism*. London: Verso, 1986.

Bailey, F. G. *Humbuggery and Manipulation: The Art of Leadership*. Ithaca, N.Y.: Cornell University Press, 1988.

Blondel, Jean. *Political Leadership: Towards a General Analysis*. London: Sage, 1987.

Burns, James MacGregor. *Leadership*. New York: Harper & Row, 1978.

Chirot, Daniel. *Modern Tyrants: The Power and Prevalence of Evil in Our Age*. New York: Free Press, 1994.

Downton, James V., Jr. *Rebel Leadership: Commitment and Charisma in the Revolutionary Process*. New York: Free Press, 1973.

Folkertsma, Marvin J., Jr. *Ideology and Leadership*. Englewood Cliffs, N.J.: Prentice-Hall, 1988.

Gardner, John W. *On Leadership*. New York: Free Press, 1990.

Greenfeld, Liah. *Nationalism: Five Roads to Modernity*. Cambridge, Mass.: Harvard University Press, 1992.

Hobsbawm, E. J. *Nations and Nationalism Since 1780: Programme, Myth, Reality*. Cambridge: Cambridge University Press, 1990.

Kellerman, Barbara, ed. *Political Leadership: A Source Book*. Pittsburgh: University of Pittsburgh Press, 1986.

Oliver, Robert T. *Leadership in Asia: Persuasive Communication in the Making of Nations, 1850–1950*. Newark: University of Delaware Press, 1989.

Rejai, Mostafa, and Kay Phillips. *Loyalists and Revolutionaries*. New York: Praeger, 1988.

Rosenbach, William E., and Robert L. Taylor, eds. *Contemporary Issues in Leadership*. Boulder, Colo.: Westview Press, 1993.

Willner, Ann Ruth. *The Spellbinders: Charismatic Political Leadership*. New Haven, Conn.: Yale University Press, 1984.

Wills, Gary. *Certain Trumpets: The Call of Leaders*. New York: Simon & Schuster, 1994.

Part I

China

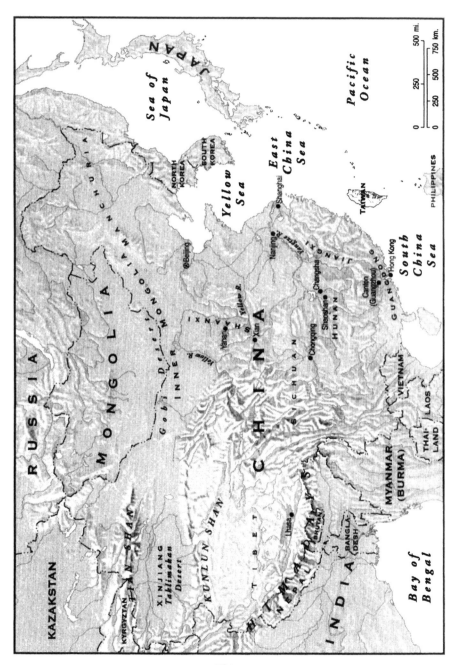

China

China Timeline

1700–1100 B.C.	Shang dynasty. Agricultural civilization flourishes in the Yellow River valley of north China.
1100–156 B.C.	Chou dynasty. Confucius and other philosophers define Chinese "high" civilization.
221–206 B.C.	Ch'in dynasty. Totalitarian rule.
202 B.C.–A.D. 220	Han dynasty. The classical age of China.
618–906	T'ang dynasty. At first militaristic, but then produced a great flowering of culture.
960–1279	Sung dynasty. Delicate and refined but fell to the Mongols.
1279–1368	Yuan (Mongol) dynasty.
1368–1644	Ming dynasty. The last "native" Chinese dynasty.
1644–1911	Manchu (Qing) dynasty.
1840–42	First Opium War.
1864	Taiping Rebellion crushed.
1893 Dec 26	Mao Zedong born in Hunan.
1894–95	Sino-Japanese War.
1898	Hundred Days of Reform.
1900	Boxer Rebellion.
1905	Sun Yat-sen founds "General League" in Tokyo.
1908	Emperor dies, Empress Dowager selects a three-year-old replacement and then dies herself the next day.
1911–12	Chinese "revolution" of Sun Yat-sen.
1912 Feb 12	Sun Yat-sen resigns in favor of Yuan Shikai.
1915 Jan	Japan's "21 Demands."
1916	Various provinces declare independence of Beijing; warlord period begins.
1919	May Fourth Movement.
1921 Jul 1	Chinese Communist Party (CCP) founded, Shanghai (fifty members).

1923	Tactical alliance between CCP and Sun Yat-sen's Kuomintang (KMT).
1925 Mar	Sun Yat-sen dies; Chiang Kai-shek becomes KMT leader.
1926 Nov	Mao returns to Hunan.
1927 April	Chiang massacres workers in Shanghai.
1927 Sept 9	Mao organizes "Autumn Harvest Uprising" in Hunan; it fails.
1930 Sep	Japanese invade Manchuria.
1931 Nov	Mao chairman of Jiangxi Soviet.
1934 Oct	Long March begins.
1935 Oct	8,000 of original 96,000 Long Marchers arrive in Shaanxi.
1936	Mao establishes base at Yanan.
1937	Rape of Nanjing.
1938	Mao writes *On the New Stage, On the Protracted War,* and *Strategic Problems in the Anti-Japanese War.*
1939	Mao marries Jiang Qing.
1940 Jan	Mao writes *On New Democracy,* justifying the united front policy.
1945 Aug	Japan surrenders, ending World War II.
1945–49	Renewed civil war.
1949 Apr	People's Liberation Army crosses the Yangtze and takes Nanjing.
1949 Oct 1	Proclamation of the People's Republic of China (PRC).
1950 June 25	Korean War begins.
1957 May–Jun	Hundred Flowers Movement at its height; a severe shock to CCP.
1958 Feb	Great Leap Forward announced.
1959 Jul–Aug	Lushan plenum (Mao criticized).
1960 Summer	Soviet technicians withdrawn from China.
1960–62	Widespread famine in PRC.
1962	Sino-Indian War.
1964 May	First publication of *Quotations from Chairman Mao Zedong.*
1964 Oct	China detonates first atomic bomb.
1966	Great Proletarian Cultural Revolution begins.
1969 Mar	Chinese and Soviet forces clash on the Ussuri River.
1971 July	Secretary of State Henry Kissinger in Beijing.
1971 Sept	Lin Biao incident.
1972 Feb	President Richard Nixon visits.
1976 Jan 8	Death of Zhou Enlai.
1976 Sept 9	Mao dies.
1976 Oct 6	Gang of Four arrested.

1977 July	Deng Xiaoping rehabilitated politically.
1978 Dec	Communist Party commits to economic modernization.
1979 Jan	Deng visits Washington.
1979 Feb	China invades Vietnam.
1986	Pro-democracy demonstrations in Beijing.
1989	Tiananmen massacre.
1992	Deng tours special economic zones.
1997 Feb 19	Deng dies.
1997 Jul 1	Hong Kong peacefully reverts to Chinese sovereignty.
1998 Jun 27	President Bill Clinton meets President Jiang Zemin in Beijing.

The Chinese Setting

China has always excited the curiosity of Westerners. Centuries before Europeans knew anything specific about "Cathay," they perceived that a great civilization lay in the Far East, one with large cities, ancient learning, and the ability to produce fine luxury goods such as silk and porcelain. Everything about China seemed exotic. The country had a wall around it. Its provinces had poetic names such as Peaceful Honor and Prosperity Found. Its people spoke a tonal language that sounded to Europeans like singing. Chinese calligraphy was complex but beautiful. Public buildings had multiple roofs that curved upward. Written descriptions by Marco Polo, who reached China overland in the thirteenth century, and accounts by later explorers and missionaries, gave rise to an odd duality in Western opinions of China: It was either an earthly paradise or a land of unspeakable barbarity. Even today our thinking is clouded by this old incongruity.

China's physical immensity, its impressively large population, and its highly refined culture give it weight and centrality in East Asian affairs. Indeed, China's name for itself, Chung-kuo (Central State) connotes a sense of cultural superiority as well as geographic centrality. The Chinese knew no equals, only "barbarians." As the distinguished China scholar Lucian Pye has written:

> China is not just another nation-state in the family of nations. China is a civilization pretending to be a state. The story of modern China could be described as the effort by both Chinese and foreigners to squeeze a civilization into the arbitrary, constraining framework of the modern state, an institutional invention that came out of the fragmentation of the West's own civilization.[1]

GEOGRAPHY

China's boundaries fluctuated with the fortunes of its dynasties, and they were not delineated until modern times. The country has always been very large compared to its immediate neighbors. The area of the People's Repub-

lic of China (PRC) is slightly greater than that of the United States. Its range
of climate and topography is correspondingly wide. The Yellow River valley
of northern China is considered the country's cultural core. This region has
cold winters and hot summers. It is prone to periodic droughts but also to
terrible floods that, however great their toll, renew the land. Manchuria, the
northeast part of the PRC, was until recently (half a millennium is recent in
Chinese history) not a part of China at all but a great forest harboring fierce
nomads who sometimes broke through the Great Wall. Southern China,
from Shanghai to the Vietnamese border, is a subtropical region of jagged
mountains and fertile valleys, where proper terracing and irrigation paddies
have yielded rice for a score of centuries with no need for fallow years. The
southern China coast has many fine deepwater ports, but this was unimportant to the introspective empire—until the arrival of Westerners. Neighboring countries (Vietnam, Tibet, Mongolia, Korea) acknowledged Chinese su-
zerainty, but not sovereignty, by sending periodic tribute missions bearing
the special products of their lands to the Han court.[2]

CULTURE

China never had an institutionalized religion that stood in opposition to the
state, the way Christianity and Islam did in lands further west. What we call
"Chinese religion" is a syncretic mixture of Daoism, Confucianism, and
Buddhism, with a strong dose of native superstition thrown in. In Chinese
society the individual was subordinate to the group, particularly to the patriarchal family, which was the basic social unit. Relations within the family
followed a rigid hierarchy, from the eldest male, who was revered for generations after his death, to the youngest female, who might be drowned if necessary to leave enough food for the others.

   Politically, the Confucian state had three elements: the villages, the bureaucracy, and the emperor. At the bottom lay innumerable villages isolated
by mountain ranges and bad roads. These villages were governed by elders
and headmen, and were terra incognita to the central authorities, who usually left them alone as long as they paid their taxes and supplied labor for
public works, particularly flood control dikes. At the county and province
level, authority rested with the world's most highly elaborated bureaucracy.
The meritocratic Chinese civil service was open to scholars who proved their
mastery of Confucian classics in demanding written examinations. These bureaucrats usually dominated the national government, too, leaving the emperor to perform rituals that put the country in harmony with the heavens. If
the emperor performed the correct sacrifices, there would be good harvests,
prosperity, and social peace. But if there came a drought, a flood, pestilence,
or an earthquake, that showed that the emperor no longer enjoyed the   man-

date of heaven." Rebellion was justified until a new dynasty arose to set things right.

Rebellion against a failing dynasty in China was not the same thing as ideological dissent in the West: "The political, ideological and cultural worlds have always coincided, and they make up a monolithic whole. Beyond that whole, there was no alternative for the individual conscience: to reject the orthodoxy in power meant not only to exclude oneself from society, but also to turn one's back on civilization, to reject the human condition."[3]

Confucian culture favored males over females. Women were taught obedience and respect. Even an old woman was considered lowly compared to her young son. Chinese females faced possible infanticide, foot-binding, and arranged marriages. Mao Zedong strongly favored the liberation of Chinese women, and the communist regime took many steps toward this end, including granting Chinese women the right to divorce. But the only woman who exercised real power in recent times was Mao's wife, who was popularly referred to as "the white-boned demon." The advent of ultrasound technology shows that old attitudes persist in China. Couples who learn that they are expecting a girl may opt for an abortion in the hope that the next conception will bring a boy.

HISTORICAL CONTEXT

Recent archaeological discoveries have confirmed what the Chinese people always believed, that theirs is one of the oldest civilizations on earth and that it achieved a very high level of sophistication at an early date. A set of bells unearthed in 1978 from the fourth century B.C. tomb in Hubei Province were found to be tuned accurately with respect to one another and to an absolute standard governed by powers of two. Swords found in the astonishing tomb of Emperor Qin Shihuang (buried 210 B.C.) are made of copper, tin, and thirteen other elements including nickel, magnesium, and cobalt. The Chinese invented gunpowder, paper, the magnetic compass, the wheelbarrow, and cast iron. But these they regarded as less important than their poetry, art, and above all their Confucian doctrine, which, if followed, promised social harmony.

In 1793 when the Qing (Manchu) dynasty was at the zenith of its power, the emperor sent an edict to King George III of England, rejecting British demands for diplomatic and commercial relations. Its tone was haughty but tragically naive:

> If you assert that your reverence for Our Celestial dynasty fills you with a desire to acquire our civilization, our ceremonies and code of laws differ so completely from your own that, even if your Envoy were able to acquire the rudi-

ments of our civilization, you could not possibly transplant our manners and customs to your alien soil. . . . As your Ambassador can see for himself, we possess all things. I set no value on objects strange or ingenious, and have no use for your country's manufactures.[4]

Because of its supreme self-assurance, China was ill-prepared for the inevitable confrontation with European powers. During the First Opium War, the Chinese asked themselves why their cannons, on firm ground, were inaccurate while British guns, on bobbing ships, hit their mark. They concluded that it must be due to the evil sorcery of the barbarians' religion.

China never lost its formal independence but through a series of unequal treaties was reduced to the status of a semicolony. Guangdong Province in the south was a British sphere of influence; Yunnan was for the French, Shandong for the Germans, Manchuria for the Russians, and Taiwan for the Japanese. The humiliations are remembered—and resented—today. Most galling was the burning of the summer palace by British troops in 1860.

Even remote villages were bankrupted because the outflow of silver to pay reparations every time China lost a battle eventually debased the currency. In addition, the cottage industries that sustained self-sufficient peasant families during the slack season were ruined by imported cloth and tools. Landlords collected rent years in advance and took the money to the port cities where they traded with the foreigners. Those cities swelled with refugees from the countryside who came looking for any way to feed themselves. Some men went abroad to work as laborers. They built railroads across the American West and dug the Panama Canal.

Amazingly, despite all the misfortunes that befell China during the centuries of Western ascendancy, the population tripled from an estimated 150 million in 1600 to 450 million in 1900. Whole new social classes developed that had no place in the traditional Confucian social order. Because few Westerners other than missionaries were interested in, or capable of, learning to speak and write Chinese, interpreters were needed, as well as foremen, bookkeepers, and go-betweens. The immiseration of the peasantry deepened. In theory any family could rise to wealth and social prominence if a gifted son could pass the civil service entrance examinations. But most often village families remained for generations illiterate, superstitious, submissive, politically powerless, and very poor.

By the early twentieth century, Chinese intellectuals were in despair. It was clear that the old regime was tottering, but what would follow? The European powers might divide China into separate colonial states, never to be reunited. Thomas Huxley's *Evolution and Ethics* was enormously influential; if the Social Darwinists were correct, the Chinese race might even become extinct. Some people thought China had already Westernized too much and must return to ancient traditions to save itself. However, the ghastly aftermath of the Taiping Rebellion (1851 64) and the blind hopelessness of the Boxer Rebellion (1900) forever discredited that line of thinking. Other people thought that Japan showed the way: Asians must imitate the West in order to fend off the West. If the Japanese, whom the Chinese called "dwarf barbarians," could modernize in thirty years, then China should be able to modernize in only three! At least that was the theory behind a brief reform movement in 1898. Many young Chinese forsook study of the Confucian classics for Western medicine, mathematics, engineering, and European languages. Inevitably, some used their command of French, English, and German to read Voltaire, Montesquieu, Locke—and Marx.

Young men who studied abroad and then returned to China were especially influential. They knew that there was nothing magical about Western culture, except that the emancipation of the common man or of the "masses," as the Marxists phrased it, unleashed hitherto undreamt-of power that could make even a small country like Belgium great. Perhaps a political revolution could restore lost greatness to the Central Kingdom.

In the early decades of the twentieth century all politically active Chinese were revolutionaries; the only question was what path to follow. One way seemed well marked: Karl Marx and his followers claimed to have discovered the scientifically correct laws of history. Mao Zedong and other Chinese communists believed they needed only to master Marxism and then modify it as necessary to suit Chinese conditions. The non-Marxist path, chosen by Sun Yat-sen and Chiang Kai-shek, was more indefinite. Sun and Chiang were never able to articulate a clear ideology; their Kuomintang (KMT) propounded a vague and sometimes contradictory mixture of nationalism and socialism, authoritarianism and democracy. As time went by, the KMT's ideological formulas became less important than its social base, which consisted of landlords and military officers. By contrast the Chinese Communist Party (CCP) drew its support from Chinese peasants. The latter constituted fully 80 percent of the Chinese population and were, in Mao's famous phrase, "poor and blank."

Mao Zedong and his communist followers forged a new China, but one of his lieutenants, a diminutive man named Deng Xiaoping, understood that rigid Marxism had to yield to a market economy for China to keep up with the rest of the world.

NOTES

1. Lucian W. Pye, "China: Erratic State, Frustrated Society," *Foreign Affairs* 69 (fall 1990), p. 58.

2. The term *Han*, referring originally to a dynasty contemporaneous with the Roman Empire, has acquired a racial connotation. Han Chinese, the "sons of the

Yellow Emperor," are distinguished from non-Han citizens of the People's Republic of China, such as Tibetans, Mongols, Manchus, Uighurs, and Tai.

3. Simon Leys, *Chinese Shadows* (New York: Penguin, 1978), p. 205.

4. "An Imperial Edict to the King of England," as reproduced in *East Meets West* (San Francisco: Field Educational Publications, 1969), p. 35.

2

Mao Zedong: The Utopian Warrior

Everything is turning upside down. I love great upheavals.

Mao Zedong, 1966

Mao Zedong directly affected more people than anyone else in the twentieth century. Some say even that he influenced more people than anyone since Mohammed. Mao Zedong, through sheer force of personality, left his horribly flawed but undeniably original imprint on an entire nation. He created a new China, not in his image, but as he thought it should be. The leader of China's revolution quickly evolved into its capricious, arbitrary dictator. Of his many titles, the one that fit him best was "the Great Helmsman." Did he liberate the Chinese people, enslave them, or both?

EARLY SOCIALIZATION

When Mao was born on December 26, 1893, China was pitifully weak, humiliated, and close to disintegration. Mao's father was a poor peasant who had spent some years as a soldier but whose fortunes had risen as he became a petty grain merchant and a hard-nosed moneylender in Shaoshan, a village in Hunan Province. The family's two and a half acres of land made them—in a category Mao would later invent—rich peasants.

Mao loathed his domineering father, a sentiment utterly contrary to Confucian norms, but remembered his mother as kind, generous, and sympathetic. He rebelled against another pillar of Confucianism, his elementary school teacher. Running away from home became a pattern, beginning when he was only ten years old. At age thirteen Mao threatened to throw himself into a pond after his father denigrated him in front of guests. He noted that his tactics paid off: "When I defended my rights by open rebellion, my father relented, but when I became meek and submissive he only cursed and

Mao Zedong, 1925

*Mao Zedong with
Richard Nixon, 1972*

beat me more."[1] Mao's father arranged a marriage for him to a local girl, but Mao did not consider her his wife and paid no attention to her.

Mao was insatiably curious, although education was not valued in the boy's home. He had to quit elementary school to work on the family farm, but at age fifteen went for one year to the Dongshan Higher Primary School in a neighboring county, then to a middle school in Changsha, the Hunan provincial capital, forty miles away by foot and boat. Here he first came into contact with ideas from the West. His study was always impetuous and undisciplined, and now he indulged himself in tales of heroes and bandits, warriors and emperors from Chinese history, and nation-builders such as Peter the Great, Napoleon, and George Washington from the West.

Mao's early education left him with a lifelong uneasiness about intellectuals. At first he, like they, thought manual labor unbecoming, but soon he changed his outlook radically. Later in life he consigned intellectuals to what he called the "ninth stinking category" (lower than landlords, small property owners, evil men, rightists, counterrevolutionaries, traitors, bad people in the party, and capitalists). Mao often said that the more books one read, the more stupid one became. He estimated in 1957 that the Chinese Communist Party (CCP) had already killed 400,000 intellectuals, and found that no cause for sorrow. Mao remained his entire life a provincial man with peasant habits. He never spoke a foreign language and only left China twice, both times on state visits to Moscow.

Mao first became interested in politics in 1911. The Manchu dynasty was crumbling, and rebellion broke out in Changsha. The Manchus had required all men to wear their hair in pigtails as a gesture of submission. Mao and a friend cut off theirs and, in a fit of enthusiasm, those of a dozen other youths. Mao enlisted in a local unit of Sun Yat-sen's army and spent six months as an orderly in the officers' mess.

As an adolescent, Mao Zedong was energetic and idealistic but unfocused. He tried various vocational programs. (How different the twentieth century would have been had he stuck with the soap-making school!) Before long he gravitated to the Changsha provincial library where at the age of eighteen, he later claimed, he spent six months reading translations of Western classics including *The Wealth of Nations* and *The Origin of Species*, and saw a map of the world for the first time.[2]

In the spring of 1913 Mao entered a teacher training school in Changsha, and remained there for five years. Here he gained his first experience in politics, helping establish several student organizations, including a "New People's Study Society." This was a time of extraordinary political turmoil in China. Sun Yat-sen's revolution had gone badly astray after the respected leader resigned in favor of Yuan Shikai, a general who quickly dissolved Parliament and began offering sacrifices at the Temple of Heaven, in the manner of a traditional emperor. Such a man could not rally Chinese resistance to

Japan's "21 Demands" of 1915, by which Tokyo sought to make China into a protectorate. Yuan Shikai died, central authority completely broke down, and China's warlord period commenced. The warlords (provincial military men) collected taxes for many years in advance; some even printed their own money. Many depended on foreigners for weapons.

The evolution of Mao's political thinking at this time is unclear, but we know that in 1916 he toured Hunan on foot and that by the following year he had become highly critical of the Chinese past and enthusiastic about grafting modern Western trends onto Chinese roots. Even his first published work was energetic: an article promoting the importance of physical education that concluded with a complete set of exercises. In 1918 Mao graduated from the teacher's college, made another walking tour of Hunan, and by September found himself at Beijing University, the intellectual center of China, working as a librarian's assistant. It was menial work, and he had to share a single room with seven other people, but finally his restless patriotism found its focus.

The Bolsheviks had just seized power in Russia, proclaiming the imminent fall of capitalism and the dawn of a new, much better—indeed perfect—age. Marxism appealed to many young Asians, particularly its Leninist version that emphasized the international aspects of imperialism. Communism offered intellectuals scientific certitude and an exciting historical role to play. It seemed a way to actually jump ahead of the European capitalist countries. Chinese students could now be modern and anti-Western at the same time. The twenty-four-year-old Mao was strongly influenced by Li Dazhao, a committed Marxist, and Chen Duxiu, a dean of literature in Beijing.

In 1919 a boatload of students (including Zhou Enlai and Deng Xiaoping) left Shanghai to work and study in France. Mao may have considered going, but in the end he only waved them off from dockside. He returned to Hunan that summer to try to organize students, merchants, and workers. All China was inflamed by the May Fourth Movement, which began as street demonstrations against the Versailles peace settlement that awarded former German concessions in China to Japan and escalated into a nationwide boycott of Japanese goods. Mao's mother died in October that year, and his father the following March, but these personal losses seemed less important than the revolutionary ferment in Changsha.

A disturbing element of Mao's personality was by now apparent: He knew how to make friends but not how to keep them. Instead, he bound people to him by exploiting their vulnerabilities. After his death, his personal physician wrote, "Mao was devoid of human feeling, incapable of love, friendship, or warmth."[3] Rivals were to be eliminated, subordinates humiliated.

RISE TO POWER

From 1919 to 1922 Mao worked in Hunan as a schoolteacher and headmaster at a primary school. In the summer of 1920 he married Yang Kaihui, the daughter of his former ethics teacher. She quickly bore him two sons. But politics was Mao's first, and warmest, love. He organized a Marxist study group, the New People's Study Society, and then a branch of the Socialist Youth League. When Vladimir Lenin decided that the East was ripe for revolution, he dispatched an agent named Gregory Voitinsky to help organize a Chinese Communist Party. Mao attended its founding congress in Shanghai in July 1921; in October he became secretary of the Hunan branch of the party, and in 1923 was elected to the CCP central committee. The Comintern favored a "united front" policy under which the CCP was to cooperate with the Kuomintang (KMT), China's nationalist party, for reasons of Russian national interest and because Soviet Marxists believed that China had to pass through a prolonged period of capitalism before it would be ready for socialist revolution. Thus Mao, a communist, worked in the KMT propaganda department. Hounded by the Hunan provincial government for his political activities, Mao spent parts of 1924 and 1925 in Shanghai and Canton.

In March 1925 Sun Yat-sen, founder of the Kuomintang, died, and Chiang Kai-shek, Mao's lifelong rival and bête noire, became the new KMT leader. In accord with the united front policy, Mao returned to Hunan to organize peasant support for the KMT. In January 1926 he published his first important treatise, *Analysis of the Different Classes of Chinese Society*. That year Chiang launched a "Northern Expedition" that was intended to defeat all warlords and unite China under KMT rule. The peasants of China were indeed ready for an end to warlords, and landlords as well.

In Mao's home province, peasant unrest escalated into a jacquerie. Mao analyzed these events in his 1927 *Report on an Investigation into the Peasant Movement in Hunan*. He predicted that "several hundred million peasants . . . will rise like a tornado or tempest—a force so extraordinarily swift and violent that no power, however great, will be able to suppress it. . . . They will send all imperialists, warlords, corrupt officials, local bullies, and evil gentry to their graves."[4]

In April 1927 Chiang Kai-shek broke the united front by suddenly and treacherously ordering KMT troops to massacre CCP members in Shanghai. Mao took to the hinterlands of Hunan and in September tried to organize an "Autumn Harvest Uprising." It was a fiasco. Mao was captured by provincial troops and might have been executed, but he broke away, hid in tall grass, and managed to escape. He fell out of favor with the CCP leadership but led a band of peasants to an inaccessible mountain range on the Hunan-Jiangxi border, where he forged an alliance with the leaders of local bandit gangs. At this time Mao started living with a pretty comrade named He Zizhen, although he was still married to Yang Kaihui, mother of his sons, who had stayed in Changsha while Mao was up in the mountains. In 1930 Yang Kaihui was tortured and publicly executed by the KMT. Genuinely saddened by this, Mao penned a sorrowful poem, "The Immortals," in Yang's memory, but he quickly married He Zizhen. His sons fled to Shanghai where they lived on the streets by their wits.

Mao was too deeply embroiled in party disputes to devote time to his family. The politburo and central committee were dominated by returned "students" trained in Moscow. This ideologically orthodox faction, led by Li Lisan, favored conventional military strategies. Li's attempt to capture several cities for the communists failed disastrously. Meanwhile, up in the mountains, Mao benefited from an alliance with a wily military genius named Zhu De. They conquered enough territory in Jiangxi Province to declare a Chinese Soviet republic in 1931. Mao became the chairman, a title he cherished for life.

In 1933 Chiang Kai-shek instituted a blockhouse strategy of encircling and slowly strangling Mao's mountain "Soviet." In October 1934 Mao's men (and women) broke through KMT lines and fled for their lives, at first with no clear destination. Thus began the heroic epic known to history as the Long March, which became the bond uniting all high-ranking CCP leaders for the next half century.[5] Mao was suffering from malaria when the Long March began, but at an emergency party meeting at Zunyi, Guizhou Province, in January 1935, he won a showdown with the Moscow-oriented faction, and took charge of the CCP. He and his followers faced appalling hardships as they crossed treacherous ravines while under fire, climbed across the eastern ranges of the Himalayas, and fought off primitive nomad tribes in the Tibetan borderlands, to arrive 368 days and 6,000 miles later in the dry country of northwest China. Of 96,000 people who left Jiangxi, only 8,000 survived. The communists established their "capital" at Yanan, in Shaanxi Province, an area so remote as to be unreachable by KMT (or Japanese) troops.

The communists lived spartan yet spirited lives at their Yanan base. The area was characterized by loess soil, wind-deposited dust that erodes vertically and is very easy to work. It is fertile if watered, and caves suitable to live in can be carved from hills as well as underneath cultivated fields. Here the communists rested, indoctrinated their troops, and even established a "Resist Japan University." Pictures of Mao at this time show him writing at a desk inside his well-lit cave, the entrance covered by paper walls and windows.

Mao's personal life became more adventurous in Yanan. He Zizhen bore Mao a girl, but Mao lost interest in his wife and began to consort with glamorous young women. In 1937 He Zizhen beat Mao with a flashlight when she caught him sneaking into the cave of an actress named Lily Wu. Mao decided his wife must be crazy and sent her to Moscow for psychiatric treatment. Then he divorced her and married another actress, Lan Ping, later called Jiang Qing. Mao's politburo colleagues were wary of her and approved of this marriage only on condition that Mao never allow his new wife to wield political power. To the sorrow of all China, Mao broke that promise thirty years later.

In July 1937 Japanese forces launched all-out war against China. The seven-week rape of Nanjing, which began in December, was one of the worst atrocities of the war. By one estimate, Japanese soldiers murdered 12,000 civilians and 30,000 fugitive soldiers, and raped 20,000 women.[6] Chiang Kaishek's KMT forces retreated to Chongqing in southwest China. There, far from the front lines, Chiang's reactionary generals hoarded supplies from the United States for renewed warfare against the communists, while waiting for U.S. forces to defeat Japan. In northern China the communists expanded their armies to more than half a million and, more important, established political control over villages behind Japanese lines. Like U.S. forces in Vietnam twenty-five years later, the Japanese occupiers could control major cities but never the villages. The CCP and KMT were again formally allied, against the Japanese, but neither side regarded the coalition as anything more than a temporary strategic necessity.

The war years were a good time for Mao. He had time to read and think and produced some of his most original and creative ideological tracts, *On Practice* and *On Contradiction* (1937), *On Protracted War* and *Strategic Problems in the Anti-Japanese War* (1938), and *On New Democracy* (1940). In 1942 and 1943 he launched his first rectification campaign to eliminate foreign dogmatists (Chinese communists too subservient to Josef Stalin). Many of Mao's enemies within the party were destroyed politically. By March 1943 his position within the party was unassailable, and he was elected chairman of the secretariat and of the politburo. Now he was in a position to implement his own personal interpretation of Marxism. Its bold originality distinguished what his growing legion of followers called "Mao Zedong Thought" from the lifeless dogmas of Stalinism.

After Japan surrendered, Mao spent six weeks in Chongqing negotiating with Chiang Kai-shek, but few people were surprised that the wartime united front dissolved and the civil war between the KMT and the CCP resumed. It was a slow slide downward for the KMT. Chiang's forces could not hold Manchuria. Hyperinflation demoralized everyone. On January 31, 1949, the citizens of Beijing welcomed their People's Liberation Army (PLA) "liberators." Chiang and the remnants of his army and government fled to Taiwan. On October 1, 1949, standing atop the Gate of Heavenly Peace in Beijing, Mao proclaimed the existence of the People's Republic of China.

POLITICAL IDEOLOGY

Ideas mattered more in communist China than in the other two classic twentieth-century totalitarian dictatorships, Adolf Hitler's Germany and Stalin's

Russia. All three systems employed a combination of propaganda and force to eliminate political opposition, but whereas Hitler and Stalin relied more heavily on their secret police, Mao scourged his people with the printing press and the radio. For Mao, human will could overcome almost any obstacle. By eliminating the "four olds" (old thoughts, old culture, old customs, and old habits), the Chinese people could create their own communist future very quickly, even without passing through the capitalist stage considered essential by Karl Marx, Lenin, and Stalin. To clarify the diverse, ambiguous, and even self-contradictory elements of Mao Zedong Thought, it will be best to consider him as a nationalist, a communist, a populist, an anarchist, a traditional Chinese thinker, a utopian dreamer, a military strategist, and a theorist of economic development. Finally, we must not forget that he turned into a megalomaniac.

Mao As a Nationalist

Marx and Lenin were internationalists. They thought that people should feel bonds of fellowship based on class. German workers should not fight British workers; rather, they should join together to overthrow their common enemies, the capitalists. The "nation" was an artificial construct. Patriotism, like religion, was a fraud, just another way for the ruling classes to deceive the proletariat (factory workers). When communism triumphs worldwide, as it ultimately must, borders will fall, and all humankind will be one. In the meantime, those on the "progressive" side of history must renounce allegiance to "nations" and devote themselves to the interests of world communism.

Mao never thought that way. He was, like almost all his contemporaries, first and foremost a Chinese patriot. He valued many things in China's past, as expressed clearly in his 1940 essay *The Chinese People*, in which he described the Chinese as one of the great peoples of the world. Mao wanted China to modernize, not Westernize. In his attitude toward the outside world, too, he was typically Chinese in combining a sense of cultural superiority with deep distrust of foreigners' intentions toward China. Whatever sins he committed along the way, Mao Zedong made China strong again. He put it simply, in 1949: "Our nation will never again be an insulted nation. We have stood up."[7]

Mao's thinking was strongly influenced by Social Darwinism, that illegitimate ideological child of biological Darwinism, which held that nations and races, like species, must conquer or be conquered, grow or decline. This explains his early dedication to physical fitness and self-strengthening. In his essay *A Study of Physical Education* (1917), he wrote that primary schools should develop children's bodies as well as their minds. In this regard, his beliefs accorded with those of Benito Mussolini and Hitler. All Mao's writings are permeated by a martial spirit, a glorification of struggle.

Mao As a Communist

Mao Zedong's sinification of Marxism was creative, original, even brilliant. China's class structure hardly resembled the European industrial societies described by Karl Marx and Friedrich Engels. For one thing, even the old ruling classes in China felt shamed by their country's humiliation. For another, if Chinese Marxists had to wait to launch their revolution until a factory system had been created, had matured, and had reached the crisis stage that Marx prophesied, they never would have lived to see it. Mao believed that China could skip stages. This presumptuous challenge to the creed annoyed the Soviets, who considered themselves to be in the vanguard of world communism.

Mao was a Leninist before he knew much about Marx. How familiar he was with the canon is a matter of debate. By one account, Mao read *The Communist Manifesto* more than a hundred times. However, Li Zhisui, his confidante as well as his physician, claims he had never read *Das Kapital*. Mao's outlook was less mechanistic than that of Marx or Lenin; for him even people of a "bad class background" could be reeducated to join "the people."

Mao based his revolution not on factory workers (who have hardly ever been revolutionaries in any place or time) but on peasants. This was heresy. Marx, and even Lenin, regarded peasants as at best a "fraternal" class, objectively speaking, allies of the only authentic revolutionary class, factory workers. They believed that peasants were unreliable, for they were rural idiots, prone to superstition, incapable of understanding their true interests, and easily manipulated by reactionaries. Mao knew better. "Whoever wins the peasants will win China," he told Edgar Snow in 1936. "Whoever solves the land question will win the peasants."[8]

Another distinctive feature of Mao Zedong Thought was the doctrine of protracted revolution, continuous revolution, or many revolutions. Marx and Lenin viewed socialist revolution as a one-time event; once capitalism was overthrown and the means of production (that is, farms and factories) distributed to the workers, socialism, a temporary stage, would evolve into true communism, defined as timeless and eternal. Mao suspected, and experience confirmed, that capitalism, like original sin, had a way of reappearing. Eternal vigilance was necessary, lest new bourgeois elements appear. The only way to prevent this was to keep the revolution going. If the communists turned into a new ruling class, another revolution would be required, and then another. Mao, like Fidel Castro, was unable to stop being a revolutionary.

All Communist governments must choose between "reds" and "experts," that is, between unskilled but ideologically committed cadres and well-trained technicians who may be less enthusiastic about the revolution. For Mao the choice was clear: It was better to be red. Li writes, "Mao believed in socialism for the sake of socialism. His highest ideal was not wealth or production but collective ownership, life in common, equality, a primitive form of sharing."[9] This fit with Mao's belief that the human personality could be remade, even perfected.

Mao and his disloyal deputy Lin Biao styled themselves as leaders of the entire Third World anti-imperialist movement. The "world countryside" (Asia, Africa, and Latin America) would surround the industrialized countries, just as the Chinese communists, from their rural bases, had surrounded China's cities in the struggle against the Japanese and then against the KMT. In the 1960s and 1970s, young leftists in many countries called themselves Maoists. This distinguished them from more hidebound, less revolutionary, Marxists, Leninists, Stalinists, and Trotskyists. It also excused their dreamy, undisciplined thinking.

Mao As a Populist

Mao always believed in the people, or, to use the term he preferred, and which is unintentionally revealing, "the masses." The masses could never be wrong, but they might need guidance. Thus we have the doctrine of the "mass line," as Mao explained in *Questions Concerning Methods of Leadership* (1943):

> In all the practical work of our Party, all correct leadership is necessarily "from the masses, to the masses." This means: take the ideas of the masses (scattered and unsystematic ideas) and concentrate them (through study turn them into concentrated systematic ideas), then go to the masses and propagate and explain these ideas until the masses embrace them as their own.

There was a problem here. The masses were infallible, but Mao himself was also infallible. What would happen if the masses failed to think or act the way Mao thought they should? For example, sometimes when he wanted people to speak out, they were fearful; at other times—as during the Hundred Flowers campaign of 1957—when people did speak their minds, Mao didn't like it. The only solution was to remold the people's thoughts to harmonize with his. Note that whatever stood between Mao and the masses, the government, the army, the bureaucracy, even the Communist Party itself, was most fallible indeed. This brings us to the next facet of Mao Zedong Thought.

Mao As an Anarchist

All serious political thinkers know that power corrupts, but all political action implies power. How, then, can a government be prevented from abusing its citizens? The liberal answer is to design the machinery of constitutional democracy so as to keep the holders of power from becoming intoxicated by it. Power must be divided (for example, into its executive, legislative, and judicial components) and elections must be held regularly so that citizens can turn out abusive officials. The anarchist answer is simpler: Why not just destroy all authority? Human life would then be chaotic, most people would reply. Genuine anarchists deny this, believing the human soul to be wholly good. Less innocent anarchists advocate replacing the remote, unfeeling state with small-scale, face-to-face groups or communes, where everyone is equal, leaders are elected by a show of hands, and life's joys and sorrows are shared. In practice, Mao never went so far as to actually abrogate wage scales. During the Great Proletarian Cultural Revolution, the PLA made a show of abolishing military rank, but naturally this could not be implemented.

Mao's attempt to turn China's villages into communes during the Cultural Revolution may seem evidence of his anarchism, but he never was willing to go all the way. The nationalist in him was not prepared to watch China disintegrate, and the communist in him could not truly permit people to act spontaneously. In 1968 he called out the army to impose order and end the chaos his own policies had unleashed. Therefore, it would be wrong to call Mao an anarchist, although his ideas did sometimes tend that way. This is one of many inconsistencies and incongruities to be found in Maoism.

Mao As a Traditional Chinese Thinker

If Mao was neither an anarchist nor a liberal, how did he propose to prevent the Communist Party members from oppressing the people? He drew on the resources of China's long history. The elaborate civil service system that evolved in China, that had governed the country while dynasties waxed and waned, gave officials nearly unlimited power. They were not constrained by written, immutable law. The way to make these powerful mandarins moral was to require them to thoroughly master Confucianism before entering government service. Years spent studying and copying the works of the master, it was hoped, would make men virtuous.

Mao's solution to the dilemma of power was similar: Moralize the holders of authority. But because Confucianism was officially designated as one of the "olds" to be eliminated, all bureaucrats were enjoined to thoroughly master Mao Zedong Thought. Then they would never forget the three words that each cadre must internalize: Serve the People. Frequent in-service training programs in memorizing and reciting Mao's words, amounting to hours per day during the Cultural Revolution, were required.

Mao As a Utopian Dreamer

There was a strain of romanticism in Mao's thought. The world could be changed because people could be changed. Human nature was absolutely malleable. The world did not have to be accepted as it was because the masses could accomplish anything if properly led and propagandized. One popular slogan was, "If you have great courage, you'll have great grain production." Mao rejected Thomas Malthus's warnings of a global imbalance between population and resources and never seemed to worry about China's gargantuan population problem. Sometimes he would even speak loosely about nuclear war, saying it wouldn't be such a bad thing to lose half the population, because the surviving half would build a civilization thousands of times more beautiful.

In fairness we should remember that all communists, if they really believe in Marx's "scientific materialism," are utopian dreamers with millennial visions. But Mao's flights of fancy were less anchored by material realities than were those of Lenin, Stalin, or Ho Chi Minh.

Mao As a Theorist of Economic Development

Mao's strategy for building China's economy is judged by many Chinese to have failed miserably. That would be a correct verdict if Mao's goal had been to maximize China's production of goods and services. If, however, the purpose of economic development is to create social and economic equality throughout society, or to build communism, then Maoist economic prescriptions make sense, and may be considered a partial success. They may be reduced to these principles.

1. Never trust so-called experts. They are probably tainted by bourgeois training. Put faith in the power of "red thought" to solve all problems. Those experts, in fact, have a lot to learn from the uneducated people they scorn. Experts should be sent out periodically to live and work in the poorest villages in China.
2. China's coastal provinces are more industrialized and in other ways more advanced than the inland provinces. This should be evened out, too.
3. In the workplace, laborers are more important than the boss.
4. China is too big for Beijing to manage everything. Let provinces, counties, towns, and villages decide for themselves how to build communism (deriving their inspiration from Mao Zedong Thought).

5. People who work for selfish reasons have the wrong attitude. The factory worker and the farmer, as much as the political cadre, should think only of how to "serve the people." Until such time as wages can be fully abolished, wage differentials should be reduced to a minimum.

6. Women are equal to men. They "hold up half the sky." Many Chinese women supported the CCP because of its strong stand in favor of liberating women from the constraints of Confucianism. In practice, though, the CCP showed itself hardly less patriarchal than the old regime or the KMT.

Mao As a Military Strategist

Without a doubt, Mao created a mighty Red Army from scratch. His strategy and tactics were perfectly suited to conditions in China in the first half of the twentieth century. He might even be considered a brilliant military thinker, except that Zhu De collaborated with him on his military writing, and that many of Mao's military principles are derived from classical Chinese texts, notably Sun Tzu's *Art of War*. Mao and Zhu, probably for didactic purposes, reduced the precepts to four easily remembered maxims:

> The enemy advances, we retreat.
> The enemy halts and encamps, we harass.
> The enemy seeks to avoid battle, we attack.
> The enemy retreats, we pursue.

Where Mao broke fundamentally from traditional strategists was in the purpose of warfare: The Red Army would fight not merely for the sake of fighting, but exclusively to agitate among the masses, to organize them, to arm them, and to help them establish political power. It is *the people* who win the war; the army only organizes them. If they are fearless, victory will be theirs. Even if the people suffer reversals, struggle itself is good, especially class struggle.

Mao As a Megalomaniac

By the time Mao reached middle age, a psychological disorder was discernible, and it became more conspicuous as he got older, namely his sense of personal omnipotence. Mao never doubted the wisdom of his own leadership. After the rectification campaigns inside the Communist Party in the early 1940s only a few other powerful leaders dared criticize him, and they were silenced in the Cultural Revolution. Toward the end of his life, Mao could only imagine enemies, for none dared show themselves. Mao became accustomed to flattery and never discouraged the personality cult that his sycophants constructed. In 1958, Mao wrote: "China's 600 million people have two remarkable peculiarities; they are, first of all, poor, and secondly, blank. That may seem like a bad thing, but it is really a good thing. . . . A clean sheet of paper has no blotches, and so the newest and most beautiful words can be written on it, the newest and most beautiful pictures can be painted on it."[10]

The obvious question was, Who was going to paint those pictures? Mao himself, and no one but Mao. As he told Edgar Snow, in human affairs there is always "the desire to be worshipped and the desire to worship."[11]

POLITICAL STYLE

Mao's political style was ostensibly modest and humble. He did not favor fancy uniforms as did his rival Chiang Kai-shek but preferred a plain tunic when he had to dress up, or sometimes an army uniform. Usually he looked rumpled. He spoke in metaphors, often repeating old Chinese proverbs to make a point. He sometimes wrote poetry, and often alluded in his speech or writing to characters from the classics. He could be blunt and direct, even scatological at times, or he could be so vague that no one was sure what he intended.

Mao preferred to give a series of orders and then to withdraw and observe how they were executed. This was what he called "luring out the snakes." People who deliberately or inadvertently misinterpreted his will revealed themselves as enemies to be destroyed. Mao would sometimes issue a vague command such as "Dig tunnels deep" and then sit back and watch millions of people spend all their spare time honeycombing the bedrock under Beijing with air-raid tunnels at the eight-meter level and the twenty-two-meter level. Once when he called for deep plowing, crops all over China were planted incorrectly.

Politics in Mao's China has been described as theater with constant drama, albeit in a tiresome Chinese style. The chairman was a master manipulator of public sentiments. Mao knew how to hate. There were always plenty of enemies. Political life was an incessant stirring of emotions, as the whole society careened first in one direction and then another. Because drama requires constant change, the chairman never held to one policy very long but swung back and forth between contradictory approaches. This was particularly true of his periodic mobilization campaigns—eventually the masses would get too carried away and would have to be calmed down again. Drama also requires heroes and villains, and these were in ample supply, with the interesting twist that one often turned into the other. This was served up with a dollop of paranoia about foreign intervention.

EARLY YEARS IN POWER

After a century of havoc and bloodshed, rebellions and revolutions, invasions and civil wars, famines and floods, the Chinese people craved effective government above all else. Any government that could bring peace and order to their vast country would be given the benefit of the doubt. The communists came to power amidst a wave of relief, patriotism, and, if not optimism, at least a feeling that things couldn't get much worse.

As China was in need of money and technical assistance, and the international situation was threatening, Mao Zedong journeyed to Moscow in December 1949. It was the first time in his life he had been outside China. Stalin received him coldly, and all that China got after months of bargaining was a $300 million loan—not a grant—and some blueprints for factories. Stalin later sent China technical advisers who designed some truly massive hotels in Beijing and a hydroelectric project that never produced a single kilowatt of electricity.

The Chinese threw themselves into flood-control projects (always the first order of business in a new dynasty), railway repair, and bridge building. Bombed-out factories had to be rebuilt. Currency speculation had to be wiped out and prices controlled. And all this was only the beginning—the old society had to be shattered. Mao's favored technique was the mass campaign. There was a Three Antis Movement and a Five Antis Movement (both against corruption), and a Thought Reform of Intellectuals Campaign. There was a campaign against counterrevolutionaries and another to eliminate foreign influence.

The communists' land reform campaign was supposed to proceed gradually, but it developed a momentum of its own. The communists' procedure was to stage public "trials" of landlords, all of whom were deemed oppressors. Peasants and sharecroppers stood up and shouted accusations. The landlords were shot on the spot. Mao welcomed this revolutionary justice, for it not only liquidated a class enemy but, more important, it changed the peasant forever. He vented his rage, got his hands bloody, cast off his former meekness. He became a red. Zhou Enlai once estimated that 830,000 people were killed in these campaigns between 1949 and 1956. Mao estimated 2 million to 3 million. More benign, but perhaps just as significant, was the Marriage Reform of 1950 that established legal equality between the sexes. Women were no longer to be considered chattel. For Confucian China, this was the real cultural revolution. Marriage reform, combined with land reform, ended the 2,000-year domination of Chinese society by the patriarchal clan. It is staggering to remember that all these internal campaigns were carried out while China, drawn into the Korean War against its will, fought the United States to a stalemate.

By the mid-1950s, Mao's new China had registered impressive economic gains, but Mao the revolutionary was restless. There were people in the party who favored a more conventional approach to nation building. Mao's response, which was becoming a habit, was to mobilize the "masses." In 1956 he launched the so-called Hundred Flowers campaign, which derived its name from one of his aphorisms, "Let a hundred flowers bloom; let a hundred schools of thought contend." In other words, Mao was offering the Chinese people free speech and encouraging them to criticize the Communist Party! At first, no one believed this possible, but when Mao ordered the party to really invite criticism, he got far more than he wanted, so he let the pendulum swing back with an Anti-Rightist Campaign in 1957. Every work unit had to find 5 percent of its members guilty of being rightists, which was hard because everyone professed to be an enthusiastic communist.

Mao was in one of his manic phases when he visited Moscow in November 1957 for celebrations marking the fortieth anniversary of the Bolshevik revolution. He was the master of his country in a way that his host, Nikita Khrushchev, could hardly match. Khrushchev was ebullient over the successful launch of Sputnik, and Mao formulated a poetic metaphor for the occasion: "The east wind prevails over the west wind." Then Mao proposed that the Soviets give the People's Republic some atomic bombs. Khrushchev demurred. Mao showed no curiosity about Russian culture, and walked out of a ballet performance.

LATER YEARS IN POWER

For a mix of reasons that must have included his ideological and personal rivalry with Khrushchev, Mao Zedong launched China into a "Great Leap Forward" on February 1, 1958. If the whole nation made a superhuman effort, production of everything would shoot up, and within fifteen years China would surpass Great Britain in industrial output. That would show the Soviets (and the "rightists," his ideological rivals on the CCP politburo) what could be achieved with imagination and energy.

In July 1958 the first communes were formed. Farmers were supposed to expand agricultural output by planting crops closer. They were also supposed to construct backyard smelters to expand China's production of pig iron. Because the poor farmers hadn't enough ore, they finally fed their pots and pans and farm implements into the crude ovens—to be melted down to produce new pots and pans and implements. The hills were deforested for fuel for the village smelters. China's rail system became clogged with trainloads of useless low-grade metal. Factories across the country closed. Hunger set in. According to recent estimates 30 million people may have starved to death as a result of the Great Leap Forward. While they were dying, the propaganda machine was claiming to the world that China had now out-stripped the United States in wheat production.[12]

By June 1959 Mao could no longer pretend that the Great Leap was succeeding. He went back to his home village, Shaoshan, for the first time since the 1920s, and learned, from talking to his relatives, what his courtiers dared not tell him. He still admitted no error, but more level-headed party members resolved to move against him at a party conference held at a mountain resort in July and August 1959, transcripts of which "show Mao suffering from a verbal battering which at times left him gibbering almost incoherently to the point where his replies are almost impossible to translate into English."[13] For the next few years Mao largely withdrew from active politics, letting others take responsibility for running China on a day-to-day basis, while he plotted a comeback. If the party had turned against him, there was still the army.

As the 1960s opened, Chinese foreign policy was in no less dire straits than domestic affairs. Mao had so offended the Russians that they abruptly withdrew their technicians, leaving industrial projects half finished. The people of Tibet rebelled, and the Dalai Lama fled to exile in India. A war with India broke out in 1962, and Moscow unmistakably leaned toward Delhi. China won that war, but now Chinese strategists saw that the Central Kingdom was literally surrounded by enemies at a time when the Kennedy administration was committing the United States to fight in Vietnam. How should the PLA prepare for an all-front war? Mao's answer was that it must revert to the guerrilla strategy that had proved successful in the 1930s. First, the masses would have to be mobilized. The party was infested with rightists; therefore everyone would have to learn from the PLA, which was commanded by a veteran of the Long March eager to show himself more Maoist than Mao, Lin Biao.

Before describing Mao's last hurrah, the Great Proletarian Cultural Revolution, let us pause to consider the dictator's personal life as he approached the age of seventy. It is not an attractive sight. He had always been impetuous and arrogant, but now these qualities became more salient. Moods and whimsy replaced logical thought. An insomniac for decades, he began demanding more and more barbiturates from his doctor, who complied to a point but, fearing for his own life if Mao should die, sometimes slipped him placebos. Mao never wore a watch and had absolutely no regular day-and-night schedule. His paranoia deepened. There was no one in the party he truly trusted. He restlessly traveled around the country in his private train, which would pull into a factory siding when he needed to sleep.

Mao's personal habits were simply gross. He never bathed but had himself wiped with hot towels. Because he rinsed his mouth with tea instead of brushing his teeth, his gums became infected. Despite these unpleasant habits his sexual appetite intensified. Sex was his only recreation. Young women

recruited by provincial party chiefs to be Mao's "dancing partners" were led
to his private rooms. He boasted that he "bathed" in their vaginal secretions.
Mao may have believed that constant sexual activity would postpone death.

Mao's wife, Jiang Qing, was no less peculiar. Ten years younger than Mao,
she had been raised in extreme poverty. As a teenager, she became an actress,
a profession then considered only slightly better than prostitution. She
found her way into Mao's bed at Yanan. Kept on the sidelines for twenty-
five years, she nursed dreams of revenge against party leaders who had
slighted her. Bright lights hurt her eyes, and the only color she liked was
green, so all her furniture had to be painted green. She wanted fresh air but
hated drafts. She also could not tolerate noise. Jiang Qing's husband found
younger bedmates but never divorced her. Mao had children but no normal
family life. His two sons by Yang Kaiwei, Mao Anying and Mao Anqing,
provided no comfort, for the former was killed in the Korean War and the
latter went insane. Other reputed sons and daughters were given to peasants
during the Long March and were never reunited with their parents. Li Na, a
daughter by Jiang Qing, was ignored by her father and mother. Li Min, a
daughter by He Zizhen, had a terrible relationship with Jiang Qing, who
carefully kept her away from Mao.

The Great Proletarian Cultural Revolution began in November 1965. Mao
placed Jiang Qing in charge of literature and the arts. She fed his vanity by
approving plays and operas that venerated him. Lin Biao did the same by
ordering the army to print millions of copies of the "little red book," *Quotations from Chairman Mao Zedong*. It is thought to be the only book in history to have been printed in more copies than the Bible. As a sacred book,
the *Quotations* could inspire Ping-Pong players to win matches and accomplish medical miracles. The New China News Agency reported that a cancer
patient named Wang Te-min, who conscientiously studied Mao's teachings,
declared, "Like imperialism and all reactionaries, cancer is nothing but a
paper tiger," and conquered the tumor.[14] Everyone wanted to wear a Mao
badge. Their manufacture consumed so much aluminum that production of
fighter planes was affected.[15] They came in 25,000 varieties.

The Cultural Revolution was more than mass insanity. Mao sincerely believed that the younger generation, not knowing the rigors of revolutionary
struggle, had gone soft. They could be given a taste of conflict while they
humiliated, abused, or even killed Mao's personal and political enemies.
Train conductors were ordered not to require tickets of teenagers; now
youngsters who had never in their lives been permitted to travel could go
anywhere in China for free. Forming themselves into bands of "Red
Guards," hundreds of thousands converged on Beijing in the fall of 1966
for mass rallies at which the Great Helmsman himself blessed them. Mao's
archenemy, Liu Shaoqi, the former head of state, was arrested, beaten, and
jailed. Jiang Qing publicly called for Liu to die slowly "by a thousand cuts,

by ten thousand cuts." He did die slowly, because his jailers took away his diabetes medicine. His eldest son was beaten to death and another son was kept in jail for eleven years.

While China was turned upside down, Mao "began to alternate between spurts of hyperactivity in which diverse herculean tasks should be achieved simultaneously, and periods of brooding and reluctant retirement."[16] By 1967 he was spending most of his time in Zhongnanhai, a secluded compound adjacent to the Forbidden City, in his large, dark bedroom, where the windows were covered with heavy drapes never drawn back. He wore a bathrobe, went barefoot, and took most of his meals alone. He became so lazy that on those occasions when he did have to get dressed, an orderly pulled up his trousers and socks. Jiang Qing lived elsewhere, enjoying foreign films forbidden to the masses, especially *Gone With the Wind*.

Before Mao slipped completely into senility, he double-crossed his youthful devotees, the Red Guards, who had called him "the reddest, reddest, red sun in our hearts." They were "rusticated," meaning they were sent down to faraway villages to learn from the people. Even if they could not speak the local dialect and hated farm work, they had to stay in those villages until after Mao died. Most never went to college; today they refer to themselves as China's "lost generation." Mao himself was subject to a final betrayal, by the little man he had publicly designated his close comrade in arms and successor, Lin Biao. To this day the facts of Lin's endgame in 1971 are disputed, but it appears he planned a coup, botched it, and fled. He died in a plane crash near the Mongolian border.

Mao lived another five years. They cannot have been happy ones, for he suffered from bronchitis, pneumonia, emphysema, convulsive coughing, congestive heart failure, and Lou Gehrig's disease. He was kept alive with the help of a U.S.-made respirator sent by Henry Kissinger. One of Mao's consorts, Zhang Yufeng, suddenly became a woman to be reckoned with, for she was the only one who could understand what he was saying. Even Jiang Qing had to ask Zhang Yufeng's permission to see Mao.

With this appalling vacuum at the center, the CCP from 1971 to 1976 was riven by virulent ideological and factional battles. It was a time of whispering and plotting, for high-ranking party members knew that the old man might die any day, and they wanted to be well positioned when the time came. A major foreign policy dispute was won by Zhou Enlai, who steered China toward détente with the United States and hostility toward the Soviet Union and its ally, North Vietnam. The all-important issue of succession was intertwined with left–right ideological polemics and personal vendettas. Mao wanted to name his own heir, and for a while he seemed to favor Wang Hongwen, a young man from Shanghai with no qualifications to lead China. However, Wang dropped from favor quickly. What most Chinese dreaded above all else was that the "Gang of Four" (the Jiang Qing faction) would end up in power. Mao finally settled on a little-known party boss from his home province, Hua Guofeng, to succeed him. In the heat of the Cultural Revolution, Hua had built in Hunan a factory capable of producing 30 million Mao buttons per year.[17]

On January 8, 1976, Zhou Enlai died. That April a memorial service for Zhou developed into a public demonstration in favor of his more moderate line and against the ultra-Maoism of the Gang of Four. The police forcefully suppressed the demonstrators. On April 30, 1976, Mao reportedly sent a message in his own handwriting to Hua Guofeng, saying, "With you in charge, I'm at ease." Zhu De died on July 6, and Hua delivered his eulogy. Three weeks later, one of the worst earthquakes of the twentieth century leveled the northern industrial city of Tangshan. In Chinese folk mythology this is an omen of impending dynastic change.

Mao Zedong died on September 9, 1976. A nationwide day of mourning was declared on September 18. Jiang Qing was arrested in her villa on October 6. All the pent-up bitterness of the Chinese people seemed to focus on Mao's wife, the "white-boned demon." It took the party four years to bring her to trial. Prisoners in China are supposed to confess their guilt and beg the court for mercy, but Madame Mao ranted and shouted and dared the judges to chop off her head. Her self-justification contained an element of candor. She once said that she was Chairman Mao's dog—whomever Mao told her to bite, she would bite. She committed suicide in prison on May 14, 1991, according to the Chinese government.

Mao's embalmed remains were put on display in a crystal, vacuum-sealed coffin, inside an imposing mausoleum in Tiananmen Square. The so-called rightists, led by Deng Xiaoping, gained power and reversed almost all of Mao's economic policies within five years of his death.

CONCLUSION

Mao Zedong's giant portrait still gazes out on Tiananmen Square from the entrance to the Forbidden City. It is sometimes said that Mao was China's last emperor, but no emperor possessed the tools of a twentieth-century totalitarian dictator—the cameras, printing presses, and radios that enable a despot to deify himself. Mao so dominated the CCP and the People's Republic that his successors could not decide how to evaluate his legacy. To acknowledge the enormity of his crimes would undermine their own rule, and because the CCP had so effectively monopolized power, the only alternative to continued communist rule seemed to be chaos. The official party verdict on Mao, pronounced in 1981, was that he had been 70 percent good and 30 percent bad. Which 30 percent was bad? Basically, everything after 1957.

Mao Zedong achieved many praiseworthy things in the twenty-seven years he ruled China. The worst abuses of the old society were eradicated: warlordism, the subjugation of women, and China's extreme inequality of land and wealth. China was undeniably more orderly and prosperous than it had ever been, and its people healthier. Probably, what its citizens appreciate the most is that China has recovered its self-respect and its place in the society of nations.

In the 1960s and 1970s when communist China's achievements (but not their cost) could be seen by the outside world, Mao gained a following in poor countries across Asia and elsewhere in the Third World. The Khmer Rouge revolutionaries in Cambodia were influenced by Mao's thinking, but their reign, several orders of magnitude bloodier than Mao's, was really sui generis. Maoist revolutionaries in Peru (the Sendero Luminoso) and India (the Naxalites) failed to gain power. But all the social factors that made Maoism possible still exist in many countries. It is too soon to consign his prophetic call for rural revolution to the pages of history books.

NOTES

1. Edgar Snow, *Red Star Over China* (New York: Grove Press, 1961), p. 126.

2. Stuart R. Schram, *Mao Tse-tung* (New York: Simon & Schuster, 1967), p. 36.

3. Li Zhisui, *The Private Life of Chairman Mao* (New York: Random House, 1994), pp. 120–21.

4. Edward E. Rice, *Mao's Way* (Berkeley: University of California Press, 1974), p. 37.

5. Harrison E. Salisbury, *The Long March: The Untold Story* (New York: Harper & Row, 1985).

6. Jonathan D. Spence, *The Search for Modern China* (New York: W. W. Norton, 1990), p. 448.

7. Mao Zedong, "The Chinese People Have Stood Up," speech, September 1949.

8. Quoted in Lois Wheeler Snow, *Edgar Snow's China* (New York: Random House, 1981), p. 49.

9. Li Zhisui, *The Private Life of Chairman Mao*, p. 377.

10. Stuart R. Schram, *The Political Thought of Mao Tse-tung* (New York: Praeger, 1963), p. 253.

11. Jonathan Mirsky, "Unmasking the Monster," *New York Review of Books* 41 (November 17, 1994), p. 23.

12. See Jasper Becker, *Hungry Ghosts: Mao's Secret Famine* (New York: Free Press, 1996).

13. Alan Lawrance, *Mao Zedong: A Bibliography* (New York: Greenwood Press, 1991), p. 15.

14. George Urban, *The Miracles of Chairman Mao* (Los Angeles: Nash Publishing, 1971), pp. 44–45.

15. Jose M. Tesoro and Anne Naham, "Mao-Memorabilia," *Asiaweek* (September 6, 1996), p. 31.

16. Lowell Dittmer, "Mao and the Politics of Revolutionary Mortality," *Asian Survey* 27 (March 1987), p. 334.

17. Spence, *The Search for Modern China*, p. 643.

3

Deng Xiaoping: The Leninist Capitalist

Every revolutionary ends as an oppressor or a heretic.

Albert Camus

Deng Xiaoping, the "paramount leader" of the People's Republic of China (PRC) from 1979 until his death in 1997, was a Chinese nationalist who oversaw the restoration of China's wealth and power in the late twentieth century. Deng's most important achievement was redefining communism as economic development. Deng's reforms went so deep that they are sometimes called "China's second revolution." Mao Zedong called Deng "the little man in a hurry," but Deng carefully waited for his time to come. When he was born, the Empress Dowager still ruled China. Deng rendered seventy years of service to the Chinese Communist Party (CCP). Its history mirrors his own life story.

Deng was a complex and contradictory man whose character cannot be easily delineated. He worked with Mao Zedong for almost half a century and therefore must have found it necessary frequently to hide his own opinions. In the world of communism nothing is quite what it seems, and most of Deng's speeches and writings, when published, were censored and slightly altered. An additional challenge Deng presents to the biographer is that he never liked to make details of his private life public.

EARLY SOCIALIZATION

Deng was born on August 22, 1904, in the village of Paifang, Guang'an County, in Sichuan Province. Sichuan occupies a very densely populated basin in southwest China so far away from Beijing that local governors sometimes governed as they pleased. Deng's name at birth is a matter of some dispute. It may have been Deng Xixian, meaning "aspirant for knowledge." He did not take the name "Xiaoping" until he was in his twenties.

Deng Xiaoping (right) with Mao Zedong (left), no date

Deng Xiaoping, 1978. Photo courtesy of Mike Chinoy.

The Deng family had a tradition of scholarship and public service that stretched back for generations. Paifang even displayed a memorial archway to a mandarin ancestor named Deng Shimin, which was destroyed during the Great Proletarian Cultural Revolution when the town was renamed "Anti-Revisionist Production Brigade."

The Deng family, according to some accounts, was originally Hakka, a distinctive society of dynamic wanderers. However, by the twentieth century they were culturally indistinguishable from their Sichuanese neighbors. They were not rich but occupied a large family compound built of wood and brick. Deng's father, Deng Wenming, owned about twenty-five acres of land. He seems to have been very interested in national politics. The religious atmosphere in which Deng Xiaoping was raised blended—in eclectic Chinese style—Confucianism, Buddhism, and Daoism.

Deng Wenming had four wives. The first died childless. The second, Deng Dan, was Deng's natural mother. She bore three other children. Deng Xiaoping was the eldest of three sons. He was a self-confident boy, even though he was very short, less than five feet tall. There was nothing in Deng's childhood to make him a natural rebel. When Deng was only five, his father engaged a private tutor trained in the Confucian classics, but the next year (1910) Deng was sent to a modern primary school and then to higher-level primary school. In 1916, at the age of twelve, Deng left Paifang for more private tutoring at the provincial capital, Chongqing. Here he was exposed for the first time to the intellectual ferment that was sweeping China at a time when warlords prevailed locally and revolutionaries were threatening the European order. In 1918 Deng boarded at a middle school and studied modern subjects, including mathematics, science, and world geography.

In the autumn of 1919 Deng enrolled in a school in Chongqing called the Movement for Diligent Work and Frugal Study. It was part of an imaginative plan under which Chinese youths learned some vocational skills, studied French, and—after passing a language test administered by the French consul—became eligible to continue their work and study in France. While Deng Xiaoping was thus preparing himself for travel, he was swept up in the political excitement of the May Fourth Movement of 1919, a nationwide boycott of Japanese goods to protest the award to Japan at the Versailles Peace Conference of former German concessions in China. In August 1920, Deng, in the company of an uncle not much older than he, left Chongqing by riverboat for Shanghai and Europe. He never saw his parents again. The provincial Chinese boys traveled steerage class, which meant that they were assigned no cabin but slept and ate in the open on a lower deck.

STUDY ABROAD

Deng Xiaoping was only sixteen years old when he disembarked in Marseilles. He went directly to Paris, where he stayed with other, mostly older,

Chinese students while awaiting his work assignment. In 1921 Deng entered a middle school in Normandy. However, the organization sponsoring him went bankrupt, so he moved back to Paris and took a series of unpleasant jobs. For a brief period, he was a locomotive fireman. He also worked in an armaments factory, a rubber-goods factory, and from 1924 to 1926 at a Renault automobile factory. All the while his real interest was in revolutionary politics, during which time he may have attended meetings of the French Communist Party. In June 1923 Deng was elected an officer of the Chinese Socialist Youth League. Soon after, he joined the European branch of the new Chinese Communist Party, and by the following February he was publishing a newspaper, *Red Light*, in tedious handwritten Chinese calligraphy. Other students called him "the doctor of duplication" for his tireless mimeographing. *Red Light*'s editor was a tall, handsome student named Zhou Enlai, whom Deng came to regard as his elder brother. As Zhou rose through the CCP hierarchy, he pulled Deng up with him. The two men understood and appreciated each other, even when Zhou had to publicly denounce Deng during the Cultural Revolution.

In 1925 Deng demonstrated outside the Chinese legation in Paris to protest foreign bullying of Chinese in Shanghai. He and other young Chinese communists in Paris were placed under police surveillance. Some were deported, but Deng and twenty others escaped by train to Berlin. The police raided his empty room the next day. From Berlin the idealistic youths continued eastward to the capital of the "workers' homeland," Moscow.

Deng spent about a year in Moscow, first at the University of the Toilers of the East, where all the courses were variations on a single theme (Marxism), and then at the newly created Sun Yat-sen University, which was actually a school of communist revolution where Comintern lecturers aimed to produce a graduating class of professional conspirators. Bolshevik luminaries, including Leon Trotsky, served as visiting lecturers. The students' expenses were paid by the Soviet government from funds Russia had received from China as indemnity for the Boxer Rebellion.[1] The heavy load of coursework included Marxist perspectives on history, philosophy, economics, and military science. These courses were taught in French. All students at Sun Yat-sen University had to study the Russian language, but Deng did not achieve fluency.

In Moscow, as in Paris, Deng associated almost entirely with other Chinese students, including a girl named Zhang Qianyuan whom he married two years later. Another classmate was Chiang Ching-kuo, the son of Chiang Kai-shek. Yet another was a daughter of Feng Yuxiang, the "Christian warlord" of northwest China who baptized his troops with a fire hose. Overlooking his religious bent, the Soviets provided Feng with arms, money, and military advisers. Feng visited Moscow and spoke to Deng's class in 1926.

In China, Sun Yat-sen died, and leadership of the Kuomintang (KMT) fell to Chiang Kai-shek. Chiang launched a "Northern Expedition" in 1926 to try to sweep warlords from China. At the insistence of Moscow, and despite their own suspicions, the Chinese communists joined forces with Chiang's KMT.

In December 1926 Deng Xiaoping returned to China to fight with Feng Yuxiang's troops. He took the Trans-Siberian Railway to Mongolia, then crossed the Gobi Desert on a two-month journey by truck, camel, and horseback. He arrived at Feng's headquarters in Xian in February 1927 and went to work as a political instructor with the warlord's troops. He used the opportunity to try to convert them to communism. In April the CCP–KMT coalition came unglued when Chiang Kai-shek ordered a massacre of communists in Shanghai, Nanjing, and Canton. This forced Feng Yuxiang to choose between the KMT and the communists. When he sided with the former, Deng Xiaoping left to work directly for the CCP. For the next seventy years, except when he was in temporary disfavor, Deng was part of the inner circle of Chinese communist leaders.

RISE TO POWER

Because Deng never revealed details of his private life, we know far more about his political activities than we do about his family life. In 1927 he took the name the world knows him by, "Xiaoping," which can be translated as "small and peaceful." In that same year his mother died, though he did not attend her funeral. At the age of twenty-three, Deng married the beautiful Zhang Qianyuan, his former classmate. She was as committed to communism as he. They lived briefly in the French concession in Shanghai. Yet only a year and a half after their marriage, Deng's wife died while giving birth, and the infant died, too.

Deng had been appointed a secretary of the central committee, based in Shanghai. He was responsible for handling all the private memos and orders at the heart of the CCP. His subsequent career confirms the maxim that knowledge is power. He never specialized in any single field but gained a broad overview of the Chinese economy, CCP social policy, and eventually military affairs, foreign policy, education, and science and technology. Deng forged friendships and alliances with powerful patrons, including Liu Bocheng, Liu Shaoqi, Zhou Enlai, and Mao Zedong himself. Mao, ten and a half years older than Deng, always respected the "little man's" abilities and spunk, but no real friendship with Mao was possible, for the chairman began to believe his own propaganda in which, after 1945, his thought was called "invincible." Zhou was more dependable than Mao as a friend and patron.

As he climbed within the hierarchy, Deng brought along his own clients, particularly Hu Yaobang and Zhao Ziyang.

In 1929 the CCP politburo dispatched Deng to Guangxi Province in China's far south. He helped organize an uprising in the town of Baise in December, and another one two months later. This was no small affair—Deng commanded 8,000 soldiers. At this point, for reasons unknown, the party summoned Deng to a conference in Shanghai. The CCP leader at that time was a dogmatic Marxist named Li Lisan, who believed, contrary to all evidence, that China's cities were ripe for revolution. Li ordered Deng to march eastward and take Canton. The idea was ludicrous, but Deng dutifully followed Li's instructions. Chiang Kai-shek's KMT troops turned back, pursued, and nearly annihilated Deng's revolutionists. Deng gave up on his hopeless mission and slogged northward with his troops in the winter of 1930–31 to join the Jiangxi Soviet. It was a miserable expedition, prefiguring the later ordeal of the Long March. Deng's troops were inadequately clothed for the cold mountain passes and had to cross rivers under hostile fire. Many thousands died. For some reason Deng suddenly took off for Shanghai via Hong Kong. His official biography states that he was reporting to the central committee, but his political enemies, including his Red Guard antagonists thirty-five years later, called it desertion. This incident has never been adequately explained.

In the summer of 1931 Deng left Shanghai for the red "base area," now officially designated the Chinese Soviet Republic in Jiangxi. Mao Zedong named Deng secretary of the party committee of Ruijin County, a relatively stable position that he held for the next two years. In the summer of 1932 Deng remarried, but the union was ill-starred. His new wife, Jin Weiying, was a party member who left him the next year when he fell into political disfavor, and married the man who had denounced Deng. Already one distinctive feature of Chinese communist political culture was evident: the use of newspaper articles to launch political offensives. In April 1933 Deng was demoted and exiled to Anyuan County, a remote part of the Jiangxi Soviet. He may even have been imprisoned briefly, but after he wrote "self-criticisms" he was rapidly rehabilitated. Soon he was editing *Red Star*, the CCP newspaper, and giving lectures on party history at a school for communist soldiers.

Chiang Kai-shek, now assisted by German advisers, launched encirclement campaigns to isolate and strangle the Jiangxi Soviet. Chiang might have succeeded had the communists not broken through the blockade and begun the legendary retreat known as the Long March of 1934 and 1935. The thirty-year-old Deng supervised propaganda work among the troops and continued to publish *Red Star* while on the run. At the crucial Zunyi meeting of January 15, 1935, Deng was the recorder, indicating that he must have been acceptable to all factions. This showdown ended with Mao Zedong victorious over the Li Lisan faction. Deng contracted typhoid fever but was one of the 8,000 red soldiers who survived to reach Shaanxi, of 96,000 who had started from Jiangxi.

Deng spent 1936 with Mao and the other communist leaders at their Yanan headquarters and was interviewed there by the American leftist journalist Edgar Snow. In 1937, when the Japanese invasion of China forced the KMT and the CCP to form another united front, the communist troops were designated the Eighth Route Army. Deng commanded his own base area in the Wutai Mountains, strategically located between the cities of Taiyuan and Beijing. His title was political commissar of 129th Division; what this meant in practice was that he provided political direction to the soldiers. Deng was not a soldier, although his responsibilities gave him an intimate knowledge of military affairs that served him well for the rest of his career. In the Wutai base area, Deng worked closely with Liu Bocheng, popularly known as "the one-eyed dragon" after having lost an eye in battle. The two became close political allies.

In the autumn of 1938 Deng married a woman twelve years younger than he, Zhuo Lin. Zhuo Lin devoted the rest of her life to Deng and bore five children. In 1940 Deng Xiaoping's father was brutally murdered near his home village in Sichuan. The crime was never solved, leading to speculation that the killers may have been communist guerrillas liquidating him as a landlord.[2]

From their base in the Wutai Mountains, Deng and Liu Bocheng concentrated on organizing village militias while at first avoiding contact with Japanese forces. However, by 1940 their 129th division descended to the lowlands and infiltrated villages all across the north China plain. The Japanese Army remained vulnerable to guerrilla attack for the duration of the war. Deng returned frequently to Yanan to report to Mao and to receive instructions. These two very different men seemed to enjoy each other's company, and Deng escaped criticism in Mao's first rectification campaign of 1942.

By 1945, when Japan surrendered, Deng had been made a member of the central committee of the CCP. His responsibilities were primarily military, for Japan's defeat allowed the KMT and the communists to resume their civil war. Chiang Kai-shek had described the Japanese as a disease of the skin, less dangerous than the communists, who were a disease of the heart. In the autumn of 1945 Deng and Liu defeated KMT forces in battle and took 20,000 prisoners.[3] In 1946 and 1947 they devised a strategy of deep penetration of KMT territory, exposing the logistical and political weakness of their enemy.

Chiang Kai-shek's forces were routed in late 1948 and early 1949. Communist troops occupied Manchuria, with its wheat farms and industrial infrastructure. Deng distinguished himself by orchestrating the Huai-Hai campaign. This was one of the largest Chinese land battles of the twentieth century. The result was the complete annihilation of a KMT army of half a million men by a communist force of approximately the same size. Deng organized millions of peasants (estimates range from 2 million to 5 million) into support battalions to carry supplies and dig trenches. KMT forces were driven south of the Yangtze River, and the outcome of the civil war was no longer in doubt. On October 1, 1949, Deng stood with Mao atop the Gate of Heavenly Peace in Beijing for the official proclamation of the People's Republic of China. On that triumphant day, Deng wrote, in his best calligraphy, "Remember forever that the victory of today was won with the blood of people's heroes in the long and difficult years of the past."

POLITICAL STYLE

Before analyzing the next phase of Deng's career, we shall pause to consider his political style as it had evolved over the twenty-five years from the time he joined the CCP to the communist seizure of state power. Deng was clearly very smart, with an excellent memory (honed in all-night bridge games) and a logical approach unclouded by emotion or ideology. In speeches to cadres, he could effectively summarize many facts. In political as well as in military affairs, he was a shrewd tactician who knew when to retreat. Many sudden policy reversals were necessitated by Mao's arbitrary, sometimes even whimsical, decisions. Deng frequently had to carry out policies he disagreed with, and even to pretend that he supported them enthusiastically. Deng always survived to fight another day. For this he was sometimes called a man without vision or principles, a charge that sells this complex man short.

Deng was always pragmatic. His oft-quoted remark that "it doesn't matter whether the cat is black or white as long as it catches mice," testifies to his disdain for preconceived ideology. "Seek truth from facts," Mao once said, and when the time was ripe Deng turned this all-purpose adage against the Maoists. Then he added a motto surely designed to infuriate the radicals, "To get rich is glorious." Deng was plain-spoken to the point of being abrasive. Although he did have close friends, such as Peng Zhen, the Beijing party boss and Deng's longtime bridge partner, more important were the political alliances he forged with other leaders, most particularly that with Zhou Enlai.

Deng was very tough, a quality some biographers have seen as a compensation for being so short. However, he never shrank from nastiness in his verbal attacks on domestic rivals like Mao's wife Jiang Qing, or in polemical denunciations of foreign enemies. Nor did he shrink from inciting peasants to kill landlords, even though his own father may have met his end in this way. He was resolute and never looked back, even on a decision so clearly disastrous as sending troops to disperse student demonstrators in Tiananmen Square in 1989.

Deng was notoriously stubborn. He never gave up, even when sentenced to menial work during the Great Proletarian Cultural Revolution, but instead plotted his next comeback. And he was cool under fire. Harrison Salisbury noted that during the Huai-Hai campaign Deng had a billiard table carted around the countryside so he could play at night.[4]

EARLY YEARS IN POWER (1949–66)

As soon as the new regime was established, Mao sent Deng Xiaoping and Liu Bocheng to Sichuan Province to mop up remnants of Chiang Kai-shek's army. Deng's official titles were vice chairman of the Southwest Military and Administrative Commission and first secretary of the regional party bureau. He was responsible for every aspect of political life in four provinces: Sichuan, Guizhou, Yunnan, and eastern Tibet. At the age of forty-five Deng Xiaoping was the boss of an area larger and far more populous than any European country. One of his proudest achievements was building a 300-mile railway line from Chongqing to Chengdu.

Deng's own relatives were vulnerable to the communists' anti-landlord campaigns in the early 1950s. He allowed them to be dispossessed but brought four of them (Deng Shuping, his brother; Deng Xianlie, his sister; Xia Bogen, his stepmother; and Deng Xianfu, her daughter) to live in his own official compound in Chongqing, thereby shielding them from possible violence.

In 1952 Deng was transferred to Beijing, probably at the behest of his friend and patron, Zhou Enlai. Clearly, his administrative talents were recognized, for he was named to the State Planning Commission and assigned to oversee the transport sector. In September 1953 he became minister of finance at a time when the state was imposing a monopoly on grain and cotton purchasing. These posts were in the government, not in the party. In communist political systems every government bureaucrat is supervised by a party member. Deng is thought to have helped write the PRC constitution of 1954. In June of that year he was named secretary-general of the central committee. This cumbersome title meant that he was trusted with the most sensitive personnel matters. Deng now had access to the secret files that follow every CCP member from post to post throughout his or her career.

Deng and his family moved into Zhongnanhai, the exclusive, guarded compound adjacent to the Forbidden City, where China's top leaders lived. Unlike Mao, Deng was always close to his wife and children. Ever since his father's murder, he had taken care of his stepmother, and he supported elderly relatives in his native village. Deng Xiaoping and Zhuo Lin had two sons and three daughters. The older son, Deng Pufang, was tortured and thrown from a high window during the Cultural Revolution. He survived but was crippled for life. The younger son, Deng Zhifang, was "sent down" to a village during the Cultural Revolution, but otherwise unharmed. In the 1980s, with the family's fortunes reversed, he was sent to do postgraduate work in physics at the University of Rochester in New York. The eldest daughter, Deng Lin, became an artist. Deng Nan became a physicist. Deng Rong (Maomao to family and friends) became a medical student and, although married to a man named He Ping, remained very close to her father and wrote a personal biography of him.[5] Maomao and her husband were both assigned to Washington, D.C., as foreign service officers from 1979 to 1983.

In April 1955 Deng was elected to the politburo. Now his brief included foreign affairs. In February 1956 he went to Moscow for the twentieth congress of the Communist Party of the Soviet Union, the famous session at which Nikita Khrushchev denounced Stalin. Never had any Communist Party admitted error. The Russian people had been told for thirty years that Stalin was a god; now he became a nonperson. Stalingrad was hastily renamed Volgograd. There were repercussions throughout the Communist bloc, not least of which was the Hungarian uprising eight months later. Like Stalin, Mao had begun to think of himself as infallible. At a party meeting Deng openly warned, in Mao's presence, against defying any individual. This bit of lèse majesté did Deng no harm at the time, for Deng was now outranked by only five men within the CCP hierarchy: Mao, Liu Shaoqi, Zhou Enlai, Zhu De, and Chen Yun.

In 1957 Mao committed a major blunder by inviting citizens to criticize communists in a mass movement he called the Hundred Flowers Campaign. The flowers blossomed into "poisonous weeds," so an Anti-Rightist Campaign was needed to reverse the tide. Deng, who probably agreed with some of the criticisms, nonetheless obediently attacked the rightists who had taken Mao at his word. In November Deng and Mao went to Moscow for celebrations marking the fortieth anniversary of the Bolshevik revolution. At one function, when Mao and Khrushchev were together, Mao pointed to Deng and remarked, "See that little man there? He's highly intelligent and has a great future ahead of him."[6]

Upon his return to China Mao plunged into the most destructive campaign of his career. In February 1958 he called for a "Great Leap Forward" to jump ahead of the Soviets and overtake the Western industrial democracies by making "simultaneous advances in all spheres." A miraculous doubling of China's crop yield and industrial output could be achieved if every man, woman, and child in China simply worked like a whirlwind. As a practical man, Deng must have known that this was a recipe for disaster, but he publicly supported Mao. In the summer of 1959 other top communists criticized Mao at a special party meeting at the mountain resort at Lushan, but Deng was absent because he had broken his leg, an injury that took two and a half years to heal.

Local leaders contributed to the Great Leap by doctoring their figures, so the party was in the dark about the real state of the country. By 1960 peasants were starving to death *by the millions*. Mao was in political retreat, and it seemed possible that he would be pushed into retirement and replaced as supreme leader by the more level-headed Liu Shaoqi. Deng now publicly referred to "problems in Mao's thinking."

China's domestic problems were matched by reverses in foreign affairs, chiefly the growth of a hatred between the Chinese communists and their Russian counterparts so venomous it could not be camouflaged. Part of the problem was Mao's personal contempt for Nikita Khrushchev, but the roots of the quarrel went deeper. China and Russia were struggling for geopolitical dominance in Central Asia. At three separate meetings in the years 1960–63 the Russians and Chinese tried to resolve their differences. Deng Xiaoping spoke for the Chinese side every time, and whether he was acting on orders from Mao or on his own, Deng's nasty invective only made the atmosphere worse. Mao showed his approval by greeting Deng at the Beijing airport when he returned from Moscow in July 1963.

For two months (December 1963 to February 1964) Deng served as acting premier while Zhou Enlai toured Africa and the Middle East. Deng also was dispatched to other communist countries, including North Korea and Romania, to encourage their anti-Russian tendencies. He probably was dismayed at the grotesque personality cult that flourished in Pyongyang, where the North Korean dictator Kim Il Sung was idolized. Deng was no longer enthusiastic about mass movements, no longer willing to sacrifice economic development on the altar of Mao Zedong Thought.

CULTURAL REVOLUTION

For reasons that included fear of his own aging, Mao Zedong launched his final assault on tradition in November 1965. Egged on by his vindictive wife, Jiang Qing, and his opportunistic defense minister, Lin Biao, Mao used the government's formidable propaganda machine to whip up hysteria about traitors within the Communist Party taking the capitalist road. Impressionable teenagers formed battalions of Red Guards. For the first time in their lives, they were encouraged to throw caution to the wind and bombard the party headquarters. This included breaking into and vandalizing the homes of the educated and the cultured, for such people were remnants of the old civilization that had to be eradicated. Huge rallies were held at an outdoor stadium in Beijing where victims were shamed and beaten. This escalated to open warfare carried out with guns hijacked from supply trains bound for North Vietnam. The number one capitalist roader was the former chief of state, the aloof, dignified Liu Shaoqi. The number two capitalist roader was Deng Xiaoping.

Mao had grown intolerant of the slightest criticism and complained that Deng treated him like a dead ancestor. Sensing the danger, Deng at first tried to ride out the turmoil by acquiescing in a denunciation of his old friend, Peng Zhen. As late as August 1966 Deng appeared in public with Mao and Lin Biao, but in October Mao demanded that Deng make a self-criticism. Knowing he was about to be purged, Deng advised his own children to testify against him. His public humiliation was complete. Teenagers forced him to kneel with his arms outstretched in the "airplane position." A dunce cap was placed on his head and he was driven through the streets of Beijing in an open truck. Jiang Qing was his most enthusiastic antagonist. It did not help that she knew he snickered at her revolutionary operas.

Deng's tormentors examined every detail of his past, starting with his "bad class background." In his self-criticism Deng wrote that he represented the capitalist, reactionary line. He was placed under house arrest and stripped of all party and government posts, but allowed to keep his party membership. That was crucial, for it gave him the first rung of the ladder for his later climb back to power. Some members of his family fared far worse. His brother Deng Shuping was driven to suicide by the Red Guards. Deng's other brother was sent to the countryside. Deng Pufang, who was paralyzed from the waist down, lived for three years at a home for the handicapped where he wove baskets, until he was allowed to join his parents in Jiangxi where Deng Xiaoping worked as a fitter in a tractor factory. However, there was a silver lining. Deng and Zhuo Lin worked together in their vegetable garden and read together in the evening. Deng used his time to read many books, an indication that he was being protected by some high-ranking military or political official, perhaps Zhou Enlai.

REHABILITATION

In an attempt to get back in the good graces of the only man who mattered, Deng sent Mao two letters of apology (November 1971 and August 1972). Deng groveled: "Whenever I think of the damages caused by my mistakes and crimes to the revolution, I cannot help but feel guilty, shameful, regretful, and self-hateful. I fully support the efforts to use me as a negative example. . . . No punishment is too much for a man like me."[7] Chinese politics from 1976 to 1979 were a nightmare of intrigue and backstabbing as the Maoists (Jiang Qing and the other members of the Gang of Four) and the anti-Maoists (people who thought like Deng, but were lying low) jockeyed to be in a position to strike the moment the great helmsman died. Mao would sometimes become lucid and issue edicts that swung unpredictably back and forth, first favoring the radicals, then the conservatives.

In February 1973 Deng returned to Beijing and once again lived at Zhongnanhai. This could not have happened without Mao's personal approval. Now Deng was assigned to work on foreign affairs. Zhou Enlai was diagnosed with cancer and began cobalt radiation treatment. During his incapacitation, he turned over all his important work on the state council to Deng. In April 1974, Deng presented Mao's theory of "the three worlds" to the United Nations in New York. In this formulation, China represented the world countryside that would surround and triumph over the industrial democracies and the Soviet revisionists.

Mao now leaned rightward. On January 29, 1975, Deng was made head of the general staff department of the People's Liberation Army (PLA), from which position he was able to rehabilitate his old friend Peng Zhen. In May he led a government delegation to France. It seems that the dying Zhou Enlai was grooming Deng to become supreme leader after he and Mao were gone. Deng was only seventy, not old by the standards of the Chinese communist gerontocracy, so he zestfully seized the opportunities presented. He met German chancellor Helmut Schmidt and U.S. secretary of state Henry Kissinger. Deng's self-confidence grew. The next time the leftists harangued him he turned off his hearing aid and told them he couldn't hear a word they were saying.

Zhou Enlai died on January 8, 1976. Deng delivered the eulogy at his funeral. In communist countries that is always a sign of power and standing. But the leftists—correctly guessing that Mao would be the next to "go to meet Marx"—quickly assailed Deng. Their attack began with wall posters that were reprinted in the national press. Then in April crowds gathered in Tiananmen Square to lay memorial wreaths to Zhou. The Gang of Four knew that the mourners were indirectly protesting the Maoist policies Zhou had subtly opposed, and ordered the police to disperse the demonstrators. On April 5 the crowd fought back, burning police vehicles. Two days later Deng was purged for the third time in his career and dismissed from all his official positions. He fled to Guangdong Province in southern China, where his old friend Marshal Ye Jianying provided military protection. Deng bided his time while the Gang orchestrated a national campaign to criticize him. Events were now moving toward a denouement.

Zhu De, the venerated military leader of the revolution, died on July 6 at the age of ninety. The old guard was clearly slipping away. Wang Hongwen, the youngest member of the Gang of Four, whom Mao had inexplicably elevated from obscurity, presided over Zhu's funeral, a sure sign that the radicals were in the driver's seat. Three weeks later a terrible earthquake leveled the northern industrial city of Tangshan. Many Chinese believe that an earthquake results from cosmic disharmony and foretells dynastic change. This time it was true. Mao Zedong died on September 9, 1976.

If Jiang Qing, Wang Hongwen, Yao Wenyuan, and Zhao Chunqiao (the Gang of Four) thought their moment had come, they could not have been more mistaken. Within a month they were in jail. Hua Guofeng, a colorless compromise candidate with a foot in both camps, succeeded Mao as chairman (an odd title that Deng never took). Soon kindergarten children were singing a ditty that went, "How wise Chairman Hua is! He smashed the four pests! We will follow him forever!"[8] But it was not Hua they ended up following. Deng Xiaoping had returned to Beijing.

LATER YEARS IN POWER

After decades of revolutionary turmoil, mass campaigns, and general chaos, the people of China longed for stability above all else. The economy was improving, but at a glacial pace, and citizens had become deeply alienated from politics, especially the political theater that substituted for elections. The situation called for a leader with administrative talent, not charisma. In July 1977 the central committee reinstated the seventy-three-year-old Deng to all his previous positions. This was his third political rehabilitation. He was still formally outranked by Hua Guofeng, but Deng's power was growing daily, while Hua's was eroding. Although Deng promised to obey Hua Guofeng, he overthrew him in less than a year and a half. Their battle was conducted in the peculiarly oblique style the communists had evolved. Those who affirmed the importance of seeking truth from facts were counted in Deng's corner; by November 1978 ten of the PRC's eleven military regions had so voted.[9] No euphemisms were employed in the wall posters Deng's supporters pasted up on "Democracy Wall" in Beijing: "Xie Fuchi's dead body should be whipped 300 times," read one, referring to a former minister of public security. "Kang Sheng's remains will stink for 10,000 years," read another, referring to the former head of the secret police. Deng's most audacious move was to pardon 100,000 people that he himself had jailed or sent to the countryside in the anti-rightist campaign twenty years earlier.

Deng was never China's president or premier, nor was he ever the party's chairman. At the height of his power he called himself merely a deputy prime minister; then he relinquished even that until at last his highest official ranking was honorary chairman of the Chinese Bridge Association. But the press accurately called him China's "paramount leader." Professor Lucian Pye, a lifelong China-watcher who has met Deng personally, compares him to a Chinese magician who, "in his unassuming manner and dress, is no different from his audience and whose prattle suggests that he is as surprised as the audience at the wonders taking place—not at all like the Western magician who is as much the center of attention as the feats he performs."[10] Pye explains the "vague and indeterminate process" by which Deng emerged supreme: "Deng's elevation was furthered by the extraordinary and instinctive deference the Chinese give to old age and seniority. . . . The authority of age reinforced the Chinese manner of not distinguishing between status and power. People with high status simply are powerful figures, regardless of their formal positions or offices."[11]

Other observers have compared Deng to a patriarch, a backroom politician, even to a Mafia godfather. He operated behind the scenes. He knew everyone. His wishes were so clear that his lieutenants usually could guess what he wanted. Normally phlegmatic, on occasion he could boil over with rage.

Deng's effective administrative style relied heavily on delegating authority, something Mao was always loath to do. Whereas Mao liked to intervene in the smallest details, Deng was content to make the important strategic decisions himself and leave implementation to others. A second important contrast between Mao and Deng is that the former liked to depict himself as alone with the masses (by which he meant that no other government figure was to be trusted), whereas Deng wanted people to rely on the party, not on any single leader, including himself. Mao spoke in oracular language that lent itself to widely variant interpretations; in contrast, Deng was clear and specific.

Mao grew to distrust his own Communist Party, but Deng was an organization man who insisted on Leninist norms, which meant operating through regular channels, never circumventing established state and party institutions. Mao had a vision, however dreamy, for what he wanted China to become. Deng simply did whatever he thought would make China prosperous and powerful, but he never specified what a modern China should look like. Hong Kong was a compelling example of what could be achieved; Deng designated Shenzhen, near the border with Hong Kong, a special economic zone where capitalism was encouraged and foreign investors welcomed.

DENG'S REFORMS: THE FOUR MODERNIZATIONS

Before his death Zhou Enlai had announced a "four modernizations" program consisting of agriculture, industry, science and technology, and national defense. Agriculture was the logical place to start, because 80 percent of the Chinese population lived in the countryside. Mao's rural communes had failed to raise production, so Deng boldly abolished them and decollectivized agriculture. Under the new household responsibility system, the state still owned the land, but families were issued long-term leases. Such leases were inheritable, so farm families now built their own houses, and the more ostentatious the better. After meeting their quota to the state, farmers could sell any surplus on the open market. For the first time in China's 5,000-year history, peasants saw the prospect of social mobility. Those who were unsuccessful came down with the "red eye disease," jealousy. With food prices floating upward, people on fixed incomes—factory workers, soldiers, bureaucrats, retired people—faced inflationary pressure, never a problem under the old command economy.

The second modernization was industry. The iron rice bowl (guaranteed job tenure and minimal pay differentials) had to be broken. Deng was no closet capitalist, for he insisted on retaining an important state sector. At the same time, however, he liberated the spirit of entrepreneurship and competition that lay dormant under the ice of socialism. Instead of emphasizing heavy industry, the government now promoted light industry and consumer goods. Free economic zones were established up and down the Chinese coast, and foreign companies were invited to take advantage of China's cheap, docile labor force. By 1990 capitalists from all over the world had invested $4 billion in these zones.

The third modernization was in science and technology. Rigor had to be reintroduced into Chinese schools and universities, which had ceased giving examinations or grades during the Cultural Revolution. Deng opened a window to the outside world. Having lived in Europe, he was free of Mao's xenophobia. History may record as Deng's single greatest achievement that he introduced one-fifth of humankind to the other four-fifths. Soon millions of Chinese were studying English. Western tourists, eager to see the wonders of China for themselves, poured in, bringing gadgets, clothes, ideas, and dollars. Chinese students could even study abroad. Hundreds of thousands leapt at the chance; a majority did not return to China.

The fourth modernization was national defense. Deng had no formal military training and was not a professional soldier, but he could see that Mao's romantic attachment to guerrilla war ("People's War") was dangerously unrealistic for a great power. Deng camouflaged his new strategic doctrine with the slogan "People's War Under Modern Conditions." That meant abandoning the guerrilla strategy of retreating to lure the enemy in deep, and instead deploying a forward defense to keep potential foes away from Chinese territory. This was going to be colossally expensive, but some money could be saved by reducing the PLA's excessive manpower, and funds could be generated, too, by converting military factories, of which there were many, to the production of civilian goods. Military procurement missions were sent abroad where they indulged in giddy shopping sprees. A modern army, navy, and air force depends on highly skilled technicians. This posed a problem, for most PLA troops were semiliterate farm boys. In the newly competitive economy, military conscription became difficult because young men perceived greater opportunities out of uniform. A still greater problem was military corruption. The PLA had always been self-sufficient; now regional military commands could escape civilian supervision completely, to run car smuggling rings, illegal timber operations, casinos, and even brothels.

THE FIFTH MODERNIZATION: DEMOCRACY

Did Deng see where all the economic, social, and intellectual ferment would lead? Apparently not. He seemed to think it possible to liberalize everything but the political system. He was willing to end discrimination against people of bad class background, for that included himself, but he had no use for civil liberties. "Liberalization itself is bourgeois in nature," he said. "There is no such thing as proletarian or socialist liberalization. Exponents of liberalization want to take us down the road to capitalism. That's why we call it bourgeois liberalization."[12] In 1979 a disillusioned former Red Guard named Wei Jingsheng was sentenced to fifteen years in prison for writing an essay pleading for the fifth modernization—democracy. When students demonstrated for democracy in December 1986, Deng reacted poorly. Dissident intellectuals such as the astrophysicist Fang Lizhi and the journalist Liu Binyan were expelled from the party.

As a true Leninist, Deng could not contemplate the party relinquishing its monopoly on political power. When faced with popular political ferment, he doggedly recited the four cardinal principles:

1. We must keep to the socialist road.
2. We must uphold the dictatorship of the proletariat.
3. We must uphold the leadership of the Communist Party.
4. We must uphold Marxism–Leninism and Mao Zedong Thought.

The last reference, to Mao Zedong Thought, was only a verbal gesture, as nearly everything Deng was attempting was precisely contrary to the dead dictator's thought. Even Deng's Marxism is questionable, for he discarded class struggle in favor of rapid economic modernization, and when challenged on this point he simply said that some get rich faster than others.

Leninists usually give no thought to the development of civil society, that is, aspects of life the state does not try to mold, including religion, a free market in stocks and real estate, labor unions, and an autonomous press. The concept of civil society is absent from Lenin's writings because he never contemplated the party loosening its grasp on society until the distant day when true communism would be achieved and the state could finally wither away.

Another political development Deng may not have foreseen was the devolution of power from Beijing to the provinces and cities. A federal system is considered normal in the West, but in the many centuries of Chinese history centrifugal forces have been harbingers of dynastic decline. Having lived through China's warlord period, Deng certainly had no intention of letting decentralization get out of hand. But the process, once begun, is difficult to stop.

THE TIANANMEN MASSACRE

The blackest mark on Deng's later career was his bloody suppression of the student uprising at Tiananmen Square. Why did he not sympathize with patriotic students who wanted to modernize China? Did he forget his own youthful enthusiasm during the May Fourth Movement of 1919? Part of the answer must be that he personally suffered so badly from the chaos of the Cultural Revolution that he thought anything was better than anarchy. He was dealing with people so much younger than he, with life experiences so different from his, that understanding was impossible.

In mid-1988 students at Beijing University penned large-character posters to Deng Xiaoping and two other party leaders, Zhao Ziyang, and Li Peng. The party's first instinct was to blame this impertinence on foreign agitators, an excuse lent superficial credibility when President George Bush visited Beijing in February 1989 and invited the outspoken Professor Fang Lizhi to a state dinner at the Great Wall Sheraton Hotel. (The Beijing police kept Fang away.) Two months later, on April 15, 1989, Hu Yaobang died. The former secretary-general of the CCP had once been Deng's protégé but had been made a scapegoat and fired for having allegedly encouraged bourgeois liberalization. Now, in death, Hu was mourned conspicuously, just as Zhou Enlai had been in 1976. By April 27 the estimated number of mourners at Tiananmen had reached 100,000. Students camped out in the square and refused to leave. Their demands grew. On May 4, the seventieth anniversary of the 1919 movement, the crowd numbered 150,000. Deng decided that this was a counterrevolutionary plot, not just a student movement. A state visit by Soviet leader Mikhail Gorbachev turned into a huge embarrassment for Deng. The students held Gorbachev in very high regard, but Deng could not give Gorbachev the usual ceremonial visit to the Forbidden City because the number of protesters at Tiananmen—now including office workers and laborers—reached 1 million.

On May 19 Deng decided to put an end to the "Beijing Spring." The liberal secretary-general of the CCP, Zhao Ziyang, another former Deng protégé, must have known what was coming, for he went to the students at 4:00 A.M. with tears in his eyes. Zhao begged them to go home and apologized for having come too late. On May 20 Premier Li Peng imposed martial law. On the night of June 3 and into the next morning, PLA troops entered Beijing. The carnage was broadcast around the world by color television.

The PLA ran over the people with tanks, killing hundreds, possibly thousands.

For several days there were no news programs on Chinese radio or television. Deng was rumored to be privately furious that the operation was so bloody, but he never backed down an inch. It was a "necessary military action," he reported to the nation. On June 9 he delivered a speech to commanders of the martial law enforcement troops in which he expressed his "heartfelt condolences" to the "martyrs" who had died in the fighting, referring to soldiers and police, not students. He said that the protesters were "not ordinary people" but "the dregs of society." He said their goals were "to establish a bourgeois republic entirely dependent on the West." He warned the commanders not to forget how cruel their enemies were, and added, "For them we should not have an iota of forgiveness."[13]

Worried that the massacre and its aftermath might tip the balance to conservatives and ultranationalists who opposed his reforms, Deng expressed the hope that "this bad thing will enable us to go ahead with reform and the open door policy at a more steady, better, even a faster pace."

Naturally, in reform and adopting the open policy, we run the risk of importing evil influences from the West and we have never underestimated such influences. What is important is that we should never change China back into a closed country. In political reforms we can affirm one point: We have to adhere to the system of the National People's Congress and not the American system of the separation of three powers. The US berates us for suppressing students. But when they handled domestic student unrest and turmoil, didn't they send out police and troops to arrest people and cause bloodshed? They were suppressing students and the people, but we are putting down a counter-revolutionary rebellion. What qualifications do they have to criticize us?[14]

DENG'S FOREIGN POLICY

When Deng Xiaoping ended China's isolation, he was acting in the tradition of turn-of-the-century Chinese reformers who had wanted to adopt foreign technology but retain China's essence. Although Deng feared contamination by foreign influences, China's first imports included Coca-Cola and Marlboro cigarettes. Deng's neomercantilist trade policy went way beyond consumer treats. Oil was exported to Japan in exchange for steel. China signed a deal with France to launch communications satellites. In October 1978 Deng visited Japan to sign a vacuous treaty of peace and friendship, but he also took the opportunity to visit a Nissan factory. What he saw resembled nothing in China. Other countries he visited in 1978 included Burma, Nepal, Thailand, Malaysia, Singapore, and Korea. These were not mere goodwill tours, for Deng had a specific goal: to neutralize reaction to the invasion of

Vietnam he had secretly planned. His celebrated visit to the United States must be seen in the same light.

President Jimmy Carter normalized U.S. relations with the PRC on New Year's Day 1979, formalizing the rapprochement President Richard Nixon had initiated in 1972. The American people were in a very pro-Chinese mood, mainly because the Chinese seemed like excellent allies to oppose the Soviet Union. *Time* magazine named Deng Xiaoping "Man of the Year." Deng and his wife traveled to the United States in January 1979, where he was received with a nineteen-gun salute on the south lawn of the White House, and spoke from behind a lectern thoughtfully equipped with a booster step. (The ceremony was marred by two reporters from a Maoist press service in Seattle who suddenly pulled out *Quotations from Chairman Mao Zedong*, started waving it, and screamed that Deng was a murderer.) He laid a wreath at the Lincoln Memorial and seemed instinctively to know what to do to make a hit with Americans, including kissing children and posing for humorous photos with players for the Harlem Globetrotters who were nearly twice as he tall as he.

Deng attended a reception at the National Gallery of Art and was serenaded by John Denver at the Kennedy Center. He was honored at a White House dinner of 140 guests including former President Nixon. The actress Shirley MacLaine was seated at Deng's table. She enthusiastically described a 1973 trip to China during which she had met an atomic scientist who had been sent down to a farm during the Cultural Revolution and who had assured her that learning how to grow tomatoes was as important to him as his atomic research. Deng had no time for such foolishness and simply said, "He lied to you."

Deng was given an honorary LL.D. from Temple University, and then moved on to Georgia, where he visited a Ford assembly plant and paid tribute at Martin Luther King's grave. His next stop was Houston, where he played at the controls of a space shuttle simulator and was introduced to executives who were interested in selling oil-drilling equipment. Most memorably, the leader of communist China attended a Texas rodeo and tried on a ten-gallon cowboy hat. His last stop was Seattle, where he toured the Boeing aircraft factory. Chinese government cameramen filmed all this for a nightly half-hour broadcast to television viewers in the PRC. Radio Beijing played Bob Dylan records for its Chinese listening audience, but their reaction was not reported.

Why was Deng doing all this? Probably because he had already decided to invade Vietnam and needed protection from Soviet retaliation. He said in an interview: "If we really want to be able to place curbs on the polar bear, the only realistic thing for us is to unite. . . . The true hotbed of war is the Soviet Union, not the U.S."[15] While Deng traveled around the United States, denouncing Soviet foreign policy at every opportunity, 150,000 Chinese troops were already massing on the Vietnam border.

The Sino–Vietnamese War of 1979 was Deng's decision. He seemed to hate the Vietnamese. A Thai diplomat who had been present at many meetings with Deng told a correspondent, "The moment the topic of Vietnam came up, one could see something change in Deng Xiaoping. His hatred for them was just visceral." He called the Vietnamese "dogs" and "the hooligans of the East."[16] Deng boasted that he would teach the Vietnamese a lesson, but in fact the PLA learned how far behind it had fallen. Chinese troops had to fight without air cover because Vietnam had one of the best air defense systems anywhere. The PLA was finally able to advance some miles into northern Vietnam, yet with a ghastly cost in lives. Vietnam did not even have to withdraw its main battle forces from occupied Cambodia, which was the stated aim of China's invasion.

Toward the end of Deng's life a spirit of angry nationalism was encouraged by a party faction grouped around the reactionary propagandist Deng Liqun (no relation to Deng Xiaoping). Deng Liqun encouraged fears of "dark plots." If Westerners wished China to evolve into a democracy, this was "a coup d'etat by other means."[17] The collapse of communism in Eastern Europe and the Soviet Union reinforced the Chinese suspicion that the West had a plan to overturn their political system, too. Democratic ideas were labeled "spiritual pollution." A propaganda campaign was mounted in 1990 on the 150th anniversary of the outbreak of the First Opium War, to warn citizens against "decadent bourgeois things from the West . . . the spiritual opium."

All revolutions are puritanical at first. However, the clearest sign that a reign of terror has ended is that bribery and black marketeering reappear. In the case of China, prostitution and drug addiction, which the communists claimed to have eliminated, returned. And there was a new scourge—AIDS. Corruption spread through the government, undermining the party's claim to moral superiority.

DENG'S PERSONAL LIFE AFTER 1977

Deng lived modestly in his years of unchallenged power, always preferring privacy to publicity. No statues of him were erected, no portraits hung in public places, no books of his thoughts published. He hardly ever gave public speeches and was rarely heard on radio or seen on television.

At some point Deng and his family moved out of the Zhongnanhai compound. He quietly sent his paralyzed son Deng Pufang to Canada for surgery that restored partial movement to his arms. Today Deng Pufang is the president of China's Disabled Persons Federation and also a businessman who has cashed in on his name. Indeed, the roster of Deng's relatives who traded on their influence grew longer as Deng aged. The younger son, Deng Zhifang, who had studied physics in the United States, was investigated for corruption in the mid-1990s. Deng's niece Ding Peng, likewise, fell under a cloud when her Australian business partner was convicted of corruption by a Chinese court.

Deng is an example of an overstaying leader. He had told Gorbachev that "the only thing that can't be brought to pass is the abolition from the system of lifelong positions for leaders. This is one of the system's biggest problems."[18] Deng could not retire because no one else had the prestige to keep China on its course of economic reform. He feared that others wanted a "bird cage economy" in which the free market would be confined inside a state plan. Ironically, Deng in his last years seemed to grow distrustful of the party, as Mao had. His famous southern tour to the special economic zones, undertaken in January 1992 when he was eighty-seven years old, was a dramatic way to endorse continued economic reform.

Deng's last years were troubled by worries about the army, too. At the Fourteenth Party Congress in 1992, Deng dropped his old bridge partner and political ally, General Yang Shangkun, from the Central Military Commission because of well-founded fears that Yang, though only four years younger than Deng himself, planned to start his own dynasty. Yang was replaced by another superannuated officer, Admiral Liu Huaqing, whom Deng recalled from retirement. Admiral Liu had been a party member for sixty years.[19]

As Deng slipped into his dotage, his public appearances grew rarer, and after 1994 they ceased entirely. He still relaxed occasionally by swimming but was unable to walk well, perhaps due to Parkinson's disease or diabetes. His doctors worried that even a cold might kill him. The party began preparing the public for his death. On his ninety-second birthday in 1996 the Xinhua News Agency released a 3,000-line poem, "Ode to Deng Xiaoping."

As always happens where there are no elections or fixed procedures for succession, the sharks began to circle. President Jiang Zemin expressed the wish to be declared Chairman Jiang, the ultimate honorific title. Prime Minister Li Peng, deeply unpopular for his role in the Tiananmen Massacre, positioned himself for the coming power struggle. Li's general outlook may be deduced from his State Council Proclamation Number 129 (October 1993), which outlawed the purchase or possession of satellite dishes, of which there were already an estimated half million in China.

Deng Xiaoping died on February 19, 1997, at age ninety-two. His designated successor, Jiang Zemin, assumed power smoothly. That in itself showed that China had entered a new era. The peaceful incorporation of Hong Kong into the PRC, which occurred in July 1997, was another legacy of Deng's pragmatism, patriotism, and patience. Any assessment of Deng

Xiaoping's life must be equivocal. If we consider only China's economic progress, Deng was a hero. If we consider only human rights, he was a tyrant. Deng Xiaoping's place in history depends to a large degree on what happens to China in the coming years. Perhaps we should let Deng's own words serve as his epitaph: "My life belongs to the Party and the state."[20]

NOTES

1. Ching Hua Lee, *Deng Xiaoping: The Marxist Road to the Forbidden City* (Princeton, N.J.: Kingston Press, 1985), p. 37.

2. Harrison E. Salisbury, *The New Emperors: China in the Era of Mao and Deng* (Boston: Little, Brown, 1992), pp. 33–34.

3. Richard Evans, *Deng Xiaoping and the Making of Modern China* (New York: Penguin, 1995), p. 98.

4. Salisbury, *The New Emperors*, p. 59.

5. Deng Maomao, *Deng Xiaoping, My Father* (New York: HarperCollins, 1995).

6. Alan Lawrance, *Mao Zedong: A Bibliography* (New York: Greenwood Press, 1991), p. 18.

7. Lucian W. Pye, "An Introductory Profile: Deng Xiaoping and China's Political Culture," in *Deng Xiaoping: Portrait of a Chinese Statesman*, ed. David Shambaugh (Oxford: Oxford University Press, 1995), p. 30. Pye found this confession in a mimeographed copy of Red Guard materials at Harvard's East Asian Research Library.

8. Salisbury, *The New Emperors*, p. 377.

9. June Teufel Dreyer, "Deng Xiaoping: The Soldier," in *Deng Xiaoping: Portrait of a Chinese Statesman*, p. 136.

10. Lucian W. Pye, "Leader in the Shadows: A View of Deng Xiaoping," *Current History* 95 (September 1996), p. 246–47.

11. Pye, "Leader in the Shadows," p. 249.

12. Deng Xiaoping, "Remarks at the 6th Plenary Session of the Party's 12th Central Committee," September 28, 1986, *Beijing Review* 32 (July 17–23, 1989), pp. 21–22.

13. "Deng's Talks on Quelling Rebellion in Beijing," *Beijing Review* 32, no. 28 (July 10–16, 1989), pp. 18–21.

14. "Deng's Talks on Quelling Rebellion in Beijing," pp. 18–21.

15. *Time* (February 5, 1979), p. 32.

16. Nayan Chanda, *Brother Enemy: The War After the War* (New York: Harcourt Brace Jovanovich, 1986), p. 261.

17. "The West's Peaceful Evolution Examined," *Beijing Review* 32, (October 23–29, 1989), pp. 13–14.

18. Patrick E. Tyler, "Chinese Issuing What May Be Deng's Final Book," *New York Times*, November 4, 1993, p. 3.

19. Roderick MacFarquhar, "Deng's Last Campaign," *New York Review of Books* 39, no. 21 (December 17, 1992), pp. 27–28.

20. Deng Xiaoping, "Letter of Resignation to CPC Political Bureau," *Beijing Review* 32, no. 47 (November 20–26, 1989), p. 22.

For Further Reading

Barmé, Geremie. *Shades of Mao: The Posthumous Cult of the Great Leader*. New York: M. E. Sharpe, 1996.

Baum, Richard. *Burying Mao: Chinese Politics in the Age of Deng Xiaoping*. Princeton, N.J.: Princeton University Press, 1994.

Becker, Jasper. *Hungry Ghosts: Mao's Secret Famine*. New York: Free Press, 1996.

Brown, Lester R. *Who Will Feed China? Wake-up Call for a Small Planet*. New York: W. W. Norton, 1995.

Ch'i, Hsi-Sheng. *Politics of Disillusionment: The Chinese Communist Party Under Deng Xiaoping, 1978–1989*. Armonk, N.Y.: M. E. Sharp, 1991.

Deng Maomao. *Deng Xiaoping: My Father*. New York: HarperCollins, 1995.

Evans, Richard. *Deng Xiaoping and the Making of Modern China*. New York: Penguin, 1995.

Franz, Uli. *Deng Xiaoping*. Boston: Harcourt Brace Jovanovich, 1988.

Goldman, Merle. *Sowing the Seeds of Democracy in China: Political Reform in the Deng Xiaoping Era*. Cambridge, Mass.: Harvard University Press, 1994.

Hsü, Emmanuel C. Y. *The Rise of Modern China*. 5th ed. New York: Oxford University Press, 1995.

Li Zhisui. *The Private Life of Chairman Mao*. New York: Random House, 1994.

Lieberthal, Kenneth, and Michael Oksenberg. *Policy Making in China: Leaders, Structures, and Processes*. Princeton, N.J.: Princeton University Press, 1988.

Lifton, Robert Jay. *Revolutionary Immortality: Mao Tse-tung and the Chinese Cultural Revolution*. New York: W. W. Norton, 1976.

Rice, Edward E. *Mao's Way*. Berkeley: University of California Press, 1974.

Spence, Jonathan D. *The Search for Modern China*. New York: W. W. Norton, 1990.

Terrill, Ross. *Madame Mao: The White-Boned Demon*. New York: Bantam Books, 1986.

———. *Mao: A Biography*. New York: Harper & Row, 1980.

Yang, Benjamin. *Deng: A Political Biography*. Armonk, N.Y.: M. E. Sharp, 1998.

Part II

Vietnam

Vietnam

Vietnam Timeline

111 B.C.	China annexes Nam Viet.
A.D. 39	Trung sisters lead rebellion against Chinese rule.
43	Rebellion crushed; Trung sisters drown themselves; Vietnam is a province of China for the next 900 years.
939	Ngo Quyen declares Vietnamese independence; defeats Chinese invading force; founds Ngo dynasty.
981	Le Hoan defeats Chinese invasion.
1009–1225	Ly dynasty; Buddhism flourishes in Vietnam.
1225–1400	Tran dynasty.
1254	Mongols invade Vietnam but are repelled.
1284	Mongols invade Vietnam again but are repelled again.
1407–27	Chinese occupy Vietnamese towns but cannot control countryside.
1418–28	Le Loi leads war of national liberation; Chinese expelled.
1858 Sep	French seize Danang.
1883 Aug	French protectorate over Annam and Tonkin; Cochin-China is a colony directly ruled by France.
1890 May 19	Ho Chi Minh born.
1901 Jan 3	Ngo Dinh Diem born.
1917–23	Ho spends six years in France.
1919	Ho pleads for Vietnamese independence at Versailles peace conference.
1920 Dec	Ho Chi Minh founding member of French Communist Party.
1930 Feb	Ho Chi Minh creates Indochinese Communist Party in Hong Kong.
1931 Jun	Ho Chi Minh arrested in Hong Kong; he spends one year in prison, where he contracts tuberculosis.
1932	Bao Dai ascends throne under French tutelage.
1933 May	Bao Dai appoints Ngo Dinh Diem minister of the interior; he resigns two months later.

1940 Sep 22	Japan occupies Vietnam with consent of French.
1941 Feb 14	Ho Chi Minh returns to Vietnam from thirty years in exile.
1945 Sep 2	Ho Chi Minh declares Vietnamese independence.
1946 Nov 22	French attack Haiphong, killing 6,000.
1950 May 30	U.S. economic mission established in Saigon.
1954 May 7	French defeated at Dien Bien Phu, despite having received more than $2 billion in U.S. aid.
1954 Jul 24	Geneva peace accords signed.
1955	Republic of Vietnam established; Ngo Dinh Diem president.
1955 Dec	Radical phase of land reform in North Vietnam.
1957 May 8–19	Diem visits United States and addresses a joint session of Congress. President Dwight Eisenhower calls him the "miracle man" of Asia.
1957 Oct	Communist insurgency begins in South Vietnam.
1959 May	First U.S. advisers sent to Vietnam.
1960 Dec 20	National Liberation Front formed.
1961	President John F. Kennedy begins clandestine war against North Vietnam and Laos.
1962	9,000 U.S. military advisers in South Vietnam.
1963 Jun 11	Buddhist monk Thich Quang Duc immolates himself in ritual suicide to protest Diem's suppression of the Buddhists.
1963 Nov 2	Ngo Dinh Diem and his brother are overthrown and killed.
1964 Aug 2	Tonkin Gulf incident.
1965 Dec	200,000 U.S. troops in South Vietnam.
1966 Apr 11	B-52s bomb North Vietnam.
1966 Dec	400,000 U.S. troops in South Vietnam.
1968 Jan 31	Tet offensive.
1969	543,000 U.S. troops in South Vietnam.
1969 Sep 3	Ho Chi Minh dies.
1975 Apr 30	Saigon falls to the communists, Vietnam reunited.
1979 Jan	Vietnam invades Cambodia.
1979 Feb	China invades Vietnam.
1986	Sixth Party Congress allows economic reforms.
1989	Economic renovation; land returned to peasants, foreign investment encouraged.
1995 Jul	United States normalizes diplomatic relations with Vietnam.
1997	Washington sends Douglas Peterson, a former prisoner of war, as ambassador.

1997 Dec 29	Le Kha Phieu elected general secretary of Communist Party; shares power with President Tran Duc Luong and Prime Minister Phan Van Khai.
1998 Mar	Vietnam eligible for U.S. financial aid and from World Bank agencies.
1998 Aug	Vietnam experiences worst drought in a century.

The Vietnamese Setting

To Americans the name "Vietnam" conjures up nightmarish images of burning villages, wounded soldiers, and a mob of terrified people trying to climb into a helicopter on the roof of the U.S. embassy in Saigon. Vietnam was America's great twentieth-century trauma. To today's college students the Vietnam War is history, but it is still so disturbing and controversial that most high school history classes skip over it lightly. The war is best symbolized by a black marble wall engraved with 58,000 names, the most visited tourist site in Washington, D.C. All this from a small, poor, faraway nation whose people had never heard of the United States until fifty years ago, a mere eye blink in their 2,000-year history.

GEOGRAPHY

Today, the Socialist Republic of Vietnam (SRV) is united from its border with China in the north to the Ca Mau Peninsula in the south. A Communist government attempts to maintain control over 78 million citizens. Vietnam's long border with Laos, demarcated by the French, runs along the Annam Cordillera. Border disputes with China and Cambodia have plagued Vietnam throughout its history. Even the maritime frontier is contested; both the Vietnamese and Chinese navies maneuver for advantage in the South China Sea.

The shape of Vietnam has been likened to a bamboo pole with baskets of rice hanging from both ends. It is an apt metaphor, for the only broad lowlands in Vietnam are the Red River delta near Hanoi and the Mekong delta near Saigon. These river deltas are densely populated; fewer people live in the center of the country, which is mountainous. Vietnam is slightly smaller than California but more than twice as populous.

Hanoi is the capital, but Saigon, officially renamed Ho Chi Minh City, is larger and more dynamic. The north may be considered the heartland of traditional Vietnamese culture, whereas the south is actually a frontier zone only relatively recently settled by the Vietnamese who, in their thousand-year-long southward march, displaced Chams and Khmers (Cambodians). South Vietnam was more Westernized than North Vietnam; first because Saigon was the seat of French colonial administration, and second because South Vietnamese elites turned to the United States for protection against the North Vietnamese communists.

Vietnam has a tropical monsoon climate. It is warm year-round but has pronounced wet and dry seasons. Rice is the staple food of the Vietnamese. Plantations (now nationalized) produce a variety of tropical commodities, including rice, rubber, fruit, sugar, and coffee. There are deposits of phosphates, iron, manganese, bauxite, zinc, and tin. These, plus some large coal mines, are mostly located in the northern mountains. After economic reforms in the 1990s, Vietnam has emerged again as a major rice exporter.

The ancestors of today's Vietnamese people migrated into the Red River delta from southern China beginning in the second century B.C., bringing with them rice cultivation, irrigation technology, and a culture based on organized cooperative labor. Whenever a strong dynasty arose in China, Chinese armies marched down to occupy Vietnam. Indeed, China counted Vietnam as one of its own provinces for a thousand years. But the Vietnamese clung tenaciously to their language and culture.

Today ethnic Vietnamese make up 85 percent of the country's population. The remainder is accounted for by Montagnards (mountain tribes), ethnic Chinese, and ethnic Khmers. The Chinese are only partly assimilated. They tend to be urban merchants and entrepreneurs. The government has closed most Chinese-language schools and bans the wearing of Chinese dress. Many Chinese became "boat people" after 1975 when the victorious communists tried to destroy private enterprise.

CULTURE

Vietnamese is a tonal language difficult for Westerners to master. Chinese ideographs were used to write Vietnamese until the seventeenth century when a Jesuit priest devised a way to write Vietnamese in the Western alphabet using special diacritical marks. This made Vietnam's existing scholarly class obsolete, and those who learned the new system were cut off from their own classical civilization.

Vietnam is a Confucian society, and in this respect resembles East Asia (China, Korea, and Japan) more than its neighbors in Southeast Asia. Confucianism is a code of ethics and morals that promotes social harmony by stressing the need for everyone to follow authority and be satisfied with one's place in life, no matter how lowly. Confucianism emphasizes mutual obligations between father and son, husband and wife, elder brother and younger brother, teacher and student, and ruler and subject. Under Confucian principles of government, political authority is concentrated in the emperor. Bureaucrats (mandarins) govern the state in his name. As long as he performs his rituals correctly, the state will be in harmony with the cosmos. Conversely, floods, earthquakes, famines, plagues, or invasions were interpreted as signs that heaven no longer smiled on the emperor, that he had lost the "mandate of heaven." It becomes a self-fulfilling prophecy, and soon revolutionaries "succeed in everything as if miraculously."[1] Many Vietnamese sensed a shift in the mandate of heaven when Ho Chi Minh declared Vietnamese independence in 1945. Over the next thirty years the seemingly unstoppable drive of the North Vietnamese and their southern partners convinced many that resistance was hopeless.

Vietnamese can be Confucians and Buddhists at the same time, for Confucianism may be considered more a philosophy than a religion. The Vietnamese, like the Chinese, are Mahayana (Greater Vehicle) Buddhists. Theravada (Lesser Vehicle) Buddhism is practiced in Cambodia, Thailand, and Burma. One difference between the two schools is that Mahayana Buddhists believe in bodhisattvas, beings somewhat like saints, who stopped just short of perfect enlightenment to help other struggling mortals. Buddhists proclaim the Four Noble Truths: (1) life is suffering; (2) suffering stems from greed; (3) suffering ceases when greed ceases; and (4) to achieve nirvana (release from suffering) one must follow the Eightfold Path of moderation in all behavior. Neither Confucianism nor Buddhism includes the concept of an anthropomorphic God. The Vietnamese have integrated animism and ancestor worship into their belief system. Spirits are present everywhere, in trees, rocks, waterfalls, and rice fields. The spirits of dead people can inhabit the bodies of animals. Spirits are so pervasive and so dangerous that they must be constantly propitiated by special ceremonies.

Approximately 7 percent of the people of Vietnam are Roman Catholic. Vietnamese emperors recognized in Christianity a mortal threat to the Confucian system over which they reigned. Catholics in South Vietnam were in a favored position in the government of Ngo Dinh Diem (1954–63). After 1975 the communists discriminated against Catholics, whom they regarded as unpatriotic. Vietnam today is overwhelmingly secular, but some churches are again filling with parishioners.

In rural Vietnam, time is measured by the rhythms of the seasons, and punctuality is not highly valued. Personal relationships are often more important than formal titles, and patron–client ties (personal, hierarchical, and reciprocal dyadic bonds between people unequal in power or resources) are the structural underpinning of society. These alliances act as the strands of a web that binds society together.[2] This web of personal ties exists in a state of tension with the universal, impersonal norms upheld by Confucians and Marxists alike. The centralized, hierarchical structure of a Marxist–Leninist state bears more than a passing similarity to that of an ideal Confucian state. Both require that those who hold power—because they are unchecked—be indoctrinated to act morally.

Vietnam is a Confucian society, but Vietnamese women have played a strong role in their country's history. Perhaps in the distant past proto-Vietnamese tribes were matriarchal. Vietnam's first independence war was led by two women, the Trung sisters. Under classical Vietnamese dynasties women had a right to inherit property; nonetheless the ideal Confucian family was patriarchal and authoritarian. In modern times women contributed heavily to the war effort. The Communist Party promotes equality of the sexes in health care benefits and education, but the party itself is heavily male at the upper reaches.

HISTORICAL CONTEXT

The name "Vietnam," as used in this book, refers to three of the five states of former French Indochina, those that faced the South China Sea: Tonkin, Annam, and Cochin-China. (The other two parts of French Indochina were Laos and Cambodia.) Tonkin was the northernmost part of Vietnam, centered on the Red River delta. Annam constituted the central part of Vietnam, mostly mountainous but with some small delta areas where short steep rivers flowed to the sea. Cochin-China in the south was a jungly, frontier zone, too remote for the emperor to effectively control. Ho Chi Minh and other nationalists used the name "Vietnam" to include all three colonies. When he proclaimed the independence of Vietnam in August 1945, he asserted the right to a united country. The Geneva accords of 1954 temporarily divided Vietnam into two zones but did not create two separate countries named North Vietnam and South Vietnam.[3]

The cradle of Vietnamese culture and history is the Red River delta, where immigrants from southern China intermarried with indigenes, including the Chams who once occupied much of the territory we know as Vietnam. Chinese troops of the Han dynasty conquered Vietnam in 111 B.C., and for the next thousand years it was considered an outlying province of China. The Vietnamese absorbed many features of Chinese civilization, including Confucianism, Buddhism, and Chinese concepts of art, architecture, poetry, science, and statecraft, but the Vietnamese never thought of themselves as Chinese and never gave up their distinct language.

The Vietnamese may be counted among our world's first nationalists, alongside the Hebrews and the Greeks. According to the Vietnamese founding myth, which may not be entirely accurate, Trung Trac and her sister, Trung Nhi, led a rebellion in A.D. 39 to avenge the murder of Trac's husband by a Chinese commander. When the insurrection failed, they drowned themselves in a well. Almost 2,000 years later, Vietnamese still commemorate the Trung sisters' sacrifice. Vietnam's next rebellion took place in A.D. 939, when the Chinese T'ang dynasty was in decline. An official named Ngo Quyen proclaimed Vietnamese independence and defeated a Chinese naval expeditionary force by implanting iron-tipped spikes in the Red River estuary and luring the Chinese in at high tide. When the tide went out, the Chinese ships were impaled. Ngo Quyen's men emerged from the riverbanks and slaughtered the Chinese. Ngo Quyen founded a dynasty that lasted for thirty years until a new Chinese dynasty once again incorporated Vietnam into China.

When the Mongols conquered China, they tried to extend their control down into Vietnam but were defeated twice, in 1254 and 1284. Vietnam was thoroughly ravaged in the fighting. When a new Chinese dynasty, the Mings, arose in the late fourteenth century they naturally invaded Vietnam. Ming commanders set up garrisons at strategic locations.

> Ming armies systematically ravaged the country, carrying off to China the Viet fleet, soldiers, horses and war elephants, plus thousands of craftsmen and scholars. . . . Vietnamese were required to learn to speak Chinese, to adopt Chinese costume, hairdress, religious practices, ceremonies, and customs. Tattooing, tooth-blackening, and betel-chewing were prohibited. Following a general census, identity cards were required to assure that no man escaped military draft. Heavy taxes were imposed, and the mines and forests were exploited with forced labor.[4]

The Chinese found they could not control the Vietnamese villages, where a resistance force arose under the leadership of a scholar named Le Loi. Le Loi proclaimed victory in 1428 after a ten-year war of national liberation. His successors placated the Chinese by entering into a tributary relationship under which Vietnam acknowledged Chinese superiority. (The Vietnamese emperor Gia Long wrote to the Chinese emperor in 1802, "I am not more than a tiny tributary of your Empire and my strongest desire is to be sprinkled by the rain of your generosity.")[5] Such flowery words concealed the reality that Vietnam was autonomous.

The French arrived in force in Vietnam in the mid-nineteenth century, acquiring territory mindlessly at first but then consolidating their holdings. They controlled all of Vietnam by 1884. A French governor general ruled Indochina (Vietnam, Cambodia, and Laos) from a magnificent palace in Hanoi. The French had two choices in Vietnam: to rule indirectly through the enfeebled Vietnamese authorities or to "assimilate" Vietnam into France, on the principle that "no greater honor could befall a people than to absorb the ideas and culture of France."[6] The solution was to prop up a puppet Vietnamese emperor but to allow him no real authority. Out in the villages the

French relied on local headmen to collect taxes and mobilize labor. These village chiefs became notorious for their extreme corruption.

French colonialists were interested in extracting Vietnam's natural resources, opening new markets for French products, and winning converts to Christianity. They expected Vietnam to remain part of the French empire forever thus made no effort to prepare the people for independence. In traditional Vietnam many people were literate, but the French replaced Vietnamese schools with a French educational system that created a new class of Francophile clerks and bureaucrats. Schooling was not intended for the masses—only 2 percent of the population received even elementary education. The French built one university and eighty-three prisons.[7] To sum up, Vietnam under the French was a society of impoverished peasants ruled by foreign bureaucrats and a small class of native collaborators. This is not to say there was no progress. Roads were built and canals dug. Swamps were drained and jungles cleared, especially in the Mekong delta where the flat land and fertile soil were perfect for large-scale plantation agriculture. But the price of these improvements included 25,000 laborers who died building a 300-mile railroad line from Haiphong up to the coal mines of Yunnan, China.

In the light of Vietnamese history, it was inevitable that this situation should produce a Vietnamese underground. One early nationalist was Phan Boi Chau, a famous scholar who had traveled all over Vietnam. In the first decades of the 1900s he founded various patriotic organizations but focused principally on the elite classes while ignoring the peasants who made up more than 80 percent of the population. Ho Chi Minh emerged as the leader of the Viet Minh, a guerrilla army that defeated French, Japanese, and U.S. troops. Ho blended Marxism–Leninism with Vietnamese patriotism, creating an irresistible force that slowly swept all before it. He was prepared to govern the entire country when the Japanese surrendered in 1945, but France tried to reconstitute its empire. War between the French and Ho's army broke out in December 1946 and lasted for eight years. By 1954, even with the United States financing 80 percent of the cost of the war, the French were ready to quit. The final blow was the Battle of Dien Bien Phu, where the French were routed by the communist general Vo Nguyen Giap, a military genius. (Twenty-one years later Giap planned the final spring offensive that crushed the army of South Vietnam.)

MODERN HISTORY

South Vietnam had some unique characteristics that distinguished it from North Vietnam but not enough to generate a viable southern nationalism. Southerners were less traditional and more cosmopolitan than northerners, for Saigon was the port through which modern ideas came to Vietnam. At the 1954 Geneva Conference, Ho Chi Minh agreed to a temporary partition of Vietnam at the seventeenth parallel in the belief that the rival southern government would quickly collapse. Elections were supposed to be held by 1956 to reunite Vietnam. However, the United States decided to back Ngo Dinh Diem—a Catholic in a Buddhist country, an Annamite in the South, and a mandarin amidst peasants. With American encouragement, Diem proclaimed the Republic of Vietnam with himself as the first president. Diem's regime grew more corrupt and oppressive with every passing year. The Viet Minh guerrillas reorganized, with guidance from Hanoi, under the banner of the National Liberation Front (NLF), better known to Americans as the Vietcong. Northerners sent south by Hanoi gradually took control of the NLF.

When Ngo Dinh Diem proved incompetent, the U.S. ambassador encouraged a coup d'etat against him, but Diem's successors fared no better. The United States found itself shouldering a greater share of the financial and military burden, even sending civilian advisers to show Vietnamese how to govern their own country. Why did U.S. presidents invest so much blood and treasure in a distant corner of the globe? First, because they subscribed to the domino theory, according to which the fall of South Vietnam would inevitably lead to communist takeovers in one country after another. Second, they escalated their rhetoric until the war in Vietnam became a test of American credibility. With the situation so defined, to withdraw became unthinkable.

President John F. Kennedy viewed Vietnam in the context of the cold war, as a direct, and personal, challenge by Soviet premier Nikita Khrushchev. In fact, the Russians had almost no role in directing North Vietnamese moves. President Lyndon Johnson, who inherited this unpromising situation when President Kennedy was assassinated, was so unfamiliar with Southeast Asia that he sometimes said "Indonesia" when he meant "Indochina." Johnson campaigned on a peace platform in 1964, even while planning to escalate the war after the election. By 1966, 200,000 American troops were in Vietnam; by 1967 the number had increased to over 500,000. U.S. spending on the war rose to $2 billion per month. Large parts of Vietnam were cratered by bombs, and still the Vietcong and the North Vietnamese refused to surrender. Anti-war groups in the United States argued that the struggle was actually a civil war, not a takeover of one country by another; that no end justified destroying an entire country; and that Southeast Asia was not even strategically important to the United States.

Richard Nixon was elected president in 1968. He claimed to have a secret plan to end the war, but fighting went on for seven more years. Nixon ordered the bombing of Cambodia to destroy the NLF headquarters and disrupt communist supply routes. Neither goal was accomplished, however, but the unrelenting B-52 raids created roving bands of orphans who found new lives as cadres of the Khmer Rouge, the Cambodian communist army that was so secretive that no one in Washington, D.C., even knew the name of their leader—Pol Pot.

As Nixon gradually withdrew U.S. forces, asking only that the North Vietnamese allow a "decent interval" before taking over the South, it became clear that the South Vietnamese Army and government would collapse. The end came in the spring of 1975, six years after the death of Ho Chi Minh. Vietnam was in ruins. Roads, railroads, and bridges were demolished. Two-thirds of the villages were damaged. The imposition of a socialist command economy on South Vietnam only made matters worse. Industries were nationalized, land was confiscated, and entrepreneurs (especially ethnic Chinese) were harassed. Many people fled the country on flimsy fishing boats. Vietnam became dependent on handouts from the Soviet Union, while the United States organized an international economic boycott of the Socialist Republic of Vietnam. Floods, droughts, and typhoons further worsened conditions. The victorious communists sent their enemies, real and perceived, to "reeducation camps," denying the nation the services of many skilled technicians and administrators.

More than a decade passed before the communists admitted the extent of their failures, which included isolating Vietnam from the world, imposing deadening controls on the economy, and wasting human resources in the reeducation camps. By then China and the Soviet Union had both embarked on thoroughgoing reform, so Vietnamese communist reformers felt less isolated. In 1986, Hanoi announced a policy of *doi moi* (renewal). The peasants were given back their land and allowed to sell their produce on the open market. Shops were privatized. Foreign investors, even U.S. oil companies, were welcomed. In the 1990s Vietnam enjoyed one of the highest rates of economic growth in the world. In 1980 Saigon traffic consisted mostly of bicycles, but by 1990 there were many motorcycles, and by 1998 the streets were clogged with Japanese cars. Many new factories have been built in Vietnam with overseas capital. Yet even with economic progress, 40 percent of Vietnamese children under the age of five suffer from malnutrition.

Vietnam's record on human rights is depressing. Freedoms of speech, press, assembly, and religion are tightly circumscribed. The government remains contemptuous of Western-style democracy on both ideological and cultural grounds.

In 1994 President Clinton lifted the U.S. economic embargo of Vietnam, and in 1995 he normalized diplomatic relations. In 1997 Douglas Peterson, who had spent seven years as a prisoner of war in North Vietnam, returned as the new U.S. ambassador.

NOTES

1. John T. McAlister, Jr., and Paul Mus, *The Vietnamese and Their Revolution* (New York: Harper & Row, 1970), p. 65.

2. Clark D. Neher, *Politics in Southeast Asia* (Cambridge, Mass.: Schenkman, 1987), pp. 143–45.

3. See Joseph Buttinger, *Vietnam: A Dragon Embattled* (New York: Praeger, 1967), p. 437.

4. Chester A. Bain, *Vietnam: The Roots of Conflict* (Englewood Cliffs, N.J.: Prentice-Hall, 1967), p. 62.

5. Quoted in J. Davidson, *Indo-China: Signposts in the Storm* (Singapore: Longman, 1979), p. 13.

6. Stanley Karnow, *Vietnam: A History* (New York: Viking Press, 1983), p. 113.

7. Robert T. Oliver, *Leadership in Asia: Persuasive Communication in the Making of Nations, 1850–1950* (Newark: University of Delaware Press, 1989), p. 202.

4

Ho Chi Minh: The Communist Patriot

A revolution is a thought in one man's mind.

Ralph Waldo Emerson

Ho Chi Minh, the creator of modern Vietnam, was a man of mystery. Biographers are unsure of the most basic facts: When was Ho born? How many brothers and sisters did he have? What happened to his mother and father? What turned him into a revolutionary? Did he ever marry? Even his real name is a matter of dispute. Here is a partial list of the more than 100 names, nicknames, and aliases that he had: Nguyen Sinh Cung, Nguyen Tat Thanh, Lin, Tran, Old Chen, Nguyen Ai Quoc, Vuong, Ho Quang, Thau Chin, Ba, Ly Thuy, Vuong Son Nhi, Truong Nhuoc Trung, Nilovsky, Tong Van So, Ho Khach Minh, and Hong Quoc Tuan.[1] We use the name "Ho Chi Minh" (He Who Enlightens) throughout this chapter, although he did not adopt it until 1942. Ho made secrecy a habit. He told the French scholar Bernard Fall, "I like to hold on to my little mysteries."[2] To the French he was a revolutionary outlaw. He would not have survived long unless he knew how to cover his tracks well.

Unlike Mao Zedong, Ho Chi Minh did not pose as a great thinker. He was too active to write treatises on revolutionary theory, but the government in Hanoi has published his prison diary and collections of pamphlets, speeches, and poems. Vietnamese accounts of Ho's life tend to be infected by hero worship. A definitive record of Ho Chi Minh's life cannot be written until Vietnamese historians feel free to follow the facts wherever they lead.

Ho Chi Minh's entire seventy-nine-year life was single-mindedly dedicated to achieving Vietnamese independence. This aloof, soft-spoken man inspired his countrymen to resist French imperialists, and he organized an army whose secret strength was its grasp of Vietnamese psychology—and also that of the French and the Americans. Ho Chi Minh proved that a well-motivated army could overcome huge material disadvantages.

Ho Chi Minh, no date

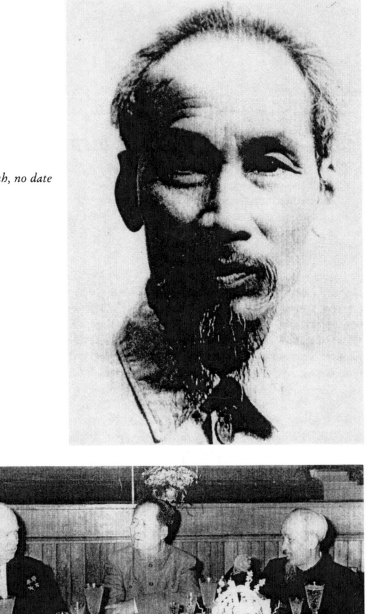

Ho Chi Minh (right) with Nikita Khrushchev (left) and Mao Zedong (center), 1959

HO CHI MINH AND HISTORY

A self-conscious patriotism is the dominant theme of Vietnamese history. Invaded and occupied repeatedly by China, the Vietnamese never lost their sense of nationalism. In the course of the twentieth century, Vietnam was invaded by four of the world's great powers—France, Japan, the United States, and China—and overcame them all. When Deng Xiaoping sent Chinese troops into Vietnam in 1979, the Vietnamese expelled them without even using their main force troops, which were otherwise busy in Cambodia. Few lessons of history are more obvious than this: It is a foolish statesman indeed who decides to invade Vietnam.

Ho Chi Minh's indignation at humiliations imposed by French imperialists was the catalyst for his revolutionary struggle. The French had destroyed many important Vietnamese institutions and traditions, and Catholic missionaries had condemned Confucianism as "ancestor worship." The Vietnamese government consisted of an emperor and a bureaucracy of mandarins (scholar-administrators). But the emperor became a tool of the French, and the mandarins were of no use to the government of French Indochina, which required the services only of native clerks and technicians.

For the ordinary Vietnamese farmer, the worst feature of French rule was the loss of village autonomy. That had been his only protection in hard times, and in monsoonal Southeast Asia hard times may be expected about one year out of three, when the rains come early or come late, when they are too skimpy or else too copious. The traditional Vietnamese state taxed villages—not individuals—and these taxes were paid in the form of rice and compulsory labor. Village headmen deliberately undercounted the inhabitants and underreported the harvest, so as to retain a surplus for the next year. The French conducted new censuses and land surveys, and they demanded taxes in cash, in good years or bad.[3] Some Vietnamese gained advantage by collaborating with the colonial rulers. A new elite class of landowners emerged, but their unpopularity was heightened by a taint of treason—they had begun to ape the foreigners.

Educated Vietnamese felt stranded. They were not regarded as "real" Frenchmen in Saigon or in Paris, and they could not return to their native villages, for they had changed too much. Such marginal men were ripe for revolution.

Ho Chi Minh was the son of a mandarin who had resigned rather than work for the French. Ho saw that Confucianism, nationalism, and Marxism had certain things in common, including that they all urged individuals to forsake their personal interests for the good of the state. The French brutally suppressed Vietnamese nationalist uprisings in the early years of the twentieth century, when Ho was a teenager. As a result, his outlook evolved from simple nationalism to revolutionary Marxism. Whether he really believed

Marxism to be scientifically correct is unclear, but he saw that it could be a powerful force in the service of Vietnamese independence.

Emperor Bao Dai, whose name meant "keeper of greatness," was born in 1913. He, too, was caught between the cultures of France and Vietnam. With his French education, he wanted to break away from the intrigues of his decadent court and reform and modernize his country, but the French restricted him to traditional ceremonies and smothered him in luxuries. He loved champagne, women, jazz, and hunting. Bao Dai was a genuine patriot but was fatally compromised and could never compete with Ho Chi Minh for popular affection. When he abdicated in 1945, ordinary Vietnamese saw in this act proof that the mandate of heaven had shifted to Ho Chi Minh.

EARLY SOCIALIZATION

Ho Chi Minh was born May 19, 1890, in Hoang Tru village, near the city of Vinh, in Nghe An Province, Tonkin. It was a poor area with a long history of producing rebels. Ho's mother died when he was still a child. His father was a poor but patriotic scholar who entered the imperial bureaucracy in 1901 after finally passing a national examination based on the works of Confucius, but who quit the imperial court, abandoned his family, and became an itinerant teacher who also practiced traditional Chinese medicine. He is thought to have died about 1930.

Ho went by the name of Nguyen That Thanh (Nguyen Who Will Be Victorious) from age ten. He delivered messages for the anti-French underground, and his family was suspected of stealing French weapons to turn over to insurgents.[4]

When he was fifteen years old Ho entered the Lycée Quôc-Hoc, an experimental high school in the old Annamese imperial capital at Hue, founded by Ngo Dinh Kha, a high official at the imperial court in Hue and father of South Vietnam's future president Ngo Dinh Diem. Courses were taught in French, but the emphasis was on Vietnamese patriotism. Two other students, besides Ho and Diem, later figured prominently in modern Vietnamese history: Vo Nguyen Giap, one of the true military geniuses of the twentieth century; and Pham Van Dong, the future premier of North Vietnam. Ho did not stay to receive a degree, perhaps for lack of money. He taught for a while at the Lycée Dac Phan in Phan Thiet, a coastal town 100 miles east of Saigon. Next he attended merchant marine school in Saigon for three months to learn navigation, in the hope of working aboard a ship and seeing the world. The prominent Vietnamese nationalist Phan Boi Chau met Ho and advised him to go to Tokyo. However, Ho was skeptical about Phan's elitist outlook and suspicious of his reliance on Japanese aid and thus ignored his advice.[5]

HO CHI MINH'S THIRTY YEARS ABROAD (1911–41)

In 1911 Ho Chi Minh sailed for Marseilles aboard the *Latouche-Treville*, a French merchant ship. Far from being a navigator, Ho was a cook, or perhaps only a mess boy. To conceal his identity, he adopted his first alias, Ba, and did not return to Vietnam for thirty years.[6] The young man spent two or three years at sea. Although working conditions below decks were ghastly, he traveled all around the Mediterranean and saw many French and Portuguese colonial port cities on the Africa runs. He probably got to Boston and New York. He later wrote passionate tracts graphically describing Ku Klux Klan lynchings in the southern United States, but he probably did not witness such atrocities; rather, as his political outlook grew steadily more radical, he was eager to denounce "the ugliness of American capitalism."[7]

When Ho quit his job with the French steamship line, he went to London and took odd jobs: He helped the chef at the Carlton Hotel, and in winter he shoveled snow off sidewalks for the London school system. He enjoyed political liberties unknown in the Indochinese colonies and joined an anticolonial group called the Overseas Workers' Association that devoted its attention to a broad range of colonial issues, including the Irish demand for home rule. These political experiences focused and strengthened his anticolonial views.

By 1917 Ho Chi Minh was living in Paris, where again he survived by taking a variety of odd jobs: kitchen boy, waiter, gardener, coal fetcher, oven stoker. He became a photographer's assistant, retouching photographs using Chinese calligraphy. And in his off hours he embarked on a remarkable adventure in self-education. His aptitude for language was impressive—Ho was fluent in Mandarin, Cantonese, and French, in addition to his native Vietnamese. He learned passable Russian, English, and German and also spoke some Portuguese, Japanese, Czech, and Thai. He is said to have read "Shakespeare and Dickens in English, Lu Hsün in Chinese, Victor Hugo and Émile Zola in French. His favorite author became Leo Tolstoy."[8]

In Paris Ho adopted the name Nguyen Ai Quoc (Nguyen Who Loves His Country) and made contact with leftist organizations and intellectuals. From them he learned how to organize meetings, distribute propaganda, and mobilize co-conspirators. It was always an eye-opener for Asians from the colonies to visit the mother country. Europeans may have acted like gods in Indochina, but Vietnamese who worked in France (80,000 did so during World War I) could see that the French were just ordinary mortals. The myth of European superiority was shattered by the senseless brutality of World War I. One imagines that the Vietnamese military policemen who, in 1917, acting on orders, fired into mutineering French troops, were changed men when they returned to Indochina.

Ho wrote politically pointed plays for cabarets, including a satire of

French colonialism called *Le dragon de bambou* (*The Bamboo Dragon*). Meanwhile his political outlook underwent a metamorphosis. From being merely anticolonial he became more ideologically anticapitalist, and his enthusiasm for Marxism swelled after the Bolshevik seizure of power in Russia in 1917.

Little is known about Ho's private life in Paris. If he had any romantic involvements, they are lost to history. His only known vice was an appetite for cigarettes, any kind; the dark French tobaccos or the lighter American brands he somehow had smuggled into Hanoi even while the United States was raining bombs on North Vietnam. Photographs of Ho Chi Minh show a man with intense, piercing eyes. He was very thin, almost frail. With his high forehead, receding hair, and long, wispy goatee, he might have been taken for a scholar instead of the dedicated revolutionary he was. Ho had one odd physical characteristic by which the French police could identify him from photos, no matter how often he changed his name to make them think he had died: His left ear was rounded, while his right ear was pointed.

In 1919 statesmen of the victorious Allies met at the Versailles Palace outside Paris to lay the foundation for a new international order. People from colonies were especially hopeful about President Woodrow Wilson's Fourteen Points, which seemed to promise the breakup of colonial empires and their replacement by free, sovereign nations. Ho borrowed a black suit and a bowler hat and went out to Versailles. He had drafted a moving, eight-point plea for justice for the people of Indochina, entitled *Cahiers de revendications du peuple vietnamien* (*List of Claims of the Vietnamese People*). "All subject peoples are filled with hope by the prospect that an era of right and justice is opening to them," he wrote.[9] He asked for legal equality between French and Vietnamese, basic civil liberties such as free speech and free press, more schools, and permanent representation in the French Parliament. This last point is significant: Ho was not demanding independence for Vietnam but merely a better deal for his country within the French empire. The assembled dignitaries laughed at the way the borrowed suit hung loosely on his delicate frame. The next year this shy Annamite with the permanently haunted expression became one of the founders of the French Communist Party.

European socialists were optimistic. History seemed to be moving their way, as Marx had said it would. Already the Bolsheviks, proclaiming themselves the vanguard of world revolution, occupied the Kremlin in Moscow. But French socialists seemed uninterested in what, for Ho, was the only question that really mattered: When would Vietnam become free? Some socialists even argued that France was developing and modernizing its colonies. To irritate them, Ho took to calling himself Nguyen O Phap (Nguyen Who Hates the French). Ho later said that all he wanted to know was which political group sided with the people of the colonial countries. When French socialists split into moderate and radical wings at their 1920 conference at Tours, Nguyen Who Loves His Country formally became a communist. Only the communists advocated immediate independence for the colonies, with no compromises. In 1921 Ho helped organize the Union Intercoloniale, an organization whose purpose was to educate the French public about abuses in the colonies, and in 1922 he worked for a left-wing propaganda newspaper called *La Paria* (*The Outcast*). When Ho read Vladimir Lenin's *Thesis on the National and Colonial Questions*, it struck him like a religious conversion:

> There were political terms difficult to understand in this thesis. But by dint of reading it again and again, finally I could grasp the main part of it. What emotion, enthusiasm, clear-sightedness, and confidence it instilled in me! I was overjoyed to tears. Though sitting alone in my room, I shouted aloud as if addressing large crowds: "Dear martyrs, compatriots! This is what we need, this is the path to our liberation!"[10]

Lenin's victory must have appeared almost miraculous to Ho. The mighty czarist empire crumbled before the Bolsheviks. Perhaps their ideology really did illuminate the path to victory. Ho devoured Lenin's extensive writings and admired his disdain of luxury and his love of labor. He agreed with Lenin's strategy for promoting a socialist revolution in the precapitalist (feudal) East by forging a three-way alliance between the peasants, the factory workers, and the national bourgeoisie (native capitalists whose patriotism impelled them to rebel against their European colonizers). In a later essay, Ho wrote: "At first patriotism, not yet Communism, led me to have confidence in Lenin. . . . I gradually came upon the fact that only Socialism and Communism can liberate the oppressed nations and the working people throughout the world from slavery."[11]

Ho observed how Mohandas Gandhi, the nonviolent Indian nationalist, had gained the attention and respect of the world with his sincerity and candor. Ho's strategy, of course, was totally different, but some of his personal traits echoed those of Gandhi: honesty, humility, and simplicity. Like Gandhi, Ho hated European clothes and preferred to sit on the floor and eat with his fingers.

The French Communist Party sent Ho to Moscow in 1922 as its delegate to the Fourth World Congress of the Communist International (Comintern). In 1923 he traveled to Moscow again, to attend the First Congress of International Peasantry (Krestintern) and was elected to its presidium. He did not return to France but stayed in Moscow to study Marxism and the Russian language at the so-called University of the Toilers of the East. Ho may have crossed paths with a young Chinese revolutionary named Deng Xiaoping, also recently arrived from Paris, but if so, we have no record of it.

Ho was in Moscow when Lenin died on January 21, 1924. He wrote a tribute that appeared in *Pravda*. That summer he attended the fifth Comintern Congress, where he publicly criticized the French Communist Party for not opposing colonialism more vigorously. Ho proclaimed a doctrine that would later be called "Maoism," namely, that peasants—those illiterates that Marx called "rural idiots"—could, if properly motivated, become the driving force for Asian communist revolutions. But while Ho was in Moscow theorizing, other Indochinese were taking direct action. On June 19, 1924, a terrorist named Pham Hong Thai detonated a bomb in the French concession in Canton, China. The intended target, Governor-General Martial-Henri Merlin, escaped, but five French businessmen were killed.[12] The time for words was passing.

The Comintern sent Ho Chi Minh (under a new alias, Ly Thuy) to Canton in December 1924 to work with Moscow's point man, Mikhail Borodin. Borodin's assignment was to lay the groundwork for communist revolution in China by manipulating Chiang Kai-shek, and Ho was fluent enough in Chinese to act as Borodin's interpreter. In 1925 Ho and the Indian communist leader M. N. Roy established the League of Oppressed Asian Peoples (which, like the Krestintern, was hardly ever heard from again). He also created the Revolutionary Youth League, the first organization of communist Vietnamese. It started with only eight members.

In China Ho met Pham Van Dong, the son of a mandarin, who became Ho's lifelong comrade in arms. Ho Chi Minh and Pham Van Dong embodied the qualities Confucius praised: rectitude, probity, sincerity, modesty, courage, and self-sacrifice. Ho's personification of the Confucian ideal of the superior man proved powerfully attractive to educated Vietnamese.

During his years in China, Ho became the acknowledged leader of expatriate Vietnamese Marxists. As a hardboiled communist revolutionary, he understood politics as war by other means. But was he treacherous? A longstanding rumor to the effect that Ho Chi Minh betrayed the conservative Vietnamese nationalist Phan Boi Chau to France's Brigade de la Sûreté for 100,000 piasters has not been confirmed by recent research. Phan Boi Chau was arrested in China in 1925 and tried in Vietnam. He was sentenced to death, but because of widespread public protest, the sentence was commuted to life under house arrest.[13]

Ho's two-and-a-half-year stint in China ended abruptly. The Chinese Communist Party (CCP) had been under orders from Stalin to cooperate with Chiang Kai-shek's Kuomintang (KMT) on the assumption that China was not ready for communist revolution but must first pass through a bourgeois revolution. This advice proved disastrous when Chiang suddenly turned on the communists in April 1927, slaughtering them by the thousands. Ho fled to the Soviet Union, where the Comintern had other assignments waiting. It is difficult to sort out his movements in these years, but he seems to have been in Brussels and Paris in 1928. Next the Comintern sent him to Siam (Thailand) where he traveled around disguised as a Buddhist monk. Exactly what he did to organize Vietnamese workers in Siam remains obscure. He published a Vietnamese-language newspaper and exhorted Buddhist priests to become more involved in the "social gospel." He showed the way by carrying bricks and mixing mortar to build schools for his fellow expatriates. From this obscure posting, the Comintern sent Ho in the summer of 1929 to Hong Kong to become director of its Asian bureau, supervising communist conspiracies in India, Southeast Asia, China, and Japan.

Ho's Revolutionary Youth League broke into factions while he was away on other business. However, after the stock market crashed on Wall Street in 1929, waves of economic depression reached all the way to Asia, and the Comintern sensed the time was ripe to escalate the revolutionary effort. When the squabbling factions balked at cooperating, Ho went to Hong Kong to straighten matters out. (Vietnamese revolutionaries plotted from China, for their lives were too much at risk in their homeland.) The Revolutionary Youth League changed its name to Vietnam Communist Party, but the Russians thought that "Vietnam" was too nationalistic; they preferred the internationalism implied by the name "Indochina," even though to Vietnamese this was a humiliating colonial appellation. So in February 1930 the name was changed again, to Indochinese Communist Party (ICP).

The ICP boldly exhorted Vietnamese workers and peasants to throw out the French imperialists. In the summer of 1930, spontaneous uprisings broke out across Vietnam, although these were not inspired or guided by the ICP. French repression was brutal and effective. Seven hundred rebels were shot. In June 1931 British authorities in Hong Kong arrested Ho, who had been condemned to death in absentia by the French. He spent more than a year in prison, filling the hours by composing poems in his head and memorizing them. Ho noted his teeth were beginning to fall out: "I looked at myself once and tried never to look again. I was skin on bones, and covered with rotten sores. I guess I was pretty sick."[14] Ho contracted tuberculosis. False rumors of his death sent his friends in Vietnam into mourning. Indeed, he would have been finished if the French had succeeded in extraditing him, but he was released from a prison hospital in 1932, with help from a leftist British lawyer in Hong Kong.

By 1933 Ho was in Moscow again. Stalin's horrifying purges were under way; already millions of Ukrainian farmers were starving, not from crop failure but from a deliberately engineered famine. This raises important questions: What did Ho Chi Minh know about Stalinism, and when did he know it? Could he have lived in Moscow from 1933 to 1938 and remained blithely unaware of the Great Terror? Did he simply ignore it because he needed Russian help for his own revolutionary purposes? Did he approve? We do not know the answers.

Ho was exposed to the dangers of life on the political left. For advocating a broad alliance between factory workers, peasants, and students, he was denounced by orthodox Marxists, who insisted that factory workers (proletarians) were the only revolutionary class. That might seem questionable, given how few factories there were in Vietnam, but among communists ideological battles assume a theological importance. Ho never recanted his belief in the need for communists to build broad coalitions with other progressive elements, even with class enemies if the situation demanded it. This flexibility was potentially dangerous in Moscow in the 1930s, but Ho was merely ignored, not sent to Siberia. A letter found by Sophie Quinn-Judge in newly released Comintern files gives us a window into Ho Chi Minh's mood in the summer of 1938, when he was forty-seven years old: "Dear Comrade, Today is the seventh anniversary of my arrest in Hong Kong. It is also the beginning of my eighth year of inactivity. I write to ask you to change this painful situation."[15]

Ho was the chief ICP delegate to the Seventh Comintern Congress of 1935. The next year Stalin decreed a "popular front" policy (an alliance between communists and democrats against fascists), which Ho had advocated for some time. A leftist government under Léon Blum came to power in France, and for a while leftists in Indochina could operate more freely. But the Blum government fell in 1937, and the pendulum in Indochina swung back toward repression. The colonial authorities ruthlessly crushed the Vietnamese nationalists. Prisons were filled with political dissidents. Thousands, perhaps tens of thousands, were executed.

Ho Chi Minh probably left Moscow in 1938 and visited Mao Zedong at Chinese communist headquarters at Yanan, in China's dry northwest, but his activities for the next two years are a mystery. On June 14, 1940, France surrendered to Germany. The Vichy regime of Marshal Pétain ordered French administrators in the colonies to cooperate with the Axis. On September 14, 1940, Japanese troops marched into Vietnam unopposed by the French colonial bureaucrats, who actually ran Vietnam, Cambodia, and Laos as part of Japan's Greater East Asia Co-Prosperity Sphere for the next three and a half years. The French even allowed the Japanese to use their naval and air bases. This, of course, meant that the French in Southeast Asia were enemies of the United States, which entered the Pacific War the day after Japan attacked Pearl Harbor. Because Ho Chi Minh was fighting the French, he was an ally of the United States in World War II.

THE VIET MINH AND VIETNAMESE INDEPENDENCE (1941–46)

In December 1940 Ho organized a training camp for party cadres in Jingxi, China, just twenty-five miles from the Vietnamese border. On February 14,

1941, he returned to Vietnam for the first time in thirty years and set up headquarters at Pac Bo, a very defensible mountain base area near the Chinese border where only the local Nung tribes knew all the footpaths. Ho's reputation as a patriot had preceded him. Because he had been living abroad, he had been able to write freely, while nationalists in Vietnam had been jailed or killed. (Indeed, according to one report, Ho had taken a wife, Nguyen Thi Minh Khai, who was arrested in 1940 and executed by a French firing squad in 1941.)[16] Ho marked his fifty-first birthday, May 19, 1941, by founding the Vietnam Doc Lap Dong Minh Hoi (Vietnam Independence League, or Viet Minh, for short). Three other leading figures at the core of the Viet Minh were Truong Chinh, Pham Van Dong, and Vo Nguyen Giap. In June Ho issued his famous *Letter From Abroad*, a stirring call for national insurrection. Here are some excerpts:

> Elders! Prominent personalities! Intellectuals, peasants, workers, traders, and soldiers! Dear Compatriots! . . . Our people suffer under a double yoke: they serve not only as buffaloes and horses to the French invaders but also as slaves to the Japanese plunderers. Alas! What sin have our people committed to be doomed to such a wretched plight? . . . Now the opportunity has come for our national liberation. . . . National salvation is the common cause of our whole people. Every Vietnamese must take part in it. . . . The hour has struck! Raise aloft the insurrectionary banner and guide the people throughout the country to overthrow the Japanese and French! The sacred call of the Fatherland is resounding in your ears; the blood of our heroic predecessors who sacrificed their lives is stirring in your hearts! Let us rise up quickly! Victory to Vietnam's Revolution! Victory to the World's Revolution.[17]

Except for the final sentence of *Letter From Abroad*, which confirms communist authorship, everything is couched in terms of the united front strategy: All patriotic Vietnamese, without regard to class background, are invited to join, even "patriotic landowners." But the communists were careful to reserve the "leading role" for themselves. (Ho would use the same tactic two decades later to camouflage his control of the National Liberation Front of South Vietnam.) One reason the Communist Party enjoyed such prestige in the eyes of ordinary Vietnamese is that exploitation of Vietnam was inseparable from French (and world) capitalism. Economic development in Indochina had produced a distorted form of capitalism, one in which the emergence of a native middle class was impossible. Joseph Buttinger summarizes the situation: "The deepest roots of Communism in Vietnam can therefore be found in the specific form of colonial capitalism, whose chief characteristics were unrestrained exploitation of the lower and economic deprivation of the middle classes, combined with a ruthless exercise of foreign rule."[18] A third reason why communists were able to dominate the Vietnamese independence movement was that the French police had infiltrated and broken less secretive patriotic clubs and organizations.

Ho creatively blended Marxism with Vietnamese tradition. By contrast with Chinese culture, in which soldiers were always considered lowly, many Vietnamese myths feature the mandarin-warrior as hero. Ngo Quyen and Le Loi are outstanding examples. Ho Chi Minh placed himself and the Viet Minh squarely within this national tradition, relating it to the present and reinterpreting it in the light of communist ideology.[19]

In 1942, while on a mission to China, Nguyen Who Loves His Country began using the name Ho Chi Minh, perhaps because it had a Chinese sound. If this new name was a device to avoid detection, it failed, for on August 28, 1942, Ho was abducted and jailed by Chang Fa-kwei, the warlord of Guangxi Province. This time Ho spent thirteen (some say eighteen) months in jail. Conditions were horrible. "Before obtaining the status of a political prisoner, he was for many weeks dragged from prison to prison, his head immobilized in a cangue (a large square board locked around the neck), his feet chained. He was linked to another prisoner who eventually died by his side."[20] Again he wrote verses in his head. Paradoxically, he expressed himself not in Vietnamese "but in Chinese—the beautiful classical Chinese of the great Tang Dynasty."[21] These poems were later published in English by the Foreign Languages Publishing House in Hanoi. One of the most affecting is called "The Leg-Irons":

> With hungry mouth open like a wicked monster,
> Each night the irons devour the legs of people:
> The Jaws grip the right leg of every prisoner:
> Only the left is free to bend and stretch.
>
> Yet there is one thing stranger in this world:
> People rush to place their legs in irons.
> Once they are shackled, they can sleep in peace.
> Otherwise they would have no place to lay their heads.[22]

Ho finally convinced Chang Fa-kwei to release him by promising to help Chang preserve his personal power base in the Chinese–Vietnamese border region. However, as soon as Ho was free he resumed his work with the Viet Minh, living and working in caves near Cao Bang. He grew closer to Vo Nguyen Giap, twenty years younger than himself, whose job it was to fuse Ho's political ideas with his own instinctive grasp of military strategy. Ho Chi Minh used to call Giap "Volcano Covered with Snows," for his thundering rages and stony silences, and *"kui,"* or devil, for his courage.[23]

As World War II ground on, Ho extended his control over more and more territory. By 1944, the Viet Minh claimed 500,000 supporters, mostly in north and central Vietnam, although only 1 percent were members of the

ICP. In 1944 Ho made contact with the American Office of Strategic Services (OSS), the precursor to the Central Intelligence Agency (CIA). The OSS supplied Ho with arms and equipment and even coordinated strategic parachute jumps into Tonkin, all with the intent of aiding his struggle against the Japanese. In return Ho gave Washington precious information and helped the OSS evacuate American flyers downed over south China. Such mutually beneficial exchanges led Ho to believe that the U.S. government would look favorably on Vietnamese independence. President Franklin D. Roosevelt did think that the French had egregiously misruled Indochina, but he seemed to believe that the Vietnamese were not ready for independence. On March 27, 1943, the United States proposed that after the war an Allied government be named to rule Indochina in place of the French.

In 1944 a terrible famine struck Tonkin and Annam. About 2 million Vietnamese died. The French made the situation worse by confiscating large quantities of food for their own use, which was one of many reasons why the French lost their last shred of political legitimacy in Vietnam. Furthermore, the way the Japanese bullied the French shattered any illusions about "white superiority" and "yellow inferiority."

The Nazis evacuated Paris in August 1944, and Free French leader Charles de Gaulle took power. Now the Japanese worried that the French administrators of Indochina, who had so cravenly done their bidding for the previous four years, might switch sides. On March 9, 1945, the Japanese suddenly clapped all the French in Vietnam into prison. Two days later Emperor Bao Dai proclaimed a Japanese-sponsored independence for Vietnam, but this made little difference, for the people's hearts were now with Ho and the Viet Minh. "With the French out of the way after March 9, 1945, the Viet Minh became more active. The Japanese did not bother to send troops into the northern provinces of Tonkin and the Viet Minh took over the region for itself."[24]

In July 1945 the Allied leaders, assembled at Potsdam, decided that Chiang Kai-shek's KMT would take the Japanese surrender in Vietnam north of the sixteenth parallel and that British troops would be landed to accept the surrender in the south. No one considered turning Vietnam over to the Vietnamese. In fact Harry S. Truman, Winston Churchill, and Josef Stalin hardly thought about Indochina at all, so absorbed were they in planning for postwar Europe.

The United States dropped an atomic bomb on Hiroshima on August 6, 1945, and a second one on Nagasaki three days later. The stunned Japanese did not comprehend what had happened and did not formally surrender until August 14. This was the moment Ho Chi Minh had been waiting for. On August 16 Ho issued an appeal for a general insurrection. The Viet Minh were able to take control of most of Tonkin, including Hanoi, within days, even though their army numbered only a few thousand poorly trained guerrillas, due to their careful planning and broad base of popular support. There was little fighting. In Cochin-China the Viet Minh had to share power with other nationalist groups, religious sects, and even criminal gangs, but in Hanoi a red banner with a gold star, the Viet Minh flag, was raised over the governor-general's palace.

After years in the political wilderness, Ho entered Hanoi on August 26, 1945. He wore shorts and a pith helmet and carried a walking stick. Many people had heard of the famous revolutionary Nguyen Who Loves His Country, but few had heard of Ho Chi Minh. When journalists asked Ho who he was, he replied simply, "I am a revolutionary. I was born at a time when my country was already a slave state. From the days of my youth I have fought to free it. That is my one merit. In consideration of my past, my colleagues have voted me head of government."[25]

Emperor Bao Dai sent a telegram to Ho stating his wish to abdicate, and a Viet Minh delegation journeyed from Hanoi to Hue to accept his resignation. The march became a triumphal procession. Bao Dai endorsed the Viet Minh, perhaps in the belief that Ho enjoyed full U.S. support, and that conferred legitimacy. The mandate of heaven had shifted. Ho magnanimously (and cleverly) invited Bao Dai to come to Hanoi and serve as "supreme counselor" to the Viet Minh government. Bao Dai had few duties during the six months he served the Viet Minh, and he left Vietnam in March 1946 to live in Hong Kong.

On September 2, 1945, Ho Chi Minh declared the independence of the Democratic Republic of Vietnam (DRV) to a jubilant crowd at Ba Dinh Square in Hanoi. Wearing a threadbare khaki tunic and white rubber sandals, Ho stood before his countrymen and read words already familiar to Americans:

> All men are created equal; they are endowed by their Creator with certain unalienable Rights; among these are Life, Liberty, and the pursuit of Happiness. [The French imperialists] have enforced inhuman laws. They have built more prisons than schools. They have mercilessly slain our patriots; they have drained our uprisings in rivers of blood. A people who have courageously opposed French domination for more than eighty years, a people who have fought side by side with the Allies against the fascists during these last years, such a people must be free and independent.[26]

Ho's borrowing from Thomas Jefferson was deliberate: He knew the French would want to take back their colonies, and he hoped Washington would prevent them from doing so. He spoke favorably of the United States, which he said had no territorial interests in Vietnam. Indeed, American planes flew low over the independence day celebrations, giving the impression of American support. In this fluid and chaotic situation the Viet Minh could not prevent the entry into southern Vietnam of 20,000 British troops under General Douglas Gracey and into northern Vietnam of 200,000 Chinese troops commanded by KMT general Lu Han. This rapacious horde was Ho's biggest worry.

The Allies betrayed the Viet Minh. General Gracey disobeyed orders not to interfere in local politics and let the French raise the tricolor again in Saigon. The local French population, newly freed from Japanese internment camps, irrationally took out their anger on Vietnamese, who they could see were not grateful for France's "civilizing" rule. "In this atmosphere of revenge the French invented a new crime: to be Vietnamese. Old men, women, and children had their ears boxed by French matrons trying to reestablish the 'natural' order in Saigon."[27]

A fundamental rule of politics and war is to decide who is your number one enemy and build a coalition against him. Ho Chi Minh defended his controversial decision to compromise with the French by saying, "I would rather sniff French dung for a few years than eat Chinese dung for a thousand."[28] Actually, Chiang Kai-shek was not interested in occupying Vietnam; his real goal was to force France to renounce its unequal treaties with China. Once that was achieved, he handed Tonkin back to the French.

Ho opened negotiations with the French in October 1945. He needed to play down his communist affiliation so included many non-Communist parties in the Viet Minh government. He even went so far as to dissolve the ICP in November. The Viet Minh won 230 of 300 seats in the National Assembly in elections held January 6, 1946.

President Roosevelt, who had deep misgivings about French misrule in Vietnam, had died in office and been succeeded by his vice president, Harry S. Truman, a machine politician from Kansas City who knew almost nothing about Indochina. In February 1946 Ho wrote to President Truman eight times, reminding him that it was the Viet Minh, not the French, who had fought Japan in Indochina. He noted that all the Western leaders had promised independence to oppressed peoples, and he charged that French aggression was tantamount to what the Germans had done in 1938. Truman probably never even saw those letters, which went unanswered.

The National Assembly elected Ho president of the Democratic Republic of Vietnam on March 6. French troops landed in Haiphong the very next day. Looking desperately for any way to avoid war, Ho Chi Minh met with Admiral Thierry d'Argenlieu aboard the cruiser *Emile Bertin* on March 26, and soon thereafter went to Paris for prolonged negotiations. Ho knew well how to deal with the French, and for their part, they recognized Ho's greatness. The chief French negotiator, Jean Sainteny, wrote: "From the time of our very first meeting I acquired the conviction that Ho Chi Minh was a personality of the first class. . . . His most striking features were his eyes—lively, alert, and burning with extraordinary fervor; all his energy seemed to be concentrated in those eyes."²⁹ Sainteny went so far as to compare Ho with the apostle of nonviolence, Mohandas Gandhi, but this was a serious misreading of Ho's character. Although Ho was always gentle in his personal relations and preferred compromise to fighting, in the end, he was willing to pay any price for Vietnamese independence.

THE FIRST INDOCHINA WAR (1946–54)

Ho agreed to postpone his dream of a united, independent Vietnam if the French would recognize his government, and for a time it appeared that war could be avoided. Ho was now on the defensive politically from impatient nationalists who thought him too weak. He defended himself: "I, Ho Chi Minh, have always led you on the road to freedom. . . . I would prefer to die rather than sell out the country. I swear to you that I have not sold you out."³⁰ Ho spent the summer of 1946 in Paris negotiating with the French, but Admiral d'Argenlieu, the French high commissioner for Indochina, effectively torpedoed the conference by proclaiming a separate government for Cochin-China. Ho begged the French not to send him home empty-handed, but their position hardened as they became more confident that the United States would not pressure them to meet Ho halfway. Ho left France on September 19 and was so discouraged that he took a slow boat to Saigon rather than fly. On the eve of his departure, he met his friend David Schoenbrun, an American journalist, and predicted exactly how the now-inevitable, long war would go:

> It will be a war between an elephant and a tiger. If the tiger ever stands still, the elephant will crush him with his mighty tusks. But the tiger will not stand still.
> . . . He will leap upon the back of the elephant, tearing huge chunks from his side, and then he will leap back into the dark jungle. And slowly the elephant will bleed to death. That will be the war of Indochina.³¹

Tension was in the air when Ho reached Hanoi on October 21. The French were waiting for an incident they could use to demonstrate their superior firepower. That occasion came on November 20 in the form of a dispute over whether the French or the Viet Minh would collect customs duties in Haiphong. On November 23 at 7:00 A.M. Colonel Debés, commander of the French troops at Haiphong, gave the Viet Minh two hours to get out of the city. At 9:45 Debés "threw everything [he] had into the battle for the streets of Haiphong—infantry, tanks, artillery, airplanes, and even the naval guns of the cruiser *Suffren*, all of which directed their fire at Vietnamese parts of the town where there was no fighting at all."³² The First Indochina War had begun with 6,000 pointless civilian deaths. Admiral d'Argenlieu sent a message to his deputy, General Jean Valluy, that read: "I have learned with indignation of the recent attacks at Haiphong and Langson. Our troops were once more victims of criminal premeditation. I bow down before our great dead soldiers."[33]

The Viet Minh retreated to the hills, the standard tactic of Asian rebels since time immemorial. On December 19 they attacked French units. The French responded by bombing Hanoi. Ho told his people to prepare: "If you don't have a sword, arm yourselves with axes and sticks." Ho traveled surreptitiously around the country, mobilizing his "people's army." The key to victory was to merge the army with the people, he said. Soldiers would help peasants bring in the harvest and teach in country schoolrooms, and the villagers helped the Viet Minh in a hundred different ways. Ho was in constant motion, going from one to another clandestine meeting with his political officials and Giap's army officers. Ho and Giap worked closely on military strategy, but Ho sometimes overruled the general.

In 1947, the French sent an envoy named Paul Mus to offer Ho Chi Minh peace, but Ho found the terms insulting. There were no more peace talks for seven years. The French found it psychologically impossible to admit that their empire was finished; even French Communist Party leader Maurice Thorez supported the reimposition of French sovereignty in Vietnam. The French tried to resurrect the discredited Vietnamese emperor Bao Dai, but when Bao Dai returned to Vietnam in 1949 no one greeted him. He spent most of his time in the mountain town of Dalat and could never rid himself of the stigma of being a French puppet.

The First Indochina War may be divided into two stages: From 1946 to 1950 the Viet Minh achieved a strategic stalemate; from 1950 to 1954 the United States poured money and advisers into Vietnam, but gradually the tide of battle shifted in favor of the communists. The watershed that divides the two phases was the outbreak of war in Korea in June 1950. Even without the congressional declaration of war that the U.S. Constitution seemed to require, President Truman decided to send troops to Korea. At the same time, because Ho Chi Minh was a communist, the United States would pay for France's war. A Military Assistance Advisory Group under General Francis Brink was established in Saigon in October 1950 to supply the French and their colonial troops with rifles, automatic weapons, ammunition, riverboats, coastal patrol vessels, jeeps, aircraft, and hospital supplies. Washington spent over $400 million per year (78 percent of the total cost of the war) from 1950 to 1954. Despite this largesse, the French deeply distrusted the Americans, who made no secret of their belief that France's day was done. The United States tried to supply aid directly to the Bao Dai government, a tactic the French obstructed at every turn. The Viet Minh now had foreign supporters, too, for ever since Mao Zedong's People's Liberation

Army swept through southern China in late 1949, Ho had the advantage of a secure base area.

In 1950 the French Army suffered severe defeats in the north near the Chinese border. In 1952 they were driven from the town of Hoa Binh, only forty miles west of Hanoi. In 1953 U.S. secretary of state John Foster Dulles stated that the war could be won the next year. And in November 1953 French general Henri Navarre made his fateful decision to concentrate French forces in a remote valley known as Dien Bien Phu. Navarre believed he could lure Viet Minh troops into his "meat grinder," yet it was one of the greatest military blunders of all time. General Giap staged diversionary actions at distant spots around the country. Then the Viet Minh disassembled their artillery, and porters carried the separate pieces up jungle paths to the ring of mountains surrounding the Dien Bien Phu valley. There they quietly reassembled their artillery. The siege began March 13, 1954. The French could only resupply their troops by air, and the landing strip made a perfect target for Viet Minh gunners. It was, to use the title of Bernard Fall's definitive book on the siege, "Hell in a Very Small Place."[34] One French colonel committed suicide with a hand grenade, saying, "I am completely dishonored."[35]

The desperate French begged the United States for relief. Admiral Arthur Radford, chairman of the Joint Chiefs of Staff, proposed using B-29 bombers for air strikes on Viet Minh positions, and Secretary of State Dulles supported this. Vice President Richard Nixon actually proposed using atomic bombs. But in the end President Dwight Eisenhower decided to do nothing, saying he "could conceive of no greater tragedy than for the United States to become involved in an all-out war in Indochina."[36]

The French surrendered on May 7. Viet Minh timing was impeccable—the Indochina phase of the Geneva Conference opened May 8. Two delegations from Vietnam were seated, one from Ho Chi Minh's DRV and the other from Bao Dai's "State of Vietnam." For reasons not yet fully understood, Ho settled for less at the conference table than he had won on the battlefield. Probably he was under pressure from Chinese foreign minister Zhou Enlai, who was pursuing a conciliatory policy toward the West in 1954. Ho may have thought Bao Dai's unpopular "state" would crumble soon in any case.

The communists accepted a temporary partition of Vietnam at the seventeenth parallel, with communist forces to regroup north of the line, and anticommunist forces to the south. This was explicitly not to be considered the permanent creation of two states called North Vietnam and South Vietnam. Nationwide elections were to be held within two years, for a government to rule over a united Vietnam. The United States was a reluctant participant at Geneva—Secretary Dulles refused to shake hands with the Chinese or Vietnamese diplomats. The United States did not sign the Geneva accords but agreed to abide by them and promised not to use force to disrupt them. Once the cease-fire took effect, Vietnamese not wishing to live under one regime could transfer to the territory of the other. Hundreds of thousands of people, many of them Catholics, fled northern Vietnam rather than live under Ho's communist regime. The U.S. Navy transported them to South Vietnam, where they became a mainstay of the anti-Communist government that emerged in Saigon. The seventeenth parallel, which was supposed to divide the two zones for only two years, in fact divided the "two Vietnams" for twenty-one years. That is what the Second Indochina War, known to Americans as the Vietnam War, was about.

BUILDING THE DEMOCRATIC REPUBLIC OF VIETNAM
(1954–60)

Ho rode into Hanoi in a captured French Army truck on October 9, 1954. Characteristically, he wore simple clothes. Most North Vietnamese had never seen their sixty-four-year-old leader. He was greeted with curiosity and quiet enthusiasm by all but the city's merchant class. Ho Chi Minh never claimed to be an all-around genius, like so many other communist dictators (such as Stalin, Mao Zedong, Kim Il Sung, and Nicolae Ceausescu). Ho was not a brilliant orator, but he played brilliantly the role of Uncle Ho, the folksy but wise patriarch of the Vietnamese family, at once scholarly and good-humored.

Until his death in 1969, Ho lived in the gardener's cottage of the former French governor-general's palace in Hanoi. Ho was the embodiment of Charles de Gaulle's observation that great leaders always stage-manage their effects. He almost always wore rubber sandals instead of shoes. Was it an act? General Bui Tin, who knew Ho well but later turned against him, wrote:

> It is true he lived very simply and honestly. He loved children and sympathized with women, as well as the poor. He hated vanity, ostentation, and formality. He was also very discerning and subtle with everybody, no matter what their experience and standing. But I entirely reject any suggestion that he was a clever actor. It has to be recognized that he was a cultured and well-travelled man, as well as somebody who was very human. In fact he was very much a human being and certainly not a saint.[37]

Ho was loyal to his revolutionary comrades, unlike Mao Zedong who sooner or later turned on all those who had fought beside him. He left most military matters in Giap's very capable hands and did not interfere in tactical decisions. Giap and Pham Van Dong remained influential in North Vietnam to the ends of their long lives. Ho believed in group decisionmaking. There were no sweeping purges of top leaders. Ho's primacy was never challenged by other Vietnamese communists, even when sharp differences of opinion arose over land reform, the nationalization of the economy, or, later, the conduct of the war against the United States. Rather, Ho smoothed over rivalries, even though a new constitution adopted by the DRV in 1960 gave him almost unlimited power to settle disputes by decree. He was unafraid to delegate some powers to local party cadres but, as in all other communist states, the party insisted on a monopoly of power and reserved all high level positions for itself.

There was nothing unique about the DRV government. The blueprints for its structure seem to have been taken straight out of the Leninist textbook. The North Vietnamese regime resembled closely the totalitarian machines that had proven so brutally effective in the Soviet Union and China, where peasant societies were forcefully industrialized. Only through heavy doses of propaganda, extensive surveillance, and the occasional resort to naked terror could potential opponents be silenced. North Vietnam was ruled by three hierarchies: the Communist Party, the state bureaucracy, and the army, with a considerable overlap at the top. Ultimate power lay with "an oligarchy of revolutionaries."[38]

Land reform in North Vietnam began with a rent reduction decree issued in January 1953 and picked up steam in 1955 under the direction of Communist Party secretary-general Truong Chinh, one of Ho's circle of loyal lieutenants but also an advocate of learning from China and of pursuing the same radical policies being imposed there by Mao Zedong. Landowners in North Vietnam were branded as reactionaries. Their land was confiscated, and perhaps as many as 15,000 were killed.

What was Ho Chi Minh's role in this brutal business? Was he blind to the terror in Tonkin, as he had somehow failed to notice people disappearing in Moscow in the 1930s? When the peasants started fighting back (even in his home province of Nghe An), Ho sent in troops. He demoted Truong Chinh and assumed the post of party boss himself. On August 18, 1956, Ho went on radio to claim the "successful completion of land reform" while admitting certain "errors": "Land reform is a class struggle against the feudalists, an earth-shaking, fierce and hard revolution. Moreover, the enemy has frenziedly carried out sabotage work. A number of our cadres have not thoroughly grasped the land reform policy or correctly followed the mass line. . . . All this has caused us to commit errors.[39]

While agriculture was (and still is) the mainstay of the Vietnamese economy, the communists knew that in the modern world industry is the true source of national power and wealth. "With a touch of megalomania which was not diminished by their victory over the French, the Viet Minh leaders embarked upon their self-imposed task, a truly monstrous task, since even its fragmentary realization required inhuman means."[40]

Recovery from the eight-year war meant first of all repairing roads, bridges, and railroad tracks. Some French factories remained intact, but spare parts were out of the question. The Soviet Union and China contributed some foreign aid but not on a generous scale. Small shopkeepers were put out of business by ruinous taxes of 50 percent on soap, 25 percent on canned goods, and 20 percent on textiles. Then they were made employees of state cooperatives.

Ho had expected to become president of a united Vietnam no later than 1956. He withdrew many Viet Minh soldiers from the south, as specified by the Geneva accord. But it was hard to say who was an official member of the Viet Minh and who was merely a sympathizer. Many people in South Vietnam had fought alongside Ho against the French; after 1954 they remained in their native southern villages and were Ho's fifth column against Diem.

The exact moment when Ho Chi Minh decided to support renewed insurgency in South Vietnam is not known. The National Liberation Front (NLF)—to give the Vietcong its proper name—was officially formed in December 1960, but in some villages in South Vietnam, particularly those remote from Saigon, a quiet insurrection had already begun. The rebels were farmers or schoolteachers by day, NLF soldiers and organizers by night. These were the same men and women who had fought the French. In Saigon, the Diem regime was composed largely of Vietnamese who had taken the side of the French against their own people. At first the NLF used guns they had hidden under farmhouses in 1954. Soon they graduated to U.S. weapons purchased from Diem's corrupt soldiers. Later, when the war had escalated far beyond anything that anyone in Washington or Hanoi had foreseen, the Vietcong were issued modern automatic rifles from the Soviet Union, sent by train across China and brought down the Ho Chi Minh Trail through the Annamite Mountains on cargo bicycles.

The DRV went on a war footing in 1960. A military draft was instituted in April. Ho Chi Minh knew that to fight the United States he would need help. He did not want Russian or Chinese troops, yet money, weapons, and threats of retaliation from Moscow and Beijing were of inestimable benefit. Despite public proclamations of fraternal solidarity, Ho had no reason to trust the Russians or the Chinese. After all, Soviet premier Nikita Khrushchev had proposed in 1957 the permanent division of Vietnam and the admission of North and South Vietnam to the United Nations as separate states—exactly what Ho was fighting against. And under any dynasty or regime, as Ho well knew, China seeks to control countries around its border.

To the deep dismay of the Vietnamese communists, the Soviets and the Chinese were squabbling; indeed, their mutual denunciations had gotten quite nasty. Ho tried to mediate the dispute at a 1960 conference of eighty-one Communist parties in Moscow, but the differences between Moscow and Beijing were deep. First, Mao Zedong and Nikita Khrushchev disliked each other viscerally. Second, there were unresolved territorial disputes at many points on the long border between the Soviet Union and the People's Republic of China. Third, there were serious ideological differences between them. Sobered by the possession of atomic bombs, the Russians were speaking of peaceful coexistence with the United States while the Chinese were in a breathing fire. Ho Chi Minh did not want to have to choose between Moscow and Beijing, so he tried to maintain a balance, leaning first this way, then that way. In May 1963 Ho joined Chinese president Liu Shaoqi in denouncing "revisionism," a code word for "Khrushchevism." And when China detonated its first atom bomb in October 1964, Ho congratulated Mao for strengthening the forces of the socialist camp, while Moscow remained pointedly silent. But three years later, when Mao's China slid into the chaos of its Cultural Revolution, and when the DRV needed advanced air defense radars and anti-aircraft missiles, Hanoi leaned toward Moscow. The Russians flattered Ho by awarding him the Order of Lenin, their highest decoration.

HO CHI MINH DURING THE AMERICAN WAR (1960–69)

Vietnam's national agony is partly traceable to the rivalry between Soviet premier Nikita S. Khrushchev, who on January 6, 1961, proclaimed support for "wars of national liberation" anywhere in the world, and U.S. President John F. Kennedy, whose inauguration speech two weeks later contained a vow to pay any price to meet that threat. In other words, a civil war (or a revolution—it had elements of both) in a small country very remote from both Washington, D.C., and Moscow was going to be made the symbolic battlefield of two ideologies, two economic systems, two nuclear superpowers.

Ho's thoughts and actions in his final decade are shrouded in deliberate mystery and official secrecy. He turned seventy in 1960. Most likely he was actively involved in political decisionmaking for a few more years, but Bui Tin reports that during 1964 and 1965 Ho Chi Minh's health declined markedly and that he was not consulted about day-to-day political decisions. Bui Tin says that Ho wrote a political will, a message of farewell and advice to the Vietnamese people, on his seventy-fifth birthday (May 1965) and revised it annually until his death.[41] He was rarely seen in public after 1967, although he was reported to have sent a New Year's greeting to Americans opposed to the war on December 30 of that year, thanking them for their support, and adding: "We shall win, and so will you. . . . No Vietnamese has ever come to make trouble in the United States. Yet half a million U.S. troops have been sent to South Vietnam, who together with over 700,000 puppet and satellite troops, are daily massacring Vietnamese people and burning down Vietnamese towns and villages."[42] Ho took heart from the growing anti-war movement in the United States, especially because there were clear signs that it was no longer confined to the political fringe. In December 1967 retired Marine Corps commandant General David M. Shoup denounced the war as a civil conflict between crooks in Saigon and Vietnamese nationalists striving for a better life.

But one wonders: Did Ho ever sink into despair? He knew that the sundry regimes in Saigon could never win legitimacy because they were fatally tainted by U.S. sponsorship. But did he really believe that North Vietnam could survive the bombing and win the war, as it ultimately did six years after his death?

The "Rolling Thunder" bombing campaign against North Vietnam began on February 24, 1965. Giant B-52 bombers, designed for waging nuclear war against the Soviet Union, were used after April 1966 to drop conventional bombs on North Vietnam and communist-controlled areas of South Vietnam. In July 1966 Ho candidly told the people of North Vietnam that "Johnson and his clique" might well destroy "Hanoi, Haiphong, and other cities" and that the war might last another "ten, twenty years, or longer" but that "the Vietnamese people will not be intimidated! Nothing is more precious than independence and freedom."[43]

If Ho were lucid to the end, he would have had good reason to despair. The Paris peace conference opened in May 1968, but American and North Vietnamese diplomats quickly got mired in a dispute about the shape of the negotiating table, whether it should be square or round. President Richard Nixon was inaugurated in January 1969 and began secretly bombing Cambodia in March. Also in March, North Vietnam's two foreign sponsors, China and the Soviet Union, nearly went to war with each other after border clashes on Damansky (Chen-pao) Island in the Ussuri River left hundreds of dead and wounded on both sides.

Ho Chi Minh died of a heart attack on September 2, 1969, but the announcement of his death was delayed one day so as not to have it coincide with Vietnam's National Day.[44] In the final version of his will he asked to be given a modest funeral so as not to waste the people's money. However, 250,000 people gathered to mourn Ho in Ba Dinh Square, where he had proclaimed Vietnam's declaration of independence twenty-four years earlier. He also requested that agricultural taxes be suspended for one year as a gift to the people, but the politburo excised that item before it published his last will. The South Vietnamese Army finally fell apart in April 1975. Vietnam was unified as the Socialist Republic of Vietnam (SRV) in 1976, and Saigon was renamed Ho Chi Minh City.

CONCLUSION

Ho requested that his ashes be divided into three urns, to be scattered in the north, center, and south of his country. But his body was embalmed and placed in a large, cold mausoleum, in the style of Lenin and Mao. In other ways, too, his successors let him down. Instead of welcoming southerners with a display of national reconciliation, Hanoi decreed harsh terms in reeducation camps for those contaminated by association with the former Saigon regime and its American patrons. Vietnam was united and independent, but it was not free.

NOTES

1. See the index of Thomas Hodgkin's *Vietnam: The Revolutionary Path* (New York: St. Martin's Press, 1981), p. 413.

2. David Halberstam, *Ho* (New York: Random House, 1971), p. 16.

3. Charles Fenn, *Ho Chi Minh: A Biographical Introduction* (New York: Scribner's, 1973), p. 12.

4. Bernard B. Fall, *Last Reflections on a War* (New York: Schocken, 1972), p. 63.

5. Marilyn A. Levine, *Ho Chi Minh and Ngo Dinh Diem: A Comparative Study* (master's thesis, University of Hawaii, 1978), p. 12.

6. N. Khac Huyen, *Vision Accomplished? The Enigma of Ho Chi Minh* (New York: Macmillan, 1971), p. 6.

7. Bernard B. Fall, *The Two Vietnams: A Political and Military Analysis*, rev. ed. (New York: Praeger, 1964), p. 87.

8. Andrew C. Skinner, "Ho Chi Minh," in *Great Lives From History*, vol. 3, ed. Frank N. Magill (Pasadena, Calif.: Salem Press, 1990), p. 1041.

9. Stanley Karnow, *Vietnam: A History* (New York: Penguin, 1984), p. 121.

10. Quoted in Neil Sheehan, *A Bright Shining Lie: John Paul Vann and America in Vietnam* (New York: Random House, 1988), p. 157.

11. Ho Chi Minh, "The Path Which Led Me to Leninism," in *Ho Chi Minh: On Revolution*, ed. Bernard B. Fall (New York: Praeger, 1984).

12. Hodgkin, *Vietnam*, p. 221.

13. See Robert F. Turner, *Vietnamese Communism: Its Origins and Development* (Stanford, Calif.: Hoover Institution Press, 1975) pp. 8–9; and P. J. Honey, ed., *North Vietnam Today* (New York: Praeger, 1962), p. 4.

14. Huyen, *Vision Accomplished?*, p. 59.

15. Sophie Quinn-Judge, "Ho Chi Minh: New Perspectives from the Comintern Files," *The Viet Nam Forum: A Review of Vietnamese Culture and Society* (Yale University Council on Southeast Asia Studies), No. 14 (1994), p. 74.

16. Quinn-Judge, "Ho Chi Minh," p. 76.

17. The full text may be found in Fall, *Ho Chi Minh*, pp. 132–34.

18. Joseph Buttinger, *Vietnam: A Dragon Embattled* (New York: Praeger, 1967), p. 211.

19. Neil Sheehan writes persuasively on this point. See his *A Bright Shining Lie*, pp. 160–63.

20. Jean Sainteny, *Ho Chi Minh and His Vietnam: A Personal Memoir* (Chicago: Cowles, 1972), p. 35.

21. Jean Lacouture, *Ho Chi Minh: A Political Biography* (New York: Random House, 1968), p. 80.

22. Ho Chi Minh, *Prison Diary,* 4th ed. (Hanoi: Foreign Languages Publishing House, 1967), p. 34.

23. Oriana Fallaci, "Giap," in *Interview With History* (New York: Liveright, 1976), p. 75.

24. Ellen Hammer, *The Struggle for Indochina 1940–1955* (Stanford, Calif.: Stanford University Press, 1955), pp. 98–99.

25. Lacouture, *Ho Chi Minh,* pp. 106–07.

26. These sentences have been excerpted. For the full text, please see Fall, *Ho Chi Minh,* pp. 143–45.

27. Edward Doyle, et al., eds., *Passing the Torch* (Boston: Boston Publishing, 1981), p. 14.

28. Bui Diem, with David Chanoff, *In the Jaws of History* (Boston: Houghton Mifflin, 1987), p. 44.

29. Sainteny, *Ho Chi Minh and His Vietnam,* pp. 51–52.

30. Marilyn B. Young, *The Vietnam Wars: 1945–1990* (New York: HarperCollins, 1991), pp. 15–16.

31. Quoted in Doyle, et al., *Passing the Torch,* p. 23.

32. Buttinger, *Vietnam,* pp. 427–28.

33. Buttinger, *Vietnam,* p. 428.

34. Bernard B. Fall, *Hell in a Very Small Place: The Siege of Dien Bien Phu* (Philadelphia: Lippincott, 1967).

35. Karnow, *Vietnam,* p. 195.

36. Quoted in Doyle, et al., *Passing the Torch,* p. 68.

37. Bui Tin, *Following Ho Chi Minh: The Memoirs of a North Vietnamese Colonel* (Honolulu: University of Hawaii Press, 1995), pp. 16–17.

38. David Steinberg, ed., *In Search of Southeast Asia* (New York: Praeger, 1971), p. 361.

39. Fall, *Ho Chi Minh,* pp. 304–06.

40. Buttinger, *Vietnam,* p. 898.

41. Bui Tin, *Following Ho Chi Minh,* p. 65.

42. *Facts on File Yearbook 1967. The Index of World Events,* vol. 27 (New York: Facts on File, 1967), p. 546.

43. Ho Chi Minh, "Fight Until Complete Victory" (a speech broadcast by Radio Hanoi, July 17, 1966) quoted in Fall, *Ho Chi Minh,* pp. 379–81.

44. Bui Tin, *Following Ho Chi Minh,* p. 67.

5

Ngo Dinh Diem:
The Conservative Nationalist

The leader is one who tries to turn his followers into children.

Eric Hoffer

Ngo Dinh Diem, the leader of South Vietnam from its creation in 1954 until his assassination in 1963, was a puzzling, contradictory man. Former U.S. secretary of defense Robert McNamara wrote, "Diem was an enigma to me. . . . Even today I do not know what long-term objectives he envisioned for his nation and his people."[1] Diem was both hero and hireling, a fervent nationalist but a lackey to the United States. An old-fashioned mandarin (a scholar-bureaucrat who had mastered the Confucian classics) in a peasant society, he was also a devout Catholic who ruled a Buddhist country. Diem was an improbable man in an impossible situation, and his virtues became the vices that destroyed him.

To understand the modern history of Vietnam, one must explore the personal characters of two men: Ho Chi Minh and Ngo Dinh Diem. As the French historian Philippe Devillers writes, "In our age of mass society, where all history seems to be determined by forces so powerful as to negate the individual, the Vietnamese problem has the originality to remain dominated by questions of individuals."[2] Both Diem and Ho were staunch patriots and ascetic men who cultivated an aura of personal mystery. But they were fated to be lifelong enemies.

Robert Shaplen, who observed Diem closely, writes that there were few men in public life who provoked so many strong opinions, pro and con,

In the Vietnamese usage, family name comes first. Thus, it would be correct to refer to Ngo Dinh Diem as "Mr. Ngo." However, because so many U.S. newspapers and magazines wrongly assumed that "Diem" was the South Vietnamese leader's family name, it became standard usage. Readers pursuing further research are advised to look under both names: Ngo and Diem.

Ngo Dinh Diem (second from right) with family, 1963

Ngo Dinh Diem (right) with Henry Cabot Lodge, 1963

and yet there was a peculiar impersonal quality to everything that was said about Diem, as if everyone were talking about a figure in history, already remote and shadowy. The words one heard—"courageous," "proud," "patriotic," "cold," "detached," "uninspiring"—sounded like clichés rather than characteristics of a living, breathing man who held his country's future in his hands. The image was oddly wooden, the portrait unreal, as if there were some doubt as to its authenticity.[3]

Diem moved in an awkward way, like a puppet being pulled on strings by some outside force. Even his preferred mode of dress, immaculate white sharkskin suits, made him appear unreal to the Vietnamese. Few South Vietnamese dared to dress like Diem, who seemed the direct opposite of Ho Chi Minh in his simple khakis and slippers. Diem believed that a ruler should maintain an unbridgeable distance between himself and his subjects. He was rigid and self-righteous, sure of his opinions on all matters, and uninterested in the views of others. Diem did not want to be loved by his people, only to be respected by them. But in the end he received neither love nor respect.

FAMILY AND CHILDHOOD

Diem's ancestors had been converted to Roman Catholicism by Portuguese missionaries in the seventeenth century. Diem claimed that his family had always been influential, but according to some sources his grandfather was a fisherman. Diem's father, Ngo Dinh Kha, rose to the highest ranks of the mandarinate, serving as minister of rites, grand chamberlain, and keeper of the eunuchs at the court of Emperor Thanh Thai. As Catholics, the Ngo family was suspected of pro-French sympathies by the vast majority of Vietnamese who retained their traditional religion—a mixture of Buddhism, Confucianism, and animism. Had he not been studying abroad, Diem's father probably would have been burned alive inside a Catholic church along with his relatives during an anti-Catholic pogrom in 1870.

Jean Baptiste Ngo Dinh Diem (Burning Jade) was born January 3, 1901, in Hué, the once-grand imperial capital that had become a quaint museum city in the new French Indochina. The traditional social order was disintegrating; indeed the nationalist Phan Boi Chau launched an abortive uprising in the same year Diem was born. Diem had five brothers, all of whom became famous, and three sisters about whom little is known. Ngo Dinh Khoi, Kha's oldest son, became governor of Quang Nam Province in French Indochina; his murder by the Viet Minh in 1945 put the seal on Diem's lifelong hatred of communism. The next oldest boy was Ngo Dinh Thuc, who imbibed his father's fierce Catholicism to become an archbishop of the Roman Catholic Church, personally ordained by the Pope. Diem was the third son. His younger brother Ngo Dinh Nhu later became his most influential adviser and, along with Nhu's notorious wife, hastened Diem's doom. The second youngest brother was named Ngo Dinh Can. In the 1950s he ruled over central Vietnam from Hué, not necessarily following instructions from Diem. And the youngest of the Ngo brothers, Ngo Dinh Luyen, became an international spokesman for the Diem regime.

Diem's childhood was disrupted by political strife. When he was six years old the French deposed Emperor Than Thai for having balked at some of their demands. Diem's father, Ngo Dinh Kha, an ardent nationalist and a supporter of Phan Boi Chau, resigned in protest and retired to his land as a gentleman farmer. Kha founded a private school in Hué, the prestigious Lycée Quôc-Hoc, that combined Eastern and Western learning. Young Diem was left at Hué under the care of Nguyen Huu Bai, another high-ranking mandarin. The boy was sent to a French Catholic school where he rose at 5:00 every morning to pray. For the rest of his life he was deeply (some say mystically) religious. Diem studied both French and Chinese classics. Ho Chi Minh attended the Lycée Quôc-Hoc, too, but as Ho was considerably older, he and Diem probably never met as boys.

When he was fifteen years old Diem decided to become a priest and entered a monastery. Although he quickly changed his mind, perhaps it was during this period of intense religiosity that Diem took a lifelong vow of chastity. He never married and is not known ever to have had a lover. Diem scored so highly on a French high school equivalency examination that he was offered a scholarship to Paris. However, he turned it down "on the pretext that his father was ill, but in truth because he did not wish to place himself under French tutelage."[4] Diem entered the Hanoi School for Law and Administration in 1917, emerging four years later with a law degree, and graduating first in his class.

BUREAUCRATIC SERVICE (1921–33)

Diem entered the imperial bureaucracy as a mandarin of the ninth (lowest) grade assigned to the Royal Library at Hué, but he rose quickly due to his intelligence, dedication, energy, and honesty. He became district chief of about seventy villages near Hué, then was given responsibility for a larger area of about 300 villages. He made inspection trips on horseback, eschewing the traditional palanquin borne by coolies. He dressed in a mandarin's silk robe and wore a conical straw hat. He functioned as tax collector, director of public works, sheriff, and judge.[5] While performing these duties Diem encountered Ho Chi Minh's Revolutionary Youth Association, the prototype for the Indochinese Communist Party. Diem planted agents among the revolutionaries and arrested some. He remained at war with the communists for the rest of his life. At the age of twenty-eight Diem was named governor of Phan Thiet Province. In 1930 he was made responsible for Quang Tri, a coastal district just north of Hué, and in 1932 he was named chairman of a commission of inquiry into corruption of high government officials.

While Diem was diligently administering his districts, Vietnam seethed with peasant unrest. Spontaneous outbreaks of violence spread across the countryside when ripples of the Great Depression reached Southeast Asia. The French ruled Annam and Tonkin, the central and northern parts of Vietnam, indirectly: A forlorn gentleman named Bao Dai reigned as "emperor" from Hué, when he was not in France; however, Bao Dai's reign was a façade for French control. The French even forbade him from traveling inside his own country.

In May 1933, on French instructions, Bao Dai appointed Ngo Dinh Diem minister of the interior—an extraordinarily high position for a man only thirty-two years old. Diem demanded that the Chamber of People's Representatives, an impotent legislative group, be given real power. When this was refused, Diem resigned (exactly as his father had twenty-six years earlier) to protest French meddling in Vietnam's internal affairs. According to historian Stanley Karnow, Diem sank into despair because he could already see the future of his country. "The Communists will defeat us," he predicted, "not by virtue of their strength, but because of our weakness. They will win by default."[6] Diem publicly accused Bao Dai of being nothing but an instrument in the hands of the French authorities and returned all the titles and decorations he had been given by the emperor and by the French.

TWENTY YEARS OF POLITICAL INACTIVITY (1933–53)

Diem's resignation created little stir. No other mandarins followed his example. A mystery of Diem's character is how this active man could sink into self-imposed idleness. For more than a decade he lived at the family home in Hué with his mother and his brother Ngo Dinh Can. He went to mass every morning, "and passed the rest of the day either reading or engaging in one of his four hobbies, riding, hunting, gardening, and photography."[7] His absence from public life strengthened his reputation as an incorruptible nationalist. He corresponded with Phan Boi Chau but refused to have anything to do with Ho's agitators. Diem was always a patriot but never, by any stretch of the imagination, a revolutionary.

Japanese troops peacefully occupied Vietnam in September 1940. Now the Vietnamese people had three layers of government: The Japanese controlled the French who in turn controlled Bao Dai. Diem considered accepting a Japanese offer of nominal Vietnamese independence, but this only resulted in his being placed under surveillance by the French police. Declared a subversive in 1944, Diem hid with friends in Saigon. In March 1945 Bao Dai declared Vietnamese independence, at Japanese prodding. Diem knew that Japan's impending defeat made it imprudent to have anything to do with Bao Dai. Diem's brother Ngo Dinh Khoi collaborated with the Japanese, and for this he was shot and killed by the Viet Minh. To make an example of his treachery, the Viet Minh burned Khoi's house, destroying Diem's personal library.

World War II ended on August 15, 1945. Ho Chi Minh proclaimed a provisional government two weeks later and wanted to persuade, or force, Diem to be part of it. But Diem was never one to give in to pressure, even when Viet Minh agents arrested him and took him to a communist "liberated zone" near the Chinese border, where he lay sick in bed for months with malaria and dysentery. Ho Chi Minh respected Diem as an administrator and a nationalist. In February 1946 Ho met with Diem and offered him the same position he had held in the early 1930s—minister of the interior. Ho hoped thereby to gain the support of Vietnamese Catholics, who were suspicious of any government dominated by communists. Here are the actual words the two leaders exchanged, or at least the version of them that Diem recounted fifteen years later:

Diem: What do you want of me?

Ho: I want of you what you have always wanted of me—your cooperation in gaining independence. We seek the same thing. We should work together.

Diem: You are a criminal who has burned and destroyed the country, and you have held me prisoner.

Ho: I apologize for that unfortunate incident. When people who have been oppressed revolt, mistakes are inevitable, and tragedies occur. But always, I believe that the welfare of the people outweighs such errors. You have grievances against us, but let's forget them.

Diem: You want me to forget that your followers killed my brother?

Ho: I knew nothing of it. I had nothing to do with your brother's death. I deplore such excesses as much as you do. How could I have done such a thing, when I gave the order to have you brought here? Not only that, but I have brought you here to take a position of high importance in our government.

Diem: My brother and his son are only two of the hundreds who have died— and hundreds more who have been betrayed. How can you dare to invite me to work with you?

Ho: Your mind is focused on the past. Think of the future—education, improved standards of living for the people.

Diem: You speak a language without conscience. I work for the good of the nation, but I cannot be influenced by pressure. I am a free man. I shall always be a free man. Look me in the face. Am I a man who fears oppression or death?

Ho: You are a free man.[9]

Diem's political inactivity continued another five years, for he found both sides of the First Indochina War, the French and the communists, equally abominable. He organized a political group known as the Nationalist Extremist Movement, which advocated simultaneous resistance against the French and the Viet Minh, but it met little success and soon disbanded. France gave the ever-pliable Bao Dai back his throne in 1949 after he agreed to reign over the nominally independent "Associated State of Vietnam." Diem refused Bao Dai's offer of the prime ministership. The Viet Minh, sensing that Diem's stubborn refusal to serve the French might make him a viable nationalist rival to Ho, sentenced him to death in absentia in the spring of 1950. Diem asked for protection from the French police but was informed that they had more pressing tasks, so he prudently embarked on a religious pilgrimage to Rome.

Diem first went to Japan to confer with the exiled nationalist Cuong De, then proceeded to Europe where he was granted an audience by the Pope. He spent some time in France and Switzerland before arriving in the United States in January 1951. He seems to have had a dual purpose. On one hand he lived a spartan life of prayer and menial chores at the Maryknoll Seminary in Lakewood, New Jersey. Other seminarians were impressed by Diem's piety. At 5:30 in the morning he would already be in a pew, praying and meditating. On the other hand Diem traveled around the United States on lecture tours. It was the height of the McCarthy period and Americans were receptive to Diem's message that to defeat communism in Southeast Asia the United States would have to force the French out of Vietnam and then support a genuine anti-Communist Vietnamese national government.

Diem's friends in the U.S. Catholic hierarchy, particularly the influential Francis Cardinal Spellman, introduced him to political heavyweights such as Congressman Walter Judd, Supreme Court Justice William O. Douglas, Senator Mike Mansfield, and a young senator from Massachusetts whose life became fatefully entangled with his own, John F. Kennedy. But Diem did not yet have enough influence with the incoming Eisenhower administration to meet with Secretary of State John Foster Dulles.

Henry Luce, the publisher of *Life* and *Time* magazines, championed Diem's cause and praised him effusively as the best hope for his country. Diem also made friends in academia, including Professor Wesley Fishel of Michigan State University (MSU). The Central Intelligence Agency (CIA) paid Diem's expenses while he was on a temporary appointment at MSU.

Ngo Dinh Diem left the United States in the summer of 1953 to live in a Benedictine monastery in Belgium. The task of building political support for him in the United States was carried on energetically by a group that called itself the American Friends of Vietnam (AFV). General William J. Donovan, the founder of the Office of Strategic Services (OSS, the predecessor agency to the CIA), was honorary chairman. Other AFV luminaries included Admiral Richard E. Byrd; Angier Biddle Duke; Norman Thomas, an American socialist leader; Joseph Buttinger, a historian; and the aforementioned Professor Fishel.[9]

While Diem was abroad the war ground on in his country. The story is by now drearily familiar: The French could never consolidate their political control. The Viet Minh infiltrated their civil administration and secretly organized villagers. France won many battles, to judge by statistics of killed and wounded, but lost the war. The French had their own version of the domino theory, which they called the "tenpin theory." If Vietnam became independent, then other French colonies, most especially Algeria, would want the same, and the mighty French empire would collapse like a set of tenpins struck by a bowling ball. But by 1954 the game was up, for France at least. The communist siege of Dien Bien Phu left the proud French with no alternative but to ask the United States for help. They suggested that the United States bomb communist positions, perhaps even with nuclear weapons, but President Dwight Eisenhower declined. As a result of the 1954 Geneva Conference, Vietnam was temporarily divided (for two years) into a northern zone controlled by Ho Chi Minh and a southern zone under the discredited Bao Dai.

PRIME MINISTER OF THE STATE OF VIETNAM (1954–55)

In June 1954 Emperor Bao Dai asked Diem once more to form a government in South Vietnam. Diem finally agreed, once he was convinced that the French were really on their way out and after Bao Dai granted him absolute civilian and military power. Diem then took an oath of loyalty to Bao Dai and to his son, swearing to preserve the throne. But Bao Dai lacked political legitimacy, for the people of Vietnam could see that he was hardly the embodiment of rectitude that Confucianism required in an emperor.

Diem was well known to the elite class of wealthy French-speaking Vietnamese: landowners, bureaucrats, bankers, and priests. But unlike his rival, "Uncle Ho," Diem was unknown to Vietnamese peasants and workers. His return to Saigon, after four years abroad, was anything but triumphal. He stepped from the airplane on June 26, 1954, tense and unsmiling, barely acknowledging a small band of supporters who greeted him—some French colonial officials, a few reporters, and his own family. Neil Sheehan writes, "The manner in which he rode into Saigon from the airport on the day of his arrival was characteristic. He sat in the back of a curtained car. None of the curious Saigonese who had gathered along the route for a glimpse of the new prime minister could see him, and he was not interested in looking out."[10]

Ngo Dinh Diem had been appointed leader of a nonexistent nation by a repudiated emperor. The tragedy of his situation was its sheer futility: Diem's genuine, passionate nationalism was fatally compromised by his abject dependence on U.S. support—diplomatic and political, financial and military, open and covert. Even his patrons had misgivings. The U.S. ambassador in Paris cabled Washington on May 24, 1954, with the message, "On balance, we are favorably impressed [by Diem] but only in the realization that we are prepared to accept the seemingly ridiculous prospect that this yogi-like mystic could assume the charge he is apparently about to undertake only because the standard set by his predecessor is so low." The American chargé d'affaires in Saigon was even less enthusiastic: "Diem is a messiah without a message. His only formulated policy is to ask for immediate U.S. assistance in every form, including refugee relief, training of troops, and armed intervention. His only present emotion, other than a lively appreciation of himself, is a blind hatred for the French."[11]

In Washington, the director of the CIA decided to send to Saigon the CIA's star operative in Asia, Colonel Edward G. Lansdale. Lansdale's exploits were legendary; indeed, he was the model for two fictional characters: Colonel Hillandale in the novel *The Ugly American* and Alden Pyle in Graham Greene's *The Quiet American*. Lansdale was not a typical spy—he had previously worked for an advertising agency—but he performed a political miracle in the Philippines by engineering Ramon Magsaysay's rise from obscurity to the presidential palace. Lansdale was credited by his superiors with having found the answer to communist insurgency: install a pro-U.S. president who identifies with the common man and then impress on him the urgency of land reform. Lansdale's close friendship with President Magsaysay was widely known in Manila, where Filipinos laughingly called him Colonel Landslide for his management of Magsaysay's 1953 election campaign.

Lansdale arrived in Saigon on June 1, 1954, three weeks before Diem. His cover was an assignment as assistant air attaché; his orders, "Do what you did in the Philippines."[12] Lansdale ingratiated himself with Diem and offered the Vietnamese leader much advice, some of which Diem accepted. Lansdale felt sorry for Diem: "To me he was a man with a terrible burden to carry and in need of friends, and I tried to be an honest friend of his."[13]

The first big problem Diem faced was settling refugees from the north. Lansdale saw this as an opportunity to score propaganda points. The more people who fled the northern zone, the worse it would look for Ho Chi Minh. Lansdale arranged for propaganda leaflets to be dropped from airplanes over Catholic villages in Tonkin, claiming that "Christ has gone to the South" and "the Virgin Mary has departed from the North." A popular account of this human drama, Thomas A. Dooley's *Deliver Us from Evil*, described for American readers the determination of Vietnamese Christians to escape Ho Chi Minh's "ruthless communist dictatorship." Nine thousand Catholics, about half of the northern Catholic community, abandoned their ancestral villages for South Vietnam, more than 300,000 of whom were transported by the U.S. Navy. Entire parishes settled in the south together. Many Catholic refugees were sent to places "regarded by Diem and his advisers as strategically important—in a belt surrounding Saigon and in certain areas of the highlands inhabited by non-Vietnamese tribal groups."[14] These tightly knit communities led by Catholic priests "were in fact regarded with a hostility that they returned with interest; they remained strangers" in South Vietnam.[15]

Bao Dai still officially reigned as emperor, and he tried to undercut Diem, using as his instrument Nguyen Van Hinh, chief of staff of the National Army, who plotted to overthrow Diem. In the nick of time, Colonel Lansdale generously paid Hinh's top officers to fly to Manila to learn from Filipinos how to handle communist insurgents. Lansdale also told Hinh that Washington would cut off all aid if he overthrew Diem. Hinh knew that South Vietnam would quickly collapse without a steady influx of dollars.

In February 1955 France transferred command of the South Viet Nam National Army to Diem, whose actual authority "hardly extended beyond a tiny island of government buildings surrounding the palace."[16] The countryside was enemy territory; in fact the Viet Minh controlled about two-thirds of the villages in South Vietnam. Furthermore, entire provinces in the Mekong delta were controlled by two religious sects, the Cao Dai and the Hoa Hao. The 1.5 million members of the Cao Dai followed their own "Pope," who proclaimed a doctrine that blended elements of Christianity, Buddhism, and Confucianism, and who commanded a 30,000-man army in Tay Ninh Province on the Cambodian border. The Hoa Hao, founded in 1939, may be considered a mystical offshoot of Theravada Buddhism. About 1 million South Vietnamese were members of Hoa Hao, which fielded a militia of 10,000 men. Colonel Lansdale secretly provided Diem with huge sums of money to buy peace with the sects. For $1 million the Cao Dai strongman General Trinh Minh placed his troops under Diem's command.

Diem still could not control his own capital city, which was firmly in the grip of the Binh Xuyen, a secret society of gangsters that dominated all Saigon's rackets: gambling, prostitution, and narcotics. The Binh Xuyen actually controlled the Saigon police force "ever since Bao Dai sold it the concession for forty million piasters."[17] A showdown between the Binh Xuyen and Diem's soldiers began on April 28, 1955, when the gangsters launched a mortar attack on the presidential palace. For more than a week, open warfare raged on the streets of Saigon. Diem emerged victorious, which saved his career, because Secretary of State Dulles had become alarmed by the turmoil and was ready to dump Diem.

To oust Bao Dai, Lansdale advised Diem to organize a referendum in which the people of South Vietnam would be asked to choose between himself and the emperor. The vote was scheduled for October 23, 1955. Diem controlled the government radio station. Villages were flooded with propaganda leaflets. Ballots for Diem were printed in red, regarded as a lucky color, while ballots for Bao Dai were printed in green, traditionally considered the color of a cuckolded man.

Colonel Lansdale advised Diem to settle for 60 or 70 percent of the vote, but Diem thought it would look better if he got 100 percent. His soldiers supervised the voting and the counting of ballots. Diem was said to have received 98.2 percent of the votes. In Saigon, 450,000 registered voters cast 605,025 votes.[18] Diem thus proclaimed South Vietnam a republic and changed his title to president. Bao Dai, who had not bothered to return to Vietnam to campaign, remained in comfortable exile in France for the next forty-two years, until his death in 1997.

Diem believed that he now enjoyed the mandate of heaven. This Confucian principle was interwoven with his Catholic practice of praying to God for guidance and following His will. Neil Jamieson explains why Diem's thinking remained so impenetrable to Westerners:

> For Diem the moral order manifested itself as a mixture of the Neo-Confucian concept of *ly* and a militant, conservative Catholicism. . . . *Ly* refers to "the nature of things," intended to provide harmony in the system by specifying the proper form of all relationships. The concept of *ly* rationalized and legitimated the hierarchical order of society and of nations, making hierarchy itself part of the intrinsic structure of the universe, a state of affairs that was both "natural" and unalterable.[19]

THE SLOW SLIDE DOWN (1956–60)

The United States paid the salaries of South Vietnamese soldiers, policemen, and civilian bureaucrats. American money flowed so freely that it changed the class structure of South Vietnam, creating a middle class that had never existed before and that depended entirely on U.S. largesse. Most of the economic aid came through the Commercial Import Program (CIP), the essential mechanism of which

> was an import subsidization scheme whereby the United States supplied dollars to the Saigon government, which sold them to local importers for South Vietnamese piasters at about half the official exchange rate. . . . The select group of firms and individuals to which the government granted the highly prized import licenses were assured such immense profits that their gratitude and political loyalty was almost automatically assured.[20]

By 1956, the United States was spending about $270 million a year to shore up Diem. The U.S. Military Assistance Advisory Group (MAAG) trained South Vietnamese troops, and MSU sent faculty members from its School of Police Administration to professionalize law enforcement. Any doubts about the need for this were dispelled by an attempt on President Diem's life in February 1957. Men standing near Diem were hit by a spray of machine-gun bullets, but the president, "seemingly unperturbed, to the wonderment of spectators, continued to the rostrum and delivered his speech as if nothing had happened."[21]

Sure now of U.S. support, Diem promulgated a new constitution, Article 3 of which stated simply, "The President is vested with leadership of the nation." In May 1957 Diem paid a two-week state visit to Washington. President Eisenhower met him at the airport, an honor bestowed only rarely. Diem spoke to a joint session of Congress. The State Department wrote Diem's speeches to make him sound like a believer in Western-style democracy, for nothing could have been further from the truth. Diem believed that government was the business of men at the top and that the people simply had a duty to obey. But Diem was saying what Americans wanted to hear, and for the most part, the U.S. press ignored his political repression and arbitrary arrests. Newspaper editorials praised his "firm concept of human rights" and his "Jeffersonian stance."[22] Senator John Kennedy stated that Vietnam was the "cornerstone of the Free World in Southeast Asia," and a "proving ground of democracy." A *New York Times* profile of Diem entitled "An Asian Liberator" praised his efforts to "save his country from falling apart," describing the way he "tirelessly toured the countryside" so that the people would get to know him and perhaps "like him more than Ho Chi Minh."[23]

Diem's political base consisted of five groups: (1) Vietnamese Catholics, who were given free tracts of land in the Mekong delta; (2) wealthy landowners who hoped that Diem would save them from the communists; (3) salaried employees of the government whose livelihood depended on Diem's continued success; (4) members of the new urban middle class, who thrived on the influx of money and consumer products from the United States; and (5) officials in the U.S. Embassy, who attempted to control Diem's every move.[24] Diem tried to place members of his own family in positions of leadership of the first four groups.

Diem's favoritism toward Catholics was a sore point. He gave them government appointments and choice tracts of land. Some peasants complained that Diem's police even forced them to smash ancestral altars and profess allegiance to Catholicism. In 1959 Diem formally dedicated South Vietnam to the Virgin Mary, even though 90 percent of his people were tribal animists, followers of the syncretic sects, or Buddhists.[25]

Probably the greatest frustration for Diem's American supporters, including Colonel Lansdale, was his refusal to implement land reform. Diem was afraid that land reform would undermine traditional social structures. He managed to antagonize both the landlords and their tenants, though very little land actually changed hands, even in the Mekong delta, where 2 percent of the people owned 45 percent of the land. Diem's minister of agrarian reform was a large landowner himself. Incredibly, Diem actually restored to landowners fields that the Viet Minh had already parceled out to peasants during the 1946–54 war. In the province of Long An, while Diem's government fiddled with a cosmetic land reform program for two years, the communists, operating clandestinely, redistributed land in only three months.[26]

There were other ways that Diem defeated himself in the villages. One was his persecution of former Viet Minh supporters, many of whom were not communists. Colonel Lansdale advised Diem to "clean up" insurgents. Hence, thousands were arrested, imprisoned, and tortured. By 1956 most Viet Minh units were smashed, but people in South Vietnam were living in terror. Because the name "Viet Minh" had a patriotic ring to Vietnamese, U.S. advisers persuaded the Saigon media to substitute the name "Vietcong" (shorthand for "Vietnamese Communists"). To honor the dead is a sacred duty to Vietnamese, but Diem's men desecrated Viet Minh war memorials and cemeteries and denied honorable burials to suspected communists.[27]

Vietnamese villages traditionally ran their internal affairs with little interference from the state, but Diem wanted to personally appoint district administrators and provincial chiefs. Often these appointees were Catholics from Tonkin and Annam, who seemed pushy and aggressive to the more slow-moving southerners.

THE RAPID SLIDE DOWN (1960–63)

There are many reasons why South Vietnamese disliked their regime more with each passing year:

1. President Diem shut himself off from the world.
2. Diem did not relate well to his own people.
3. He relied excessively on members his own family, some of whom were corrupt schemers.
4. Diem's ideology of Personalism was too vague for people to understand.
5. He was intolerant of democratic opposition.
6. His regime employed police-state tactics to repress opponents.
7. The Americanization of the war undermined Diem's status.
8. The Vietcong spread their control throughout the countryside, while Diem's political base remained urban.
9. Diem's American patrons began to lose confidence in him.

1. *President Diem shut himself off from the world.* Ngo Dinh Diem preferred to spend his days inside the presidential palace. When he did venture out, it was usually in a motorcade with a police escort, sirens wailing. His American advisers constantly urged him to get out and mix with the people, but he was shy and never felt comfortable doing so. Diem found idle ways to fill up his days, almost as if he wanted to avoid the job of leading his nation. One journalist wrote that "after an entire afternoon of listening to his monologue, I stepped into the fading tropical twilight bewildered by the fact that, with his country in crisis, he could devote half a day to a reporter."[28]

2. *Diem did not relate well to his own people.* He constantly spoke of the people's duty to the government. He refused to delegate power or even listen to advice. Frances FitzGerald considered Diem to be not a traditional ruler but a reactionary who "idealized the past and misconceived the present. His whole political outlook was founded in nostalgia—nostalgia for a country that did not exist except in the Confucian texts, where the sovereign governed entirely by ritual and the people looked up to him with a distant, filial respect."[29] To avoid hearing differing opinions, Diem simply filibustered. As his regime declined, his monologues grew longer and longer. By 1961 "they passed all bounds, frequently lasting six, seven, even twelve hours."[30]

3. *He relied excessively on members his own family, some of whom were corrupt schemers.* President Diem's brothers jockeyed with each other for power, but they knew how to present a united front when necessary. Ngo Dinh Nhu, described as Diem's "brains and hands," was nine years younger than Diem. American diplomats, who found Nhu's demeanor insincere, sarcastically called him "Smiley." Nhu amassed more power with each passing year. Nhu's Can Lao Party resembled a traditional oriental secret society with some modern totalitarian touches. It operated through a secret hierarchy of five-man cells strategically placed throughout the bureaucracy, a government within a government, ready to report any dissent to Nhu, who ran the secret police. Nhu also led the Republican Youth Movement, a martial organization of about 1 million members that acted as his private army. The budgets of the Youth Movement and the Can Lao Party were the source of much of Nhu's huge personal fortune. Nhu took control of the mass media and made no secret of his admiration for Adolf Hitler.

Nhu's wife was worse yet. Madame Nhu was smart, ambitious, and very pretty. She thought of herself as a reincarnation of the famous Trung sisters, who had rallied Vietnamese resistance against China 1,900 years earlier. (She had her own face sculpted onto a statue commemorating the Trung sisters, but angry crowds destroyed this monument after Diem was overthrown.)[31] In a drive to restore traditional morality, she outlawed prostitution, marital infidelity, divorce, contraception, gambling, fortune-telling, beauty contests, dancing, and the singing of sentimental songs.[32]

Madame Nhu organized a paramilitary Women's Solidarity Movement and lavishly funded it with money expropriated from corporations, banks, trading companies, and government agencies. The Women's Solidarity Movement was mobilized for spontaneous demonstrations against Buddhists, who constituted about 80 percent of the population. Madame Nhu encouraged her brother-in-law to purge the cabinet of those who resisted her. As a result, no member of Diem's 1954 cabinet remained in his post in 1963.

Diem's other brothers included Monsignor Pierre Martin Ngo Dinh Thuc, the senior Catholic bishop, who survived the 1963 coup only because he was at the Vatican when the plotters struck; Ngo Dinh Can, the uneducated warlord of central Vietnam; and Ngo Dinh Luyen, who represented Diem abroad. Diem brooked no criticism of any member of his family.

4. *Diem's ideology of Personalism was too vague for people to understand.* Ngo Dinh Nhu proclaimed as the regime's official ideology a doctrine he called "Personalism." This creed was a porridge of misapplied ideas from French Catholic intellectuals such as Emmanuel Mounier and Jacques Maritain, who criticized liberal democracy on the grounds that it left people alienated. According to Personalism, people must accept traditional values, remember their civic duties, and believe in God. Rather than trying to exercise political power themselves, they should obey those who exhibit superior moral fiber.

Personalism was incompatible with democracy, which assumes that people are equal and capable of reasonable thought, but it was consistent with Confucianism, and that is what appealed to Diem. U.S. diplomats and advisers insisted that Diem describe his regime as democratic, so he redefined democracy to mean acceptance of traditional customs and principles, especially those taught by Confucius. The vagueness and irrelevance of Personalism contrasted sharply with the simple tenets of communism as interpreted by the Vietcong—distribute land to the people and neutralize corrupt officials.

5. *He was intolerant of democratic opposition.* Because Diem was certain that he was always right, he saw no point in compromise. Therefore, Diem could never unify the many different South Vietnamese factions who opposed communism. Had he been able to do so, the outcome might have been different.

South Vietnam's Parliament had little power, for its members were afraid to defy Diem. They confined their legislation to such minor matters as setting their own internal parliamentary rules and regulating pharmacists.[33] In 1960, a group of respected South Vietnamese, including former cabinet members, signed a manifesto asking Diem to liberalize his regime. Diem responded by jailing them.

6. *His regime employed police state tactics to repress opponents.* Diem's power base was narrow, and he deliberately kept it so. People who had

served with the Viet Minh were banned from government jobs, while those who had fought alongside the French against their own people were eligible for any position. In 1957 Diem's police arrested 65,000 people, mostly middle-class citizens. It was a downward spiral—the worse Diem's misrule grew, the more people worried that his political failures would deliver the country to the communists. Under the terms of the infamous Law 10/59, issued in May 1959, military tribunals were given a free hand to execute with portable guillotines anyone *suspected* of subversion. By mid-1962 Diem worried so much about unauthorized public meetings that his National Assembly passed a law requiring citizens to apply for permission to celebrate weddings and funerals.[34]

7. *The Americanization of the war undermined Diem's status.* Diem relied on U.S. money, weapons, and advisers, a decision that was ultimately counterproductive, for it made Diem look like an American hireling. In fact, that is precisely how the State Department saw matters. Ambassador Frederick E. Nolting was instructed to tell Diem that Washington wanted a much closer relationship than one of acting in an advisory capacity only and would expect to share in the decisionmaking process in the political, economic, and military fields as they affected the security situation.[35] By 1961 the connection between Diem and the Americans had become so deeply embedded in the minds of villagers that they sometimes politely addressed officials as "My-Diem" (American-Diem).

Diem knew that the Americans had left themselves little leverage when Secretary of State Dulles said that Washington had to support Diem wholeheartedly lest he become "another Kerensky." By jailing his opponents, Diem made sure that the Americans would have no alternative but to prop him up indefinitely, even if he rejected all their pleas to initiate reforms. Thus did the tail wag the dog.

By 1963 the United States was spending $1.5 million a day on South Vietnam, yet Diem resented Americans, distrusted them, found them "rude," and looked on them as "great big children." Sometimes he would even mimic the way they wagged their fingers in his face. To placate Washington, Diem constructed a façade of democracy. "What do Americans know of mandarins?" he asked.[36]

8. *The Vietcong spread their control throughout the countryside while Diem's political base remained urban.* The Military Assistance Advisory Group that the Pentagon sent to train the South Vietnamese Army initially misconceived the entire situation, which they likened to that on the Korean peninsula, where a viable government (South Korea) needed to deter a conventional military thrust across a demilitarized zone. Circumstances in Vietnam, of course, were fundamentally different. There were no front lines, and the "enemy" was to be found in every village.

Former Viet Minh fighters resumed their insurgency in 1957. They employed terror in a selective way—ordinary villagers had little to fear, but officials of the Saigon government were marked for execution. Approximately 2,500 people were assassinated from mid-1959 to mid-1960.[37] The southern revolutionaries were eager to fight Diem even before Ho Chi Minh was ready; Hanoi withheld official approval and support until 1960 and then endorsed the "war of national liberation" mainly because the northern communists did not wish to seem too timorous. By late 1961, the National Liberation Front (NLF), as the communist-led Vietcong was officially known, attracted peasants, disaffected intellectuals, and frustrated nationalists.

The North Vietnamese Army began sending guns, ammunition, and other necessities of war down a long supply line called the Ho Chi Minh Trail, which ran through Laos and eastern Cambodia to South Vietnam. North Vietnamese officers and party cadres professionalized the Vietcong but gradually took away its separate southern identity. Troop mobility was a problem for the South Vietnamese Army. Diem's forces stayed on main roads while the Vietcong used remote footpaths. U.S. helicopters could be used to ferry Diem's troops to distant villages, but Ngo Dinh Nhu worried about attacks on the palace and insisted that no troop movements take place without his prior approval.

One of Diem's worst blunders was his approval of the "agroville" (later called "strategic hamlet") program urged on him by American advisers who believed that the tactic of separating villagers from armed guerrillas explained British success in suppressing a communist insurgency in Malaya. Under this relocation scheme peasants were forced to abandon their homes and villages, where the bones of their ancestors were buried, and move to barren new settlements, often far from their fields. The strategic hamlets, surrounded by moats and barbed wire, resembled prison camps. They were quite ineffective, for there were always Vietcong informers and agitators inside. Diem fatuously called the strategic hamlet program "the point of impact of a political and social revolution" and the "base of a new scale of values, founded essentially on civic virtues and dedication to the common good."[38] The man Diem placed in charge of the agroville scheme, Colonel Pham Ngoc Thao, was actually a communist agent whose enthusiasm for the strategic hamlets stemmed from his certainty that it would turn peasants against Diem.[39]

9. *Diem's American patrons began to lose confidence in him.* President Kennedy promised in his inaugural address of January 20, 1961, to "pay any price, bear any burden, meet any hardship, support any friend, oppose any foe to assure the survival and success of liberty." For Kennedy the most important thing was for the United States to demonstrate its credibility, defined as the ability and willingness to defeat communist wars of national liberation. America's reputation seemed gravely endangered by the Bay of Pigs fiasco in April 1961. Now Kennedy and his advisers could see that Diem

was losing the war. Hence, they urged on him a list of reforms that included depoliticizing the officer corps and firing corrupt officials. Above all, the Americans insisted, Diem must win the "hearts and minds" of South Vietnamese peasants. This, of course, Diem saw no need to do.

In May 1961 Kennedy sent Vice President Lyndon B. Johnson to Saigon to size up the situation. Johnson lavished praise on Diem, calling him "the Churchill of Asia." Later, on board the vice presidential airplane, Johnson was asked if he had really meant it. "Shit," Johnson drawled, "Diem's the only boy we got out there."[40] Within two years Washington had found other "boys" to back. In December 1962 President Kennedy asked Diem's old friend Senator Mike Mansfield to investigate the situation. Mansfield reported that the Diem regime was "less, not more, stable, than it was at the outset" and "more removed from, rather than closer to, the achievement of popularly responsible and responsive government."[41]

THE DOWNFALL OF NGO DINH DIEM (1963)

Diem's open favoritism toward Catholics angered Buddhists, but their protests only brought repression, for Diem and Nhu suspected Buddhist leaders of collaborating with the communists. Tensions rose when Buddhist demonstrators displayed religious flags in defiance of a government ban. (Archbishop Ngo Dinh Thuc was allowed to fly Catholic flags in Hué, however.) A cycle of escalation began: The more harshly the police put down one demonstration, the larger was the next one. On June 11, 1963, an elderly Buddhist monk named Thich Quang Duc sat down in a busy intersection in Saigon, poured gasoline over himself, and lit a match. This protest suicide seemed heroic to many Vietnamese but not to Madame Nhu, who said, "We shall clap our hands at more monk barbecues," nor to her husband, who offered to furnish the Buddhists with gasoline.[42] Vietnamese Buddhists were deeply impressed by the fact that Thich Qang Duc's heart would not burn, though it was set on fire two more times.

Now Nhu's special police attacked pagodas, firing tear gas into the sanctuaries. More than a thousand monks were arrested. Buddhist shrines were sealed. Americans were horrified. As Diem's support in Washington began to melt away, he offered this defense:

> I cannot seem to convince the embassy that this is Vietnam—not the United States of America. We have had good reason to ban street demonstrations in the middle of the war. This is not child's play; I am not inventing Viet Cong terror. Yet when I try to protect the people of this country—including the Americans—by good police work, keeping control of the streets, I am accused of persecuting the Buddhists![43]

President Diem's political base was eroding as rapidly in Saigon as it was in Washington. Ngo Dinh Nhu summoned seven generals to the Gia Long Palace for consultations on August 20, 1963. Six of these seven were already plotting against him and his brother.[44]

Kennedy recalled Ambassador Nolting, who was on friendly terms with Diem, and replaced him with Henry Cabot Lodge. Before Lodge had even presented his credentials to the South Vietnamese president, he received a telegram from the State Department instructing him to tell Diem to remove Ngo Dinh Nhu and Madame Nhu from his government. Since Diem was unlikely to comply, Lodge was ordered to "urgently examine all possible alternative leadership and make detailed plans as to how we might bring about Diem's replacement if this should become necessary."[45] Lodge was to inform generals who might be plotting against Diem that U.S. economic and military support would continue after a coup, and that if the coup failed, the United States would help their families escape Diem's retribution. Not all American diplomats and military officers were ready to betray Diem. General Paul Harkins found it incongruous to summarily dump Diem after eight long years of supporting him. But the die was cast. On August 29, Lodge cabled Washington: "We are launched on a course from which there is no turning back: the overthrow of the Diem government."[46]

Ironically, while Diem's generals were conspiring with the Americans to overthrow him, Diem was sending peace feelers to Ho Chi Minh, asking if it would be possible to create a loose federal government that would leave Ho in power in the North and Diem in power in the South. The Kennedy administration strongly opposed any such negotiated settlement, believing that it would be interpreted as a foreign policy defeat. Such a settlement, if it actually could have been reached, might have kept the communists from conquering South Vietnam.

Two South Vietnamese officers plotting against Diem were General Tran Van Don and General Duong Van ("Big") Minh. They were baffled to learn that General Harkins opposed a coup at the same time that Lucien Conein of the CIA was urging quick action. At a secret meeting at the Saigon airport, early on the morning of October 27, Tran Van Don asked Lodge if Conein spoke for him. Lodge replied that indeed he did. That was the signal the officers were waiting for. For his part, Lodge asked for and received assurance that after Diem was gone the generals would still welcome U.S. military assistance.[47]

Ambassador Lodge met with Diem at 10:00 A.M. on November 1, 1963. Diem told Lodge, "I know there is going to be a coup but I don't know who is going to do it."[48] Lodge falsely told Diem that there was nothing to worry about. The CIA knew very well that the coup was already under way, as its Saigon station chief Lucien Conein declared years later in a television interview,

During the whole reporting period, through my own channels, I was reporting every one of the developments leading up to and including the time of the coup. Every one of the meetings, every one of the negotiations, the discussions that were held with general Big Minh, with General Don and General Kim and any other military leaders who were participating in the coup was completely reported to Washington, D.C., and I received many times guidance of what I was to discuss with these individuals and the limits of which I could discuss these problems with them.[49]

The coup unfolded as planned, but Diem and Nhu managed to escape from the palace through a secret tunnel. They hid in the home of a friend in the Cholon District of Saigon. Diem telephoned Ambassador Lodge to ask where the United States government stood. Lodge dissembled again, saying that because it was the middle of the night in Washington, the United States government could not have an opinion one way or the other. Diem knew then that he had been betrayed.

The next day, November 2, was All Souls' Day in the Catholic calendar, the Day of the Dead. Diem and Nhu negotiated with General Minh for safe passage to exile. Minh sent an armored personnel carrier to take the brothers into custody. They were forced inside the vehicle, and their hands were tied behind their backs. Then they were sprayed with machine-gun fire and, for good measure, repeatedly stabbed. President Kennedy expressed shock, but neither the U.S. nor the South Vietnamese government conducted an investigation into the killings, which were greeted with popular jubilation in South Vietnam.[50] Political prisoners were released, and the city's nightclubs reopened. The communists were pleased, and the leader of the NLF called the assassination "a gift from heaven for us."[51]

President Diem was given no public funeral. He and his brother were buried in unmarked graves inside a military compound. Madame Nhu was out of the country and never returned to Vietnam. Archbishop Ngo Dinh Thuc was also abroad, so he was spared, too. Ngo Dinh Can, Diem's younger brother, took refuge in the U.S. consulate in Hué but was delivered into the hands of the new regime and executed.

President Kennedy was assassinated in Dallas three weeks later. To many Vietnamese, Kennedy's death put events "in balance." President Lyndon B. Johnson, pointing to a picture of Diem, said, "We had a hand in killing him. Now it's happening here."[52]

Diem's assassination led to chaos in Saigon. General Minh's regime lasted only three months, and none of the next seven governments of South Vietnam enjoyed political legitimacy. The war escalated to new levels of ferocity ending with a complete victory for the communists in April 1975. There are no statues or monuments in Diem's honor anywhere in Vietnam. The mandate of heaven had changed.

NOTES

1. Robert S. McNamara, *In Retrospect: The Tragedy and Lessons of Vietnam* (New York: Times Books, 1995), pp. 41–42.

2. Philippe Devillers, *Histoire du Viet-Nam de 1940 à 1952* (Paris: Editions du Seuil, 1952) p. 469.

3. Robert Shaplen, *The Lost Revolution: The U.S. in Vietnam, 1946–1966* (New York: Harper & Row, 1966), p. 104.

4. Joseph Buttinger, *Vietnam: A Dragon Embattled,* 2 vols. (New York: Praeger, 1967), p. 1254.

5. Robert Shaplen, "Diem," *The New Yorker* 38 (September 22, 1962), p. 103

6. Stanley Karnow, *Vietnam: A History* (New York: Penguin, 1984), p. 216.

7. Shaplen, "Diem," p. 108.

8. This exchange (as it was recounted by Diem) is found in Karnow, *Vietnam: A History,* pp. 216–17.

9. Joseph G. Morgan, *The Vietnam Lobby: The American Friends of Vietnam, 1955–1975* (Chapel Hill: University of North Carolina Press, 1997), p. 161.

10. Neil Sheehan, *A Bright Shining Lie: John Paul Vann and America in Vietnam* (New York: Random House, 1988), p. 175.

11. Both quotes are from George McT. Kahin, *Intervention: How America Became Involved in Vietnam,* rev. ed. (Garden City, N.Y.: Anchor, 1987), p. 78.

12. Cecil B. Currey, *Edward Lansdale: The Unquiet American* (Boston: Houghton Mifflin, 1988), p. 136.

13. Edward Doyle, et al., *Passing the Torch,* The Vietnam Experience Series (Boston: Boston Publishing, 1981), p. 126.

14. Kahin, *Intervention,* p. 77.

15. Ellen J. Hammer, *A Death in November: America in Vietnam, 1963* (New York: E. P. Dutton, 1987), p. 19.

16. Doyle, et al., *Passing the Torch,* p. 122.

17. Shaplen, "Diem," p. 120.

18. Kahin, *Intervention,* p. 95.

19. Neil Jamieson, *Understanding Vietnam* (Berkeley: University of California Press, 1993), pp. 16, 235.

20. Kahin, *Intervention,* pp. 86–87.

21. Doyle, et al., *Passing the Torch,* p. 148.

22. Frances FitzGerald, *Fire in the Lake: The Vietnamese and the Americans in Vietnam* (Boston: Little, Brown, 1972), p. 87.

23. These quotes are drawn from Marilyn B. Young, *The Vietnam Wars: 1945–1990* (New York: Harper Perennial, 1991), p. 58.

24. See George Donelson Moss, *Vietnam: An American Ordeal* (Englewood Cliffs, N.J.: Prentice-Hall, 1990), p. 79.

25. Kahin, *Intervention,* p. 101.

26. Jeffrey Race, *War Comes to Long An: Revolutionary Conflict in a Vietnamese Province* (Berkeley: University of California Press, 1972), pp. 167–68.

27. Sheehan, *A Bright Shining Lie,* p. 190.

28. Karnow, *Vietnam,* p. 214.

29. FitzGerald, *Fire in the Lake*, p. 133.

30. Doyle, et al., *Passing the Torch*, p. 182.

31. Tran Van Don, *Our Endless War: Inside Vietnam* (San Rafael, Calif.: Presidio Press, 1978), p. 55.

32. Buttinger, *Vietnam*, pp. 957–58.

33. Kahin, *Intervention*, p. 95.

34. Shaplen, "Diem," p. 122.

35. U.S. Department of State, Deptel 619, November 15, 1961, as quoted in Hammer, *A Death in November*, p. 37.

36. Marguerite Higgins, *Our Vietnam Nightmare* (New York: Harper & Row, 1965), pp. 166–67.

37. Doyle, et al., *Passing the Torch*, p. 152.

38. Quoted in Marilyn A. Levine, *Ho Chi Minh and Ngo Dinh Diem: A Comparative Study* (master's thesis, University of Hawaii, 1978), p. 123.

39. Doyle, et al., *Passing the Torch*, p. 159.

40. Karnow, *Vietnam*, p. 214.

41. Kahin, *Intervention*, p. 146.

42. Buttinger, *Vietnam*, p. 995.

43. Quoted in Higgins, *Our Vietnam Nightmare*, p. 167.

44. Hammer, *A Death in November*, p. 166.

45. Hammer, *A Death in November*, p. 179.

46. Hammer, *A Death in November*, p. 191.

47. Anne E. Blair, *Lodge in Vietnam: A Patriot Abroad* (New Haven, Conn.: Yale University Press, 1995), p. 66.

48. Hammer, *A Death in November*, p. 282.

49. Hammer, *A Death in November*, p. 285.

50. *The Pentagon Papers: The Defense Department History of United States Decisionmaking on Vietnam*, vol. 2 (Senator Mike Gravel edition), (Boston: Beacon Hill Press, 1971), p. 270.

51. Francis X. Winters, *The Year of the Hare: America in Vietnam, January 25, 1963–February 13, 1964* (Athens: University of Georgia Press, 1997), p. 111.

52. Quoted in Winters, *The Year of the Hare*, p. 113.

For Further Reading

Blair, Anne E. *Lodge in Vietnam: A Patriot Abroad.* New Haven, Conn.: Yale University Press, 1995.

Bouscaren, Anthony. *The Last of the Mandarins: Diem of Vietnam.* Pittsburgh: Duquesne University Press, 1965.

Brocheux, Pierre. *The Mekong Delta: Ecology, Economy and Revolution, 1860–1960.* Madison: University of Wisconsin Center for Southeast Asian Studies, 1995.

Bui Diem, with David Chanoff. *In the Jaws of History.* Boston: Houghton Mifflin, 1987.

Bui Tin. *Following Ho Chi Minh: The Memoirs of a North Vietnamese Colonel.* Honolulu: University of Hawaii Press, 1995.

Buttinger, Joseph. *Vietnam: A Dragon Embattled.* 2 vols. New York: Praeger, 1967.

Currey, Cecil B. *Edward Lansdale: The Unquiet American.* Boston: Houghton Mifflin, 1988.

Davidson, Phillip B. *Vietnam at War: The History 1946–1975.* New York: Oxford University Press, 1988.

Doyle, Edward, et al. *Passing the Torch.* The Vietnam Experience Series. Boston: Boston Publishing, 1981.

Duiker, William. *Vietnam: Revolution in Transition.* 2d ed. Boulder, Colo.: Westview Press, 1996.

Fall, Bernard B. *Hell in a Very Small Place: The Siege of Dien Bien Phu.* Philadelphia: Lippincott, 1967.

———. *Ho Chi Minh on Revolution.* New York: Praeger, 1967.

———. *Last Reflections on a War.* New York: Schocken, 1972.

———. *Street Without Joy.* Harrisburg, Penn.: Stackpole, 1961.

———. *The Two Vietnams: A Political and Military Analysis.* 2d ed. New York: Praeger, 1967.

———, ed. *Ho Chi Minh on Revolution.* New York: Praeger, 1967.

FitzGerald, Frances. *Fire in the Lake: The Vietnamese and the Americans in Vietnam.* Boston: Little, Brown, 1972.

Halberstam, David. *Ho.* New York: Random House, 1971.

Hammer, Ellen. *A Death in November: America in Vietnam, 1963.* New York: Oxford University Press, 1987.

———. *The Struggle for Indochina, 1940–1955.* Stanford, Calif.: Stanford University Press, 1955.

Kahin, George McT. *Intervention: How America Became Involved in Vietnam*. New York: Knopf, 1986.

Karnow, Stanley. *Vietnam: A History*. New York: Viking, 1983.

Lacouture, Jean. *Vietnam: Between Two Truces*. New York: Random House, 1966.

McAlister, John T. Jr., and Paul Mus. *The Vietnamese and Their Revolution*. New York: Harper & Row, 1970.

McNamara, Robert S. *In Retrospect: The Tragedy and Lessons of Vietnam*. New York: Times Books, 1995.

Morgan, Joseph G. *The Vietnam Lobby*. Chapel Hill: University of North Carolina Press, 1997.

The Pentagon Papers: The Defense Department History of United States Decision-making on Vietnam. Boston: Beacon Hill Press, 1971.

Sheehan, Neil. *A Bright Shining Lie: John Paul Vann and America in Vietnam*. New York: Random House, 1988.

Wright, Gwendolyn. *The Politics of Design in French Colonial Urbanism*. Chicago: University of Chicago Press, 1991.

Part III

Cambodia

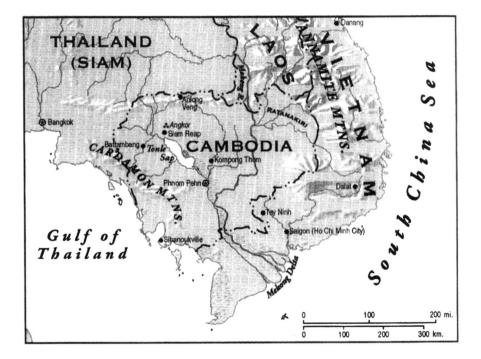

Cambodia Timeline

9th century	First great Cambodian empire under Jayavarman II.
1000–1250	Period of artistic and cultural brilliance; magnificent stone temple-cities built at Angkor.
1431	Thais invade and sack Angkor.
19th century	Thais and Vietnamese repeatedly invade Cambodia.
1864	France establishes protectorate over Cambodia.
1885–87	Insurrections against French.
1922 Oct 31	Norodom Sihanouk born.
1925 Jan	Pol Pot born.
1936	First high school in Cambodia.
1941 Apr 21	French install Sihanouk as king of Cambodia.
1949	Pol Pot awarded scholarship to study in France.
1953 Jan	King Sihanouk dissolves National Assembly.
1953 Nov 9	Cambodian Independence Day.
1955 Mar 2	King Sihanouk abdicates to enter politics.
1960 Sep	Pol Pot reorganizes Cambodian communists.
1965	Sihanouk allows Vietnamese communists to station troops in eastern Cambodia.
1966	Pol Pot visits China.
1967	Peasant uprising in Battambang savagely repressed.
1969 Mar	United States starts bombing Cambodia.
1970 Mar 18	Sihanouk overthrown by Lon Nol.
1970 Apr 30	U.S. and South Vietnamese troops invade Cambodia.
1973 Feb	U.S. bombing intensifies.
1975 Apr 17	Phnom Penh falls to Khmer Rouge; beginning of fanatical revolutionary transformation of Cambodian society.
1976 Apr 4	Khmer Rouge arrest Sihanouk; they subsequently kill many members of his family.
1978 Dec 25	Vietnam invades Cambodia; establishes puppet government under Heng Samrin.

1980s	The Khmer Rouge wage guerrilla war from remote jungle bases against Vietnamese-supported government in Phnom Penh.
1991	Peace accords signed, but factional fighting continues.
1993 May	Elections held under United Nations supervision.
1996 Aug	Defections from Khmer Rouge inner circle; movement crumbling.
1997 Jun 9	Pol Pot orders brutal murder of longtime ally Son Sen.
1997 Jul 25	Pol Pot's comrades turn against him and subject him to a show trial.
1998 Apr 15	Pol Pot dies, allegedly of natural causes.
1998 Jul 26	Election in Cambodia won by Hun Sen using strongarm tactics.

The Cambodian Setting

GEOGRAPHY

Cambodia is located in the heart of mainland Southeast Asia, between Vietnam and Thailand. The worldview of the Cambodian people (the Khmers) is shaped by this geographical reality. The Cambodians believe, not without historical justification, that their neighbors want to swallow them. Consequently, they have considered four options: (1) allying themselves with Thailand against Vietnam; (2) allying themselves with Vietnam against Thailand; (3) finding a distant protector to guarantee Cambodia's frontiers against both; or (4) turning inward, rejecting all foreign influences. All options have been tried, but none has proven satisfactory. Ravaged by war and revolution, Cambodia today is the poorest nation in Southeast Asia.

Cambodia has no natural borders to define its national area and thwart invaders. Moreover, the country has extensive tracts of fertile land. In some areas peasants can harvest three rice crops annually. Cambodia is also rich in aquatic resources. After monsoon rains the Mekong River, 500 miles of which flow through Cambodia, becomes so swollen that it cannot flow out to the sea fast enough and so backs up into a natural catchment basin, Tonle Sap, the largest fresh-water lake (drained by the Tonle Sap River) in Southeast Asia. Cambodians do not need to catch fish—they can harvest them. With such a bounteous source of protein, no Khmer need ever starve.

Cambodia's exports are all primary products: rice, sugar, coffee, cotton, rubber, spices, and timber, although the natural forest cover is shrinking rapidly, as hardwood logs are illegally exported to Thailand and Vietnam. Two other products—gems and marijuana—are easily smuggled across the border for ready cash.

Cambodia's climate is tropical. The rainy season starts in June and runs until October. During this time Cambodia's unpaved roads are a mass of wet, red clay, and military campaigns are postponed. Cool, dry weather from November to March is followed by very hot, dry days until the life-giving monsoon comes once more.

Cambodia's population of 10.8 million (mid-1998 estimate) would be greater if so many people had not died from overwork, starvation, and execution during the terrible years from 1975 to 1979, under the regime of the fanatical Khmer Rouge communists, led by Pol Pot. Khmers (ethnic Cambodians) account for more than 80 percent of the population; the remainder includes Chams, Vietnamese, Chinese, Siamese (Thai), and various tribal groups (Khmer Loeu) living in the northeast near the Laotian border and in the Cardamom Mountains and the Elephant Range to the southwest. The Khmers have historically regarded the hill tribes as savages and taken them for slaves.

The Cambodian educational system is poorly developed. The French regarded their upriver colony as a quaint realm that would only be spoiled by modernity; hence, they built few schools and not a single college. When Cambodia became independent in 1954, only 144 citizens had completed high school. Under King (later Prince) Norodom Sihanouk, from the end of World War II to the mid-1960s, 11,000 young people studied at new colleges in Phnom Penh or abroad. All schools were closed by the Khmer Rouge, who also killed most educated people. Schools have now reopened, but their quality remains low.

Cambodia's once-gracious capital, Phnom Penh, located at the confluence of the Mekong and Tonle Sap Rivers, has been nearly ruined by the wars and political turmoil of recent decades. First the city swelled with refugees from U.S. bombs between 1969 and 1973. Then more people squeezed in to escape the Khmer Rouge, who advanced relentlessly until they completely surrounded Phnom Penh. The communists shelled the city prior to their final assault of April 1975, then immediately evacuated it and scattered the city dwellers all across the countryside. Phnom Penh was essentially vacant for four years. Since 1979 it has been repopulated, and now more than 1 million people live there. Sanitary conditions are poor and crime is rampant.

CULTURE

Khmer civilization was defined by its glorious Angkor period, from the ninth to the thirteenth centuries. The Khmers blended Indian (Hindu) beliefs and practices with their native animism. The god-king, or *deva raja*, performed sacred ceremonies in his temple, which was regarded as the very axis of the universe. Theravada Buddhism spread to Cambodia from Thailand in the thirteenth century. Buddhism's theoretically egalitarian doctrine was modified to incorporate the *deva raja* symbolism "with the god-king conceived as an emergent Buddha or Bodhisattva."[1] The village temple is the center of social and religious life for most Cambodians, and the Buddhist monks are highly respected as religious and secular teachers and arbiters of disputes.

Buddha (c. 563–c. 483 B.C.) taught that life is suffering, caused by needless desires. Conquering desire requires following the "Middle Path" and eschewing all extremes. One's present life is only one of an endless series of rebirths, and one's station in society indicates the balance of merit and demerit accumulated from past lives. Merit can be acquired by giving alms or food to monks, refurbishing a temple, or performing other good deeds. Eventually, with enough merit, a soul may escape from the cycle of birth and death. This release from suffering is called "nirvana."

Buddha is not considered a god, nor is he worshipped. Instead he is revered for having achieved nirvana and for showing his followers the path to enlightenment. Buddhists venerate all life, for even insects are part of the infinite cycle of rebirths. It is therefore difficult to explain how people who are taught such a gentle creed could behave with such cruelty. Part of the answer may be that Khmers are taught to defer to authority. Government policies emanate from elites who inform and instruct their subjects. Consequently, there is a tendency to view alternatives dichotomously, as black and white rather than in shades of gray. Cambodians do not negotiate well, for they may see compromise as a sign of weakness. What is more, there is no tradition of noblesse oblige.

Cambodian art forms stem from Hindu legends such as the *Ramayana* and the *Mahabharata* and from Buddhist parables used to teach morality. Complex, stylized dancing is a central element in Cambodia's high civilization, as can be observed in the bas reliefs of Angkor Wat. The finest dancers were those of the royal court, but few survived Pol Pot's fury. An essential element in Cambodia's national recovery is the revival of classical dance as an art form.

Khmer women were expected to be soft-spoken and well-mannered. The fact that a wife's behavior could cause her husband's status to rise or fall gave women a certain degree of leverage within the family. Under the Pol Pot regime, women suffered along with men but died in fewer numbers. The result is a demographic imbalance between the sexes today. Khmer society still suffers from the deep wounds inflicted by the Khmer Rouge.

HISTORICAL CONTEXT

From the third to the sixth centuries a state known as Funan dominated the area of present-day Cambodia. A successor state, Chenla (A.D. 550–800) left the earliest known Khmer-language inscriptions. Classical Cambodian civilization is considered to have begun in the early ninth century with the reign of Jayavarman II, who established the *deva raja* cult and invited *Saivite* (Shiva-worshipping) priests from India to live at his court.

Indravarman I (877–89), the next important king of Angkor, introduced the worship of Vishnu, a different Hindu manifestation of God, and began a systematic program of temple building. Great reservoirs were dug to store monsoon rains, and canals were dug to the hills where the huge stones used to build monuments were quarried. These works were performed by enslaved battle captives and peasants conscripted for corvée labor.

By the year 1000 Cambodia had become a powerful empire, controlling most of mainland Southeast Asia. Under Suryavarman I (1011–50) and Suryavarman II (1113–50), Cambodia achieved new heights of artistic and cultural brilliance. Magnificent sacred cities arose, built of solid stone. The Angkor temples are the largest and, in the opinion of many, the finest religious monuments in the world. Each Angkor king had his own sacred image placed in a great temple in his honor. The Angkor temples represent physical proof that religion lay at the center of the Khmer civilization. The Khmer scholar-priests were proficient in Sanskrit, producing many original works of literature and poetry, and arguing subtle points of philosophy.

The lower classes, of course, had to support the priests, artists, architects, and engineers who designed the temple complexes. There may have been as many as a million farmers and fishermen who contributed food and labor for the glory of the god-king. Many of the temples feature bas-reliefs showing scenes of everyday life—thereby giving us a glimpse of Angkor society. There are market scenes, portrayals of cockfights, and fish harvests. We can see that oxcarts used a thousand years ago are identical to those used today. These picturesque carvings were not for the eyes of commoners, for Angkor Wat was a sacred space, a physical and metaphysical link between heaven and earth. Hindu cosmology, with its numerous hierarchically organized gods, has remained an essential underpinning of Cambodia's status culture. Serge Thion makes this important point:

> Southeast Asian Theravada societies never had an institutional framework of hierarchical relations, like the Hindu caste system, but they had other means for building up pyramidal relations, namely, patronage and slavery, which complemented each other. The very elaborate system of slavery has formally disappeared, but it has left a deep historical imprint. It is fascinating to consider how quick and easy it was to turn Khmer society into a system having so much in common with the old slavery, with its hierarchical layers of slaves.[2]

In the fourteenth century Cambodia declined culturally, and its empire contracted. Various explanations have been offered: Perhaps the people were exhausted by all the monument-building; or maybe military campaigns to suppress distant rebellions reduced the number of men available to maintain the hydraulic system, or perhaps the society had simply grown top-heavy with its 300,000 priests and temple servants. Certainly internecine dynastic struggles contributed to the decline of Angkor, for the Khmers never evolved a regular, predictable method of designating the next king. Pretenders to the throne often sought help from outside powers. The Siamese and Annamese were only too eager to help. A Siamese army invaded Angkor in the middle 1300s; the once-proud city was sacked and looted in 1431. Khmer civilization went into eclipse and nearly disappeared, although Angkor was not completely abandoned. Theravada Buddhism became the main religion, and huge Hindu temples were no longer needed.

By the 1500s, when the first Europeans penetrated Cambodia, the capital had been moved south to the area of Phnom Penh, where the Tonle Sap River meets the Mekong, a more defensible location and one conducive to trade. Khmer "kings" became mere vassals of the Siamese. In the 1600s they were doubly humiliated, subordinated to Vietnam as well. But for their racial and linguistic distinctiveness, the Khmers might have been assimilated by the Siamese who, by the eighteenth century, "dominated every area of political life, including administration, court rituals, education, kinship alliances, and royal chronicles."[3] Modern Cambodians call these centuries their dark ages.

Khmers consider the Vietnamese to be their hereditary enemies. In the words of Norodom Sihanouk, the Vietnamese "will not sleep peacefully until [they] have succeeded in pushing Cambodia towards annihilation."[4] There is some historical basis for this view. In the early 1800s Vietnamese troops invaded Cambodia and virtually ran the country before being driven out by the Siamese.

French intervention seemed to give Cambodia a degree of domestic stability. To the French, Cambodia was unimportant in itself, but it made an excellent buffer between their valuable Vietnamese colonies and the aggressive Siamese. King Norodom readily accepted France's offer of protectorate status. As a result, Cambodia's foreign affairs and defense were handled by the French while internal decisions were left to the king. French policies did not have much impact on the daily lives of most Cambodians, though they tended to undermine the king's position. In 1884 Norodom signed away most of his remaining powers at gunpoint. He took to opium, and lived out his remaining years an embittered man.[5]

The French abolished slavery in Cambodia. However welcome that decision may have been to the common people, it so infuriated the provincial elite that a three-year rebellion broke out (1885–88). Norodom's brother Sisowath sided with the French, and when Norodom died in 1904 they engineered Sisowath's succession to the throne.

The French did not wish to transform Cambodia; indeed, they prized its slow, gracious pace of life. Devoted French scholars worked to reconstruct Cambodia's glorious history. French archaeologists and engineers directed the laborious restoration of the Angkor temples. For those Frenchmen who romanticized their Southeast Asian backwater, "Cambodia would always be a beautiful and graceful country, shrouded in Oriental mystery and ruled by a divine king, flanked by dancing *apsaras*."[6] Yet transformation was inevitable. Modernization brought roads, steamships, rubber plantations—and a new bureaucracy staffed in the middle ranks largely by French-speaking Vietnamese. Chinese lived in Phnom Penh and in the provincial capitals, where they operated stores and banks.

MODERN HISTORY

While Vietnam seethed with nationalist rebellions, Cambodian life remained placid. Hardly anyone thought it odd that when King Sisowath died in 1941, Europeans picked his successor. They chose an eighteen-year-old schoolboy named Norodom Sihanouk who seemed innocent and malleable, but as Sihanouk matured he metamorphosed into a strong nationalist who insisted on independence for his country.

Japan occupied Indochina during World War II, but life in Cambodia was not greatly affected by the war. In 1946 France granted Cambodia a small measure of autonomy within the French Union, but this only whetted the Cambodians' appetites for real independence. The pace of events was forced by the success of the Viet Minh in the First Indochina War (1946–54). Seeing that an exit from Vietnam was inevitable, Paris gave Cambodia complete independence on November 9, 1953.

In March 1955 Sihanouk "abdicated" the kingship to enter politics. For the next thirty-eight years (until 1993) he was known as Prince Sihanouk. Sihanouk's political power derived from the fact that Cambodian peasants continued to revere him as a *deva raja*, and some (but not all) middle-class people respected Sihanouk's nationalism. Under Sihanouk's somewhat erratic rule Cambodia enjoyed fifteen years of peace from 1955 to 1970, while war raged just a few miles away in South Vietnam.

Prince Sihanouk was deposed in March 1970 by his prime minister, Lon Nol, a conservative army general who jettisoned Sihanouk's neutralism and sided with the United States in its war against the Vietnamese communists. It was a fatal error because President Richard Nixon and his national security adviser, Henry Kissinger, had already concluded that the Vietnam War could not be won, and they proceeded to coldly bomb Cambodia to purchase time for what they hoped would be a graceful exit from Southeast Asia. The bombing raids thoroughly disrupted life in eastern Cambodia. Cratered fields could not be flooded for planting rice. Worst of all, the bombs created a horde of orphans with no one to follow but Pol Pot.

For five years (1970–75) the area controlled by Pol Pot grew while that controlled by Lon Nol shrank, until finally Phnom Penh was completely surrounded. The Khmer Rouge walked into the city on April 17, 1975. To the surprise of the populace, most of the soldiers were mere teenagers— unsmiling, barefoot, and very well armed. The years from 1975 to 1979 were Cambodia's nightmare. In fact, the English language does not contain words to adequately describe the horrors of Pol Pot's Cambodia. Suffice it to say that the Khmer Rouge abolished education, money, religion, and the family.

In December 1978, Vietnam invaded Cambodia. The well-trained Vietnamese troops quickly took Phnom Penh, where they set up a puppet government. Pol Pot and his most loyal soldiers retreated to the western borderlands, where for the next twenty years they carried on a guerrilla war against the Vietnamese-backed Communist government in Phnom Penh.

The warring sides declared a cease-fire in 1991 and agreed to hold elections. Twenty thousand United Nations troops administered the polls and otherwise helped Cambodia get back on its feet. Sihanouk reassumed the title of king, but by now he was old and ill. Pol Pot was sick, too, from malaria, but fought on until his summary trial by his own comrades in the summer of 1997. Pol Pot died in April 1998.

CONCLUSION

The tragedy of Cambodia's modern history is that although the Khmers wanted only to be left alone by the rest of the world, their country was fought over as if it were the most precious real estate on earth. Not only Cambodia's two aggressive neighbors (Thailand and Vietnam), but also most of the world's great powers (France, Japan, the United States, the Soviet Union, and China) either fought in Cambodia or backed one side in Cambodia's seemingly endless civil wars.

Cambodia at the end of the twentieth century was described by King Sihanouk as "an island of war, insecurity, self-destruction, poverty, social injustice, arch corruption, lawlessness, national division, drug trafficking, and AIDS."[7] The Cambodian people's agony has not ended, for its population of amputees grows daily, a consequence of children herding water buffalos in a country still littered with land mines. But the resilient Khmers are rebuilding their society and are determined that the killing fields not return.

NOTES

1. John F. Cady, *Southeast Asia: Its Historical Development* (New York: McGraw-Hill, 1964), p. 89.
2. Serge Thion, "The Pattern of Cambodian Politics," in *The Cambodian Agony*, ed. David A. Ablin and Marlowe Hood (Armonk, N.Y.: M. E. Sharpe, 1987), p. 162.

3. Thion, "The Pattern of Cambodian Politics," p. 151.

4. Gary Klintworth, *Vietnam's Intervention in Cambodia in International Law* (Canberra: Australian Government Publishing Service, 1989), p. 3.

5. Ian Mabbett and David Chandler, *The Khmers* (Cambridge, Mass.: Blackwell, 1995), p. 232.

6. Thion, "The Pattern of Cambodian Politics," p. 149.

7. Associated Press dispatch, October 12, 1997.

6

Norodom Sihanouk:
The Populist Prince

I have to always swim between hot and cold water, so I must be a fish like that.

Norodom Sihanouk

The mercurial political prince Norodom Sihanouk is central to modern Cambodian history. For well over half a century, since Sihanouk was crowned in 1941, Cambodian politics has revolved around his whims, his Machiavellian political strategies, his erratic ideological shifts, and his puzzling choices of domestic allies and foreign patrons. No one has ever been able to predict what Sihanouk will do next. The Italian journalist Oriana Fallaci simply gave up: "It seems to me," she writes, "that the most astounding thing to be said about Norodom Sihanouk is that the more you listen to him, the more you follow his actions, the more you discuss him, the less you understand about him."[1] But perhaps there is a key: Sihanouk is a patriot. Whatever he says or does, he has the best interests of Cambodia at heart. Yet he is accused of having led his people to Pol Pot's killing fields.

Depending upon the situation, Sihanouk can be charming, tenacious, revengeful, ebullient, stubborn, wily, intolerant, megalomaniacal, autocratic, shrill, or playful. At all times he is volatile and unpredictable and makes it a regular practice to conceal his intentions. Dangerously parochial, Sihanouk is an emotional man of boundless energy whose main motivation throughout his long political life has been to keep his people independent of outside powers. He seems brilliant at times, ridiculous at others.

Any assessment of Sihanouk will be controversial. To his supporters, he is the only man capable of uniting the fractious Khmer people. His detractors call him a naïf, a man so conceited that he let himself be duped by Pol Pot into providing a cloak of legitimacy for the abominable Khmer Rouge re-

Norodom Sihanouk, 1941

Norodom Sihanouk, no date

gime that killed an estimated 1.7 million Cambodians, including many members of Sihanouk's own family.

FAMILY AND BACKGROUND

Sihanouk is descended from a long line of royalty. Cambodia has been ruled by kings since the time of the great Angkor empire, but new dynasties were established every time that invading Vietnamese or Thais found a pliable Khmer to advance their interests. King Norodom, Sihanouk's great-grandfather, reigned for forty years. He gladly accepted French protection but later bitterly regretted that choice. The Cambodian royal family (which includes many hundreds of princes and princesses and their children) agreed to French guidance because they were allowed to live in splendor with no duties at all.

When Norodom died in 1904 the kingship should have gone to his eldest son, Prince Sutharot, but the French instead gave the throne to Norodom's pliable half-brother Sisowath, who reigned until his death in 1927. The French then placed Sisowath's dissipated, corrupt son Monivong on the throne. When Monivong died in April 1941 the choice of successor came down to Prince Monireth (of the Sisowath line) or Prince Suramarit (of the Norodom line). The French decided against Monireth, who had been heard to speak of reforms, but they bypassed Prince Suramarit and arranged the coronation of Suramarit's adolescent son, Norodom Sihanouk, a direct descendant of both lines of succession. The next king of Cambodia was a mere schoolboy at the time.

CHILDHOOD AND EDUCATION

Norodom Sihanouk's childhood was lonely. When his father was not occupied with royal ceremonies and rituals, he engaged in light social pastimes and sexual liaisons with his many wives. Suramarit was estranged from Queen Kossamak, and Sihanouk was the only child born of this union. On the advice of an astrologer Kossamak gave her son to an elderly relation who turned the boy over to a nanny. A pattern in Sihanouk's life was that "he lived in a world in which the word and comforting presence of women was a dominant feature."[2] The boy attended a French-language elementary school, the Ecole François Baudoin in Phnom Penh, and then was sent to the prestigious Lycée Chasseloup-Laubat in Saigon, to study for a baccalaureate in rhetoric. The curriculum emphasized French history and culture. Sihanouk's guardian was a French customs official. His royal status inhibited other Khmers from approaching him, but he became friendly with French students. Sihanouk never completed high school because at age eighteen he found himself the king of Cambodia.

SIHANOUK AS KING UNDER THE FRENCH (1941–53)

The French colonial administrators expected that the inexperienced Sihanouk would prove malleable. However, the extent of their miscalculation was not apparent for a decade. At first Sihanouk followed French advice in all matters. Knowing little of affairs of state, he devoted most of his time to music and study. The boy-king had little real power. Not even his French masters held ultimate control, for they answered to the Japanese, who occupied Indochina in World War II. The Japanese recognized Sihanouk's formal position, but the young monarch was rarely seen outside the palace walls.

Gradually, Sihanouk began to assert himself. He refused luxurious gifts from the French and thwarted French plans to romanize the Cambodian alphabet to replace the traditional Cambodian calendar with the Gregorian calendar used in Europe. The new transliteration system devised by two renowned scholars, George Coedès and Georges Gautier, was intended to be a step toward modernization, but to Cambodians it seemed an attack on their culture. Sihanouk threatened to abdicate if the writing system were changed. This tactic worked, and he used it repeatedly for the rest of his life, most recently in 1997.

Sihanouk was taking on the role of protector of Cambodia's traditions, values, and culture.[3] He traveled around the countryside with the blessing of the French, who wanted to advance the king's status as a foil against a less compromising nationalist, Son Ngoc Thanh. The Japanese arrested all French administrators in Indochina on March 9, 1945, and proclaimed Cambodian independence (but at the same time demanded that Cambodia join Japan in the war). Sihanouk later wrote:

> I had no intention of doing this, but I was determined to squeeze every scrap of advantage I could out of our newly acquired status. Before I could do anything concrete, I explained to the Japanese High Command, I must have the documents establishing *de jure* independence. This produced an endless series of exchanges between Phnom Penh and Tokyo. I was thus able to keep Cambodia out of the war, and to later use the status of "independence" as a bargaining counter with the French.[4]

After Japan's surrender Sihanouk became a crusader for real Cambodian independence. He presented his case theatrically, orating in a shrill voice to the Cambodian people and the world. The stimulus for Sihanouk's transformation from compliant monarch to ardent patriot may have been his bitter personal rivalry with Son Ngoc Thanh, who argued for a republican form of government. Thanh had spent the war years in Tokyo. The Japanese installed him as foreign minister in March 1945. In August 1945, Thanh staged a coup, placed Sihanouk under palace arrest, declared himself prime minister, and proclaimed Cambodia an independent republic. When the French returned, they exiled Thanh to Saigon, where he continued to oppose Sihanouk and eventually joined the Khmer Issarak (Free Khmer) insurgents, who fought against the French.

Sihanouk felt personally humiliated by Thanh's criticism and resolved never again to leave himself open to the charge of being insufficiently patriotic. Yet Sihanouk also savored French culture and said that France and Cambodia had a special relationship. On January 1, 1946, in Paris, Sihanouk signed an agreement under which Cambodia achieved "autonomy" within the French Union. However, responsibility for the national budget, foreign policy, and defense remained in French hands. The king's response to complaints from Khmer nationalists was that more time was needed to achieve real independence. So to maintain credibility, Sihanouk led a crusade for independence.

The first Cambodian political party was formed in March 1946. The Democratic Party espoused uncompromising nationalism. In fact it was the political arm of the Khmer Issarak, noncommunist Cambodians who fought alongside the communist Viet Minh to push the French out of Indochina. Sihanouk's enemy Son Ngoc Thanh was the Democratic Party leader. Sihanouk's strategy was to force the French to make numerous incremental concessions, while waiting to see what happened on the battlefields of Viet Nam. Sihanouk (with advice from French experts) fashioned a new constitution calling for male suffrage and elections to a constituent assembly, but with certain powers reserved for the king.

When the first National Assembly elections were held in 1947 the Democrats captured nearly all the seats and won the right to form a new government. Sihanouk became more and more unhappy with constitutional politics. Political factions, usually based on personal ties, not ideology, quarreled endlessly in the National Assembly while the Khmer Issarak fought France in the countryside. In September 1949 King Sihanouk dissolved the National Assembly and for the next two years issued decrees himself. The French were not yet out of the picture, but internal politics in Cambodia was for them definitely a minor matter. Their attention was fixed on Vietnam, where Ho Chi Minh's communist revolution drew strength from the victory of communists in China in 1949. There were Cambodian communists, too, fighting under the banner of the United Issarak (Freedom) Front (UIF), but they were few in number.

Sihanouk continued to chip away at the edifice of French administration. By the terms of a 1949 agreement with Paris, Cambodia was given a freer hand diplomatically, but the French continued to supervise Cambodia's budget and national defense. In the National Assembly elections of 1951, enthusiastic crowds lined the streets in support of Son Ngoc Thanh's Democratic Party, which won overwhelmingly. But the elected legislature was essentially toothless because neither Sihanouk nor the French were willing to cede to it any real power. By the spring of 1952 Thanh had concluded that legislative politics was a dead end, so he left Phnom Penh to join Issarak insurgents in the outlying provinces.

Cambodian politics began to polarize between left and right in the early 1950s, a split that spawned a national nightmare a quarter century later. In September 1951 Ho Chi Minh dissolved the Indochinese Communist Party and replaced it with three national Communist parties (those of Vietnam, Laos, and Cambodia). The communist Khmer People's Revolutionary Party (KPRP) started with about 1,000 members. The Khmer communists believed that independence should be accompanied by a complete restructuring of society to eliminate the distortions of imperialism. Some Cambodian radicals had studied in Paris, where they read Marx, Lenin, and Stalin in French translation. Pol Pot, Ieng Sary, Son Sen, and Khieu Samphan, all now infamous for their actions in the Khmer Rouge regime, were KPRP members.

By 1952 much of rural Cambodia was in the hands of insurgents. In June, King Sihanouk dramatically preempted the communists and the Issarak by seizing power for himself in a coup against his own constitutional government. Sihanouk named himself prime minister, dismissed the National Assembly, and promulgated laws himself. "I am the natural ruler of the country," he said, "and my authority has never been questioned."[5]

To arouse his people's concern, Sihanouk announced that he was temporarily leaving Cambodia for medical reasons. Pronouncements of deteriorating health became a standard tactic. It worked as long as the people viewed him as a god-king, because the *deva raja* was supposed to stay in his capital performing ceremonies. In an impulsive decision in the spring of 1953, Sihanouk left by car for Bangkok and vowed not to return until the French granted Cambodia complete independence. However, Sihanouk found the Thais less than cordial, and he quickly retreated to Battambang, a provincial town in northwest Cambodia.

Next Sihanouk launched an emotional *croisade royale pour l'indépendance* that took the handsome thirty-year-old king to Bangkok, Tokyo, Paris, and Washington. An incident with John Foster Dulles, the U.S. secretary of state, soured him on Americans for the rest of his life. Sihanouk says that Dulles told him, "Go home, your majesty, and thank God that you have the French. Without them, Ho Chi Minh would swallow you in two weeks. Good-bye." Sihanouk never forgot that. "From that day on I have detested them," he wrote, "them and their fake democracy, their fake freedom, their imperialism put through in the name of Christian civilization."[6] Sihanouk portrayed himself as the fighting king, a leader willing to simultaneously take on the French, the Khmer Issarak, and the Thais and Vietnamese.

Sihanouk argued to the French that he knew how to cooperate with them, but that unless he were given immediate, complete independence Khmer Issarak extremists would prevail. As a result, in October 1953 France transferred authority over judicial and police matters to the government in Phnom Penh. These concessions were forced by the deteriorating military situation in Vietnam and by public opinion in France, which favored a rapid exit from Indochina. November 9, 1953, was celebrated as Cambodian Independence Day. It was a moment of sweet triumph for Norodom Sihanouk, whose nationalist credentials now surpassed those of his rival, Son Ngoc Thanh. The communists, however, maintained that liberation had not been achieved because Cambodia's feudal social structure and economy remained intact. A leading proponent of this view was Pol Pot, newly returned from France along with other implacable Khmer communists, including Ieng Sary, Hu Nim, and Hou Youn.

SIHANOUK AS LEADER OF INDEPENDENT CAMBODIA
(1954–70)

Sihanouk was in full command by 1954. Son Ngoc Thanh's Democratic Party had weakened, while people loyal to the king grew more influential. Cambodia was recognized as a sovereign country within its French-drawn borders at the Geneva Conference of 1954. The Geneva accords also called for elections to be held in Cambodia. This would be a test of Sihanouk's political skill, for most Cambodian peasants were no better off as subjects of a sovereign king than they had been under the French. Sihanouk feared that the well-organized Democrats or even the newly formed pro-communist Krom Pracheachon (People's Group) might win many votes.

In a Machiavellian masterstroke, King Sihanouk abdicated the throne on March 2, 1955, and took the title of prince. His father, Norodom Suramarit, became king and wore the royal regalia, but Prince Sihanouk nevertheless "retained as many royal trappings as possible, and there was no question for the population as to who the real king was."[7]

Sihanouk was now free to enter electoral politics as a private citizen. He founded the Sangkum Reastr Niyum (People's Socialist Community), which was something more like a mass movement than a political party. Sihanouk mobilized the entire bureaucracy to support the Sangkum and paid candidates from rival parties to join it. The press was required to report positively on the Sangkum.

Sihanouk could hardly have lost the election. Most villagers still thought of him as a *deva raja* able to move in both earthly and celestial orbits.[8] Sihanouk was able to convert his people's awe of his royal presence into popular adoration. His relationship with the people became uniquely personal, without all the pomp and ceremony of the kingship. Sihanouk began referring to himself as "Samdech Sahachivin" (Prince Comrade) or "Samdech Ou" (Prince Daddy). Not leaving anything to chance, Sihanouk's party workers stuffed ballot boxes. The Sangkum won every single seat in the National Assembly. Sihanouk also conducted a national referendum to ask Cambodians if they approved of his leadership. One ballot bore a picture of Sihanouk and the word "Yes." The "No" ballots were printed on black paper. According to official figures, of 927,000 votes cast, 925,000 (99.8 percent) were affirmative.

The 1955 elections marked the beginning of a political era personally dominated by Sihanouk. He portrayed himself as a private citizen fighting for Cambodian dignity, while he still basked in the royal aura of his former kingship. The combination was irresistible. Sihanouk's only detractors were certain dissatisfied members of the royal family, Son Ngoc Thanh's followers, and the communists. The latter were patronizing and were referred to by Sihanouk as "my little red Cambodians (Khmer Rouges)." He co-opted the moderate left by using their own words in his speeches. The prince staged annual congresses that turned into spectacles of adulation for himself. He often traveled in the countryside, "scattering bales of cloth and sacks of food in remote hamlets of Ratanakiri, standing in village squares and mopping the sweat from his face as he swapped raucous jokes with the delighted peasantry, exploiting both his semidivinity and his obvious humanity in a unique brand of personal populism."[9]

Prince Sihanouk loved international diplomacy and was in good form at the 1955 Bandung Conference of Asian and African nations, where he chatted on friendly terms with Jawaharlal Nehru of India, U Nu of Burma, Sukarno of Indonesia, and Zhou Enlai, the Chinese foreign minister. This last contact was important. The enduring friendship between Zhou and Sihanouk was a critical factor in Sihanouk's decision to back the Khmer Rouge after 1970.

From Bandung Sihanouk went to Manila, Tokyo, and Beijing. In China he was treated with the deference he craved. By contrast, his relations with the United States were filled with problems. Perhaps Sihanouk had imbibed some of the French disdain for American culture, and perhaps his prickly sense of pride perceived insults where none were intended, but the main problem was that American diplomats vocally disapproved of Sihanouk's neutralist foreign policy. President Dwight Eisenhower and Secretary of State Dulles distrusted all of Sihanouk's newfound friends: Nehru, Sukarno, Josip Broz Tito (the Yugoslav dictator), Gamal Abdel Nasser of Egypt, and most especially the Chinese communists. The Americans, for their part, seemed to go out of their way to offend the prince. For example, the U.S.

ambassador to Cambodia, Robert McClintock, who considered his posting to Phnom Penh beneath his status, lectured Sihanouk and "openly displayed his contempt by [calling on Sihanouk] in shorts or, on other occasions, with a walking stick and his Irish setter."[10] Notwithstanding such atmospherics, U.S. economic aid made up 30 percent of the kingdom's defense budget in some years.

Prince Sihanouk received a hero's welcome when he returned to China in 1956. Chinese foreign aid came with no strings attached, albeit with ulterior motives. Zhou Enlai and Sihanouk signed a Sino-Cambodian friendship pact, under which China offered Cambodia protection against South Vietnamese military incursions. Sihanouk extended diplomatic recognition to the Soviet Union in 1956 and to the People's Republic of China in 1958.

Some Cambodians remember the late 1950s as a golden age of political and economic stability. But this superficially peaceful era was the calm before the storm, for Sihanouk undermined the political center by taking all power into his own hands and stifling legitimate political opposition. In 1957 Sihanouk retreated to a monastery near Angkor Wat to become a monk. However, this was a ploy to demonstrate his indispensability, for less than two weeks later he was back in Phnom Penh.[11] Then he moved against his political enemies in the Democrat Party, even instigating soldiers to beat up party leaders. He organized new elections and won 99 percent of the vote against the only competing party, Krom Pracheachon. The communists, realizing that they could not compete against the omnipotent Sangkum organization, decided to go underground.

Sihanouk's father, King Suramarit, died in April 1960. Sihanouk decided not to appoint a successor but instead set up a regency council, which named him chief of state, and he retained the title of prince. In a formal sense his decision temporarily ended the thousand-year-old monarchy. Sihanouk now dominated nearly all aspects of life in Cambodia. Schools, temples, clinics, bridges, and roads were named in his honor. He led a public discussion in the press about leadership in Cambodia, making it clear that he alone symbolized the unity of his country. To strengthen his image as a man of the people and to show his disdain for the Americans, he courted various left-wing groups, welcoming their endorsement of "socialist" programs such as the nationalization of banks and foreign trade. But he was foolishly inconsistent in his policies toward the Cambodian left. His biggest mistake was sending a squad of ten policemen to humiliate the future Khmer Rouge leader Khieu Samphan, beating him up in the street, stripping him naked, and photographing him.[12]

While it lasted, Sihanouk's balancing act was brilliant, but by the mid-1960s he found it increasingly hard to juggle the interests of the very diverse elements of Cambodian political life—peasants, urban intellectuals, bureaucrats, army officers, royalists, shopkeepers, and radical nationalists. He tacked with the wind, moving first right, then left, then right again. In 1963 he swung way left with public denunciations of American meddling in Cambodian affairs. Sihanouk broke off diplomatic relations with Washington altogether in 1963, when *Newsweek* magazine accused his mother, Queen Kossamak, of running Phnom Penh bordellos and being "money-mad."[13] He railed against the Central Intelligence Agency (CIA) for its involvement with his old enemy Son Ngoc Thanh and for its ceaseless plotting against him. When Sihanouk read foreign newspaper articles he deemed unfriendly, he invariably wrote a reply directly to the editors.

For Sihanouk, as for all Cambodian leaders past and present, safeguarding Cambodia's territorial integrity was the highest priority. It galled him that the United States relied on Thailand and South Vietnam, Cambodia's two traditional enemies, to support its policies in Southeast Asia. He railed at an American journalist in 1968, "You have agreed to respect Cambodia's territorial integrity: we want you to add 'within the present frontiers.' The reason you balk at these words, of course, is because your satellites, Thailand and South Vietnam, continue to make completely unjustified territorial claims against us, and you are afraid to offend them."[14]

Prince Sihanouk was shocked and frightened by the assassination of South Vietnamese president Ngo Dinh Diem on November 2, 1963, which he suspected had been arranged by the CIA. Sihanouk had detested Diem but worried that something similar might happen to him. On November 6 he terminated all U.S. military and economic aid programs in Cambodia. Three men Sihanouk disliked died within a month of one another: Diem, U.S. President John F. Kennedy, and Thai prime minister Sarit Thannarat. Sihanouk proclaimed over Radio Phnom Penh that "all would meet in hell."[15]

The prince decided to cast his lot with North Vietnam and the Vietcong. He allowed the North Vietnamese to resupply their troops in South Vietnam via the Ho Chi Minh Trail (and later permitted Chinese and North Vietnamese ships to use the newly built port of Sihanoukville, from where supplies were taken by train and truck to the front lines). Sihanouk waited until May 1965 to formally sever diplomatic relations with the United States, perhaps because his own army harbored deep reservations about his leftist diplomacy. Sihanouk's domestic policies also showed a leftward tilt, which, however, stopped far short of economic leveling. When he nationalized trade and banking, he called it "Buddhist socialism," but the main effect was to frustrate the emerging bourgeois class in Phnom Penh.

Sihanouk was reacting to moves on the global chessboard over which he had little control. The ferocious escalation of the war in Vietnam affected Cambodia in ways that no one could have predicted. Tens of thousands of Vietnamese communist troops used eastern Cambodia as a protected area from which they could attack South Vietnam. Retaliation by the South Vietnamese and the Americans was only a matter of time. The prince believed that if the United States, the Soviet Union, and China would jointly guaran tee Cambodia's neutrality, the Cambodian communists would never be strong enough to threaten him. Sihanouk's verbal leftism must not be taken at face value, for he often spoke about the failures of communism and opined that Cambodia ought to stop sending students to France, where they became communists, and instead send them to Peking, where seeing communism in practice would turn them into anticommunists.

A pleasant interlude from Cambodia's crisis occurred in 1966 when Sihanouk's idol, French president Charles de Gaulle, visited Cambodia. De Gaulle and Sihanouk agreed fully on the need to counter U.S. power while at the same time resisting communism. De Gaulle, who approved of Cambodian neutralism, was given a magnificent welcome in Phnom Penh and an outdoor feast on the terraces of Angkor Wat. Sihanouk flattered himself by comparing his own reign with that of King Jayavarman VII from classical times (1181–1219).

But the underlying polarization of Cambodian politics could no longer be ignored. The Cambodian communists changed their party's name from "Worker's Party of Kampuchea" to "Communist Party of Kampuchea" (CPK), an indication that they thought that their struggle had reached a more advanced stage. Meanwhile, many conservatives who resented the loss of U.S. economic and military aid were elected to the National Assembly. Sihanouk had not nominated candidates from his Sangkum Reastr Niyum. Candidates generously supported by the army gained enough seats to name their own prime minister, General Lon Nol, in November 1966.

Sihanouk maintained Cambodian neutrality and maneuvered in every possible way to keep Cambodia out of the war. He attempted to appease both sides, sometimes speaking well of the Americans in public, but then secretly cooperating with the North Vietnamese. Convinced that the communists would win, he wanted to avoid alienating them. Beset by antagonistic forces on all sides, he was reduced to denouncing extremism of the left and the right. But he never found solutions to his country's serious problems: economic deterioration, growing factionalism, rising insurgency, and discontent in the armed forces. Sihanouk's rhetorical and tactical contradictions made him appear merely farcical; his shrill denunciations of all his domestic and foreign enemies began to sound desperate.

Prime Minister (also General) Lon Nol was supported by the Cambodian Army and the urban middle class. Although Prince Sihanouk formally endorsed him, he simultaneously began releasing news bulletins with a markedly leftist tone. Cambodian politics turned into a bizarre, factionalized circus. Lon Nol offered to resign, but Sihanouk rejected his offer while continuing to undermine his position. In 1967, resorting to an old trick, Sihanouk flew to France, believing that all the squabbling factions would beg him to return. As Milton Osborne writes, "Sihanouk never once entertained the idea that he might not remain the indispensable centerpiece of Cambodian politics."[16] In reality, he was becoming irrelevant.

While Sihanouk focused on foreign affairs, ominous rumblings of peasant rebellion could be heard in Battambang Province, where farmers lashed out at Chinese moneylenders and at Lon Nol's men, who used heavy-handed tactics to force the people to sell rice to the state at fixed prices. Sihanouk returned from France to deal with the insurrection, which became known as the Samlaut Rebellion. Sihanouk told Lon Nol to end the revolt, and the general carried out his orders with enthusiasm and brutality. Military violence against the peasants of Battambang only generated increased sympathy for the insurgents and lent credence to their claims that Sihanouk's rule was repressive. The Samlaut Rebellion was spontaneous, not the result of a communist plot.

Concluding that the communists now presented a more serious challenge than Cambodian rightists, Sihanouk again shifted course. In a move he intended as a diplomatic opening to Washington, Sihanouk invited former first lady Jacqueline Kennedy to visit Cambodia. He had heard that she had always dreamt of seeing Angkor Wat, and he received her in grandiose style. It was in effect a state visit, for Mrs. Kennedy arrived in Phnom Penh in a U.S. Air Force C-54 from Bangkok and stayed in Khemarin Palace, a state guest house. In hope of inaugurating a new era in Cambodian–U.S. relations, Sihanouk designated a street in Sihanoukville as Avenue President Kennedy.

The world press gave intense coverage to the war in Vietnam but tended to downplay or ignore events in Cambodia. Few international journalists were allowed to enter the country, and most of the world failed to recognize the extent of Sihanouk's cooperation with the North Vietnamese. By secret agreement he allowed them to station troops and build military depots on Cambodian territory. However, the U.S. government knew. So when Richard Nixon entered the White House in January 1969, he and his national security adviser, Henry Kissinger, laid plans to bomb Cambodia, using Sihanouk's duplicity as a pretext. Although the B-52 bombing campaigns were kept strictly secret from the American public, they could scarcely be kept secret from the Cambodians. Sihanouk was never asked to approve the raids, but Kissinger thought that Sihanouk would tolerate them. William Shawcross writes:

> It is possible that Prince Sihanouk was indeed a party to the conspiracy. It would have fitted in with his policy of playing enemies off against one another, with his dislike of the Vietnamese and with his move back toward Washington. It is certainly true that while Phnom Penh continued to denounce American defoliant attacks, artillery barrages and tactical airstrikes against Cambodian villages throughout 1969, it made no public protest that specifically mentioned B-52 strikes.[17]

Sihanouk claims that he was never asked to approve the B 52 campaign and never did so. In any case, Sihanouk could do nothing to stop either the Americans or the North Vietnamese from violating Cambodian neutrality. The Nixon administration tapped telephones and falsified reports to conceal the extension of the war into neutral Cambodia. In his memoirs Nixon admitted that one reason for the secrecy "was the problem of domestic antiwar protestors."[18] U.S. policymakers, preoccupied with the situation in Vietnam, did not care if the bombings undermined Sihanouk.

Sihanouk decided to establish normal diplomatic relations with the United States in 1969, but he hoped to appease the North Vietnamese as well. He sometimes repeated a Cambodian proverb: "When elephants fight, ants should stand aside." Trying to maintain his balancing act while the war closed in on him and his people, the prince inevitably failed.

THE DOWNFALL OF SIHANOUK

In the early 1960s it seemed impossible that Sihanouk could be overthrown, for he had cleverly co-opted his opponents on the left and right and was practically worshipped by peasants. Son Ngoc Thanh was discredited. To those who might have conspired against him, he seemed indispensable. The economy was sluggish but stable. But Sihanouk's excessive self-confidence blinded him to signs of serious discontent. The army was making little headway against Cambodian communists and was worried by Vietcong and North Vietnamese troops on Cambodian soil. The generals had not forgiven Sihanouk for breaking relations with the United States and refusing U.S. military assistance.

In Phnom Penh public opinion was turning. Citizens resented the spreading corruption in Sihanouk's administration, especially that which they attributed to his wife, Monique. Gambling casinos were built in Phnom Penh at the government's expense, and many influential people lost their fortunes at the gambling tables. Sihanouk entertained himself by playing piano, accordion, and saxophone. He wrote military marches and popular songs ("The Evening I Met You," "Passion," "Regret") and produced his own movies. *The Enchanted Forest*, directed by Norodom Sihanouk and starring Norodom and Monique Sihanouk, won an award at the Moscow Film Festival in 1967, inspiring jokes that the category must have been films produced and directed by heads of state. In *Shadow Over Angkor* (1968) the prince thwarted an American plot against Cambodia. All these antics tended to erode the natural respect Khmers accorded their prince and furnished a pretext for the army to move against him.

Sihanouk's nationalization of foreign trade undermined the small class of Cambodian entrepreneurs and gave them a strong incentive to trade on the black market. An economic ripple effect from the bottleneck in trade reached down to farmers whose rice was grown for export. When Sihanouk concluded that there was little he could do to improve the economy, he delegated responsibility for economic policy to Lon Nol, who bore the brunt of complaints formerly directed at Sihanouk. By 1969 the economic situation had grown serious. Tens of thousands of farmers migrated to Phnom Penh. At first they were fleeing rural indebtedness. Later they were fleeing American bombs. The sleepy capital city found it hard to accommodate so many new residents. Even the tiny industrial sector of the Cambodian economy went into decline, adding urban unemployment to the nation's list of woes. Sihanouk seemed oblivious to these crises and refused to initiate reforms. He called the Cambodian people his children. It was a revealing phrase, for he really did not think them capable of making rational decisions.

Sihanouk's opening to the United States confused rural people and irritated Phnom Penh intellectuals. Nonetheless, he defended his political oscillations bluntly: "All national leaders must be Machiavellian in the interest of their people. And I must maneuver as best I can for Cambodia."[19] Deputy Prime Minister Sirik Matak, Sihanouk's cousin, began plotting to replace the prince with someone more acceptable to Cambodia's elite. The mild-mannered prime minister, Lon Nol, was being pressured by the army to expel Vietnamese communist troops from Cambodia.

Sihanouk's swelling vanity attracted critical public notice. He insisted that the entire foreign diplomatic corps turn out to greet him whenever he returned to Phnom Penh from his frequent trips abroad. Any journalist who wrote a negative word about him could expect to receive a deportation notice. Later, he looked back on his behavior with regret:

> I had, let's say, a rather extravagant lifestyle. I was a rather unusual head of state and not really a socialist. I liked racing cars, I gave myself up to the pleasures of life, I led a jazz band. Usually, kings and presidents do not play the saxophone and the clarinet. I composed songs and traveled through the provinces to sing them with my people. . . . Even worse: I forced the diplomatic corps to sing them.[20]

Relying on his old ploy of leaving the country during hard times (with the object of being begged to return), Sihanouk went to France in January 1970 for his annual medical exam and to enter an obesity program. This time his ruse did not work. On the contrary, it provided his enemies with a perfect opportunity. Lon Nol and Sirik Matak moved quickly. They closed the gambling casinos and privatized banks. Sirik Matak flew to Hanoi to demand the removal of Vietnamese troops. (He was infuriated when Vietnamese officials showed him documents signed by Sihanouk agreeing to a Vietnamese presence on Cambodian soil.)[21]

In early March 1970, some citizens of Phnom Penh, with direct encouragement from Lon Nol, rioted in front of the North Vietnamese Embassy. Sirik Matak, after listening to a tape-recorded press conference from Paris in which Sihanouk threatened to execute him and Lon Nol as soon as he returned to Phnom Penh, convinced Lon Nol to depose the prince. On March 18 Lon Nol publicly demanded that all Vietnamese forces leave Cambodia. The National Assembly voted to remove Sihanouk as chief of state and abolish the monarchy. Sihanouk, on his way back to Phnom Penh via Moscow, was informed by Soviet premier Alexei Kosygin that he had been overthrown. Instead of going home and rallying to his side the rural people who still revered him, he went to China and lobbied for support from the French, Russians, and Chinese. Only the Chinese were interested, for they had a separate agenda for Cambodia. China had fought border skirmishes with the Soviets in the spring and summer of 1969 and feared that in the event of a North Vietnamese victory, a united Vietnam might follow pro-Soviet, anti-Chinese policies. Needing a proxy to exert leverage on Hanoi, China began playing a double game: Zhou Enlai catered to Sihanouk's elevated ideas of his own status and so was publicly committed to restoration of the monarchy in Cambodia; but he covered his bets by increasing Chinese support for the Cambodian communists, the Khmer Rouge. Sihanouk was completely taken in. He described Zhou as "the truest friend I ever had."[22]

Sihanouk believes his ouster was planned by the CIA, especially because only six weeks later 50,000 U.S. and South Vietnamese troops invaded Cambodia in an unsuccessful search for the Vietcong's secret headquarters. No convincing evidence of CIA involvement in the Cambodian coup has come to light. In 1970 Sihanouk was actually leaning toward the Americans and away from the North Vietnamese. The immediate reasons for the 1970 coup were the multiple frustrations of army officers, businessmen, bureaucrats, and intellectuals. These people were not pro-Vietnamese, pro-Chinese, or pro-American, but they all had concluded that they would be better off without Prince Sihanouk. Sihanouk tried to ignite an uprising against Lon Nol with a radio broadcast but was disappointed at the lack of response. Lon Nol encouraged people to take out their frustrations on a despised minority—Vietnamese shopkeepers, fishermen, and farmers living in Cambodia. The army itself joined in these racial pogroms.

Sihanouk became depressed and unable to sleep in his Beijing exile. He claims to have received a message from his mother in Phnom Penh warning him that Lon Nol had planted assassins in the Royal Guard. He was condemned to death in absentia by a military court in Phnom Penh; his wife, Monique, was sentenced to life imprisonment; and Queen Kossamak was placed under house arrest. Sihanouk was running out of options. There was obviously no possibility of returning to Cambodia as long as Lon Nol's military regime remained in power. He therefore formed a government in exile, the Royal Government of National Union which, under pressure from China, included the Khmer Rouge, the same communists he had formerly hunted down. Sihanouk's hatred of Lon Nol, whom he described as a "complete idiot," knew no bounds. "He never understood a damn thing, always stared at me with those ox's eyes and spent all his time praying. Worse, before he blew his nose he would consult the soothsayers to find out whether the stars were favorable to that activity." His described his cousin Sirik Matak as intelligent, but "nasty, perfidious, a lousy bastard, and jealous."[23]

SIHANOUK'S FIRST EXILE (1970–75)

Lon Nol's seizure of power marked the beginning of a disastrous decade for the people of Cambodia. Lon Nol, a weak and not especially astute man, mistakenly thought that with U.S. military aid Cambodia could expel Vietnamese communist troops and defeat the Khmer Rouge, but his political dilemma was precisely the same as that of South Vietnamese president Nguyen Van Thieu: To fight with foreigners against your own people is politically delegitimizing. Lon Nol could not avoid looking like a lackey of the Americans who, after all, controlled his budget. He was incapable of curbing the galloping wartime corruption that engulfed his administration.

Lon Nol suffered a stroke in 1971. To the frustration of his American advisers, he was more likely to listen to mystics and astrologers than to them. Lon Nol's army launched its last offensive in the summer of 1971 and then remained on the defensive, gradually losing control of the countryside, for the next four years. To appease the Nixon administration, which wanted to depict him as a democrat to the American public, Lon Nol conducted a fraudulent election in 1972 and assumed the title of president of the Khmer Republic.

The Khmer Rouge might have taken control of the entire nation in 1973 if the United States had not unleashed a massive bombing campaign against their strongholds. Though it halted them temporarily, this bombing ultimately hardened and fanaticized those who survived it and produced three other effects: First, it drove the Khmer Rouge out of their base area in the east and encouraged them to build new bases in other parts of the country. Second, by making large tracts of the countryside unlivable, it generated an influx of refugees to Phnom Penh that the floundering Lon Nol regime was ill-equipped to deal with. Third, it produced many, many orphans. Wandering bands of Cambodian children found a new father—Pol Pot. The Khmer Rouge were exceedingly secretive, but by 1973 peasants coming into Phnom Penh reported that when the communists took over a village, they drove people into the forest, forcibly collectivized the land, and executed anyone who might by any stretch of the imagination be considered a rightist.

While his countrymen slid into an agony of war and revolution, Sihanouk was practically immobilized in Beijing. Yet it was not unpleasant. When interviewed by Italian journalist Oriana Fallaci in 1973, he offered the following reassurance:

The Chinese treat me splendidly. They have put at my disposal an enormous house, as large as a palace, and I have all the rooms I want—for myself, my family and my officials. By now there are a hundred of us Cambodians at Peking, and besides the palace I have a number of guest houses. I even have a beautiful covered swimming pool, with cold water in the summer and hot water in the winter. Zhou Enlai had it built for me.[24]

For all the amenities, the prince was kept on a short leash, with a Khmer Rouge informer following him around day and night. Ieng Sary, one of the top Khmer Rouge leaders, went to Beijing to see how Sihanouk could be used to advance the communist cause; the leaders determined that it would be a boost to the morale of all anti–Lon Nol forces if Sihanouk visited the "liberated" areas of Cambodia. He did so in 1973, incongruously clad in the simple uniform and checkered scarf that Khmer Rouge soldiers customarily wore. On this secret journey Sihanouk was photographed with Ieng Sary and another Khmer Rouge leader, Khieu Samphan. Why did Sihanouk lend his aura of semidivinity to the most brutal, fanatical communist movement in history? Fallaci posed that question. Sihanouk's answer reveals his mixture of patriotic and selfish motives: "I have no other way of rescuing my country and of not losing face."[25]

Sihanouk had discounted reports of Khmer Rouge outrages, including the total evacuation of all cities, the executions of thousands of people identified as supporters of Lon Nol and the United States, the closing of schools, widespread disrobing and even killing of monks, and putting the entire population to work at forced labor. Sihanouk said that none of this was true—it was all imperialist lies. It is hard to tell how much of what he said was deliberate falsification and how much was simply naiveté. For example, he was quoted as saying: "Khieu Samphan told me not to call him and his comrades Communists. He is a Cambodian nationalist and anti-imperialist who fights for independence, neutrality, democracy and social revolution. You can say he is a socialist with the same basic ideology as the Swedish Prime Minister. The work he is heading inside Cambodia is fantastic."[26]

When he actually returned to Cambodia in September 1973 and could see life in the liberated zones with his own eyes, he became deeply troubled but did not alter his public posture of unstinting support for the Khmer Rouge.

When not in exile in China, Sihanouk had an alternative residence in the capital of a country that would hardly seem likely to welcome a monarch, North Korea. Despite all their differences, Sihanouk and North Korean dictator Kim Il Sung shared certain attitudes: a taste for personalized rule, extreme distrust of the United States, and a desire to avoid total dependence on China. Kim provided Sihanouk with his own palace and the same sorts of luxuries the prince had been given by the Chinese. He dreamed that after the Khmer Rouge took power, he would be able to continue a life of idle luxury: "I will go back and live in a small villa in Angkor like a retired country gentleman. I can be a public relations man for my country and have my jazz parties and do some filming."[27]

On April 17, 1975, just two weeks before the end of the Vietnam War, glowering young Khmer Rouge soldiers marched into Phnom Penh and embarked on their horrifying plan to take Cambodia back to the "year zero." Their new state was named Democratic Kampuchea (DK). To create a wholly new society it would be necessary to eliminate all vestiges of the old. The era of the killing fields had begun. Sihanouk lauded the Khmer Rouge victory and rejoiced at the defeat of "American imperialism." His archenemy Lon Nol went into humiliating exile in Hawaii. Sihanouk believed his honor had been restored. But he had to choose between permanent exile and returning to his country as it underwent communization.

PRISONER OF THE KHMER ROUGE (1976–79)

Sihanouk visited Phnom Penh briefly in September 1975, at which time he was allowed to conduct a funeral ceremony in the royal palace for his mother, Queen Kossamak, who had died in Beijing. He then traveled to New York to claim Cambodia's seat at the United Nations (UN) and to praise the Khmer Rouge's decision to evacuate the cities. On December 31, 1975, he and Princess Monique returned to DK. For the next three years they were held in the "gilded prison" of the royal palace. Sihanouk was given no role whatsoever in the new regime. The two were under constant surveillance, but he and Monique listened to the Voice of America anyway. Bright spotlights were trained on his house every night. Once, in despair, he asked the Khmer Rouge to shoot him. They would have done so without a second thought, except that he had a certain utility in lending their fanatical, reclusive regime a trace of international legitimacy. Probably Pol Pot was pressured by Zhou Enlai to spare the prince. Sometimes Sihanouk's guards would trot him out to show to startled peasants working in the fields under the guns of Khmer Rouge guards.[28]

Although Pol Pot did not kill Sihanouk or his wife, other royal relatives were judged useless and executed. These included no less than five of Sihanouk's children (two sons and three daughters) and an estimated fifteen to twenty grandchildren. One of Sihanouk's sons, Narindrapong, saved himself by singing the praises of the Khmer Rouge. Plagued by insomnia, Sihanouk had a supply of barbiturates, which his wife rationed to prevent him from committing suicide.[29] His consolation then (and later in Beijing) was a little white-haired pet dog named Miko. His sole gesture of protest was resigning as figurehead chief of state in 1976. Rather than admitting that he never should have allied himself with the Khmer Rouge, Sihanouk said his relatives were killed only because of his 1976 resignation:

> When I knew the truth [about the death of my children], I said to myself that my refusal to serve Pol Pot's Kampuchea from April 1976 carried with it some responsibility for the elimination of my relatives. But in working with the Khmer Rouge I would have betrayed the confidence of the millions of my compatriots who were the victims of worse horrors. I torture myself thinking about this.[30]

The remorse and confusion Sihanouk expresses here are as close to a confession of guilt as he has ever provided. Never has he publicly apologized for his support of the Khmer Rouge from 1970 to 1976. Even while a palace prisoner, he flattered the Khmer Rouge leaders, possibly hoping to convince them to moderate their cruel policies, possibly hoping for better treatment for himself. He blamed the United States for Cambodia's tragedy on the grounds that U.S. support for Lon Nol's "lackey" regime "created the Khmer Rouge."[31]

By 1978 border skirmishes between DK and the Socialist Republic of Vietnam (SRV) escalated, and China increased its arms shipments to the Khmer Rouge. As a war between Vietnam and Cambodia loomed, Pol Pot instituted a purge of DK cadres in the Eastern Zone that turned into mass slaughter. Some of the Khmer Rouge fighters targeted for execution, including a man named Heng Samrin and another named Hun Sen, slipped across the border and sought protection and backing from the Vietnamese, who recognized this as a golden opportunity to cultivate an alternative government for Cambodia—one that would be totally dependent on them. After first securing their rear by signing a treaty of peace and friendship with the Soviet Union, the Vietnamese launched a full-scale invasion of Cambodia on Christmas Day 1978. They rolled steadily westward and took Phnom Penh in two weeks.

The Vietnamese hoped to capture Sihanouk and use him as a figurehead for their puppet government. Whether Sihanouk would have cooperated is a moot point, for on January 2, 1979, a Khmer Rouge soldier told Sihanouk and Monique they had fifteen minutes to prepare to evacuate. Sihanouk feared he was about to be executed, but the Khmer Rouge sent him in a convoy of cars to Battambang, thence to Sisophon, the last Cambodian town before the Thai border. Then, inexplicably, they took Sihanouk all the way back to Phnom Penh where, on January 5, he met Pol Pot, whom he had not seen since his visit to the liberated zones six years earlier. Pol Pot was self-effacing, gentle, and to Sihanouk's amazement Pol Pot used respectful court language when speaking to the prince, actually referring to him as "your servant."[32] Pol Pot asked Sihanouk to denounce the Vietnamese invasion to the UN. Sihanouk asked that his family and retainers be allowed to accompany him. On January 6, Sihanouk left for New York, just hours before Vietnamese troops took Phnom Penh.

In New York Sihanouk showed once again how unpredictable he could be. He denounced the Vietnamese invasion yet at the very same press conference said of Pol Pot that he might be a patriot, "but he is a butcher. He treats the Cambodian people as cattle good for forced labor and pigs good for the slaughterhouse."[33] While in New York City, Sihanouk escaped his Khmer Rouge bodyguards with an elaborate scheme worthy of one of his films. He slipped out of his hotel room at 2:00 A.M. with the help of a sympathetic security guard and requested asylum from U.S. officials. The United States was embarrassed by the defection because Washington was trying to improve relations with Beijing, and the state department did not know how Sihanouk's escape would be perceived. Moreover, it would be difficult to justify granting political asylum to someone so notoriously anti-American. When the state department decided not to grant asylum, Sihanouk flew to France, where he was told he could stay if he agreed to refrain from all political activity. Sihanouk angrily rejected this condition and went to China, where he was welcomed triumphantly.

SIHANOUK'S SECOND EXILE (1979–97)

Life for the Cambodian people was immeasurably better under the communist regime headed by Heng Samrin and Hun Sen, officially called the People's Republic of Kampuchea, than it had been under the fanatical Khmer Rouge. Pol Pot and his men were pushed to the most remote corners of Cambodia, well away from the Tonle Sap and Phnom Penh. For the shell-shocked survivors of Pol Pot's experiment in forcible utopia, life slowly returned to some degree of normalcy. Cities were repopulated, Buddhist temples and schools reopened, money was used again for the first time in five years, and small-scale trade in rice and commodities was revived.

During the 1980s Sihanouk stayed at his guest houses in Beijing and Pyongyang when not traveling abroad to promote his anti-Vietnamese political party, known by its the French acronym FUNCINPEC (National United Front for an Independent, Neutral, and Peaceful Cambodia). There were now four political forces in Cambodia: (1) the Sihanoukists (FUNCINPEC); (2) the rightists (Son Sann's Khmer People's National Liberation Front (KPNLF); (3) the Khmer Rouge, unregenerate and unrepentant, still controlled by Pol Pot, Ieng Sary, and Khieu Samphan; and (4) the Vietnamese-supported communist regime in power in Phnom Penh. Sihanouk headed a coalition of the first three of these forces against the fourth, even though it meant once again embracing the murderous Khmer Rouge.

The three resistance groups united under the banner of the Coalition Government of Democratic Kampuchea (CGDK), which they claimed to be the legitimate government of Cambodia, and which was recognized as such by the UN. Sihanouk, the leader of the coalition, conceded that it was a "pact with the devil," thereby confirming the penetrating insight of a *Life* magazine reporter who had written years earlier that the "one cardinal rule, perhaps the only absolute rule" of Sihanouk's conduct is that "Sihanouk says or does whatever he feels Cambodia's national security demands at the moment."[34]

Sihanouk's life was pleasurable again. He was always treated well in Pyongyang where Kim Il Sung, who knew of the prince's love of films, equipped his guest's palatial residence with a private movie theater and encouraged Sihanouk to produce more films by underwriting production costs. As a result, two love stories, *Mysterious City* and *Adieu, Mon Amour*, were produced in Korean with English subtitles.[35] Sihanouk's lifestyle seemed nonchalant when he visited New York in 1982 and was observed singing along with a Cambodian band flown in from Paris.

The military and political situation in Cambodia remained stalemated for ten years, with the PRK government of Heng Samrin and Hun Sen controlling most of Cambodia, but with the Khmer Rouge—the only one of the three resistance groups that had a credible army—lurking in the jungle, waiting for a second chance to build utopia. By 1989 Vietnam withdrew the last of its soldiers. Sihanouk and Hun Sen entered negotiations, but, amazingly, the prince still preferred the Khmer Rouge: "The Khmer Rouge are tigers, but I would rather be eaten by a Khmer Rouge tiger than by a Vietnamese crocodile, because the Khmer Rouge are true patriots. Oh, they are vicious, they are cruel; they are murderers. But they are not traitors like Hun Sen."[36] As all sides edged toward a peace agreement, Sihanouk shuttled back and forth between Cambodia, where he was protected by a squad of North Korean bodyguards, and Paris, where he charmed reporters—but perhaps not other negotiators—by bringing his pet poodle to the negotiating table.

On October 23, 1991, all sides to the Cambodian conflict signed a formal agreement to stop fighting and prepare the country for free elections. The UN was invited to run the country pending the formation of a new government. The mission of the United Nations Transitional Authority in Cambodia (UNTAC) was breathtaking in scope. UNTAC managed Cambodia as if it were a bankrupt company in receivership. It was the biggest UN operation in history, involving 20,000 soldiers and 5,000 civilian advisers. The total cost exceeded $2 billion.

THE RETURN OF SIHANOUK

Executing yet another dazzling zigzag, Sihanouk broke with the Khmer Rouge, proposed trying them for war crimes, and appeared in public in an open limousine alongside Hun Sen, whom he now called "my son." Hun Sen appointed Sihanouk president of Cambodia in November 1991. While UNTAC exercised authority, Sihanouk worked to reestablish himself politically but was hindered, at the age of seventy, by declining health. He turned over leadership of FUNCINPEC to his son, Prince Norodom Ranariddh. Sihanouk returned to China for treatment of prostate cancer in November 1992 and while there suffered a stroke.

Free elections were held in Cambodia on May 23, 1993, under the watchful eyes of UN peacekeepers. Ninety percent of the Cambodian people voted, a stunning turnout considering the many reasons why a prudent citizen might choose to stay home. Prince Ranariddh won 45 percent of the vote. Hun Sen, the runner-up, received 38 percent. Hun Sen, however, refused to go quietly, so Sihanouk decreed that Prince Ranariddh would be known as first prime minister and that Hun Sen would be second prime minister. The government ministries were effectively split between these two factions. On September 24, 1993, Norodom Sihanouk became king again, after thirty-eight years as prince. The king of Cambodia spent much of the next four years in China and North Korea. Surely the chemotherapy he needed could have been administered elsewhere. Perhaps he had grown to crave order and deference.

Ranariddh and Hun Sen carried on their rivalry. Over time Hun Sen's faction edged out that of Ranariddh. Meanwhile the Khmer Rouge army gradually deteriorated. There was little to celebrate in the new Cambodia. A few hundred families in Phnom Penh prospered, while 90 percent of the people eked out a bare existence in the countryside. Cambodia's tropical forests dwindled fast, as hard cash for illegal timber became the financial mainstay of the Khmer Rouge. Drugs and gems became Cambodia's preferred currencies.

In 1996, Co-Premiers Hun Sen and Norodom Ranariddh persuaded King Sihanouk to grant amnesty to Ieng Sary, one of the top leaders of the Khmer Rouge. There could be no moral justification for this act, but there was a compelling pragmatic motive: to split the remaining Khmer Rouge forces, thereby hastening their final collapse. After Ieng Sary's defection, hundreds of other Khmer Rouge soldiers and their families also crossed over to the government side. Sihanouk offered to stand trial alongside Khmer Rouge leaders for atrocities committed in DK. This unusual announcement created little stir, as if King Sihanouk were becoming irrelevant. In November 1996, as he departed for medical treatment in China, the king told his subjects that he had the honor to inform the entire nation and international community that, until the day of his death, he would not enter into a political campaign.

In the summer of 1997, while Sihanouk was in Beijing, Hun Sen moved against Prince Ranariddh's faction, hunting down and killing more than forty senior FUNCINPEC officials. Foreign observers who expected Sihanouk to protest the murder of his own son's followers were surprised that the old, sick king simply said, "I have no power to do anything." On August 29, 1997, Sihanouk returned to his homeland. His cancer was in remission, but he suffered from cataracts and arteriosclerosis. He was met and embraced by Hun Sen at the airport in Siem Reap, near the Angkor temples. Standing under great royal silver and gold silk umbrellas protecting him from the monsoon rain, Sihanouk said he would spend the next three months at Angkor, paying his respect to the sacred statues. He told the Cambodian people, "I am old, but I haven't died yet, because of your prayers."[37] In October 1997 Sihanouk said that if he were not a Buddhist he would kill himself, "because the end of my life is filled with shame, humiliation, and despair over the national order."[38]

CONCLUSION

How shall we judge this contradictory, baffling man? It is tempting to let his candid statement of 1973 stand as his epitaph: "I may seem devious and twisting in my diplomatic maneuvers, my intentions may seem diabolical, but the truth is that I can't even manage to be shrewd."[39] But it would not be right for American authors to do so. The Cambodian people, those whom Sihanouk said he loved so much that it was almost carnal, have through their suffering earned the right to say whether he loved them well, or wisely. We shall wait to see what their own historians say.

NOTES

1. Oriana Fallaci, "Sihanouk: The Man We May Have to Settle For in Cambodia," *New York Times Magazine*, August 12, 1973, p. 14.

2. Milton Osborne, *Sihanouk: Prince of Light, Prince of Darkness* (Honolulu: University of Hawaii Press, 1994), pp. 21–22.

3. David P. Chandler, *A History of Cambodia* (Boulder, Colo.: Westview Press, 1993), p. 170.

4. Norodom Sihanouk, *My War With the CIA: The Memoirs of Prince Norodom Sihanouk* (New York: Pantheon Books, 1972), p. 147.

5. Quoted in Chandler, *A History of Cambodia*, p. 185.

6. Fallaci, "Sihanouk," p. 16.

7. Serge Thion, "The Pattern of Cambodian Politics," in *The Cambodian Agony*, ed. David A. Ablin and Marlowe Hood (Armonk, N.Y.: M. E. Sharpe, 1987), p. 154.

8. Jean Lacouture, *The Demigods: Charismatic Leadership in the Third World* (New York: Alfred A. Knopf, 1970), p. 200.

9. William Shawcross, *Sideshow: Kissinger, Nixon and the Destruction of Cambodia* (New York: Simon & Schuster, 1979), p. 49.

10. Shawcross, *Sideshow: Kissinger, Nixon and the Destruction of Cambodia*, p. 53.

11. Osborne, *Sihanouk*, p. 105.

12. Laura Summers, translator's introduction to *Cambodia's Economy and Industrial Development* (data paper, No. 11) by Khieu Samphan (Ithaca, N.Y.: Cornell University, Southeast Asia Program, 1979), p. 9.

13. *Newsweek* (April 5, 1965), pp. 46–47.

14. William Attwood, "Sihanouk Talks," *Look* 32 (April 2, 1968), p. 66.

15. Osborne, *Sihanouk*, p. 163.

16. Osborne, *Sihanouk*, p. 189.

17. Shawcross, *Sideshow*, p. 94.

18. Richard M. Nixon, *RN: The Memoirs of Richard Nixon* (New York: Grosset & Dunlap, 1978), p. 382.

19. Attwood, "Sihanouk Talks," p. 65.

20. Fallaci, "Sihanouk," p. 14.

21. Chandler, *A History of Cambodia*, p. 204.

22. Fallaci, "Sihanouk," p. 14.

23. Fallaci, "Sihanouk," p. 16.

24. Fallaci, "Sihanouk," p. 14.

25. Fallaci, "Sihanouk," p. 14.

26. *Newsweek* 82 (July 16, 1973), p. 35.

27. *Newsweek* 82, (July 16, 1973), p. 34.

28. Thion, "The Pattern of Cambodian Politics," p. 155.

29. T. D. Allman, "Sihanouk's Sideshow," *Vanity Fair* 53 (April 1990), p. 155.

30. Osborne, *Sihanouk*, p. 236.

31. Shawcross, *Sideshow*, p. 391.

32. Nayan Chanda, *Brother Enemy: The War After the War* (New York: Harcourt Brace Jovanovich, 1986), pp. 302–03.

33. Chanda, *Brother Enemy*, p. 364.

34. Hal Wingo, "The Vexing Peace-Keeper of Cambodia," *Life* 64 (February 16, 1968), p. 38.

35. Allman, "Sihanouk's Sideshow," p. 231.

36. Allman, "Sihanouk's Sideshow," p. 158.

37. *New York Times*, August 30, 1997, p. A4.

38. Associated Press dispatch, October 12, 1997.

39. Fallaci, "Sihanouk," p. 16.

7

Pol Pot: Architect of Autogenocide

Even now you can look at me. Am I a savage person?
My conscience is clear.

Pol Pot, 1997

In the summer of 1997 Cambodians stared with a mixture of fascination and horror at television screens showing a weary old man being denounced by his former comrades. This was the first time they had seen the face of Pol Pot, one of the most infamous dictators of all time. We owe it to posterity to study the lives of tyrants such as Adolf Hitler, Josef Stalin, and Pol Pot. Were they brutal from birth? Were they capable of love? How did they induce their followers to butcher people without hesitation or regret? Were they demented, or was there some logic behind their ruthlessness? The answers are maddeningly elusive.

Pol Pot lived as a kind of phantom, always seeking power but never seeking fame. His biographers have had to laboriously piece together scattered Khmer Rouge documents and accounts by those few people who knew him. In this chapter we consider the life of this deceptively ordinary-looking man in the context of modern Cambodian politics and history.

FAMILY AND BACKGROUND

The man known to the world as Pol Pot was actually named Saloth Sar, and he adopted his nom de guerre only in 1976. Saloth Sar was born in 1925 in the village of Prek Sbauv, Kompong Thom Province, about ninety miles north of Phnom Penh. Sar's father, Pen Saloth, was a prosperous rice farmer who owned twelve hectares of land and several water buffalos. Little is known about his mother, Sok Nem, except that she had a reputation for piety. Saloth Sar and his siblings lived in a comfortable, sturdy house. Saloth Seng, a brother about thirteen years older, remembers Sar as "a very polite

Pol Pot, no date

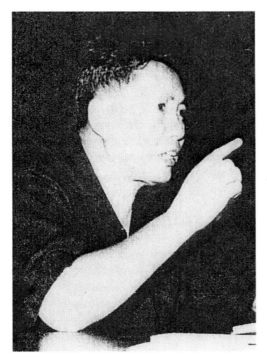

Pol Pot, no date

boy" who "never caused trouble." A younger brother, Saloth Nhep, remembered Sar the same way: "He was a nice boy, very polite. He was happy and sometimes made jokes." Sar's older sister, Saloth Roeung, said simply that she was not happy to share even a drop of his blood.[1]

The family had certain connections to Cambodian royalty. A cousin, Khum Meak, danced in the royal ballet and bore a child by Prince Sisowath Monivong. Saloth Sar was sent at the age of six to live with his older brother and other relatives in the royal palace in Phnom Penh. There is no indication that Saloth Sar suffered any trauma in his boyhood. At some point Sar lived for a year in a Buddhist monastery, as was normal for Khmer boys.

EDUCATION IN CAMBODIA

Cambodia in the 1930s was a tranquil French colony where most common people were only dimly aware of their own history. The colony's first high school, the Lycée Sisowath, was founded in 1936. In that same year the first Khmer-language newspaper, *Nagaravatta* (Angkor Wat), was published by a man named Son Ngoc Thanh. In 1937 Saloth Sar enrolled in the Ecole Miche, a private primary school in Phnom Penh where the medium of instruction was French.

While the soft-spoken, smooth-faced teenager was learning about the modern world, winds of war were blowing across Europe and Asia. France surrendered to Nazi Germany in May 1940, which made French Indochina (Vietnam, Laos, and Cambodia) an ally of Japan. In December 1940 a Cambodian independence movement called the Khmer Issarak was founded. In January 1941, Japan's ally Siam (Thailand) invaded Cambodia and annexed two provinces in the northwest, Battambang and Siem Reap. (Siem Reap Province contains the magnificent Angkor temples, the central symbol of Cambodian culture.) At this perilous juncture King Sisowath Monivong died, and the French decided to enthrone an apparently pliable schoolboy, Norodom Sihanouk. The first Japanese troops arrived in Cambodia in May 1941.

The colonial government decided to create a junior college for Khmer youth and selected twenty boys to enroll in its first class. One of them was Saloth Sar. At the Collège Sihanouk in Kompong Cham, "all the classes were conducted in French, and students were discouraged from speaking Khmer among themselves. They studied literature, history, geography, mathematics, science, and philosophy, played soccer and basketball, learned to play musical instruments (Saloth Sar's was the violin) and staged plays."[2]

Khieu Samphan, later Sar's right-hand man, was in the class behind Sar. Sar's best friend at school was Lon Non, brother of Lon Nol, the man Sar would later defeat in war. If Sar stayed at the Collège Sihanouk for five years, as seems likely, he probably first became interested in politics at that time. Later he claimed that he was influenced by Mohandas K. Gandhi, the Indian apostle of nonviolence.

In 1942 French police arrested two Khmer Buddhist monks for "spreading discord." Anti-French demonstrations broke out that gave a boost to the independence movement led by Son Ngoc Thanh. The French exiled Son Ngoc Thanh and signed a compromise agreement with King Norodom Sihanouk giving Cambodia a spurious independence that infuriated the small, but growing, circle of Khmer nationalists.

The very fact of their having once ruled all mainland Southeast Asia has given modern Khmers, whose country is weak and poor, a feeling of frustration. To compensate, certain radical Khmer intellectuals have searched for a way to recapture Cambodia's past glory. To them, Sihanouk's accommodation to foreigners' demands seemed treasonous, and the lifestyle at his royal court, of which Saloth Sar had inside knowledge, seemed decadent. Sihanouk's gradual evolution as a nationalist was dismissed by more radical Khmers as too little too late.

Because of Sar's quiet, reticent personality, he made little impression on people. Certainly he was undistinguished academically. David Chandler poses the critical but still unanswered question of Sar's personality: "Was he deliberately effacing himself, was he genuinely mediocre, or was he indifferent to making a strong impression?"[3] None of his contemporaries could have predicted that one day he would plunge Cambodia into the most extreme revolution in history.

Saloth Sar graduated from Collège Sihanouk in 1947. He applied to the prestigious Lycée Sisowath in Phnom Penh but failed the entrance exam and had to settle for vocational training at the Ecole Technique. In 1949 Sar won a scholarship to study at the Ecole Français de Radio-électricité in Paris. This put him in a rarefied group—only 100 Cambodians had ever been given such scholarships. Sar probably got the scholarship through some influential patron, perhaps either a relative with connections in the royal palace or someone in the antimonarchical Democratic Party, which Sar informally supported. It was the rainy season when Sar left Cambodia for Saigon, the port from which his ship, the S.S. *Jamaique*, would sail. Saigon was the largest city the twenty-four-year-old Sar had ever seen. He said it made him feel like a dark monkey from the mountains.[4]

YEARS IN PARIS

Saloth Sar arrived in France in September 1949. The next year he was joined by his friend Ieng Sary, a more confident, outgoing type. Sary introduced Sar to an expatriate Cambodian intellectual named Keng Vannsak, who sharpened Sar's awareness of political events inside Cambodia and internationally. Sar became interested in Marxism and attended radical discussion sessions along with Sary and two other future Khmer Rouge leaders, Son Sen and Hou Youn. At the Marxist study sessions Saloth Sar met his future wife, Khieu Ponnary.[5]

In Paris in the early 1950s, especially among the small, intellectually inbred circle of Khmer students, communism was de rigueur. After all, the Indochinese Communist Party was leading the struggle against French imperialism in Southeast Asia, and the Chinese Communist Party had proclaimed a new era in Asia. In Cambodia a communist-led movement, the United Issarak Front, was founded by a Khmer communist named Son Ngoc Minh. Communists were on the offensive in Korea, too.

In the summer of 1950 Saloth Sar volunteered to work in Yugoslavia with a student brigade that was building a highway from Zagreb to Belgrade. This may have been the first time in his life that Sar performed heavy manual labor, but it was exhilarating. He was building communism in the literal sense, an independent, national communism at that, for the Yugoslav prime minister Josip Broz (Tito) had refused to take orders from any foreign power, including the Soviet Union. Sar's overriding interest in radical politics may have been one reason why he failed his exams three years in a row.

In Cambodia the Democratic Party swept elections for the National Assembly in September 1951 on a platform of immediate independence. The Democrats also advocated retaining the monarchy only for ceremonial purposes. Thus was born Sihanouk's lifelong hatred for the Democrats and their leader, Son Ngoc Thanh. In June 1952 Sihanouk dissolved the National Assembly. Political power in Cambodia was now in his hands, except for that retained by the French. In Paris, Saloth Sar published an article entitled "Monarchy or Democracy" in a Khmer-language magazine, the *Cambodian Student*, arguing that monarchy ("a malodorous running sore") unjustly gives power to "a small group of men who do nothing to earn their living so that they can exploit the majority of the people."[6] Knowing that Sihanouk's government would revoke his scholarship if he used his real name, Sar chose an enigmatic pseudonym, "Original Khmer." Sar's scholarship was cut in 1952, and Khieu Ponnary's scholarship was terminated at the same time.[7] Sar lingered in Paris for some months before returning to Cambodia, where he probably joined the French Communist Party.

SALOTH SAR IN EASTERN CAMBODIA (1953–54)

Saloth Sar's activities upon his return to Cambodia are cloaked in mystery, not only because that was his preferred style throughout his life, but also because Sihanouk's police and the French were hunting down communists.

Immediately upon his return in 1953 Saloth Sar joined a cell of Ho Chi Minh's Indochinese Communist Party (ICP) that had ten Vietnamese and ten Khmers and soon had left Phnom Penh for the border area where the Viet Minh, not the French, were in control.[8] Here he met his future mentor, Tou Samouth.

One by one, other Cambodian students who had become communists in France returned home, including Ieng Sary, Hu Nim, and Hou Youn. France transferred residual powers to King Sihanouk in October 1953, although French troops remained in Cambodia. Cambodian Independence Day, November 9, seemed a bad joke to Sar, for a country as weak as Cambodia could never be truly independent. Furthermore, he had begun to equate genuine independence with sweeping social revolution. The entire social structure, he believed, would have to be reconstructed before Khmers could regain their dignity.

The Geneva accords of 1954 divided Vietnam temporarily at the seventeenth parallel. Now there was a secure communist base in Southeast Asia, the Democratic Republic of Vietnam (DRV). DRV president Ho Chi Minh wished to control, or at least influence, non-Vietnamese (Cambodian and Lao) members of the old ICP, which by now ostensibly had been divided into three national Communist parties. One thousand Cambodian communists were told to lie low inside Cambodia, while another thousand were disguised in Viet Minh uniforms and put aboard ships in Saigon, bound for North Vietnam. Saloth Sar remained in Cambodia. His distrust of the Khmer communists who went to North Vietnam—men with Khmer bodies and Vietnamese minds, he called them—led to their wholesale slaughter when he acquired supreme power.

Sar and other communists in Phnom Penh formed a legal political party, the Pracheachon (People's Group) to contest elections in 1955. Sihanouk abdicated his throne to campaign for his newly established party, the Sangkum Reastr Niyum, which won 99.8 percent of the vote and every single seat in the National Assembly.

SALOTH SAR IN PHNOM PENH (1954–62)

In 1954 Sar returned to Phnom Penh and went underground, using a pseudonym. The next year, according to some sources, his older brother, Saloth Suong, who served as chief of royal protocol, found a job for Sar inside the palace. This could only have intensified Sar's contempt for the idle, ostentatious Khmer royalty whose wealth contrasted so sharply with the poverty outside the palace walls. In 1956 Saloth Sar married Khieu Ponnary, eight years his senior, who had found a job teaching at the Lycée Sisowath. They picked July 14 (Bastille Day) as their wedding day.

The Cambodian communists decided to set up secret cells in the capital, and to this end they opened a private lycée that they named Kampuchea But (Child of Cambodia). Saloth Sar taught there and at another private college, Chamraon Vichea. He was gifted at teaching, "fond of his students, eloquent but unpretentious, honest, humane, easy to befriend."[9] His political radicalism and cultural nationalism were well disguised, as he taught Cambodian history in French and clearly loved French literature and poetry. Twenty years later he killed people for speaking French.

This was not a promising time for communists in Cambodia. Sihanouk was very popular, the country was at peace, and—on the surface at least—there was no reason to think the gentle Khmers would ever rise up in angry revolution. However, the communists were dealt a serious blow when a high-ranking party member named Sieu Heng betrayed his comrades to the police. Many communists were hunted down by Sihanouk's security chief, Lon Nol, and others quit the movement out of fear. This episode may explain the incessant searches for "enemies within" that characterized the Khmer Rouge years. In what must be considered one of the royal government's most egregious blunders, ten men from the security services attacked Khieu Samphan on a street in Phnom Penh in broad daylight on July 13, 1960, beat him, stripped him naked, and took photographs of him. There is no telling how many people later paid with their lives for this insult.[10]

In this crisis atmosphere the communists reorganized. At a secret party congress in Phnom Penh, Saloth Sar, Ieng Sary, and Nuon Chea were named to the central committee. The number one communist leader was Tou Samouth, who had elevated Saloth Sar through the ranks. Tou Samouth disappeared in 1962, probably tied up and thrown into the Mekong River by Sihanouk's secret police. According to one leading scholar of the Khmer Rouge, Ben Kiernan, Saloth Sar tipped off the police as to Samouth's whereabouts to get rid of him. However, this interpretation is disputed by other scholars.[11] Sar became acting secretary of the central committee at the next party congress in 1962. The next year, seeing his name on a list of communists published by the government, Sar fled to the jungle.

IN THE JUNGLE (1963–69)

Sar's life in the 1960s is poorly documented. He may already have been pursuing his odd blend of unlimited power and anonymity, for his comrades now referred to him as "Brother Number One." It seems that in 1964 Sar was at a secret zone called "Office 100" in eastern Cambodia that was controlled by the Vietnamese communists he distrusted. As the Vietnam War escalated, Prince Sihanouk came to terms with the Vietcong and North Vietnamese, especially once he convinced himself that the Americans planned to set him up for assassination. In 1965 Sihanouk allowed the Vietnamese communists to station troops in lightly populated areas of eastern Cambodia and even permitted the transshipment of war supplies through Cambodia's sole seaport, Sihanoukville.

Saloth Sar and Ieng Sary did not like the way they were received on a visit to Hanoi in 1965. Evidently the North Vietnamese perceived that the Khmer communists did not intend to subordinate their own interests to those of Hanoi. Sar and Sary stayed in North Vietnam for nine months. No doubt they met the Cambodian communists who had gone to North Vietnam after the Geneva accords nine years earlier. Perhaps they suspected that these men were being carefully trained to carry out Vietnamese directives. Such cadres might be needed, Sar reasoned, but would have to be watched closely. Ultimately, they would have to be eliminated.

From Hanoi Saloth Sar went to China, just as the Chinese were plunging into the so-called Great Proletarian Cultural Revolution, the main theme of which was erasing the "four olds": old ideas, old culture, old customs, and old habits. Perfect social equality was another goal of the Cultural Revolution. (The Chinese Army formally abolished all military ranks.) A third theme of the Cultural Revolution was that people could achieve miraculous production goals if only they were properly enthused and indoctrinated with correct thought. Education and technical training were unnecessary if the people were only "red" enough in their thinking. China, Mao Zedong believed, could reach the utopia that lies at the end of history—true communism—before the Soviets, with their plodding ways, their excessive caution, their compromises with the capitalist world. Another feature of the Chinese Cultural Revolution was a dual standard of civility in which young people were exhorted to show "boundless love" for the party and the leader, and "boundless hate" for all designated enemies, who were described as parasitic worms and poisonous snakes.

When he returned to Cambodia in September 1966, Sar secretly changed his party's name from Workers Party of Kampuchea to Communist Party of Kampuchea (CPK). But Sar was not yet in a position to dictate ideological conformity. There were at the time three ideological factions among Cambodia communists: (1) a nationalist group led by Saloth Sar, chauvinist in spirit, emphasizing the countryside over the cities and shunning guidance from any foreign power; (2) a group led by Phouk Chhay and Hu Nim, also committed to radical social change and rural reform but thinking of communism as an international, not a strictly national, movement (the leaders of which were tortured and executed after Saloth Sar came to power); and (3) a pro-Vietnamese wing of the party, which was eventually wiped out in bloody purges, except for those who managed to flee to Vietnam in 1979.[12]

In 1966 Saloth Sar relocated to the most remote province in Cambodia, Ratanakiri, in the extreme northeast, close to Laos and Vietnam. The deep forests of Ratanakiri were home to tribes such as the Jarai, who did not speak Khmer and who were considered subhuman by many Khmers. During these years when Saloth Sar lived as far from Phnom Penh as possible, Prince Sihanouk's regime went into decline, its popular support quietly eroding. A warning of serious trouble, which Sihanouk and his generals underrated, came in April 1967 when angry peasants in Battambang refused to pay taxes on their rice. Lon Nol's troops savagely repressed the "Samlaut Rebellion."

Were it not for the war in Vietnam, the Cambodian communists might never have come to power. But many North Vietnamese Army (NVA) troops were stationed in eastern Cambodia. When Richard Nixon entered the White House in 1969, he quickly ordered secret bombing raids to disrupt NVA supply lines. This was a gift to the Khmer Rouge, for it showed the peasants that Prince Sihanouk could not protect them, and it created social upheaval by sending thousands of refugees into Phnom Penh, where Sihanouk could do little for them.

In late 1969 Saloth Sar went to Hanoi for six months of consultations. Chandler believes he was summoned by the Vietnamese.[13] While Brother Number One was in Hanoi, Prince Sihanouk was overthrown by General Lon Nol. Lon Nol immediately cast his lot with the Americans, a fatal mistake because Nixon had already concluded that the war in Vietnam could not be won. Sihanouk went to live, ironically, in China, the only country that supported Saloth Sar. North Vietnamese prime minister Pham Van Dong, with Sar in tow, flew to Beijing to meet Sihanouk, who obligingly announced a united front to be called the Royal Government of National Union.

CAMBODIAN CIVIL WAR (1970–75)

President Nixon ordered 50,000 U.S. and South Vietnamese troops into Cambodia on April 30, 1970, in a futile search for the underground Vietcong headquarters. The communists retreated westward, bringing the war to more provinces of eastern Cambodia. The CPK guerrillas, deceitfully proclaiming loyalty to Sihanouk, gained thousands of supporters, who were told that Lon Nol was an American puppet and that the people in Phnom Penh, Lon Nol's supporters, were corrupt. Fresh recruits to the CPK may have had no idea who Americans were, but they could look up and see the bombers. They certainly did not know what a capitalist was, but like peasants everywhere they distrusted city people.

When Saloth Sar returned from Vietnam, he moved his base to rural Kompong Thom, his home province located in the heart of Cambodia, not in the remote northeast corner. He began enforcing tougher standards in the zones he controlled. Drinking and gambling were banned. Peasants were told to stop using respectful ("feudal") terms of address. They were not told, however, that their new masters were communists, merely that they had to obey a mysterious, amorphous Angka (Organization). "One must trust completely in the *Angka* because the Organization has as many eyes as a pineapple, and cannot make mistakes."[14]

In November 1970 the North Vietnamese sent back those Cambodian communists who had been given sixteen years of Vietnamese military and political training. Lon Nol's army launched one last offensive in the summer of 1971, then fell back to Phnom Penh and provincial capitals to await its fate. The NVA fought Lon Nol's U.S.-supplied army while the Khmer Rouge concentrated on building up its forces—and worked on blueprints for utopia.

Saloth Sar's "democratic revolution" began with land collectivization and mandatory political study sessions. Showing a cynical grasp of mass social psychology, the Khmer Rouge "sealed off their zones by creating miles-wide tracts of no-man's land . . . laid with booby traps and patrolled around the clock."[15] People isolated from the world can be manipulated in astounding ways. Poor peasants were given positions of leadership for the first time in their lives. Buddhism, the central organizing principle of rural Cambodian society, was proscribed.

Evidently the fanatic scale of Saloth Sar's revolution was more than his wife could bear. Journalist Elizabeth Becker tells of a photograph of Khieu Ponnary that appeared in a propaganda pamphlet printed in Beijing: "Ponnary's hair is a shocking gray. Her thin face appears haunted. . . . Her arms dangle limply at her side. This posed photograph cannot hide her condition: Ponnary is going mad in the service of her husband's revolution."[16] Inevitably, one is reminded of Stalin's wife, Nadezhda Alliluyeva, who shot herself in the head on the fifteenth anniversary of the Bolshevik revolution.

While Sar was building communism in his "liberated zones," the constellation of international power was shifting. President Nixon went to Beijing to meet Mao Zedong, thereby creating a de facto Sino–American alliance against the Soviet Union. Hanoi signed a peace accord with Washington in January 1973 and wanted the Khmer Rouge to observe a cease-fire. Sar angrily rejected this. It cemented his hatred and distrust of the Vietnamese communists. He now tried to force North Vietnamese troops out of Cambodia by organizing anti-Vietnamese demonstrations and refusing to sell rice to Vietnamese workers on Cambodian rubber plantations.[17]

Sar was hardly alone in his hostility toward the Vietnamese; the prejudice is widely shared among Khmers. The two cultures have very little in common. To simplify their stereotypes, Vietnamese think of Cambodians as country bumpkins, and Cambodians think of Vietnamese as city slickers. But it was not yet time for an open break. On October 3, 1974, Saloth Sar wrote a letter to the North Vietnamese leaders, thanking them for their help and assuring them "in all sincerity" and "from the bottom of my heart" that he would always cherish the "great solidarity and fraternal and revolutionary friendship between Cambodia and Vietnam."[18]

After January 1973 the United States could no longer bomb North or South Vietnam, but B-52 missions over Cambodia, code-named "Arc Light," intensified and spread across the entire country except for the far west until Congress, emboldened by Nixon's dwindling popularity, cut off funds for the bombing on August 15, 1973. The United States had dropped 257,465 tons of explosives on Cambodia, which was 150 percent of the explosive tonnage dropped on Japan in World War II.[19] Cambodian society was shattered even before Saloth Sar adopted the name Pol Pot and took Cambodia back to the year zero. By 1974 the Khmer Rouge controlled most of rural Cambodia. Prince Sihanouk was taken on a tour of Khmer Rouge zones and reported that Khieu Samphan was "a socialist with the same basic ideology as the Swedish Prime Minister. The work he is heading inside Cambodia is fantastic."[20]

The Chinese (at least the Maoists, who were riding high as of 1975) agreed that the Khmer Rouge were achieving wonderful things. A delegation of Chinese journalists reported from the liberated zones, one month before the fall of Phnom Penh, "Wherever we went, we saw thousands of cheerful people working at water conservancy construction sites."[21]

> We visited many water conservancy worksites and were deeply impressed by the magnificent scenes of collective labor. On our way back from Angkor we saw a project in Chikreng District where 15,000 people were building a huge dam and a 16-kilometer-long main canal. Their broadcast system carried songs over the entire worksite, and the people were digging, hauling and building energetically, though the sun was beating down hard. In order to complete their projects before the rainy season set in, people at some construction sites continued into the cool of the night, working under electric light or flaming torches.[22]

The above-quoted Chinese propaganda booklet contains photographs of Khmer Rouge soldiers with brand-new Chinese armored personnel carriers and artillery. Their uniforms and baggy caps bear a suspicious resemblance to those worn in the Chinese Army.

A Khmer Rouge "storming attack" on Phnom Penh was beaten back in 1974, but the city, swollen to many times its prewar size by an influx of refugees, was surrounded. After the Khmer Rouge mined the Mekong River, rice and ammunition could no longer be brought upriver from Saigon. Lon Nol's army could only be resupplied by U.S. aircraft. By early 1975 even that tenuous lifeline became risky as the Khmer Rouge advanced to within artillery range of the Phnom Penh airport runways. Saloth Sar directed the bloody final offensive himself. Showing callous disregard for the lives of helpless refugees, the Khmer Rouge lobbed shells directly into the city. Washington now wanted Lon Nol out of the country in the vain hope that some kind of compromise could be reached with Sihanouk and the Khmer Rouge. Lon Nol was persuaded to go into exile in Hawaii with a sweetener of $500,000 (according to Becker) or $1 million (according to Chandler).[23] Why he should have needed such inducement is unclear, as he undoubtedly would have been killed within hours of capture.

DEMOCRATIC KAMPUCHEA (1975–78)

On April 17, 1975, Khmer Rouge soldiers, grim-faced and startlingly young, entered Phnom Penh. Nervous but hopeful citizens greeted them with smiles and waves. The victorious teenage warriors were strangely silent. They wore black shirts and shorts instead of regular military uniforms, checkered scarves instead of helmets, and rubber sandals instead of combat boots. Some were barefoot. But all were very heavily armed, with Chinese machine guns and rocket-propelled grenade launchers. Some of these young men had never been in Phnom Penh, or any other city, and were puzzled by modern inventions. One was observed trying to eat a tube of toothpaste; another shot a motorcycle he could not start.[24] Some tried to drive abandoned cars but, not knowing how to steer or shift, drove them into trees.

Saloth Sar conceived a drastic plan to evacuate the entire population of Phnom Penh. To him city people were class enemies—businessmen, soldiers of the old regime, Chinese merchants, Vietnamese tailors, aristocrats, and royalists. Not even destitute refugees from the provinces could be trusted, for they had fled rather than allowing him to liberate them. Everyone—without exception—was ordered to leave immediately on the pretext that the Americans were going to bomb the city. Even hospitals were emptied. The patients in their wheeled beds were pushed out of the city by relatives. The evacuees had to keep walking on penalty of being shot. Children who could not keep up with their mothers might not ever see them again. When people asked the guards where they were going, the answer was simply, "to the countryside." Thousands died of exhaustion or were shot.

About 600 foreigners, mostly diplomats and missionaries, some with Khmer spouses, sought refuge inside the French Embassy compound. According to François Ponchaud, who was among this group, they were loaded into the backs of trucks, driven across Cambodia, and deposited at the Thai border. As the convoy passed through provincial capitals—Kompong Chhnang, Pursat, and Battambang—Ponchaud observed that these small cities, like Phnom Penh, were ghost towns. The Khmer Rouge had taken cars, refrigerators, air conditioners—all symbols of modern life—smashed them, and piled them in heaps on the edge of the cities. A refugee told Ponclaud that the people of Battambang had been given only three hours to leave and that anyone caught in the city after that would be shot. Even the dogs would be shot.[25]

Saloth Sar entered Phnom Penh on April 23 or 24, 1975. It was the first time he had seen the city in twelve years. He must have felt triumphant but, as always, he traveled incognito, wearing ordinary black clothes. He made no announcement, no speech, no proclamation. After one month he summoned high-ranking military and civilian officials of his new government to a five-day meeting to receive the plan distributed by the center. One who was in the audience later recalled, "We saw Pol Pot's behavior and heard his words, and he did not seem to us to be a killer. He seemed kindly. He did not speak very much. He just smiled and smiled. . . . And his words were light, not strong. In general you would estimate that Pol Pot was a kindly person."[26]

Just as the Khmer Rouge had controlled people in the liberated zones by isolating them, now they isolated the whole country. They cut all international telephone, telegram, and cable connections. "There was no international mail service. All regular airline service save occasional flights from Peking and Hanoi were halted. The borders were closed and mined, the maritime boundaries were patrolled."[27] Not a single international journalist was admitted until March 1978 when, in a desperate search for communist allies against Vietnam, some Yugoslav reporters were granted entry.

Political Organization of Democratic Kampuchea

Extreme secrecy was Saloth Sar's way. No modern tyrant has so shunned publicity as this furtive, taciturn man. He ruled through the Angka, an entity intentionally nebulous so that Cambodians could not blame any individual for the terrible things that happened to them. In sharp contrast to the techniques Stalin and Mao used, Sar permitted no cult of personality, no statues, and few pictures. Most Cambodians never knew what he looked like, despite the fact that for forty-four months he controlled every aspect of their lives.

Even the elementary fact that the Communist Party had taken power was a secret. The term *revolutionary organization* was used instead. Cambodia was renamed "Democratic Kampuchea" and given a new flag, which featured a profile of the towers of Angkor Wat. Due to the exigencies of revolutionary war, the organization was decentralized before its victory of April 1975. Now Pol Pot made sure that each zone commander could communicate with him but not with any other zone commander. Democratic Kampuchea was divided into six administrative zones, each subdivided into smaller regions. Conditions varied considerably between regions. Those zones whose commanders were most closely associated with Pol Pot experienced the harshest rule. The total number of Khmer Rouge soldiers was about 100,000. Kiernan reports that there were 14,000 party members.[28]

Prince Sihanouk was nominally the head of state, but actually the Khmer Rouge held him under house arrest. When Sihanouk, who had grown suicidal, resigned, Khieu Samphan was named president of the state presidium. "Elections" were held on March 20, 1976, for a "Cambodian People's Representative Assembly." This legislature met only once, to elect a "rubber plantation worker" named Pol Pot as prime minister. No one had ever heard of him before. Not until 1977, when he was photographed on a state visit to China, did anyone—even the Central Intelligence Agency (CIA)—realize that Pol Pot was actually the obscure former schoolteacher, Saloth Sar. Ieng Sary was named minister of foreign affairs, and Son Sen was identified as minister of defense. Five of the original thirteen cabinet members were soon executed.

In a poorly understood incident that may have reflected an internal power struggle, a genuine medical emergency, or merely a ruse, Pol Pot resigned as prime minister in September 1976 and was temporarily replaced by Nuon Chea. Whether or not he was really at risk of being overthrown, he was soon back in control, and the pace of murderous purges "skyrocketed."[29]

Ideology of Democratic Kampuchea

A revolution is by definition a violent seizure of power. But few revolutionaries gloried in the imagery of bloodshed as enthusiastically as Pol Pot and his henchmen. Consider these lines from the "National Anthem of Democratic Kampuchea":

> The red, red blood splatters the cities and plains of the Cambodian fatherland,
> The sublime blood of the workers and peasants,
> The blood of revolutionary combatants of both sexes.
> The blood spills out into great indignation and a resolute urge to fight.
> 17 April, that day under the revolutionary flag
> The blood certainly liberates us from slavery.[30]

The following words, from a song called "The Red Flag" that DK cadres sang to open every political meeting, convey the flavor of Khmer Rouge propaganda:

> Glittering red blood blankets the earth,
> Blood given up to liberate the people:
> Blood of workers, peasants and intellectuals,
> Blood of young men, Buddhist monks and girls.
> The blood swirls away, and flows upward, gently, into the sky,
> Turning into a red, revolutionary flag.
> Red flag! Red flag! Flying now! Flying now!
> O beloved friends, pursue, strike, and hit the enemy.

Red flag! Red flag! Flying now! Flying now!
Don't spare a single reactionary imperialist.
Drive them from Kampuchea.
Strive and strike, strive and strike, win the victory, win the victory![31]

Few Westerners realized the scope of Pol Pot's revolution in the first year. Despite his obvious debt to Stalin, who showed how an entire country could be cowed, Pol Pot claimed that Cambodia was "building socialism without a model."[32]

Economic Organization of Democratic Kampuchea

Pol Pot went further than any communist dictator before him. Fidel Castro mused about abolishing money someday, but Pol Pot actually did it. In Democratic Kampuchea there were no wages, banks, markets, stores, restaurants, or businesses. All the land was collectivized, as in the Soviet Union and China, but again Pol Pot trumped Stalin and Mao by abolishing all personal property: "No personal clothes, pots, pans, watches, anything."[33] Each person was allowed two possessions: a bowl and a spoon.

The Khmer Rouge leaders indulged in dreamy "planning," which is a prime example of what Serge Thion calls "the deep lack of realism that has up to now been a permanent factor in Cambodian politics."[34] A four-year plan announced in 1976 called for Cambodians to triple their annual rice yield through heroic labor. This contrasted oddly with the claim broadcast by DK radio: "Thanks to the Angka, every day is a holiday."[35]

It is sometimes said that Pol Pot tried to take Cambodia back to a preindustrial era, but that is not correct. For all his fierce hatred of capitalism and of the West, Pol Pot pursued forced-draft industrial modernization.[36] The Khmer Rouge coat of arms showed factories as well as rice fields. Pol Pot accepted a limited amount of aid from China and North Korea. None of it did much good, though, because the society was practically paralyzed by terror.

Social Organization of Democratic Kampuchea

Cambodian culture lost its underpinnings. People had to follow a completely new and inhumane code of conduct, on pain of death. The population was divided into "base people" (also called "old people") and "new people." The base people were those who had been peasants before the revolution. They were considered more trustworthy than the new people who came from Phnom Penh or some other city. Because the category of new people included teachers, doctors, clerks, merchants, and bureaucrats, Pol Pot effectively destroyed Cambodia's middle class. One right-handed former dancer at the royal court survived only because when given a pencil and told to write his name, he wrote with his left hand. The resultant scrawl convinced his tormentors he had never been to school and therefore did not deserve to be killed. Others survived by carefully avoiding eye contact with Khmer Rouge cadres.

Pol Pot attacked organized religion with the same zeal shown by Stalin, Mao, and the North Korean dictator Kim Il Sung. Chapter 15 of the Constitution of Democratic Kampuchea states: "Every citizen of Kampuchea has the right to worship according to any religion and the right not to worship according to any religion. All reactionary religions that are detrimental to Democratic Kampuchea and the Kampuchean people are strictly forbidden." Monasteries were closed and monks defrocked. Every one of the country's 3,000 pagodas was desecrated if not actually destroyed. The Khmer Rouge explained that "the Buddhist religion came from Siam and it deceived the people's minds and put them to sleep."[37] Of perhaps 50,000 Cambodian monks, only 1,000 survived. A Catholic cathedral in Phnom Penh was leveled, but at least the Khmer Rouge did not deliberately attack Angkor Wat.

Pol Pot abolished education. All schools were closed, and some were used as torture centers. He abolished the family, too. In much of the country children were separated from their parents at the age of seven and thereafter were authorized to see them only once or twice a year.[38] People ate together in large dining barns and lived in dormitories. Only the Angka could grant permission to marry, and premarital sex was punishable by death. People were even given new names. Personal conversation was conducted in whispers.

Forced Labor

The Khmer Rouge put everyone to work. Base people and new people alike were made to dig canals and dams. The emphasis on vast water works suggests that Pol Pot was trying to emulate the slave society of ancient Angkor. Unfortunately, most engineers had been executed, and the uneducated Khmer Rouge cadres did not understand that dams built without spillways would collapse after the monsoon rains.[39] The use of slave labor was not new in Southeast Asia. War captives and enslaved mountain tribesmen had always been used to build monuments and dig canals. The difference this time was that Pol Pot made war on his own people.

The Killing Fields: Mass Executions

A reign of terror always spreads, as shown by the course of the French, Russian, and Chinese revolutions. People denounce others in a desperate effort to save themselves. When a tyrant promises to create a perfect society, all blemishes must be the work of saboteurs. In December 1976, Pol Pot said,

"We search for the microbes within the Party without success. They are buried."[40]

Violent revolutions turn on themselves. Thousands of Khmer Rouge cadres were arrested and sent to Tuol Sleng Prison where they were made to confess to things they had never done. Tuol Sleng, located on the grounds of a former high school, was run by a man whose alias was Deuch. Deuch answered to Son Sen. Of approximately 20,000 prisoners sent to Tuol Sleng, only 7 are known to have survived. Most could not even hope for a quick death.

> Everyone—man, woman, and child—was subjected to whippings, electric shocks, and repeated dunkings in water tanks. But there were said to be special tortures for women—their breasts were slashed; their vaginal areas were burned with hot pokers; poisonous reptiles were allowed to roam their bodies; if they were mothers they were forced to watch their children slowly tortured.[41]

Deuch kept meticulous records with name, number, and photograph of every victim. Their confessions were forwarded to Son Sen, Nuon Chea, and sometimes to Pol Pot himself. To the degree that Khmer Rouge leaders actually believed these fantastic concoctions, they were simply feeding their own paranoid delusions. Certain days were devoted to executing relatives of those previously executed.[42] Ben Kiernan of Yale University's Cambodian Genocide Program examined Tuol Sleng records and found that of 111 wardens at Tuol Sleng, 82 were aged seventeen to twenty-one.[43]

Of course Tuol Sleng was not the only place in Democratic Kampuchea where people were executed. Executions were often carried out in the middle of the night with no publicity. At other times they were carried out in front of other people. Onlookers, even relatives, were forbidden to show grief. The condemned were usually made to dig their own mass graves, then shot or, to save bullets, clubbed with poles or hatchets. There were "killing fields" in every province. As of 1997 twelve killing fields had been uncovered in Kompong Thom, Pol Pot's home province, with skeletons of more than 300,000 people.[44] Approximately 1.7 million people died under Pol Pot's rule, from execution, starvation, overwork, disease, and lack of medical care. The prewar population of Cambodia was estimated at 8 million. Therefore Pol Pot killed a greater proportion of his own population than any other tyrant known to history.

Private Lives of Pol Pot and Other DK Leaders

For all their anti-urban bias the Khmer Rouge leaders lived in Phnom Penh. Pol Pot is said to have brought along Jarai tribesmen from Ratanakiri to serve as bodyguards and to have shifted houses frequently and without notice. There were food tasters, of course. Cooks were terrified that their masters might get sick. According to Serge Thion, the families of top leaders had fruit, vegetables, and fabrics flown in on bimonthly planes from Beijing.[45] Photographs taken in China in 1977 clearly show Pol Pot with a double chin. He had gained weight while his people starved.

Kinship ties are relatively loose in Cambodia. Family loyalty may be given or withheld according to self-interest. Some relatives of Khmer Rouge leaders were privileged and influential. Pol Pot gave several nephews and nieces jobs in the foreign affairs ministry. One daughter of Ieng Sary directed a hospital, and another directed the Pasteur Institute, although neither had finished high school.[46] Other relatives did not fare so well: Pol Pot's older brother, Saloth Seng, was driven from his home, and his son (Pol Pot's nephew) was killed.

Pol Pot Provokes War with Vietnam

Pol Pot's downfall came about because he lost his ability to calculate military odds and foolishly provoked a war with the Vietnamese, whose army was larger, better trained, better led, and better equipped than his own. Pol Pot moved quickly in the two weeks between his taking Phnom Penh (April 17, 1975) and the NVA conquest of Saigon (April 30, 1975) to move Khmer Rouge troops into territory claimed by both Cambodia and Vietnam. In April 1977 he mounted raids into Vietnam. In August 1977 DK troops drove deep into the Vietnamese province of Tay Ninh, less than a hundred miles northwest of Saigon. Why was he doing this? He had grown absurdly overconfident, as evidenced by a radio address in which he claimed that one Khmer soldier was capable of killing thirty Vietnamese.[47]

In September 1977 Vietnam attacked Cambodia along the entire 650-mile border, penetrating up to ten miles before halting. This clear warning did not induce caution in Pol Pot. After delivering a five-hour public speech in which he finally revealed that he was the secretary-general of the Communist Party, he flew to Beijing, where he was promised military aid. Chinese arms shipments to DK were stepped up in January 1978. That spring the Vietnamese leaders made up their minds to invade Cambodia, overthrow Pol Pot, and replace him with a Khmer communist who understood the need for friendship with Vietnam. They took the precaution of first signing a treaty of friendship and cooperation with the Soviet Union.

On December 3, 1978, Vietnam announced the creation of a "Kampuchean National United Front for National Salvation" led by Heng Samrin. Knowing he needed allies as never before, Pol Pot began welcoming visitors from communist countries in Eastern Europe, leftists from capitalist countries, and even two objective American journalists, Elizabeth Becker of the *Washington Post* and Richard Dudman of the *St. Louis Post Dispatch*. This gambit went badly awry when Malcolm Caldwell, a British scholar who was openly sympathetic to Pol Pot, was mysteriously murdered in his hotel room in Phnom Penh.

Vietnam's full-scale invasion of Cambodia, utilizing 120,000 troops plus 15,000 anti–Pol Pot Khmers, was launched on Christmas Day 1978. The Vietnamese encountered little resistance and occupied Phnom Penh on January 7, 1979. Pol Pot escaped by helicopter to a mountain hideout on the Thai border. Soon the Vietnamese controlled most of Cambodia, except for those remote zones from which the Khmer Rouge, now down to 40,000 troops, could not be dislodged. The Vietnamese established their own satellite government, officially known as the People's Republic of Kampuchea (PRK), headed at first by Heng Samrin and later by Hun Sen, both former Khmer Rouge cadres who had fled to Vietnam to escape Pol Pot's purges. Within months, Cambodians began to rebuild their lives. The cities were repopulated, Buddhism relegitimized, and schools reopened. Massive population movements took place as people roamed the country searching for their families, so not much rice was planted in 1979. After all that had happened, the Cambodian people now faced famine.

POL POT RESUMES GUERRILLA WARFARE (1979–97)

Although relieved to be free from the Khmer Rouge, many Cambodians still distrusted the Vietnamese and resented that 200,000 Vietnamese soldiers occupied their country. Therefore, Pol Pot could still play the patriot. With clandestine support from three countries with reasons to oppose Vietnam (Thailand, China, and the United States), Pol Pot lurked in inaccessible jungle camps near the Thai border for the next eighteen years.

China invaded Vietnam in February 1979 to "teach Vietnam a lesson," as Deng Xiaoping said, and to force Hanoi to withdraw troops from Cambodia. Instead the Vietnamese taught Deng a lesson: Any country that invades Vietnam is committing a very serious blunder. The Vietnamese saw no reason to withdraw from Cambodia. Their client government in Phnom Penh tried Pol Pot and Ieng Sary in absentia on August 18, 1979, and sentenced both to death. The Chinese continued to supply the Khmer Rouge with uniforms, weapons, and ammunition. The Thais, to maintain a buffer between themselves and Vietnam, offered Pol Pot sanctuary when he needed to cross the border for medical treatment or to escape the PRK's annual dry-season offensives. Prince Sihanouk again offered his imprimatur to the Khmer Rouge cadres, although they had imprisoned him for years and killed five of his children and nine other relatives.

The Cambodian anti-Vietnam forces banded together to form what they called the Coalition Government of Democratic Kampuchea (CGDK). It was not a government at all, but three separate armed groups that cooperated only because they had to: (1) approximately 25,000 Khmer Rouge soldiers still led by Pol Pot; (2) the Armée Nationaliste Sihanoukienne with about 5,000 troops; and (3) the Khmer People's National Liberation Front with 9,000 troops under Son Sann, a conservative former prime minister. Of these three armies only the Khmer Rouge was a serious fighting force.

President Jimmy Carter, who spoke often of human rights, and President Ronald Reagan, who denounced communism, offered Pol Pot indirect support for the simple reason that the Soviet Union supported Vietnam. The United States could not be seen to support the odious Khmer Rouge, so Washington confined itself to "humanitarian" aid to the CDGK, knowing it would reach the Khmer Rouge sooner or later, and to diplomatic support in the United Nations (UN), where American diplomats lined up support for the Khmer Rouge. The world simply shut its eyes to the horrors of Democratic Kampuchea and voted year after year to allow Pol Pot's representative, Thiounn Prasith, to occupy Cambodia's seat in the UN. President Carter's national security adviser, Zbigniew Brzezinski was not ashamed to state openly, "I encouraged the Chinese to support Pol Pot. I encouraged the Thai to help the D.K."[48] For Brzezinski, a man of Polish descent who strongly identified with his homeland, anything was justified to counter Soviet moves on the global chessboard.

Khieu Samphan served as public spokesman and roving diplomat for the Khmer Rouge. Pol Pot was not seen from 1979 to 1997 except by a small inner circle that included the most notorious thugs of his old politburo: Son Sen, Ta Mok, and Ieng Sary. Many people believed he had died. Pol Pot could not leave his base except for furtive trips to Thailand and China, but he lived comfortably because the Khmer Rouge generated $12 million a month by cutting tropical hardwood trees in the Cardamom Mountains and smuggling the logs onto the world market with the aid of corrupt Thai generals. A former prime minister of Thailand claimed to have met Pol Pot several times during the 1980s and reported that Pol Pot repented nothing. According to Prince Sihanouk, who found it hilarious, when Pol Pot came down with malaria, "the Royal Army of Thailand sent a helicopter, a beautiful American helicopter, to take him from his headquarters to the best hospital."[49] With Khieu Ponnary dead or insane, Pol Pot remarried sometime in the mid-1980s. His new wife, many decades younger than he, bore him a daughter in 1985. Pol Pot was reported to be very affectionate toward the girl.

In 1991 all four warring factions (the three CGDK "armies" and the PRK government) signed a peace agreement and put Cambodia under the control of the UN Transitional Authority in Cambodia (UNTAC). In 1993 UNTAC sponsored free elections in which Prince Norodom Ranariddh, Sihanouk's son, garnered the most votes. The Khmer Rouge boycotted these elections. Hun Sen refused to abide by the results and demanded to be co–prime minister along with Ranariddh. Ranariddh and Hun Sen opened secret talks with the Khmer Rouge in May 1994, but they must have been exploiting a split in Khmer Rouge ranks because Pol Pot violently opposed negotiations. In his seventieth year, Pol Pot's slogan, according to a leader of the "new" Khmer Rouge, Tep Kunnal, was "Fight! Fight! Fight! Struggle! Struggle! Struggle!"[50]

THE DECLINE AND FALL OF POL POT (1966–98)

Ieng Sary defected to the Cambodian government in 1996, taking about one-fourth of the remaining Khmer Rouge soldiers with him. He denied responsibility for Khmer Rouge atrocities and blamed a secret committee answerable to Pol Pot, to which he did not belong. No one believed this, yet Sihanouk issued a royal pardon. Pol Pot was bitter about Ieng Sary's betrayal. In February 1997 the PRK government sent a team of fifteen officials to negotiate directly with Pol Pot at his enclave at Anlong Veng. Ten of these men were immediately led off into the jungle and shot.

Pol Pot called a meeting of his remaining loyalists on the night of June 9, 1997. When his former comrade Son Sen, who had run Tuol Sleng, failed to attend,

> Pol Pot coolly ordered his security chief, General Sarouen, to kill the "traitor" and his family. Sarouen and 20 to 30 of his men drove to Son Sen's house and shot him dead in the right temple and cheek. Then they killed his wife with shots to her left ear and right back. A dozen other family members, including a five-year-old child, were also murdered. Afterward, all the bodies were run over by a truck.[51]

Three days later General Nhek Bun Chhay, Ranariddh's top commander, flew into Anlong Veng by helicopter and discovered that Khieu Samphan had been taken hostage by Pol Pot, who had only about 300 supporters left. On June 19, Pol Pot was captured by Khmer Rouge soldiers loyal to Khieu Samphan and Ta Mok. Two of Pol Pot's soldiers "were carrying him through the jungle in a green Chinese military hammock strung on a bamboo pole. With him were his wife, a woman in her thirties, their 12-year old daughter, a niece, three other loyalists and Khieu Samphan as hostage."[52] Pol Pot was in terrible health, wracked with malarial fever, high blood pressure, and heart disease. Government negotiators asked Ta Mok if they could take a picture of him, and Ta Mok answered, "Let me throw the contemptible Pol Pot in a cage first, and then you can take his photograph."[53]

The Khmer Rouge staged an eerie show trial of Pol Pot on July 25, 1997, and invited Nate Thayer of the *Far Eastern Economic Review* to witness and film the proceedings. Thayer's video was subsequently broadcast worldwide. The accused was white-haired, stooped, and feeble, but from the eyes, shape of the head, and distinctive mole on his nose, there was no doubt that it was really Pol Pot. The world expected to see a monster, but the impassive face staring back was quite ordinary. Under a metal shed, Pol Pot sat quietly and fanned himself while the audience chanted, on cue, "Crush! Crush! Crush! Pol Pot and his clique!" The Khmer Rouge faction that was disowning him broadcast a plea to be accepted as "a liberal democratic regime."[54]

In October 1997 Thayer was invited back to Anlong Veng to interview Pol Pot. The former dictator claimed he had never heard of Tuol Sleng and spent much time complaining about his health problems. Pol Pot died on April 15, 1998. The Khmer Rouge said he had died in his sleep, but they refused to conduct an autopsy and cremated his body.

CONCLUSION

Cambodian society today is dislocated and disoriented, struggling to re-constitute itself after having been atomized. Even those who survived and emigrated cannot shake the past: There is a syndrome of psychosomatic blindness found among middle-aged Cambodian refugees who settled in California. Doctors can find nothing wrong with their eyes and say that perhaps these patients witnessed such terrible things that their brains refuse to see anymore.

How can we explain such radical evil? Here is a summary of eight different answers that have been offered:

1. *Pol Pot is to blame.* Pol Pot's dreams knew no bounds, and he simply concluded that the only way to create a perfect society was to eliminate anyone who might foil his plans. One is tempted to agree with Pol Pot's brother Saloth Nhep, who said, "My brother does not deserve to live. If he is captured, then every Cambodian should be given a razor blade and allowed to make one cut."[55] But this is too simple. Pol Pot did not kill all those people by himself.

2. *The entire Khmer Rouge leadership is to blame.* If there were justice in the world, all surviving Khmer Rouge leaders would be brought before a war crimes tribunal, and this may yet happen. Nuon Chea would be indicted, as well as Ta Mok and Khieu Samphan. Ieng Sary's pardon would be revoked. These men, of course, want to pin it all on Pol Pot. For example, Ta Mok told a reporter, "From the very beginning of the struggle to now I never issued an order to kill anyone. All orders were decided by Pol Pot alone. Pol Pot made all decisions with absolute dictatorship."[56]

3. *Norodom Sihanouk shares in the blame.* Prince Sihanouk allowed his fury at Lon Nol, who overthrew him in 1970, to blind him to the infinitely

greater evil of the Khmer Rouge. He lent his prestige to Pol Pot before, during, and after the reign of terror, in the name of patriotism. In the words of T. D. Allman, "Sihanouk was the Judas goat. He led his people to the slaughter. And now he is asking them to trust him all over again."[57]

4. *The U.S. government is to blame.* Had President Nixon not ordered the air force to bomb Cambodia, and had Congress not waited four years to call an end to the bombing, Sihanouk might not have been overthrown and Saloth Sar might have remained an obscure rebel. We shall never know. Presidents Carter and Reagan offered diplomatic support to Pol Pot after his crimes were well known.

5. *Cambodian society is to blame.* This explanation smacks of blaming the victim, but perhaps certain features of Cambodian society and culture account for the savagery of the Khmer Rouge. Scholars who are deeply in love with the country and its people have suggested that this is part of the explanation. David Chandler says that "Cambodians have this darkness, which is part of the shadow of their sweetness. Many of us who keep going there still find it hard to understand."[58] An aid worker who had spent years in Cambodia found that "there are always levels and levels—and then more levels—of intrigue and shadows."[59] François Ponchaud, a French missionary who lived in Cambodia for ten years, thinks that the Buddhist belief in karma may have made Khmer Rouge executioners fatalistic: "They believed their victims had made errors, political errors, and that killing them would allow them to be reborn as better people in their next lives."[60] Lest this explanation be written off as merely a Catholic perspective on Buddhist theology, consider what Saloth Roueng, Pol Pot's sister, said when shown a photograph of her brother in the summer of 1997: "Old, old. He looks sick. But he deserves whatever he got. The good receive good; the bad receive bad."[61] Elizabeth Becker noted that Lon Nol's xenophobia mirrored that of Pol Pot, for Lon Nol "made no secret of his dream of purifying the Khmer race, the Khmer culture, and Khmer Buddhism of the foreign pollutants he thought had sapped the country's energy and eaten away at its identity and territory."[62] And Karl Jackson reminds us that in 1970 in Kompong Cham, "two members of parliament were killed by an angry pro-Sihanouk crowd. They were flayed into pieces and their livers were grilled and eaten by the crowd."[63]

6. *Communism is to blame.* The parallels between Josef Stalin's purges, Mao Zedong's maniacal Great Leap Forward, and Pol Pot's attempt to purify Cambodia are obvious. They should serve as a permanent reminder that ideas have consequences, especially Karl Marx's idea that class struggle is the "locomotive of history"; Lenin's idea that "morality is that which serves to destroy the old, exploiting society"; and Mao's idea that power grows out of the barrel of a gun.

7. *Racism is to blame.* Along with communism and Maoism, Ben Kiernan emphasizes the anti-Vietnamese, anti-Chinese, anti-Cham, anti-Thai, and

anti-Western race hatred fomented by Pol Pot. This interpretation is challenged by others, including Chandler, who acknowledge that ethnic minorities were nearly exterminated by Pol Pot but point out that more than 1 million Khmers were killed, too.

8. *Peasant suspicion of city people is to blame.* Peasants worldwide are instinctively suspicious of people who live in the city, a crowded, confusing place where foreigners flaunt their wealth and where traditional morality breaks down. In the case of Cambodia, racism augmented the peasants' anti-urban bias because many Chinese and Vietnamese lived in Phnom Penh. In Elizabeth Becker's words, "Intellectual and peasant discovered a frightening coincidence of prejudice. They were each other's best converts to a bitter, burning hatred."[64]

Perhaps there is some truth in each of these explanations. It is a moral and political conundrum we would like to forget, but cannot.

NOTES

1. These revealing interviews are found in Seth Mydans, "Pol Pot's Siblings Remember the Polite Boy and the Killer," *New York Times,* August 6, 1997, p. 1.

2. David Chandler, *Brother Number One: A Political Biography of Pol Pot* (Boulder, Colo.: Westview Press, 1992), p. 19.

3. Chandler, *Brother Number One,* p. 22.

4. Ben Kiernan, *The Pol Pot Regime: Race, Power, and Genocide in Cambodia Under the Khmer Rouge, 1975–79* (New Haven, Conn.: Yale University Press, 1996), p. 10.

5. Elizabeth Becker, *When the War Was Over: The Voices of Cambodia's Revolution and Its People* (New York: Simon & Schuster, 1986), p. 74. The sisters were no relation to Khieu Samphan.

6. Chandler, *Brother Number One,* p. 39.

7. Becker, *When the War Was Over,* p. 78.

8. Becker, *When the War Was Over,* p. 91.

9. Chandler, *Brother Number One,* p. 52.

10. See Laura Summers, translator's introduction to *Cambodia's Economy and Industrial Development* by Khieu Samphan (data paper, No. 111) (Ithaca, N.Y.: Cornell University Southeast Asia Program, 1979), p. 9.

11. See Kiernan, *The Pol Pot Regime,* footnote 30, p. 13; and Kiernan, *How Pol Pot Came to Power* (London: Verso, 1985), footnote 135, p. 241.

12. See Ben Kiernan and Chanthou Boua, eds., *Peasants and Politics in Kampuchea, 1942–1981* (Armonk, N.Y.: M. E. Sharpe, 1982), pp. 228–29, for a detailed explanation of these groups.

13. Chandler, *Brother Number One,* p. 88.

14. William Shawcross, *Sideshow: Kissinger, Nixon, and the Destruction of Cambodia* (New York: Simon & Schuster, 1979), p. 253.

15. Becker, *When the War Was Over,* p. 164.

16. Becker, *When the War Was Over*, pp. 160–61.

17. David P. Chandler and Ben Kiernan, eds., *Revolution and Its Aftermath in Kampuchea: Eight Essays* (monograph series, No. 25) (New Haven, Conn.: Yale University, Southeast Asia Studies, 1983), p. 300.

18. Nayan Chanda, *Brother Enemy: The War After the War* (New York: Macmillan Publishing, 1986), p. 73.

19. Becker, *When the War Was Over*, p. 34.

20. "The Once and Future Prince?" *Newsweek* 82 (July 16, 1973), p. 35.

21. *Fighting Cambodia: Reports of the Chinese Journalists Delegation to Cambodia* (Peking: Foreign Languages Press, 1975), p. 37.

22. *Fighting Cambodia*, pp. 41–42.

23. See Becker, *When the War Was Over*, p. 358; and David P. Chandler, *The Tragedy of Cambodian History: Politics, War, and Revolution Since 1945* (New Haven, Conn.: Yale University Press, 1991), p. 234.

24. Kiernan, *The Pol Pot Regime:* pp. 39–50.

25. See François Ponchaud, *Cambodia: Year Zero* (New York: Holt, Rinehart & Winston, 1977), pp. 34–51.

26. Kiernan, *The Pol Pot Regime*, pp. 55–58.

27. Becker, *When the War Was Over*, p. 180.

28. Kiernan, *The Pol Pot Regime*, p. 313.

29. Kiernan, *The Pol Pot Regime*, p. 335.

30. Karl D. Jackson, *Cambodia 1975–78: Rendezvous With Death* (Princeton, N.J.: Princeton University Press, 1989), p. 72.

31. Khing Hoc Dy, "Khmer Literature Since 1975," in *Cambodian Culture Since 1975: Homeland and Exile*, ed. May M. Ebihara, Carol A. Mortland, and Judy Ledgerwood (Ithaca, N.Y.: Cornell University Press, 1994), p. 28.

32. Pol Pot is quoted in David P. Chandler, *A History of Cambodia*, 2d ed. (Boulder, Colo.: Westview Press, 1993), p. 210.

33. R. J. Rummel, *Death By Government* (New Brunswick, N.J.: Transaction Publishers, 1994), p. 183.

34. Serge Thion, "The Pattern of Cambodian Politics," in *The Cambodian Agony*, ed. David A. Ablin and Marlow Hood (Armonk, N.Y.: M. E. Sharpe, 1987), p. 150.

35. Ponchaud, *Cambodia*, p. 88.

36. Jackson, *Cambodia 1975–78*, p. 58.

37. Ponchaud, *Cambodia*, p. 131.

38. Marie A. Martin, *Cambodia: A Shattered Society* (Berkeley: University of California Press, 1994), p. 180.

39. Becker, *When the War Was Over*, p. 251.

40. Kiernan, *The Pol Pot Regime*, p. 336.

41. Becker, *When the War Was Over*, p. 235.

42. Jackson, *Cambodia 1975–78*, photo section following p. 214.

43. Kiernan, *The Pol Pot Regime*, p. 316.

44. Mydans, "Pol Pot's Siblings," p. 1.

45. Thion, "The Pattern of Cambodian Politics," p. 159.

46. Thion, "The Pattern of Cambodian Politics," p. 158.

47. Chanda, *Brother Enemy*, p. 298.

48. Becker, *When the War Was Over*, p. 440.

49. T. D. Allman, "Sihanouk's Sideshow," *Vanity Fair* 53 (April 1990), p. 159.

50. Nate Thayer, "Cambodian Peace Was Just a Day Away," *Washington Post*, August 17, 1997, p. A1.

51. Sydney H. Schanberg, "Return to the Killing Fields," *Vanity Fair* (October 1997), p. 233.

52. Thayer, "Cambodian Peace Was Just a Day Away," p. A1.

53. Thayer, "Cambodian Peace Was Just a Day Away," p. A1.

54. Radio of the Provisional Government of National Union and National Salvation of Cambodia, as reported in the *BBC Summary of World Broadcasts*, July 28, 1997.

55. Schanberg, "Return to the Killing Fields," p. 246.

56. Thayer, "Cambodian Peace Was Just a Day Away," p. A1.

57. Allman, "Sihanouk's Sideshow," p. 232.

58. David Chandler, as quoted in *Time* (August 11, 1997), p. 39.

59. Schanberg, "Return to the Killing Fields," p. 234.

60. Ponchaud, as quoted in *Time* (August 11, 1997), p. 39.

61. Seth Mydans, "Pol Pot's Siblings," p. 1.

62. Becker, *When the War Was Over*, p. 135.

63. Jackson, *Cambodia 1975–78*, pp. 71–72.

64. Becker, *When the War Was Over*, pp. 151–52.

For Further Reading

Ablin, David A., and Marlowe Hood, eds. *The Cambodian Agony*. Armonk, N.Y.: M. E. Sharpe, 1987.

Becker, Elizabeth. *When the War Was Over*. New York: Simon & Schuster, 1986.

Chanda, Nayan. *Brother Enemy: The War After the War*. New York: Macmillan, 1986.

Chandler, David P. *Brother Number One: A Political Biography of Pol Pot*. Boulder, Colo.: Westview Press, 1992.

———. *A History of Cambodia*. 2d ed. Boulder, Colo.: Westview Press, 1993.

———. *The Tragedy of Cambodian History: Politics, War, and Revolution Since 1945*. New Haven, Conn.: Yale University Press, 1991.

Ebihara, May, et al. *Cambodian Culture Since 1975*. Ithaca, N.Y.: Cornell University Press, 1994.

Etcheson, Craig. *The Rise and Demise of Democratic Kampuchea*. Boulder, Colo.: Westview Press, 1984.

Haas, Michael. *Genocide by Proxy: Cambodian Pawn on a Superpower Chessboard*. New York: Praeger, 1991.

Jackson, Karl D. *Cambodia 1975–1978: Rendezvous With Death*. Princeton, N.J.: Princeton University Press, 1989.

Kamm, Henry. *Report From a Stricken Land*. New York: Arcade, 1998.

Kiernan, Ben. *Genocide and Democracy in Cambodia: The Khmer Rouge, the United Nations, and the International Community* (Monograph Series, No. 41). New Haven, Conn.: Yale University, Southeast Asia Studies, 1993.

———. *How Pol Pot Came to Power*. London: Verso, 1985.

———. *The Pol Pot Regime: Race, Power, and Genocide in Cambodia Under the Khmer Rouge, 1975–79*. New Haven, Conn.: Yale University Press, 1996.

Kiernan, Ben, and Chanthou Boua, eds. *Peasants and Politics in Kampuchea, 1942–1981*. Armonk, N.Y.: M. E. Sharpe, 1982.

Mabbett, Ian, and David Chandler. *The Khmers*. Cambridge, Mass.: Blackwell, 1995.

Martin, Marie. *Cambodia: A Shattered Society*. Berkeley: University of California Press, 1994.

Osborne, Milton. *Sihanouk: Prince of Light, Prince of Darkness*. Honolulu: University of Hawaii Press, 1994.

Picq, Laurence. *Beyond the Horizon: Five Years With the Khmer Rouge*. New York: St. Martin's Press, 1989.

Ponchaud, François. *Cambodia: Year Zero.* New York: Holt, Rinehart & Winston, 1977.

Schanberg, Sydney H. *The Death and Life of Dith Pran.* New York: Penguin, 1985.

Shawcross, William. *Sideshow: Kissinger, Nixon, and the Destruction of Cambodia.* New York: Simon & Schuster, 1979.

Szymusiak, Molyda. *The Stones Cry Out: A Cambodian Childhood, 1975–1980.* New York: Hill & Wang, 1986.

Part IV

Indonesia

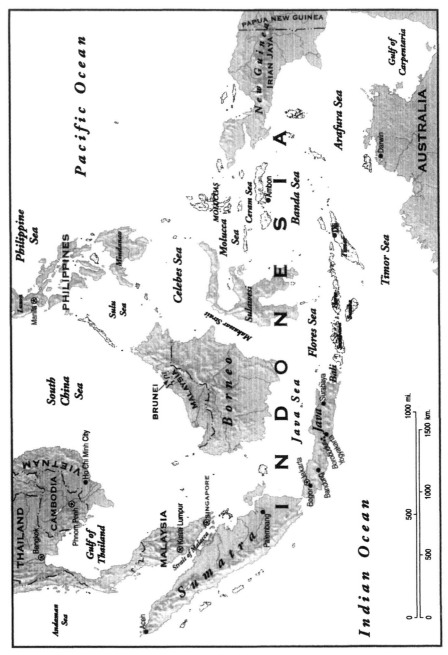

Indonesia

Indonesia Timeline

100–2500	Buddhist missionaries reach Sumatra and Java, transmitting Indian ideas of metaphysics; Brahman Hindus from India provide Indonesian kings with new, impressive court rituals.
600–1100	Buddhist Srivijaya kingdom on Sumatra.
700–900	Sailendra kingdom in eastern Java.
800	Borobudur temple complex in central Java.
1200–1500	Majapahit Empire, the last and greatest kingdom of the Hindu–Javanese period.
1500s	Islam spreads through Sumatra and Java.
1619	Dutch build fort at Batavia (Jakarta).
1700s	Dutch enforce contingency system in Java.
1825–30	Java war led by Diponegoro takes 200,000 lives.
1830	Dutch institute Cultivation System.
1890	Royal Dutch Petroleum Company formed.
1901	Dutch adopt ethical policy.
1901 Jun 6	Sukarno born.
1908	Budi Utomo, the first nationalist group in Indonesia, is founded.
1912	Omar Said Tjokroaminoto founds Sarekat Islam.
1918	Dutch create People's Council (Volksraad) in Indies.
1921 Jun 8	Suharto born.
1926	Sukarno receives engineering degree.
1927 Jun 4	Sukarno founds Indonesian Nationalist Union.
1929 Dec	Sukarno sentenced to four years in prison but released after two.
1942–45	Japanese occupation of Indonesia.
1943 Oct	Japan creates an Indonesian defense force.
1945 Aug 15	Japan surrenders.
1945 Aug 17	Sukarno and Mohammad Hatta proclaim Indonesian independence.
1945–49	Indonesian national revolution.

1949 Jan 28	United Nations demands Dutch withdrawal from Indonesia.
1949 Dec 16	Sukarno elected president of Indonesian Republic.
1949–56	Era of liberal, multiparty democracy.
1957–59	Two years of crisis in Indonesia.
1959 Aug 17	Guided democracy announced.
1962 Jan	Suharto promoted to major general.
1963	Konfrontasi policy toward Malaysia.
1965 Feb 25	Sukarno tells United States to "go to hell with your aid."
1965 Sep 30	Coup attempt fails but triggers massacre of suspected leftists and Chinese; military government comes to power.
1967 Feb 22	Sukarno turns over authority to Suharto.
1970 Jun 21	Sukarno dies at age sixty-nine.
1975 Dec 7	Indonesian armed forces invade newly independent East Timor.
1991 Nov 12	Indonesian troops fire on demonstrators in East Timor.
1993 Mar 10	Suharto unanimously reelected president for sixth five-year term.
1996 Dec	Nobel Peace Prize awarded to East Timor bishop Belo and East Timor foreign minister in exile Jose Ramos Horta.
1997	Economic crisis, Indonesian rupiah plummets, many companies and banks ruined.
1998 Mar 11	Suharto unanimously elected to his seventh consecutive five-year term.
1998 May 21	Suharto resigns; B. J. Habibie takes over.

The Indonesian Setting

GEOGRAPHY AND DEMOGRAPHY

donesia consists of about 13,000 islands (3,000 of them inhabited) strung
ong an arc 3,000 miles wide. It is strategically located between two conti-
:nts (Asia and Australia) and two oceans (the Pacific and the Indian). Indo-
:sia's history is conditioned by its control of the Strait of Malacca and the
nda Strait, the only two practical sea routes between East Asia and India,
rabia and Europe.

Indonesia contains over 200 active volcanoes, more than any other coun-
y. Their eruptions, calamitous in the short run, give Indonesia vast tracts
fertile volcanic soil well suited for growing rice, sugar, coffee, tea, tobacco,
ld rubber. The terrain includes high mountains and vast swamps. The cli-
ate is hot except at higher elevations, and rainfall depends on local topo-
aphical variations. Kalimantan (the Indonesian part of Borneo) and Irian
ya (the western half of New Guinea) are frontier zones where primeval jun-
es are being logged at the rate of 4,700 square miles per year, equal to 5.72
res per minute.

Indonesia is rich in timber, gold, tin, and oil and is the world's number
ie exporter of liquefied natural gas. Despite abundant natural resources,
donesia has a per capita gross national product of only $1,000, and that
zure was compiled before the great financial crash of 1998. Most Indone-
ans depend on rice farming and fishing. Indonesia has only a relatively
nall industrial sector, consisting primarily of small food-processing plants
ld textile mills. Many Indonesian factories are owned by local Chinese.

With 207 million people (1998 estimate), Indonesia is the fourth most
opulous country in the world after China, India, and the United States. In-
onesia's national motto, "Unity in Diversity," acknowledges its exuberant
riety of cultures. More than 250 distinct languages are spoken. Bahasa In-
onesia has taken root as a national language. The population of Indonesia
87 percent Muslim, 9 percent Christian, 2 percent Hindu, 1 percent Bud-
iist, and the remainder animists. Only about 2 percent of the population is

Chinese, but they dominate Indonesian commerce. Chinese who have assimilated are called Peranakans; those more recently arrived are called Totoks.

Java

The island of Java, 600 miles long by 100 miles wide, is the heartland of Indonesia—the cultural, political, educational, and economic center of gravity. It is densely populated, even by Asian standards. All other parts of Indonesia are collectively referred to as the "outer islands." From the perspective of a Sumatran or a Balinese, Indonesia sometimes appears to be a Javanese empire. The capital, Jakarta (formerly Batavia), is a sprawling metropolis of 10 million people with modern skyscrapers, extensive slums, and traffic gridlock.

Sumatra

Sumatra is the fourth largest island in the world but has a population less than one-tenth as dense as that of Java. Indonesia's first commercial oil was found in Sumatra and marketed by the Royal Dutch Shell Company. The extreme northwestern end of Sumatra constitutes a culturally distinct region, Aceh, where strict Muslims have historically resisted outside control.

Kalimantan

The southern two-thirds of Borneo is Indonesian territory and is called Kalimantan. Kalimantan has one of the world's largest remaining tracts of tropical rain forest, but it is being cut down for plywood. Loggers and settlers often start forest fires to clear brush. In 1997 a great pall of smoke from Kalimantan spread across Southeast Asia, causing respiratory problems for hundreds of thousands of people.

Bali

This gem of an island is a tropical paradise. Indian prime minister Jawaharlal Nehru said that having seen Bali, he now could die. The people of Bali refused to convert to Islam, and constitute the only major population of Hindus outside India. Thousands of tourists every year are attracted to Bali's lush beauty, majestic volcanoes, and elaborate temples. The government plans to construct a golf resort adjacent to one famous seaside temple, Tanah Lot.

Sulawesi (Celebes)

This unusually shaped island of four peninsulas has such rugged terrain that there are hardly any interior lines of communication. As a result, the seven major ethnic groups of Sulawesi developed in isolation from one another. The Dutch considered Sulawesi pacified by 1860 but had to suppress revolts in 1905 and 1911. Sulawesian provincial nationalists, encouraged by the United States, rebelled against the Indonesian government in 1957 but were defeated.

Timor

Timor was formerly divided into Dutch West Timor and Portuguese East Timor. The population of the east was largely Roman Catholic. After the collapse of the Portuguese overseas empire in 1975, the Indonesian Army invaded East Timor. The people did not submit easily—more than 100,000 are thought to have died from war and starvation.

Maluku (The Moluccas)

This group of approximately 1,000 small islands was the magnet that drew Portuguese, British, and Dutch adventurers to the East—the fabled Spice Islands, where cloves, nutmeg, and mace, worth more than their weight in gold on the European market, were grown.

Irian Jaya

This enormous territory contains one-fifth the land area of Indonesia but less than 1 percent of its population. Most of Irian Jaya is trackless jungle. A high central mountain range, the Maokes, contains tropical glaciers. Dutch sovereignty was purely nominal; Western explorers did not penetrate the interior until 1875, yet some tribes still live in isolation from the modern world. Indonesia annexed Irian Jaya in 1969. Although the government encourages migration from overpopulated Java, few Javanese are willing to move to an island they consider uncivilized.

HISTORY AND CULTURE

Classical Empires

The prehistory of Indonesia is poorly understood, but we know that wet-rice agriculture has been practiced on Java for thousands of years. By the early centuries of the Christian era, spices were exported to China and Arabia. There was no unified Indonesia until the twentieth century. Local kingdoms arose along the coast and were perpetually at war with one another. Buddhist missionaries reached Sumatra and Java as early as the second century. Hindu priests performed impressive court rituals that bolstered the power of local Indonesian kings. India exerted a profound influence on Indonesian culture, for people who learned to read Sanskrit could delve into Indian philosophy, politics, and statecraft, not to mention treatises on science, medicine, metallurgy, and architectural engineering.

Local potentates transformed themselves into *deva rajas,* or god-kings. Javanese and Sumatran kings now claimed to be incarnations of Hindu gods whose supernatural powers conferred political legitimacy. The political order was seen as a microcosm of the universe, wherein the royal throne was the axis of creation. It is easy to see why Indonesian rulers adopted Indian religion, but what about commoners? Their animism acquired a Buddhist and Hindu overlay but did not vanish. Even Islam, many centuries later, was for many Indonesians one more layer of belief that did not invalidate earlier gods.

The first important Indonesian empire, known as Srivijaya, flourished on Sumatra from the ninth to the twelfth centuries. Srivijaya adopted Tantric Mahayana Buddhism. The king was thought to be a bodhisattva (one who teaches others how to achieve enlightenment). Srivijaya, centered on Palembang, near the Strait of Malacca, and grew wealthy from the entrepôt trade between India, the Spice Islands, and China. In the ninth century Srivijaya controlled Sumatra, Java, and portions of Borneo and the Malay Peninsula.

Other powerful empires arose in Java, notably the Buddhist Sailendra kingdom, with its capital near the modern city of Yogyakarta. Proof of Sailendra glory endures in the massive ninth-century Borobudur monument constructed from 2 million cubic feet of stone. Unfortunately the coarse texture of its volcanic rock did not permit the Javanese to carve finely detailed bas reliefs as the Khmers did for their temples at Angkor. Eventually Buddhism, a democratic religion in the sense that all souls are believed to suffer from the same woes, undermined the hierarchical organization of the Srivijaya and Sailendra Empires.

The last great classical Javanese empire was Majapahit, centered near the modern city of Surabaya in east Java. Gajah Mada, a strong-willed Majapahit prime minister, extended Javanese rule over Bali, Sumatra, and Kalimantan in the mid-fourteenth century. Modern nationalists call Gajah Mada the first Indonesian patriot, but they are attributing to him political concepts unknown in his time.

The Coming of Islam

Eighty-seven percent of Indonesians are Sunni Muslims. Islam is an ethical religion based on the Holy Koran, which consists of the words of God (Allah) as spoken through the prophet Mohammed from A.D. 610 to 622. Islam preaches submission to the almighty and judgmental Allah. To become a Muslim, one must only profess that there is no God but Allah and that Mohammed is His Prophet. That phrase, spoken in Arabic, is so fundamental that parents whisper it into the ears of small children. Islamic law governs all aspects of life. Islamic principles recognize no separation between the secular and the sacred and therefore theoretically can be applied to family life, business operations, and politics.

Islam was brought to Indonesia by Muslim merchants from Arabia and southern India. The Buddhist and Hindu empires of Sumatra and Java had already collapsed of their own internal feuds. Arab merchants reached China at a very early date and reprovisioned themselves at the Strait of Malacca. By the late 1200s Islam had reached northern Sumatra. Within a century, people there were using the graceful, flowing Arabic script. In the 1400s Islam spread to ports on the north coast of Java and further east toward the Spice Islands.

Two main categories of Muslims exist in Indonesia. The Santri, who predominate in Aceh but who constitute only a third of the Muslims on Java, may be considered orthodox. They stress the five pillars of Islam: (1) confessing the faith; (2) praying five times every day; (3) fasting during the month of Ramadan; (4) making the *haj* (the pilgrimage to Mecca) at least once in a lifetime, if possible; and (5) paying the *zakah*, a religious tax, for relief of the poor and propagation of the faith. Most Indonesian Muslims, especially those from rural villages, consider themselves *abangan*—a loose mixture of Islam and all the preexisting layers of Javanese religion. *Abangans* observe Islamic rituals to mark passages in life, such as birth, marriage, illness, and death, but are unconcerned with doctrinal purity.

Animism (spirit worship) is an integral part of Indonesian culture. Life is full of risk, and ordinary mortals are helpless to control events except by propitiating spirits and ghosts who dwell in rice fields, homes, forests, waterfalls, volcanoes, bamboo groves, and caves. Animism is amoral. Men and women are rewarded or punished not for acts of kindness or spite but according to how skillfully they can appease evil spirits. Even today well-educated Indonesians may immerse themselves in mystical symbols. President Sukarno and his successor, President Suharto, consulted soothsayers before making policy decisions.

Society

In Indonesia, as elsewhere in Asia, society is based on an elaborate web of patron–client relationships between unequal (higher-ranking and lower-ranking) people for mutual benefit. Indonesian children quickly learn to behave deferentially toward their betters. Leaders' commands are usually followed unquestioningly because followers feel a moral obligation to obey. Such deference exacerbates the bureaucratic pathologies one finds in any country because it is unacceptable to question the decision of a superior. Indonesians may distrust someone who is overactive and respect a person who is *halus* (refined and passive). People who make demands, instigate trouble, or assert themselves are *kasar* (uncouth, emotional). Indonesians cultivate the art of *etak-etak* (telling others what they want to hear and suppressing one's own ego). Open conflict, at least within the group, is abhorred. Those who are lucky in life are expected to share their good fortune with others. For example, a man who builds a factory may feel obligated to put his entire town on the payroll, even if by doing so he flirts with bankruptcy.

In Indonesia women are customarily in a stronger position within the home than in the wider society. Often they control household finances. The constitution grants basic rights to women and men. President Sukarno recognized that women were still treated unfairly, but their position did not significantly improve under his leadership. Few women are found in top-level public positions. Megawati Sukarnoputri carried the hopes of anti-Suharto dissidents, but her political fame is the exception rather than the rule.

For Javanese, political power emanates from the ruler; it is intrinsic to him and does not depend on external factors as such as military and political resources.

> The man of power should have to exert himself as little as possible in any action. The slightest lifting of his finger should be able to set a chain of actions in motion. The man of real power does not have to raise his voice and does not have to give overt orders. The *halus*ness of his command is the external expression of his authority. The whole Javanese style of administration is therefore marked by the attempt, wherever possible, to give an impression of minimum effort.[1]

Three aspects of Indonesian culture, turned to political ends by Presidents Sukarno and Suharto, hark back to village customs: (1) *musyawarah* (long, open discussion before reaching any collective decision); (2) *mufakat* (a consensual decision, proclaimed by the village headman after all points of view have been heard); and (3) *gotong royong* (cooperating for the welfare of the entire group). Indonesia's presidents have cited the ideal of *gotong royong* as a unifying principle of the Indonesian state. President Sukarno formulated, and President Suharto reaffirmed, a doctrine known as the Panca Silz (Five Principles): nationalism, humanitarianism, democracy (based on traditional village procedures), social justice, and belief in one God. All political parties and organizations are required by law to adhere to these five principles.

COLONIAL HISTORY

Before European farmers learned to plant winter forage, they had to slaughter animals in the autumn. Spices from "the Indies," particularly nutmeg, mace, and cloves, were prized because they preserved meat. Once Vasco da Gama had rounded the Cape of Good Hope, West European merchants hoped to reap astronomical profits by cutting out Indian, Arab, and Venetian middlemen. Portuguese, Spaniards, Dutchmen, and Englishmen raced to stake a claim to the Spice Islands before their rivals. The Portuguese arrived first, capturing the strategically situated entrepôt of Malacca (on the west coast of present-day Malaysia) in 1511 and establishing an outpost on Timor. When Portuguese power declined, the Dutch moved in. Unlike the Roman Catholic Portuguese, who were interested in converting the natives as well as in monopolizing the spice trade, the Calvinist Dutch were motivated solely by commerce.

The Dutch East India Company (Vereenigde Oost-Indische Compagnie, or VOC) a private corporation of Dutch traders, was chartered in 1602. From its local headquarters at Batavia (modern-day Jakarta), a swampy and unhealthy site on the northwest coast of Java, the VOC controlled the spice trade, which remained lucrative until other European powers began to grow spices in their own tropical colonies. The VOC was granted an official monopoly on all Dutch trade east of Africa and gradually took on the trappings of a sovereign state. The VOC had modern weapons and a unified organization, advantages that enabled it to subjugate Javanese and Moluccan sultans one by one. The VOC played one king against another and took sides in disputes over royal succession. Javanese potentates were transformed into compliant vassals of the VOC, deriving a comfortable income by taxing the peasants on behalf of the company and themselves.

By the late eighteenth century, the VOC slipped into bankruptcy due to corruption, sloppy bookkeeping, and the growing cost of administering the territory it had acquired. The Netherlands government assumed direct control of the East Indies in 1799, only to be displaced by the British in 1811. When the Dutch returned in 1816 their two main concerns were to make the colony profitable again and to stamp out rebellions. For five years (1825–30) they fought a bitter war against guerrillas led by a Javanese prince named Diponegoro, who excited messianic expectations of deliverance from foreign rule and restoration of social harmony.

In 1830 Governor-General Johannes van den Bosch implemented a Cultivation System that required every village to grow an export crop such as sugar, coffee, or tea. The system was profitable indeed—the colonial government paid all its debts and used the surplus to build railroads in Holland—but it caused a growing polarization of wealth. Chinese middlemen moved into the gap that opened up between Javanese peasants and the *priyayi* class (Javanese aristocrats and officials).

In 1860 Eduard Douwes Dekker published a novel, *Max Havelaar*, which movingly exposed the abuses of the Cultivation System. For the first time Hollanders questioned the justice of their colonial policies. The Suez Canal opened in 1869. The next year the Netherlands adopted a policy of free trade that quickly transformed economy and society in the Indies. The Royal Dutch Petroleum Company was formed in 1893 and merged with the British Shell Company in 1907. The Dutch then moved to consolidate their empire by occupying all the outlying islands and remote enclaves that had heretofore remained independent. Brutal military expeditions were mounted against Aceh from 1870 to 1904. Resistance in Bali was finally extinguished in 1908.

In 1901 a newly elected liberal government in the Netherlands, wishing to make amends for the abuses of colonialism, adopted an "Ethical Policy" of improving health care and education in the Indies. It was a praiseworthy experiment but the actual results were meager.

Within Dutch colonial society a rift opened between newly arrived Europeans and older settlers who had married native women and considered the Indies their home. Part of the Eurasian community participated in the first tentative stirrings of Indonesian nationalism, marked by the founding of a reformist group called Budi Utomo (Noble Endeavor) in 1908, an Islamic party named Sarekat Islam in 1912, a Communist Party in 1920, and Sukarno's Indonesian Nationalist Union in 1927. The name "Indonesia," coined by a German geographer, so frightened the Dutch with its implication of a unitary state from Sumatra to the Moluccas, that they forbade its use. Indonesian nationalism was one part of the worldwide awakening of colonial peoples. Similar national movements were under way in China, Vietnam, the Philippines, India, Egypt, Turkey, and elsewhere.

Dutch authorities clamped down on dissent, arrested Sukarno, and kept the nationalists under surveillance throughout the 1930s, but their hold was broken by Japanese troops who occupied Indonesia in 1942. Indonesians were amazed and delighted to see white men sweeping the streets at the command of Japanese foremen. Given a taste of independence by the Japanese, Indonesians fought to prevent the Dutch from reconstituting their empire after 1945.

Before 1998 independent Indonesia had known only two presidents, the fiery demagogue Sukarno and the stolid administrator Suharto. The two could not have been more different in their paths to power, their relationship to their people, or their visions for Indonesia, but each man was, in his own way, both a patriot and a tyrant.

NOTE

1. Benedict Anderson, "The Idea of Power in Javanese Culture," in *Culture and Politics in Indonesia*, ed. Claire Holt (Ithaca, N.Y.: Cornell University Press, 1972), p. 13.

8

Sukarno: The Fiery Emancipator

> The simplest way to describe Sukarno is to say that he is a great lover.
> He loves his country, he loves his people, he loves women, he loves art,
> and, best of all, he loves himself.
>
> Sukarno, describing himself

Sukarno, known to his countrymen as the father of Indonesian independence, possessed the elusive personal magnetism we call charisma. His followers fell under his spell. Sukarno (who, like many Indonesians, used only
one name) was idolized by Indonesians, especially by Javanese peasants.
Some people thought he was omniscient, even supernatural, and he encouraged them in that belief.

Charismatic leaders such as Sukarno tend to appear when a nation is in
crisis. In 1901, when he was born, traditional society was disintegrating in
Java, Sumatra, and the thousands of other islands that made up the Netherlands East Indies because of political and economic changes brought about
by Dutch colonialism. There was no such country as "Indonesia." By 1970,
when Sukarno died, the Indonesian people were poor but proud. Those were
his twin legacies to his country: poverty and pride.

Sukarno drew inspiration from other Indonesian nationalists, particularly
Omar Said Tjokroaminoto (1882–1934) and Soetomo (1888–1938), but only
Sukarno could speak to the peasants in the folksy way they understood.[1] He
projected a vision of a glorious future and led his people toward it. Sukarno
forged a new nation from an archipelago where people spoke hundreds of
different languages. When life in independent Indonesia turned out to be less
than glorious, he mesmerized the masses with words. He designed new
mechanisms for resolving conflicts and governing a nation and reformulated
traditional values to make them relevant to twentieth-century Indonesians.
By creating a unitary Indonesian state and holding it together, Sukarno
earned his place in history.

Sukarno was complicated and unpredictable, a man of extremes. He has

Sukarno, no date

Sukarno, 1965

been described as flamboyant, brilliant, ebullient, dynamic, reckless, profligate, irrational, undisciplined, heroic, demagogic, and tendentious—and all those adjectives fit him.[2] Such a personality may inspire revolutionaries, but later the nation may require someone quite different, a stolid pragmatist such as General Suharto.

FAMILY AND BACKGROUND

Sukarno was born in Surabaya, a busy port city on the northeast coast of Java, on June 6, 1901. He was the first son of a minor Javanese aristocrat, Raden Sukemi, and his Balinese commoner wife, Ida Njoman Rai. Sukarno has told many colorful stories about his early life. He was a master showman who crafted a public persona to captivate the masses.

Sukarno's name at birth may have been Kusno Sosro Sukarno, but there are no records to confirm this. If true, the first two names were dropped while he was still a child, for he never used a family name. All his life he signed his name "Soekarno," using the Dutch spelling, saying it was too late to change, but insisting that the proper spelling should be "Sukarno" according to revised rules for transliteration. *Su* means "good," and Karna was a hero of the *Mahabharata*, an ancient Hindu epic known to every Javanese; therefore, *Sukarno* means "the best hero."

Sukarno claimed that his mother was descended from Javanese royalty, but this is widely discounted. He liked to portray his birth as the fulfillment of a prophecy that a boy named Sukarno would be born into a sultan's family and would liberate Indonesia from the Dutch. Sukarno claimed to be descended from the Sultan of Kediri. Sometimes he brazenly reversed this story and claimed humble origins. When he wanted to identify with peasants, he would tell them he had been born so poor that he had no shoes to wear and that his family "could barely eat rice once a day."[3]

Sukarno savored these contradictions, for they added to the aura of mystery that was an essential component of his image. In the early years of the twentieth century, rumors spread among Javanese that a child of Mohammed would fall from heaven to deliver them from the Dutch. Sukarno claims his mother told him, when he was two years old, the following prediction: "Son, you are looking at the sunrise. And you, my son, will be a man of glory, a great leader of his people, because your mother gave birth to you at dawn. We Javanese believe that one born at the moment of sunrise is predestined. Never, never forget you are a child of the dawn."[4] Undoubtedly, she never said any such thing—just another one of his fantasies.

Sukarno's childhood was pleasant. He always spoke warmly of his parents and was conspicuously respectful to his mother when she was an old woman and he was president of Indonesia. To grow up in Java is to be immersed in

a complex culture where legends from the *Mahabharata* and its companion
epic, the *Ramayana,* are told and retold through the theatrical medium of
the *wayang kulit,* a shadow play in which a puppet master projects the pro-
files of characters from behind a screen or sheet, accompanied by dramatic
thumping and tingling from the drums, xylophones, and flutes of a gamelan
orchestra. Sukarno recalls being spellbound as a boy by *wayang kulit* tales
of heroic warriors struggling to cast out evil invaders. He also claimed to
have supernatural healing powers: "When anyone was sick in the village or
had a running sore, Grandmother would summon me and with my tongue I
licked the affected area of the person. Strangely enough, they were healed."[5]

As a schoolboy Sukarno showed talent in academics and athletics. He performed *wayang* shows and played musical instruments. He lived with his
paternal grandparents for much of his childhood. This is not unusual in Indonesia, and he was usually indulged, if not spoiled. For example, he often
crawled into the bed of a servant woman named Sarinah, to be hugged and
comforted by her. It was a type of maternal, not sexual, bond. Sukarno later
idealized Sarinah as a symbol of kind, virtuous Indonesian womanhood. He
said Sarinah was "the single greatest influence" in his life.[6]

Schools were administered by the Dutch and reserved for privileged
Dutch and Eurasian children. Only a few Indonesians were admitted, most
of them children of the *priyayi* class of Javanese aristocrats and civil servants.
At the age of thirteen, Sukarno entered the Europeesche Lagere School at
Mojokerto where he became fluent in the Dutch language. After two years
he graduated to a Dutch-language high school where "there were three hundred European boys and only twenty Indonesians. The fist fights with
Dutch boys and the teasing he received were unbearable cruelties for the hy-
persensitive Sukarno. Apparently he tried to get even by attempting to make
love to Dutch girls."[7]

THE EMERGENCE OF INDONESIAN NATIONALISM

During Sukarno's adolescence a nationalist movement was blossoming in the
Netherlands East Indies. Political scientist Donald Seekins cites six separate
historical events and processes that inspired the Indonesians:[8]

1. Indonesian students and pilgrims returning from the Middle East
   brought back ideas for modernizing and reforming Islam.
2. The Indian National Congress, founded as a moderate reformist club
   in 1885, grew steadily more radical, asking for home rule in 1906, for
   dominion status in 1916, and for complete independence in 1929.
3. Filipinos, inspired by the martyrdom of Jose Rizal, waged Asia's first

nationalist revolution (against Spain, 1896–98) and fought a doomed guerrilla war (against the United States, 1898–1901).

4. Japan built an industrial base with surprising speed and decisively defeated czarist Russia in war (1904–05), proving that modernization was not the same as westernization.

5. A military officer named Kemal Ataturk transformed the Ottoman Empire, the "sick man of Europe," into the Republic of Turkey.

6. In Russia radicals seized power in 1917, claiming to have found a scientifically correct path to a beautiful future.

In 1908 the first Indonesian protonationalist association, Budi Utomo (Noble Endeavor) was organized. Its *priyayi* members aspired to improved status within the Dutch system. They had not yet conceived of "Indonesia" but spoke instead of "Greater Java," a term that sounded ominous to people from the outer islands. The more assertive Indische Partij was founded in 1912; but as its membership was largely Eurasian, it, too, had limited appeal. The same year Sarekat Islam (the Islamic Association) was founded by Tjokroaminoto. The talented and wealthy Tjokroaminoto was a newspaper editor, businessman, and teacher. His party recruited aggressively among both *santri* (observant) and *abangan* (nondogmatic) Muslims and claimed 360,000 members within two years. Tjokroaminoto, anticipating a tactic Sukarno later employed, played on Javanese millennialism by implying that he was the long-awaited *ratu adil* (just king) come to expel foreigners and usher in a golden age.

SUKARNO DEFINES INDONESIAN NATIONALISM

Sukarno's father was a friend of Tjokroaminoto. In 1916 he sent the promising teenager to board with the "uncrowned king of Java" and to attend the prestigious Dutch secondary school Hoogere Burger School in Surabaya. Tjokroaminoto became Sukarno's foster parent, sponsor, and guru. The Tjokroaminoto home served as a salon where intellectuals discussed politics. Sukarno soon knew, and was known by, all the prominent older nationalists. Taking advantage of a well-stocked library at the Surabaya branch of the Theosophical Society, he plunged into books of political philosophy. He could quote Thomas Jefferson and Karl Marx for the rest of his life. In his vainglorious autobiography, Sukarno claimed also to have read Voltaire, Rousseau, Lincoln, Hegel, Kant, Engels, Lenin, Mazzini, and Garibaldi.

When Sukarno was nineteen he and Tjokroaminoto's daughter Sitti Utari were wed in an arranged marriage. This must have been unsatisfactory to Sukarno for he embarked on a passionate love affair with his landlady, a married woman ten years older than he, named Inggit Garnisih. Sukarno divorced Sitti, Inggit divorced her husband, and the two lovers were married in 1923. Tjokroaminoto accepted his daughter's divorce without rancor, but his relationship with Sukarno was never the same. Sukarno's second marriage lasted seventeen years but produced no children.

Sukarno graduated from high school in 1921 and entered a technical college at Bandung. He studied architecture but was far more interested in politics. He became the student leader of the Algemeene Studieclub (General Study Club) at Bandung. Certain aspects of Marxism attracted him, particularly its explanation of imperialism, but he always believed in the importance of national struggle, not class struggle, and therefore never accepted Marxism nor joined the Partai Komunis Indonesia (PKI).

When Sukarno received his degree in 1926, he easily could have stepped into a mid-level position in the colonial administration, but he plunged into politics instead. Already he had acquired the respectful and affectionate nickname "Bung" (elder brother) and for the rest of his life was Bung Karno to his countrymen. Tjokroaminoto hoped his protégé would take over the leadership of Sarekat Islam, but Sukarno was heading down a middle path between Islam and Marxism: pure nationalism, with its actual content left vague.

Many Asian nationalist leaders, including Ho Chi Minh, Deng Xiaoping, and Mohandas Gandhi, went to Europe for higher education. London, Paris, and Amsterdam were natural incubators for nationalism, because young men and women from the colonies could see clearly that the whites, seemingly omnipotent in "the East," were ordinary people with human foibles. From the students' point of view, ethnic differences between themselves (for example, between Javanese and Sundanese) shrank beside the unbridgeable gap separating all of them from the Dutch. Many Dutch-educated Indonesians entered the nationalist movement when they returned home, but their advanced learning and high status placed a barrier between themselves and Indonesian peasants. Not so for Sukarno, who did not set foot outside the Indies until middle age.

In contrast to the situation in Vietnam and China, where people had no doubts about their identity, nationalists in the Netherlands East Indies had not only to rally people to noncooperation, then resistance, but also had to create an entirely new national identity. It could not be based on language, religion, or class. A nation was "a soul, a fundamental outlook" arising from a common history and from "a desire, and urge to live as one."[9] Sukarno used his oratorical skill to excite audiences, drawing for them a picture of a new, free republic, an Indonesia Raya (Greater Indonesia), that would embrace the entire Malay race except for Filipinos. That grand vision was the root of his later Konfrontasi (Confrontation) policy toward Malaysia, which he regarded as an illegitimate child of British imperialism in Southeast Asia. Sukarno's speeches may have been short on specifics, but he knew how to reduce complex situations to catchy slogans that unschooled peasants could easily remember.

Sukarno coined a term that signified Indonesian populism. He called it "Marhaenism" and claimed that it stemmed from an encounter with a peasant named Marhaen who worked a small plot of land that yielded too little to feed and clothe a family. Marhaen was almost certainly apocryphal, but that did not stop Sukarno from recalling the following conversation.[10]

> Who is the owner of this lot on which you now are working?
> Why, I am, sir.
> How about your shovel? Is it yours?
> Yes, sir.
> Is it sufficient for your needs?
> How could a plot so small be sufficient for a wife and four children?
> Do you ever sell your labor?
> No, sir. I must work very hard, but my labors are all for myself.

The last line was Sukarno's way of rejecting Marxism. Almost all Indonesians were Marhaenists: "A Marhaenist is a person with small means; a little man with little ownership, little tools, sufficient to himself. Our tens of millions of impoverished souls work for no person and no person works for them. There is no exploitation of one man by another." He went on to add, illogically, "Marhaenism is Indonesian Socialism in operation."[11] Sukarno told the story of Marhaen over and over. His fame spread.

On June 4, 1927, Sukarno and other nationalists founded the Indonesian Nationalist Union, which evolved into the Partai Nasional Indonesia (PNI), the springboard for Bung Karno's rise to power and the organizational vehicle for national independence. Sukarno wanted to create a mass movement and favored a policy of noncooperation. To refuse to obey the foreign authorities was to cross a Rubicon; there was no going back. The logical end was *merdeka* (freedom), but not all Indonesian nationalists were ready.

Mohammad Hatta (1902–80) and Sutan Syahrir (1909–66) were two prominent nationalists who spent much of their careers trying to restrain Sukarno's wilder impulses. However, Sukarno was less radical than the Comintern agent Tan Malaka (1897–1949) and other Indonesian communists. Tan Malaka, probably acting on orders from Stalin, tried to squelch PKI plans for armed insurrections on Java and Sumatra in 1926 and 1927. The time was not ripe, and the rebellions were easily suppressed.

The colonial government, now alert to signs of mutiny, arrested Sukarno and other nationalists in December 1929. They made the mistake of staging a public trial in Bandung District Court and allowing Sukarno to defend himself. He delivered a passionate two-day speech entitled "Indonesia Accuses." His arrest and trial, he said, were actions directed against the whole

Indonesian people. He argued that the PNI worked not for the overthrow of law and order but for the overthrow of the lawlessness of colonialism, capitalism, and imperialism. Sukarno was sent to prison. It was a shattering experience for him, not least because it entailed celibacy:

> I am a sybarite. I am a man who gratifies his senses. I enjoy fine clothes, exciting foods, love-making, and I could not take the isolation, rigidity, filth, the million little humiliations of the lowest form of prison life. . . . The last week of 1930 a fat, dirty, ugly old woman who was way over 60 waddled into the jail on her errand of mercy. She was delivering Christmas bread. I knew I was in serious shape when that pig of a fat lady looked gorgeous to me.[12]

The authorities released Sukarno on December 31, 1931. Huge crowds greeted him as he made his way home. Asked if he was beginning a new life, he responded, "A leader does not change because of a sentence. I came into prison to fight for freedom. I leave it the same way."[13]

Sukarno continued to urge noncooperation with the Dutch authorities while more moderate nationalists advocated working with them for gradual progress toward self-rule. Sukarno said that the Dutch did not fear "phrases" or "intellectualizing" but understood only the language of power: "Give me one thousand old men, and with them I shall have confidence to move Mt. Meru. But give me ten youths who are fired with zeal and with love for our native land, and with them I shall shake the earth."[14]

The PNI had broken into factions and dissolved itself while Sukarno was in prison. Picking up where he had left off, Sukarno joined the more radical contingent, Partai Indonesia (Partindo), quickly became its leader, and attracted thousands of members. In March 1933 he wrote an essay entitled "Achieving Independent Indonesia." On August 1 he was re-arrested, but this time there was no trial at all. Sukarno seemed to lose his nerve—he recanted his opinions, begged to be released, and promised to abstain from future political activity. His request for a pardon was denied, and he was sent into exile, first to a remote island and then to Bengkulu, Sumatra, where conditions were less arduous. He was separated from other nationalists but was allowed to have his wife live with him. He spent the rest of the decade in internal exile. When he was sent to the island of Flores, he took his wife and his mother-in-law, too. Oddly, the Dutch treated the moderate nationalists Hatta and Syahrir more severely, sending them to the notorious Boven Digul prison camp in the malarial jungles of West New Guinea. Sukarno took advantage of his ten-year internal exile to study Islam and to read world literature in Dutch, German, French, English, and Indonesian. He wrote plays and organized shows. But he suffered from malaria and was depressed much of the time. The Indonesian nationalist movement went dormant, and the Dutch spoke of enjoying another 300 years of colonial rule in the East Indies.

Sukarno's personal life was in turmoil. He fell in love with a much younger woman named Fatmawati and wanted to take her as a second wife, as Muslim law allowed, but Inggit would not hear of it. He wanted children, yet it was clear that Inggit could not conceive. Sukarno carried on an affair with Fatmawati for years, finally marrying her in June 1943 after divorcing Inggit.

WORLD WAR II IN INDONESIA

In the late 1930s many Javanese were excited by millennial predictions of a *ratu adil*. They expected to see the fulfillment of a prophecy popularly attributed to an eleventh-century Javanese king named Djojobojo who predicted that Java would be ruled by white foreigners who, in turn, would be evicted by yellow-skinned foreigners, and that Java would finally be free.

Adolf Hitler invaded the Netherlands in May 1940. Because the Dutch were now answerable to the Germans—who were allied with the Japanese—Tokyo demanded that the government of Netherlands East Indies supply it with the rubber and oil so desperately needed for the Japanese war machine. But Dutch colonial authorities instead froze Japanese assets and embargoed oil and rubber exports to Japan. A Japanese invasion fleet appeared off the coast of Java in February 1942. The Netherlands East Indies government surrendered on March 9, and Japanese troops occupied the islands for the remainder of the war.

Indonesians were not sorry to see Dutchmen interned and were particularly impressed to observe Europeans performing manual labor. Affairs of government were now conducted in the Japanese language or in Malay, not Dutch. The Japanese called their conquered territories a "Greater East Asia Co-Prosperity Sphere" and cast themselves in the role of the "light of Asia." While that had a certain appeal, the Japanese cult of emperor worship deeply offended Muslims.

Indonesia was Japan's richest prize in Southeast Asia. In addition to strategic resources (tin, oil, bauxite, and rubber), the islands supplied hundreds of thousands of *romushas* (manual laborers) who were used on construction projects in Burma and elsewhere.

The Japanese, in a bid for popular support, brought Sukarno back from exile and returned him to center stage. He and Mohammad Hatta agreed to cooperate with the conquerors, hoping to gain real independence (and perhaps political power for themselves) after the war. Sukarno tried to manipulate the Japanese, but they were more successful at manipulating him. He propagandized for their cause and recruited *romushas* to work on the outer islands and abroad. Sutan Syahrir, who later founded the Partai Sosialis Indonesia (PSI), led anti-Japanese partisans while Sukarno led the pro-Japanese

Indonesian puppet government. Hatta became an intermediary between Sukarno and Syahrir.

The Dutch, and some Indonesians, considered Sukarno an opportunist and a traitor, particularly when thousands of *romushas* working on the Burma Road perished from overwork, malnutrition, and beatings. Of an estimated total of 200,000 to 500,000 *romushas*, only 70,000 are known to have survived.[15] In his autobiography, Sukarno admitted, "In fact, it was I, Sukarno, who sent them to work. Yes, it was I. I shipped them to their deaths. Yes, yes, yes, yes, I am the one."[16] Sukarno's defense was that resistance to the Japanese was futile, but that by working with the Imperial Army, Indonesian nationalists could conserve their strength for the moment when Japan must surrender. Speaking in his usual direct way, he justified his role: "If I must sacrifice thousands to save millions, I will. We are in a struggle for survival. As leader of this county I cannot afford the luxury of sensitivity."[17]

When the tide of war turned, the Japanese prepared to grant Indonesia formal independence, while retaining ultimate power for themselves. In March 1943 they named Sukarno leader of the Pusat Tenaga Rakyat (Center of People's Power). Although little more than a propaganda organization, it enabled Sukarno for the first time in his life to deliver frequent radio speeches, thereby becoming much better known to his "Marhaens" throughout the islands. In October 1943 Sukarno helped the Japanese organize a volunteer defense force of sixty-five battalions of Indonesians called Pembela Tanah Air (Defenders of the Fatherland, or Peta for short) to resist a possible Allied invasion. The Allies bypassed most of Indonesia, but Sukarno's strategy paid off because the 50,000 Peta soldiers received training in weapons and tactics.

In March 1945 the Japanese allowed Sukarno to form an "Investigatory Body for Preparatory Work for Indonesian Independence." The committee met in May, adopted a national anthem, "Indonesia Raya," and declared that the new country should include all of the former Netherlands East Indies, plus West New Guinea, Portuguese Timor, Malaya, and British North Borneo. Sukarno argued for a unitary state while the more cautious Hatta thought a federal system better suited to Indonesian conditions. On June 1, 1945, Sukarno announced the Panca Silz, the Five Principles, which he said should become the basic ideology of the new nation: nationalism, humanitarianism, democracy, social justice, and belief in one God. The Pantja Sila was vague enough to allow widely varying interpretation under different circumstances.

A youthful wing of the nationalist movement known as the *pemudas* (daring youths) distrusted Sukarno. In July 1945 a youth leader named Chaerul Saleh kidnapped Sukarno to force him to declare Indonesian independence before the war ended and the Dutch came back. Sukarno was deeply embarrassed by this incident. He called the *pemudas* shortsighted and impetuous.

"We cannot force our will at this instant without being massacred by the Japanese."[18] Once again we see that for all his fire-breathing rhetoric, Sukarno was essentially a cautious man who preferred compromise to combat.

THE INDONESIAN REVOLUTION (1945–49)

The Japanese had placed Indonesians in some administrative posts previously held by Dutch, so when the war ended with Japan's surrender on August 15, 1945, a rudimentary Indonesian government was already in place. By the terms of surrender the Japanese were supposed to freeze the political status quo, so Sukarno and Hatta, on their own, declared independence on August 17. Sukarno scribbled these terse words on a piece of paper and read them to a small group assembled outside his house: "We the people of Indonesia hereby declare the independence of Indonesia. Matters concerning the transfer of power, etc., will be carried out in a conscientious manner and as speedily as possible." After Sukarno and Hatta signed the declaration, a homemade red and white flag, sewn by Sukarno's wife Fatmawati, was raised. The small group sang the new national anthem, "Indonesia Raya." August 17 was Indonesia's Independence Day. On August 18 the nationalists promulgated a constitution consisting of thirty-seven ambiguously worded articles. Sukarno became president of Indonesia and Hatta became vice president.

The Dutch intended to recover their empire and hoped to find natives willing to work with them. The first Allied force to reach Java consisted of British troops and their fiercely loyal Gurkha (Nepalese) battalions. The new Indonesian Army (Peta troops under nationalist leadership) fired on them, the first shots of a bitter four-year war. The British and the Americans "had no consistent policy concerning Indonesia's future apart from the vague hope that the republicans and the Dutch could be induced to negotiate peacefully."[19]

Sukarno desperately sought a compromise. He urged the nationalists to lay down their arms and invited the Allies to investigate the "extremists" at Surabaya. Although he promised that his republic would not seize foreigners' property, more shooting broke out, and it escalated into the Battle of Surabaya (November 1945). There were now two rival governments claiming to control the islands: Sukarno's Republic of Indonesia and the reconstituted Netherlands East Indies, the latter controlling most of the military and financial resources and territory outside Java and Sumatra. Sukarno's government was in constant jeopardy and had no real organization or even an official government building. His greatest asset was his magnificent oratory.

Sukarno moved his government to Yogyakarta in south central Java, the stronghold of republican sentiment. Indonesian cabinet members were quarreling, a symptom of the factionalism that permeated Sukarno's Indonesia. The issue in 1946 was whether to negotiate with the Dutch or fight on. Syahrir opened secret negotiations with Dutch governor-general Van Mook "on the basis of de facto Republican sovereignty in Java, Madura, and Sumatra alone, a recognition of Dutch sovereignty elsewhere, and a cooperative Dutch-Republican effort to create a federal Indonesia within a Dutch-Indonesian union."[20] More intractable nationalists learned of Syahrir's "betrayal" in June and abducted him. Sukarno sided with Syahrir and declared martial law, but the hard-liners held the prime minister captive until Sukarno, using a skill he had by now honed to perfection, went on the radio and pleaded for unity. Syahrir was released that night.

Negotiations continued, culminating in the Linggajati Agreement of November 12, 1946, according to which the Netherlands recognized an Indonesian republic with sovereignty over Java, Sumatra, and Madura but that the republic was to be subsumed into a "United States of Indonesia" that would also include autonomous states of Borneo and the Great East (Bali, Celebes, Dutch New Guinea, Moluccas, and Lesser Sundas). It was far short of the Indonesia Raya of Sukarno's dreams, but he tried to convince his people to settle for this nominal sovereignty. This he was unable to do. Fighting resumed in 1947 with a Dutch attack on Mojokerto in March and a police action (actually the resumption of full-scale warfare) in July. Jakarta was captured after two weeks of fighting. The Indonesians reverted to tactics of guerrilla war, burning their own cities and retreating to the mountains.

Sukarno was forced in September 1948 to suppress a communist uprising at Madiun in eastern Java. This was certainly not choreographed from the Kremlin, and probably not even planned in advance by the PKI. Rather, it grew out of local clashes between the two incompatible wings of Sukarno's nationalist movement: communists and Muslims. Sukarno was emphatically not a communist (although he considered himself a socialist), and in 1948 he leaned to the right. Sukarno rallied popular opinion against the PKI, and the Madiun uprising was quickly suppressed. A pogrom against the communists followed, in which Tan Malaka was captured and shot. Despite the PKI's "treachery," Sukarno continued to regard the communists as an authentic element in the Indonesian revolution. Furthermore, Sukarno prided himself on his ability to reconcile all sides, to make real differences disappear as if by magic. The PKI leader, Dipa Nusantara Aidit, later became an important player in Indonesian politics.

The Dutch were defeated by local guerrilla fighters who controlled the hinterlands of Java and the outer islands and by strong diplomatic and economic pressure from the United States. The Berlin blockade, the communist coup in Czechoslovakia, the impending victory of the communist Mao Zedong in China—combined with revelations of Soviet spying in the United States—induced a new mind-set in the Truman administration. Vietnam and

Indonesia were no longer seen as peripheral to U.S. interests but as integral to global security, as "dominoes." Seeing Asian nationalism as an incoming tide, Washington scrambled to take the side of Asian nationalists against France and the Netherlands. In Vietnam it was too late, for the communists had already appropriated Vietnamese nationalism for themselves. But in Indonesia, Sukarno seemed to be the man to back.

A second Dutch police action (so called to imply that the conflict was an internal affair of the Netherlands East Indies) in December 1948 resulted in Sukarno's capture. A storm of protest arose in the United Nations (UN). Sukarno was released in July 1949 and flown under UN auspices to Yogyakarta, where 300,000 cheering citizens hailed him. A cease-fire was called in August, and negotiations at the Hague produced a final settlement. Queen Juliana transferred full sovereignty to the Federal Republic of Indonesia (also known as the Republic of the United States of Indonesia) on December 27, 1949. The next day Sukarno told a wildly cheering crowd, "Thank God we are free." The cumbersome federal system was consolidated into the unitary Republic of Indonesia on August 15, 1950.

INDEPENDENCE AND CONSTITUTIONAL DEMOCRACY (1950–57)

Under the provisional constitution adopted at independence, the president (Sukarno) had rather little power, and the government was highly factionalized. Sukarno broke with the brilliant and forceful Syahrir over perceived personal slights. Cabinets fell six times between 1950 and 1957. Crises were frequent; once the entire cabinet resigned en masse to protest Sukarno's acceptance of U.S. aid. There were military mutinies and separatist uprisings. In 1952 the people of Jakarta, frustrated by government instability and inefficiency, demonstrated against Parliament. Ominously, army officers spoke out in support of the demonstrators and demanded more power. Facing an agitated mob at his palace gate, Sukarno was able to dampen the volatile situation:

He emerged coolly from the palace. . . . He talked to the demonstrators, ignoring the threat of the guns; he returned to the palace steps to speak to the crowd as a whole. He did so as a father to wayward children. He understood their dissatisfaction with things as they were, he said, and he assured them that elections would be held as soon as possible. But he insisted that he had no desire to be a dictator and he pointed out that to dissolve parliament would be a step in that direction. He then ordered them to disperse and without any question they obeyed him.[21]

Sukarno resented the restrictions placed on him by the 1950 constitution. He was thus forced to maintain a delicate balance between the army officers, strong Muslims, and the communists. The Muslims correctly suspected that Sukarno's religious convictions were only lightly held, while the leftists believed he had betrayed the revolution. Moderates such as social democrats Hatta and Syahrir sometimes felt they had nowhere to stand. Political parties multiplied. The strongest were the PNI, Sukarno's own party; the PKI, a highly disciplined Communist party; the Masyumi, a modernizing Muslim party; and Nahdatul Ulama, a strictly conservative Muslim party.

SUKARNO'S PERSONAL LIFE

Women

Although Sukarno's wife Fatmawati gave birth to two boys and two girls, their marriage ended when Sukarno fell in love with Hartini, the sophisticated and beautiful wife of an oil company executive. He began the affair as a second marriage but soon decided his love for Hartini was so overwhelming that he wanted her as his sole wife. He married Hartini in 1955, leaving Fatmawati in control of his summer palace at Bogor. A few years later, Sukarno met Ratna Dewi, a Japanese bar-girl, and later he met Hariati and then Yurike Sanger. It is not clear how many of these women he actually married. Most biographers say he married all but Yurike. It appears, however, that none of the marriages was formally recognized by the Muslim community.

Sukarno pretended not to understand why anyone should object to his womanizing. "The smile of a beautiful girl is God's reflection," he said. "Why is it a sin to take her?" But he played it up, deliberately, knowing that in Javanese culture sexual potency was thought to be a sign of *sekti*, or supernatural power. "People say Sukarno likes to look out of the corner of his eye at beautiful women," he wrote in his autobiography, "Why do they say that? It is not true. Sukarno likes to look out of his *whole* eye at beautiful women."[22] Another way Sukarno asserted his sexuality was by bedding Western women.

Personal Characteristics

Sukarno was a supreme egotist. The following sentence from his autobiography is typical: "I thank the Almighty that I was born with sentiment and artistry. How else could I have become The Great Leader of the Revolution, as my 105 million people call me?"[23] Sukarno always appeared fit and trim, yet he suffered from health problems, including recurring malarial fevers. He wore himself down, but insomnia prevented rest. He once claimed not to have slept in six years. He was highly intelligent and was gifted with a prodigious memory for faces and names of people he had seen years earlier. In personal encounters, he could exert "a kind of hypnotic power," as a political opponent recalled: "I went in to tell Sukarno how angry I was with what he had done. The moment I sat in front of him and looked into his eyes, something happened and what I wanted to say just disappeared. My anger also disappeared. It was well over an hour after I left his presence that I could recall what I had wanted to say to him."[24]

CHARISMATIC SPEAKER

More than any other Southeast Asian leader, Sukarno had star appeal. Indonesians compared him to Clark Gable. His personal appearance was immaculate. He liked to wear a neatly pressed uniform, a black felt Muslim hat, and sunglasses. He often carried a black baton, which some Indonesians interpreted as a symbol of sacred power. His expressive face most often showed a broad smile, but it also could be made to appear positively demonic when he launched into public tirades against neocolonialists.

Sukarno was one of the century's great orators. Even as a young man, he knew how to build suspense: "He stands for a minute, silently surveying those present. All is deadly quiet, so that one could hear a pin drop. Then as if he had finished drawing together his creative powers he opens quietly but with his voice gradually becoming more resounding."[25] His sentences were rhythmic as he moved from whispers to thunderous bellowing. He would pause, then repeat ideas over again in slightly different words. His audiences swayed to the sound of his voice and sometimes even fell into a trance.

Sukarno drew heavily on Javanese mythology. Sometimes he would identify himself with sacred and legendary figures such as Bima, a hero of the *Mahabharata*. The common people imagined Sukarno to embody Bima's bravery and determination. For the Balinese, Sukarno liked to cast himself as a descendant of Vishnu, capable of bringing rain. "The last time I flew to Bali they had been suffering from a dry spell. Just after I arrived, the heavens opened."[26] Sukarno's biographer John Legge saw "many signs that [Sukarno] did tend to think of events of the day as illustrating *wayang* themes, with himself in a *ksatria* (warrior) role" and that he interpreted the Indonesian nationalist struggle in terms of the *Mahabharata*.

Sukarno was fiercely anticapitalist because he accepted Lenin's explanation that capitalism caused imperialism, but he hated being called a communist by anyone, especially by the U.S. press. He was a modernist Muslim in the tradition of Kemal Ataturk, whom he greatly admired. Sukarno's patriotism was sincere and deep. One reason he loved to travel abroad was "to educate the foreigners and give them their first glimpse of this beloved green land of mine which winds itself around the equator like a girdle of emeralds.''[27]

Sukarno's ideology is difficult to pin down, for he believed he could weave together and harmonize antithetical ideas:

> My politics do not correspond to anyone else's. But, then neither does my background correspond to anyone else's. My grandfather inculcated in me Javanism and mysticism. From father came Theosophy and Islamism. From mother, Hinduism and Buddhism. Sarinah gave me humanism. From Tjokro came Socialism. From his friends Nationalism. To that I added gleanings of Karl Marxism and Thomas Jeffersonism. I learned economics from Sun Yat-sen, benevolence from Gandhi. I was able to synthesize modern scientific schooling and ancient animistic culture.[28]

Sukarno was not supported unreservedly by any of the three most important political groupings in Indonesia: the army, the Muslims, or the communists. Even in his own administration, technocrats concerned with efficiency and economic development grew depressed at Sukarno's chronic flightiness and ill-concealed boredom whenever the subject of finances came up. But the peasants were enthusiastic, and they were numerous indeed. In the 1955 elections, Sukarno's PNI received 22 percent of the vote, the Masyumi 20 percent, Nahdatul Ulama 18 percent, and the PKI 16 percent.

No one could challenge Sukarno's personal popularity, but he was incapable of methodical planning and preferred to delegate most administrative tasks. He generated around himself an atmosphere of vagueness and mysticism. By the mid-1950s, political deterioration was evident. Sukarno tried to give his people a sense of pride by swaggering across the world stage. He hosted an Asia–Africa conference at Bandung in 1955 and billed it as a kind of forum of the world's neutralists. The conference attracted famous Third World leaders including Zhou Enlai, Jawaharlal Nehru, Norodom Sihanouk, and Gamal Abdel Nasser. Sukarno delivered passionate speeches castigating imperialists and rhapsodizing about hurricanes of national awakening sweeping the Third World.

Sukarno took personal pleasure in telling the rich countries to "go to hell with their aid" and repudiated $1 billion in debt owed to the Netherlands. In March 1956 U.S. secretary of state John Foster Dulles was heckled by communists at the Jakarta airport. In 1957 Sukarno expelled 46,000 Dutch nationals. National security planners in Washington began to fret about a possible Jakarta–Phnom Penh–Peking–Pyongyang axis, and drew up contingency plans to destabilize Indonesia. Regional revolts flared in Sumatra, Borneo, and Sulawesi in 1956 and 1957. The Eisenhower administration recognized regional separatism as Sukarno's Achilles' heel.

GUIDED DEMOCRACY (1957–66)

The machinery of liberal democracy—political parties, elections, and parliamentary government—failed to provide political stability. Sukarno concluded that Western "50 percent-plus-one-democracy" simply did not suit Indonesia. In 1957 he proclaimed "Guided Democracy," allegedly based on indigenous concepts. Political parties were banned. Knowing that Indonesians prized harmony, Sukarno tried to govern through *mufakat* (consensus) and *musyawarah* (lengthy consultations). He urged people to remember the village tradition of *gotong-royong* (mutual self-help). His vision of harmonious village life was not entirely realistic. Because clashing interests are the essence of political life everywhere, Sukarno's effort to extinguish conflict came to resemble what Lenin called "democratic centralism": differing opinions could be voiced before a decision was reached but not afterward.

In early 1958, while Sukarno was out of the country on a five-week diplomatic tour, rebel army and political leaders in Padang, central Sumatra, proclaimed a new regime headed by Sjafruddim Prawiranegara, the Masyumi Party leader. Sukarno suspected that the rebels were instruments of foreign powers, and he turned out to be correct. The United States supplied the rebels from air bases in Thailand, South Vietnam, and the Philippines. The Indonesian Army had largely regained control by May 1958 when a B-26 bomber piloted by an American named Allen Pope was shot down over the Moluccas. Pope claimed he was merely working for the rebels, but he was carrying U.S. military identification papers, recently dated orders, and a valid post exchange card for Clark Air Force Base in the Philippines.[29] Sukarno's animosity toward the United States hardened, and he said that the fall of capitalism and imperialism was a historical certainty.

In July 1959 Sukarno issued a decree—unconstitutional in itself—abrogating the 1950 constitution and reinstating the 1945 constitution under which he, as president, had exercised wide powers. This bold stroke, he said, had exorcised "the devil of liberalism, the devil of feudalism, the devil of individualism, the devil of suku-ism, the devil of groupism, the devil of deviation, the devil of adventurism, the devil of four kinds of dualisms, the devil of corruption, the devil of scraping up wealth at one blow, the devil of the multi-party system, and the devil of rebellion."[30] For good measure, he banned the Rotary Club and the Ancient Mystical Order of Rosicrucians.

There was little protest. Most Indonesians agreed with Sukarno that parliamentary democracy had failed. The public was served a feast of slogans and neologisms: "Manipol" was Sukarno's political manifesto delivered on the occasion of his August 17, 1959, Independence Day speech. "USDEK" was an acronym compiled from words describing five different nebulous ideas, including "Guided Economy." "NASAKOM" was a fusion of *NASionalisme* (nationalism), *Agama* (religion), and *KOMmunisme* (communism).

The world was divided into "oldefos" (old, declining forces) and "nefos," (new, emerging forces). Neocolonialists became "nekolims." Sukarno loved delivering his annual Independence Day addresses and used them to give names to years: the "Year of Rediscovery of Our Revolution," the "Year of Decision," the "Year of Challenge," the "Year of Triumph." Jakarta began to sprout grandiose monuments, some personally designed by architect Sukarno. Meanwhile Indonesian exports declined, foreign indebtedness grew, and inflation got so out of hand that Sukarno went on the radio and told citizens to take out their pens and draw a line through zeros on banknotes. The National Planning Council produced an eight-year plan containing precisely eight parts, seventeen volumes, and 1,945 paragraphs (8/17/1945 was Indonesia's independence day).

The political system atrophied, and before long there was no system at all; one historian wrote that trying to describe Guided Democracy was "a process rather similar to describing the shape of an amoeba."[31] Sukarno named himself "President for Life" in May 1963. As a substitute for the defunct Parliament, Sukarno created a Dewan Perwakilan Rakjat (People's Representative Council, or DPR), the members of which were selected by Sukarno from political parties and functional groups. This was an innovation his successor, General Suharto, liked.

Assassins tried to kill Sukarno four times: in 1957, 1960, and twice in 1962. With so many problems at home, he focused on foreign affairs. He claimed to have "desperately wanted to be America's friend, but she wouldn't let me."[32] He bore a special animus toward the U.S. press, particularly the Henry Luce publications *Time* and *Life*. He observed, "The Russians never permitted anyone to jeer at me in print."[33] But as late as 1965 he claimed to want a reconciliation: "I would adore to make up with the United States of America. I once even made love to a girl who had hurt my feelings. To me there's nothing peculiar in that. And the situations seem identical in my mind."[34] He liked to invite foreign ambassadors to attend his speeches and seated them before him to give the impression that they were representatives of subordinate states showing him deference.

Sukarno savored one foreign policy triumph in May 1963 when West New Guinea was incorporated into the republic. The Dutch maintained that the people of New Guinea were racially, historically, and culturally distinct from Indonesians, but because the UN voted in favor of Sukarno's position the Dutch relinquished control of the huge territory.

In 1963 Sukarno launched a campaign to crush a newly independent neighbor, Malaysia. In his eyes, Malaysia was an artificial federation of territories (Malaya, Singapore, Sabah, and Sarawak) that ought to be part of Indonesia Raya. Worse yet, the midwives to Malaysia's birth were those nekolims, the British. Sukarno vowed to "gobble Malaysia raw." Some small-scale military engagements took place, but his Konfrontasi policy consisted mostly of violent speeches by Sukarno including a call for "21 million volunteers to help the people of Malaya, Singapore, Sarawak, Brunei and Sabah dissolve Malaysia and attain national independence."[35] The Indonesian Army initially saw Konfrontasi as a good justification for demanding a larger share of the government budget. The PKI supported Konfrontasi, too, for ideological reasons, and also because it seemed a good way to get army units transferred out of Java, where tension had been building between communists and local army commanders.

Tension was also building between Jakarta and Washington. President Kennedy, on the advice of Ambassador Howard Jones, had tried to accommodate Sukarno in order to moderate his anti-American views, but Kennedy's successor, Lyndon B. Johnson, had no patience with the Indonesian megalomaniac (who had recently "renamed" the Indian Ocean the Indonesian Ocean). Secretary of State Dean Rusk was angered by Sukarno's threats to nationalize U.S. oil companies, his ban on American movies, and most of all his apparent approval of mob violence against the United States Information Service libraries in Indonesia.

Senator Birch Bayh of Indiana spoke against "continuing to ask the American people for their tax dollars to support a man who is arrogant, insulting, incompetent, and unstable."[36] Foreign aid to Indonesia was terminated in March 1964, and Peace Corps volunteers were sent home. The State Department replaced Ambassador Jones with Marshall Green, who advocated a hard line toward Sukarno.

CENTER WEAKENS, EXTREMES GROW STRONGER

As Sukarno warmed toward the Communist bloc, he also moved closer to the PKI, the largest and best-organized political party in Indonesia, with 2 million members and another 12.5 million supporters in communist-influenced mass organizations. Thinking that the time was ripe for revolution, the PKI incited Indonesian tenant farmers to seize land. PKI leader D. N. Aidit recommended arming 5 million workers and 10 million peasants with guns thoughtfully supplied by the Chinese communists.

As the center weakened, the left (PKI) and right (the army) grew stronger. The army's prestige derived from its heroic role during the revolution of 1945–49. The fact that Sukarno had to balance the PKI against the army proves that Guided Democracy was not a totalitarian dictatorship. On the contrary, Sukarno had to treat the army and the PKI (as well as Chinese businessmen, Muslims, and university students) as rivals or partners, depending on the situation. He could not dictate policy to them but had to persuade, bargain, or manipulate. Sukarno's balancing act was similar to one being performed at the same time by Prince Sihanouk in Cambodia. When

Sukarno proposed bringing communists into his cabinet, army officers began to consider other options.

THE OVERTHROW OF SUKARNO

Only if he had truly possessed supernatural powers could Sukarno have reconciled Islam and Marx. Everyone could sense a storm coming. In his Independence Day speech of August 17, 1964, Sukarno gave the year a memorable name: The Year of Living Dangerously. In September Adam Malik, a prominent nationalist who had once been close to Tan Malaka but had since become a bitter anticommunist, organized a "Body to Support Sukarno-ism," (BPS) for the purpose of driving a wedge between Sukarno and the communists. Sukarno called the BPS a CIA plot.

Sukarno's health was deteriorating. He suffered acute pain from kidney stones but refused surgery because a soothsayer had prophesied that he would die by a knife.[37] He gained weight, and his jowls became noticeable for the first time. His sexual activity became more compulsive—as if to prove he still had vigor—and his temper grew worse. Sometimes Sukarno seemed incoherent in meetings, and his diplomacy took on an edge of dementia, as when he withdrew Indonesia from the UN in December 1964 and declared in July 1965 that Indonesia would soon produce an atom bomb.

On the night of September 29–30, 1965, a unit of soldiers from Halim Air Base kidnapped seven generals. Six were brutally murdered, and their bodies thrown down a well. One (General Nasution) escaped, but his daughter was killed. The mutineers seized several radio stations and warned that the coup was an internal affair of the army. The next morning Sukarno met with PKI leader Aidit at the Halim base, but he did not seem upset by the murders. General Suharto counterattacked with loyal army units and won a complete victory.

The Indonesian Army claimed that the PKI was behind the coup attempt and launched a nationwide pogrom against communists and their supporters. CIA officers, operating under diplomatic cover from the U.S. Embassy in Jakarta, had compiled a comprehensive list of 5,000 leading Communist Party members. They gave those lists to the Indonesian Army and later "checked off the names of those who had been killed or arrested."[38]

The terror spread until it seemed as if the entire nation was running amok. Indonesians of Chinese descent were slaughtered, ostensibly because China had supported the PKI. This was illogical, of course, for the Indonesian Chinese, far from being PKI sympathizers, were mostly petty capitalists. In East Java and Bali, people took advantage of the massacres to settle old scores and family feuds. No one can say with certainty how many people were killed. Estimates run from 80,000 to 2 million.

To this day the identity of the coup perpetrators is a subject of heated debate. Scholars from Cornell University have argued that the culprits were junior officers, not communists. Sukarno's personal role is unclear. His reaction to the coup was astounding—he prevaricated, praised the PKI, expressed no outrage at the murder of the generals, and referred to the coup as "a mere ripple in the ocean of the Indonesian revolution."[39] His precise role in the affair, if any, will probably never be known because virtually all of the people involved are now dead or remain in jail.

SUKARNO'S LAST YEARS (1966–70)

The army put Sukarno under house arrest and confined him to his summer palace in Bogor, south of Jakarta. It took Sukarno a while to comprehend that his political days were over, and he vowed to create a new Communist Party less influenced by China. On March 11, 1966, he was forced to sign an executive order giving General Suharto command of the government. On March 12, 1967, the Provisional People's Assembly voted "no confidence" in Sukarno and named Suharto acting president. However, Sukarno wanted to be tried so that he could conduct his own defense as he had almost forty years earlier when put on trial by the Dutch. But General Suharto was not about to run that risk.

In 1968 Sukarno was moved from the summer palace to a private house. As a consolation, the country's new military rulers allowed Sukarno to retain the title "Great Leader of the Revolution." Sukarno's last years were miserable. He was isolated from his friends. One by one his wives divorced him, until he was left with only one wife, Hartini. Sukarno died on June 21, 1970, of acute kidney poisoning. To avoid public protests from remaining Sukarno loyalists, President Suharto allowed him to have a state funeral. Sukarno had wanted, but did not get, a tombstone inscribed "Here lies Bung Karno, the mouthpiece of the Indonesian people."[40] Some villagers said that on the night Sukarno died they saw his face in the moon, and that there was thunder and lightning for three days.

CONCLUSION

Despite Sukarno's populist rhetoric and his revolutionary bombast, he was in some ways a conservative. He did not overturn the power structure of Indonesian society. Rather, he extolled traditional customs. Certainly he was not an economic leveler. His administration was dominated by hapless officials uninterested in, if not wholly incapable of, reform. Sukarno's place in history is a simple one: He gave Indonesians a sense of national identity and pride but left them in dire poverty.

NOTES

1. See Paul W. van der Veur, *Toward a Glorious Indonesia: Reminiscences and Observations of Dr. Soetomo* (Ohio University Monographs in International Studies, Southeast Asia Series, No. 81) (Athens: Ohio University Center for International Studies, 1987).

2. Willard Hanna, *Eight Nation Makers: Southeast Asia's Charismatic Statesmen* (New York: St. Martin's Press, 1964), p. 2.

3. Sukarno, *Sukarno: An Autobiography (As Told to Cindy Adams)* (Indianapolis: Bobbs-Merrill, 1965), p. 23.

4. Sukarno, *Sukarno: An Autobiography*, p. 17.

5. Sukarno, *Sukarno: An Autobiography*, p. 27.

6. Sukarno, *Sukarno: An Autobiography*, p. 25.

7. C. L. M. Penders, *The Life and Times of Sukarno* (London: Sidgwick & Jackson, 1974), p. 7.

8. See p. 31 of Donald M. Seekins's chapter, "The Historical Setting," in *Indonesia: A Country Study*, ed. William H. Frederick and Robert L. Worden (Washington, D.C.: Library of Congress, 1993).

9. John D. Legge, *Sukarno: A Political Biography* (New York: Praeger, 1972), p. 80.

10. Sukarno, *Sukarno: An Autobiography* pp. 61–62. This is a condensed rendering of the conversation. Many other versions exist.

11. Sukarno, *Sukarno: An Autobiography*, p. 63.

12. Sukarno, *Sukarno: An Autobiography*, pp. 97, 111.

13. Sukarno, *Sukarno: An Autobiography*, p. 115.

14. Quoted in Hanna, *Eight Nation Makers* p. 26.

15. Robert Cribb, *Historical Dictionary of Indonesia* (Metuchen, N.J.: Scarecrow Press, 1992), p. 408.

16. Sukarno, *Sukarno: An Autobiography*, p. 192.

17. Sukarno, *Sukarno: An Autobiography*, p. 193.

18. Sukarno, *Sukarno: An Autobiography*, p. 201.

19. Seekins, "The Historical Setting," p. 43.

20. M. C. Ricklefs, *A History of Modern Indonesia Since c. 1300* (Stanford, Calif.: Stanford University Press, 1993), p. 223.

21. Legge, *Sukarno*, p. 255.

22. Sukarno, *Sukarno: An Autobiography*, p. 12.

23. Sukarno, *Sukarno: An Autobiography*, p. 1

24. Ann Ruth Willner, *The Spellbinders: Charismatic Political Leadership* (New Haven, Conn.: Yale University Press, 1984), pp. 22–23.

25. Legge, *Sukarno*, p. 106.

26. Sukarno, *Sukarno: An Autobiography*, p. 4.

27. Sukarno, *Sukarno: An Autobiography*, p. 6.

28. Sukarno, *Sukarno: An Autobiography*, p. 76.

29. Audrey R. Kahin and George McT. Kahin, *Subversion As Foreign Policy: The Secret Eisenhower and Dulles Debacle in Indonesia* (New York: New Press, 1995), p. 179.

30. Legge, *Sukarno*, p. 4.

31. Ricklefs, *A History of Modern Indonesia*, p. 257.

32. Sukarno, *Sukarno: An Autobiography*, p. 295.

33. Sukarno, *Sukarno: An Autobiography*, p. 5.

34. Sukarno, *Sukarno: An Autobiography*, p. 300.

35. Paul F. Gardner, *Shared Hopes, Separate Fears: Fifty Years of U.S.-Indonesian Relations* (Boulder, Colo.: Westview Press, 1997), p. 184.

36. Gardner, *Shared Hopes, Separate Fears*, p. 184.

37. Legge, *Sukarno*, p. 385.

38. Margaret Bald, "How the CIA Helped Carry Out a Massacre," *Toward Freedom* 39 (October–November 1990), p. 10.

39. Penders, *The Life and Times of Sukarno*, p. 190.

40. Sukarno, *Sukarno: An Autobiography*, p. 312.

9

Suharto: The Impassive Administrator

In Java, there is a tremendous amount of protection from the father. If he doesn't do that, he would be no good as a father.

Clifford Geertz

President Suharto dominated Indonesian politics for more than thirty years. Before his fall in 1998 he was the senior statesman in a region noted for superannuated national leaders. Suharto (who, like Sukarno and many other Indonesians, uses only one name) was an army general not known to have harbored political ambition when he seized control of the world's fourth most populous nation in 1965.

The contrast between Suharto and the leader he pushed out, Sukarno, was striking. Sukarno was a flamboyant revolutionary agitator. Suharto was the ultimate insider, a taciturn, colorless functionary whose entire career was spent working for the state. Sukarno was a populist visionary, eloquent at the microphone but bored by details of policy. Suharto was a pragmatic leader who instinctively turned to his technocrats for moderate solutions to mundane problems of administration and economic development. Sukarno mesmerized Indonesians with his dazzling showmanship. Suharto, by contrast, was placid and phlegmatic. He concentrated on economic development and surrounded himself with specialists, including many foreigners.

Suharto was not well known to the public when he took power in the mid-1960s, and he remained enigmatic his entire three decades in power. There are few serious biographies of him, and his autobiography is a collection of self-serving anecdotes.[1] For his restrained, avuncular manner he acquired the nickname "The Smiling General." He remained a private and devoted family man. Indonesians called him *tertutup* (reserved), a quality highly respected by Javanese.[2] Suharto was formal, shy, and soft-spoken, and he ruled quietly, as if from a great distance. He confided in no one other than his family and a few close friends. His face registered no emotion except when he smiled benevolently.

Suharto with his family, no date

Suharto, 1966

In Javanese culture appearances matter. Public confrontation is regarded as unseemly. Leaders are respected for who they are, not for what they do. Suharto deliberately constructed a public image of himself as the antithesis of Sukarno, maybe because he knew instinctively that he could never achieve the kind of emotional bond Sukarno had forged with the Indonesian people. Even in retirement President Suharto presents himself as a man who is *halus* (refined). Suharto may be compared to the traditional Javanese puppet master of the *wayang* shadow puppet theater, who effortlessly and invisibly manipulates his puppets from behind a screen.[3]

In the latter years of the Sukarno regime (1960–65), Indonesia descended into chaos. The rate of inflation reached triple digits. Indonesian political life was equally frenzied. Suharto abandoned Sukarno's adventurist foreign policy, ended his Konfrontasi (Confrontation) policy with Malaysia, broke diplomatic ties with the People's Republic of China, aligned Indonesia with the West, and renewed Indonesian membership in the United Nations (UN). In addition, he discouraged Islamic extremism.

Suharto was widely acclaimed for his success in promoting economic development in Indonesia. When he took power the average annual income of Indonesians was less than half that of Indians. By 1997, the per capita gross national product ($980) was almost three times that of India. One reason for this impressive performance was that well-trained technocrats, not ideologues or political hacks, ran government ministries that supervised economic development.

When he first took power, Suharto stabilized Indonesia's currency and brought inflation under control. Indonesia achieved self-sufficiency in rice production. The national infrastructure was restored and expanded. Suharto promoted family planning and improved the public schools, with measurable gains in the literacy rate. The newly diversified economy grew at a rate fast enough to catch the attention of Western bankers and businessmen. Indonesia's international trade boomed, and other Third World leaders looked to Suharto as a model. But Suharto did not eradicate corruption—he systematized it. And Indonesians had to endure strict newspaper censorship and myriad human rights abuses. Military officers ruled rural districts like feudal lords.

CHILDHOOD AND BACKGROUND

Suharto was born on June 8, 1921, in Kemusuk, Yogyakarta, the third child of Kertosudiro, a village irrigation official, and his second wife, Sukirah. Suharto's parents separated when he was two years old, and he was cared for by his paternal grandmother until he was four. Sukirah reclaimed her son when she remarried. A short time later, Kertosudiro took the boy from his mother's house and placed him in the household of a sister until he finished primary school. His own mother then brought him back to Kemusuk. This confusion seemed to leave no psychological scars on the boy.

Little is known of Suharto's childhood. He often claimed to have risen from humble origins. His family could not afford to send him to a Dutch-language school, so all his education was in the Javanese language. He completed middle school and entered a military school at the age of nineteen.

EARLY MILITARY CAREER

Suharto enlisted in the Royal Netherlands Indies Army (KNIL), where he quickly rose to the rank of sergeant. After Japanese troops invaded Java in March 1942, the young Suharto volunteered for the Japanese-sponsored army, Pembela Tanah Air (Peta). The Japanese imperial government considered granting Java a degree of autonomy, for the Javanese seemed so reliably anti-Dutch, and they spoke of the Peta as an Indonesian independence army. In reality, they created it to serve as an auxiliary force to defend Java against a possible Allied landing.

The Indonesian national revolution lasted from 1945 to 1949. Many military officers later exaggerated the roles they had played, as Suharto did in his autobiography and his speeches. However, Suharto did plan and execute attacks against Dutch troops and was responsible for protecting the Indonesian Republic's wartime capital at Yogyakarta.

In 1947, while Suharto was still in the army, he married Siti Hartinah ("Tien"). It was an arranged marriage within the Javanese tradition. Such a union does not begin with romance, although love may ripen over time and certainly did in this case. Suharto wrote that his duties left little time for romance. He placed his faith in the Javanese saying, *Witing tresna jalaran saka kulina,* meaning "love grows through knowing one another." Siti Hartinah eventually bore him six children, three sons and three daughters. She was his adviser, confidante, and best friend until her death in April 1996. Suharto found real comfort in his family. His autobiography is filled with photographs of himself with his wife, their children, and a very large brood of grandchildren.

SUHARTO DURING THE SUKARNO YEARS (1950–65)

Suharto made a career of service in the Armed Forces of the Republic of Indonesia (Angkatan Bersenjata Republik Indonesia, abbreviated ABRI) and gained a variety of experiences, in staff work, in battle, and in intelligence-gathering. He had risen to the rank of lieutenant colonel by 1950 and was stationed in central Java for most of the 1950s, except for a six month period in 1958 when he took part in the successful campaign to crush Sulawesian separatists.

As commander of the prestigious Diponegoro Division, Suharto found that ABRI sometimes lacked money to pay his soldiers. However, an opportunity to supplement an army man's pay opened up when President Sukarno proclaimed the doctrine of *dwi fungsi* (dual function), under which the army was given responsibility for national development as well as for national defense. Officers were now free to engage in business deals. Suharto was rumored to have gone into business with Chinese traders. "Rumors of corruption in the Diponegoro Division may account for his sudden assignment to the staff and command school."[4] This reassignment marked a turning point in Suharto's career, for he moved to Bandung and became a personal assistant to the army's general chief of staff, Nasution.

Suharto was promoted to brigadier general in January 1960 and major general in January 1962. He was assigned to lead the military operation to wrest West Irian, the western half of New Guinea, from the Dutch. (As it turned out, the Dutch left peacefully.) President Sukarno appointed Suharto as the first commander of a new elite strike force, the Komando Cadangan Strategis Angkatan Darat (Kostrad). Kostrad was answerable only to the general staff. Although it became the organizational springboard for Suharto's rise to power, there is no evidence that Suharto imagined himself a future president. He was competent but shunned publicity. No one felt threatened by him.

In the early 1960s, President Sukarno found it increasingly difficult to maintain a political balance between the Indonesian Communist Party and Indonesian Army. The Partai Komunis Indonesia (PKI), emboldened by Sukarno's blossoming friendship with communist Chinese premier Zhou Enlai, began to prepare for "direct action," by which they meant a seizure of power in the countryside. ABRI was not prepared to allow this.

THE SEPTEMBER 30 COUP AND ITS AFTERMATH (1965–66)

In a confused and violent series of events on the night of September 29–30, 1965, six ABRI generals were murdered. Who planned this coup attempt? This is the pivotal question of modern Indonesian history, and it remains unanswered. Some say the killings were planned by the communists, some say by Sukarno. Others, noting that Kostrad commander Suharto was spared, believe he staged the murders as an excuse to depose Sukarno. Suharto quickly but discreetly contacted other generals to assure himself of their support for measures to counter the coup. In the aftermath of this incident, soldiers and citizens fell upon Chinese and other suspected leftists and slaughtered them indiscriminately.

It appears that the PKI and Sukarno may have had joint foreknowledge of the coup attempt, for the communist leader, Dipa Nusantara Aidit, appeared at the Halim Air base on the morning of October 1, and the PKI newspaper, *Harian Rakjat,* published an editorial praising the coup in its morning edition of October 2, even though the coup had been effectively suppressed by then. Why did Sukarno go to the Halim base, where he was seen with the coup plotters? Why did he not seem angered by the murder of six of his generals?

A report prepared by American professors from Cornell University contends that the putsch against the Council of Generals was carried out by dissatisfied low-ranking army officers and that the PKI was not involved. There is no evidence that the United States was involved. Officials at the U.S. Embassy were as surprised as everyone else. They did not know who Suharto was; the Central Intelligence Agency (CIA) could not even provide a biographical sketch of him.

Rumors persist that Suharto himself was behind the coup attempt. He was the only important general not slated for assassination. He had a motive, in that he believed that senior army generals were not effectively countering rising PKI strength. He had ties with the coup leaders and had consulted with them several times during the days immediately prior to the putsch.[5] Colonel Latief, a member of the coup group, met with Suharto on the eve of the putsch after the decision had been made to go ahead. Suharto later claimed that Latief met with him solely to keep track of his, Suharto's, whereabouts. However, Latief asserted when he was brought to trial in 1976 that he had on that occasion informed Suharto of the operation.

Suharto claimed that the murders were the work of the PKI, and that interpretation has been the official one in Indonesia ever since. Whatever the truth of the matter, from September 30, 1965, Suharto's star rose while Sukarno's fell. How could an unassuming man like Suharto gain control of an entire country? No other leader emerged to challenge Suharto. General Nasution, shocked by the murder of his daughter and by how close he himself had come to being killed, did not try to take power for himself. Nasution's indecision worked in Suharto's favor, especially because he was underestimated by potential rivals. The United States immediately announced its support for the staunchly anticommunist Suharto.

The PKI was decimated. The death toll of known or suspected communists was probably in the hundreds of thousands. In some cases villagers took advantage of the general bedlam to settle old family feuds. This bloodbath has been described as "a gigantic case of running amok; a sudden explosion of psychic pressure built up during years of privation, economic hardship, instability, fear and disorder. Old scores and vendettas were settled without any reference to the Communist issue."[6] Marauding bands of young Indonesians mounted the heads of victims on poles and paraded them through villages. Rivers in Bali became clogged with bodies of the dead. Indonesian Chinese, as shopkeepers, middlemen, and moneylenders, were made scapegoats, as happened to Jews in medieval and modern Europe. The Western press did not pay much attention to the massacres.

SUHARTO IN POWER (1967–98)

Between 1965 and 1968 Suharto maneuvered one step at a time to ease the demagogue Sukarno out of power. He gradually consolidated his authority over ABRI, the legislature, and the bureaucracy. To comprehend this approach, argues Nawaz Mody,

> one must understand the nature of the Javanese style of functioning which is essentially oblique. The governing factions prefer to pre-empt their rivals and prepare the way for eventual monopoly control of the state. It is commoner to function deviously from behind the scene, rather than face an overt confrontation. The struggle for political hegemony between Sukarno and Suharto had many characteristics of the traditional Javanese *wayang kulit* (puppet shadow play). The coup attempt was the first part, the transition represented the plot, leading finally to the downfall of Sukarno in the last part.[7]

Suharto knew that he lacked Sukarno's oratorical gifts and made no attempt to arouse the masses, but he did appropriate some of the dictator's left-wing language. One example: "God willing, the armed forces will carry out . . . a left democratic revolution with the ideals of anti-feudalism, anti-capitalism. . . . The armed forces do not wish to turn the revolution to the right as had been asserted by parasites and sponges on the revolution."[8]

Sukarno's image had to be undermined subtly and carefully. Suharto raised questions about Sukarno's affiliation with the communists and the possibility of his involvement in the coup. This caused student groups to turn against Sukarno. The U.S. ambassador, Marshall Green, was told by the prominent publisher B. M. Diah that Suharto would proceed in a Javanese way. Green interpreted this to mean "indirectness, apparent hesitation, some duplicity of language and shadow boxing that may be irritating to western observers but that will reflect the continuing Indonesian *wayang*."[9]

March 11, 1966, marked the point of no return. Sukarno reluctantly issued an executive order directing Suharto to take all necessary steps to guarantee security and calm and the stability of the running of the government and the course of the revolution. This decree was officially entitled "Surat Perintah Sebelas Maret." By taking the first syllable of each word, the decree became "Supersemar," an odd-sounding word but one with a hidden referent: Semar is the mythical founder of the Javanese race, a common man famous for getting things done, in contrast to more dazzling, confrontational leaders who often failed to satisfy the people's needs. This is how Suharto liked to portray himself.

After the army surrounded the presidential palace in Jakarta, Sukarno sought refuge at his Bogor residence. On March 12, 1967, eighteen months after the coup attempt, the Indonesian legislature designated Suharto acting president. One year later the qualifier "acting" was removed. The assembly renewed Suharto's mandate in 1973, 1978, 1983, 1988, 1993, and 1998, always by unanimous vote. Suharto cloaked his one-man rule in the mantle of constitutional legality, a subterfuge later copied by Philippine president Ferdinand Marcos and other Asian dictators wishing to maintain international respectability.

Suharto's long years in power may be divided into five periods:

1. From 1967 to 1974 he was primus inter pares in a military-dominated government with a weak and ineffectual bureaucracy. He depended on army support. This was a fluid time, when the public was still emotionally involved in politics.
2. From 1974 to 1983 Suharto ensconced himself in power. He emasculated political parties and severely censored the press. ABRI retained political power, and the bureaucracy performed more effectively. Rising revenues from oil exports eased pressure on the economy.
3. From 1983 to 1988 Suharto strengthened his position by building up a reserve of authority outside the armed forces.
4. For ten years after 1988, hardly anyone dared to challenge Suharto.
5. In 1998 Suharto found his power eroded along with the value of the Indonesian rupiah, and he had no choice but to resign.

THE NEW ORDER

Political scientists have flailed about in search of a model to describe the polity Suharto fashioned, and which he designated the "New Order."[10] Some described it as a bureaucratic polity in which administrators, technocrats, and military officers ran Indonesia as they pleased, with no input from the public or interest groups. Others called it soft authoritarianism, or corporatism. Still others sought to understand the New Order through historical or anthropological analogies; they compared Suharto to a patrimonial Javanese king. There was some truth to each of these descriptions, but the fundamental fact is that a congruence of interest linked (1) the Suharto family and its personal friends; (2) the armed forces; (3) foreign bankers, particularly those associated with the International Monetary Fund (IMF) and the World Bank (WB) (whose advice Suharto followed and whose approval of his rule was nearly unconditional until 1997); and (4) Indonesian businessmen, especially those of Chinese origin. Apart from these relatively small but coherent political blocs, the population at large was depoliticized. Note that two of the most potent political forces, the communists and the Islamists, were neutralized. The communists were killed and the Islamic movement was co-opted.

The New Order bore the clear imprint of Suharto's administrative style and his obsession with stability and order. Suharto's regime was unmistakably authoritarian but not totalitarian—this is a vital distinction. Although Suharto compelled people to obey him, he did not flood the country with propaganda. He arrested opponents and ignored human rights abuses by his policemen and soldiers but did not use terror on a wide scale except in East Timor. A real totalitarian regime, such as that of Mao Zedong or Pol Pot, stirs up the people and leads them on grand crusades against real or imagined enemies. But the last thing Suharto wanted was a mobilized population. The Indonesian social compact under Suharto was that most people tolerated Suharto's dictatorial tendencies in return for law, order, and a steadily rising income.

Another contrast between Suharto's New Order and true totalitarian regimes is that the latter always try to imprint an official state ideology in the minds of the citizens. Suharto's vague credo did not amount to an ideology. It came down to little more than reverence for the old verities of Javanese culture: obedience to superiors, respect for old people, fitting into one's place in the social pyramid, and avoiding open confrontation at all costs.[11] Obviously, if everyone observed these precepts, government officials could rest easily.

Suharto believed that a strong state was part of Javanese culture and that he was obliged, as president, to stabilize the nation—especially in view of the chaos and social disorder of the Sukarno years. However, certain of Sukarno's ideological formulations were deemed useful and were retained, notably the clever adaptation of the traditional Javanese village concepts of *musyawarah-mufakat* to twentieth-century mass politics. The ideal (not always the reality) of village government was that a practically endless discussion, open to all, would be conducted without animosity, regarding whatever issue the village faced, until a consensus was reached. Then anyone who still inwardly disagreed would acquiesce in order to maintain social harmony. It is quite a leap to apply such a model to 200 million people speaking 250 different languages and living on 3,000 islands. But Suharto maintained that there was no reason for political opposition in Indonesia because government policies were approved by elected representatives of the people, in accordance with *musyawarah-mufakat*.

Like other dictatorships, the New Order revolved around one strongman at the center. Suharto controlled all important political blocs and government institutions in Indonesia, including the Parliament, the army, and the judiciary, either directly or through his wide network of personal, familial, and financial allies. Therefore, politics in Suharto's Indonesia resembled politics at a royal court. All power emanated from the presidential palace. Access to Suharto equaled political power. Suharto rarely met with his cabinet, for he preferred to deal with ministers on a one-on-one basis. As supreme commander of the military (ABRI) Suharto personally approved promotions to high rank. He kept a sharp eye out for regionalism, the bane of the Indonesian military in times past.

Suharto did not rule by force alone but adroitly cultivated the qualities that Javanese look for in a leader. To achieve *halus* (refinement) Suharto always appeared composed, never agitated. He was unemotional and secretive. He kept his own counsel, trusting only in himself and his family. Perhaps the secret of Suharto's power was that no one knew what he was thinking.[12]

Suharto's personal belief system was hard to pin down. He was raised as a Muslim, of the *abangan*, or nondogmatic, type. *Abangan* Muslims freely mix liberal doses of Hinduism, Buddhism, and old-style Javanese mysticism into the austere monotheistic religion of Islam that emanated from a very different environment—the deserts of Arabia. On the one hand, Suharto made the *haj*, the once-in-a-lifetime pilgrimage to Mecca that is the solemn duty of every Muslim who can afford it. On the other hand, when Suharto traveled abroad in 1970, he followed the advice of soothsayers and had the head of a water buffalo buried at each tip of Indonesia, so that the nation would hold together during his absence.[13] Some people consider Suharto hardly a Muslim at all but an adherent of Kebatinan, an amalgam of animist, Hindu–Buddhist, and Sufi Islamic beliefs. Sufis are distinguished from other Muslims by their quest for personal, rapturous union with God through rituals, chants, and contact with holy men.

FACADE OF DEMOCRACY

Dictators who seek acceptance by the international community—namely, governments of the wealthy industrialized countries, the UN, the WB, and the IMF—must not rule through naked force like the brutal generals of Burma. They must maintain at least a veneer of democracy. Opposition parties must be allowed, though they may be circumscribed in various ways. Elections must be held, even if the results are predictable. There must be a legislature even if it always passes laws recommended by the chief executive. President Suharto constructed this kind of facade.

Suharto tolerated opposition political parties, watched them closely, and regulated their activities quite narrowly. He had already been in power for five years when he authorized the New Order elections of 1971. (These were the first elections held since 1955.) His own party, Golkar, won 236 of 360 legislative seats. Not satisfied with that result, Suharto two years later forced the opposition parties to amalgamate into two blocs: (1) the Partai Demokrasi Indonesia (PDI), or Indonesian Democratic Party, formed primarily of former nationalist and Christian parties; and (2) the Partai Persatuan, or Development Unity Party (PPP), which supposedly represents the Islamic community. These opposition parties were partly funded by the government.

Suharto relied on Golkar (Golangan Karya, the Joint Secretariat of Functional Groups) as his political vehicle. Golkar was actually a federation of numerous peasant groups, unions, and businesses, as well as district, provincial, and national bureaucratic agencies. The army was well represented in Golkar, of course. Golkar had "little organizational life between elections," but every five years it came to life to elect the Dewan Perwakilan Rakyat (DPR), the Parliament.[14]

In the third general election (1977) Golkar won 62 percent of the votes; in the fourth general election (1982) 64 percent; in the fifth general election (1987) 73 percent; in the sixth general election (1992) 68 percent; and in the seventh general election (1997) 75 percent. The DPR is not a real legislature. Members cannot even initiate bills themselves but may deliberate only on bills presented to them by the executive branch. In the year following these general elections, the DPR is joined by hundreds of presidential appointees to form the Majelis Permusyawaratan Rakyat (MPR), or People's Consultative Assembly, which "elected" Suharto to another five-year presidential term—always unanimously.

The New Order was not a military dictatorship. ABRI had a very broad role indeed, but it was not omnipotent. Under the doctrine of *dwi fungsi*, the army not only protected the state from internal and external enemies but also involved itself in activities that in other countries are the job of civilian bureaucrats or are carried on by the private sector. In Suharto's Indonesia, generals ran lucrative industrial enterprises. In return for this entitlement ABRI remained loyal to its patron. Although military leaders held high-level civilian administrative posts and sat on the boards of directors of many leading corporations, Suharto did not give the military everything it wanted. In fact, ABRI's role has receded. Suharto may have seized power as a general, but he usually wore civilian clothes after 1968.

If the hallmark of real democracy is acceptance of the concept of a loyal opposition, Suharto failed the test. He brooked no opposition whatsoever, although it was bound to surface from time to time. To cite some examples:

- In 1972 students protested government corruption. Student leaders were arrested and public demonstrations were banned.
- In 1974, violent demonstrations marred a visit by Japanese prime minister Kakuei Tanaka. Suharto assumed personal command of the state security agency.

- In 1977, students demonstrated again. Suharto banned seven newspapers that covered the story.
- In 1980, a group of eminent scholars, journalists, politicians, and even retired generals, including General Nasution himself, issued a "Petition of Fifty," criticizing various features of political life under the New Order. Suharto prevented these individuals from traveling abroad and took away their business contracts.

As a result of this pattern of repression, most Indonesians simply retreated from politics and concentrated on making a living.

In 1988 Suharto faced a series of challenges, including questions about his nominee for vice president, General Sudharmono. Suharto prevailed, but it seemed significant that his authority was so openly challenged. A rash of student demonstrations called for more open government, and the press began discussing politics in a spirited way. This brief interlude was known as the time of openness (*keterbukaan*, comparable to Mikhail Gorbachev's glasnost).

Philippine president Ferdinand Marcos, whose regime resembled Suharto's in many ways, fled his palace in a U.S. helicopter in 1986. Marcos was routed by an unusual coalition of Filipino aristocrats, slum dwellers, nuns, students, and military officers—with a final nudge from Washington. Concerned that Suharto might be vulnerable, and with no attractive alternative in sight, the U.S. ambassador to Jakarta, Paul Wolfowitz, called for greater political accountability to accompany economic growth. But as soon as he could, Suharto put an end to *keterbukaan*. When he felt threatened by the growing popularity of Sukarno's daughter, Megawati Sukarnoputri—who, against his wishes, was elected to lead the PDI in 1993—Suharto closed down three domestic newspapers and magazines, including the popular *Tempo*, a journal equivalent to *Time* or *Newsweek*. Naturally, Suharto opposed the globalization of information and sought ways to restrict access to the Internet.

CORRUPTION AND NEPOTISM

Until the Asian currency crisis of late 1997, the main problem with the Indonesian economy under Suharto was the debilitating prevalence of corruption at every level. All major business deals depended on access to Suharto—although he himself seemed ambivalent on this issue. He spoke forcefully about the importance of a free market system, and he knew it depended on competition, but he was also loyal to his family and friends and therefore inevitably placed expensive burdens (namely, the cost of bribery) on entrepreneurs and industrialists, foreign and domestic. An economic nationalist,

Suharto resisted advice from those who would globalize the economy. Externalization of the economy would diminish his own control over it and would force financiers to follow international rules and regulations instead of informal and often corrupt indigenous practices. An opposition politician once compared Suharto to a mafia boss who "protects himself by making everyone around him corrupt."[15]

Suharto's family itself was a major financial institution that controlled large sectors of the economy. Suharto and his late wife, Siti Hartinah (known informally as "Mrs. Tien Percent," for her usual demand), controlled at least seven major "charitable foundations" funded by Chinese businessmen seeking to buy their way into Suharto's favor. As a result, virtually unlimited funds were available for the Suharto family.[16] Suharto also set up a public-private partnership program known as Program Kemitraan, which levied a 2 percent tax on individuals and companies with high incomes, for distribution to needy families. His motives may not have been entirely altruistic, for the program greatly increased the size of government coffers, which were controlled by Suharto.

All of Suharto's six children were involved in Indonesia's most important industries: petrochemicals, computers, oil, toll roads, satellite communications, and automobile productions. The most famous presidential child was Suharto's youngest son, Hutomo Mandala Putra, universally known by his nickname, "Tommy." Tommy was given exclusive tax exemptions and tariff concessions to develop a "national" car, the Timor, which sold for about half the price of competing vehicles. The Timor was not actually manufactured in Indonesia, for Tommy's company was a joint venture with South Korea's Kia Motors.

The U.S. government protested Suharto's support for Indonesia's national car on the ground that to exempt the Timor from taxes levied against other cars sold in Indonesia constituted an unfair trade practice. Japan and several European states also criticized Suharto's son for trying to monopolize the Indonesian automobile market. Many Indonesians refused to buy the Timor, citing its poor performance. Their disdain for the car was taken as it was intended: as an oblique expression of contempt for the corruption of power. Quite apart from the economic inefficiency that must accompany nepotism, it was breathtakingly insensitive to name the car Timor at a time when the Indonesian Army was conducting a campaign of starvation and torture against the people of East Timor.

Suharto also owned the Humpuss Group, which had a share in a logging venture that was awarded lucrative timber concessions in Burma. Because of widespread violations of human rights committed by the Burmese State Law and Order Commission, Burma is a pariah state where few foreign companies conduct business. Exceptions include two oil companies: Unocal of the United States, and Total of France. Tommy went into partnership with both.

The Humpuss group controlled oil exploration, commercial aviation, toll-road construction, and agribusiness in Indonesia. In 1990, Suharto awarded Tommy a trade monopoly over Indonesian cloves and named him head of the Clove Marketing Board, a post that provided him the opportunity to generate uncountable sums. Here, too, the parallel with Ferdinand Marcos's crony capitalism is clear: Marcos claimed to have "rationalized" the marketing of bananas, coconuts, and sugar by awarding monopolies to his political allies. In 1998 Tommy said that he had deposited platinum worth $1.6 billion in the Union Bank of Switzerland.

Suharto's son Bambang Trihatmodjo also became a multimillionaire. He was the largest shareholder in Bimantara, a conglomerate with investments in ninety companies, including television stations, shipping, insurance, cocoa, timber, hotels, chemicals, and a condom factory.[17] Bambang also ran rapacious logging operations that contributed to deforestation in Burma and Cambodia. Bambang tried to edge his brother Tommy out of the national car venture.

Suharto's eldest daughter, Siti Hardijanti Hastuti Rukmana ("Tutut"), held a senior post in Golkar and sat in Parliament. She was even mentioned as a possible successor to her father. Her extensive business ventures included controlling interest in a company that collected revenues from Java's main toll roads. She controlled the Citra Lamtoro conglomerate, which was said to be worth $1 billion. Suharto's eldest son, Sigit Harjojudanto, his foster brother, Sudwikatmono, and his half-brother, Probosutedjo, were also involved in family business ventures.

Collectively, the Suharto family formed an economic dynasty with no equal in Indonesia. Hardly any major contract for infrastructure development was awarded without some relative of Suharto being involved. Critics called Indonesia the "land of the rising son . . . and daughter." The CIA estimated Suharto's personal wealth in 1989 at $15 billion and twice that sum if the rest of the Suharto family were counted.[18] *Forbes* magazine came up with a similar estimate in 1996 and placed Suharto in sixth place on the list of the world's richest people.[19]

Suharto asked why his children should not have the right to engage in business and claimed that they were nationalists countering the excessive influence wielded by Indonesian–Chinese businessmen. But, in fact, many of Suharto's business partners were themselves Chinese. The most prominent of these was Liem Sioe Liong. Suharto's daughter Tutut was a shareholder in Liem's Bank of Central Asia. Liem's personal wealth may even have surpassed that of Suharto. Accurate figures are not available, for ownership of Indonesian companies is often disguised through distant relatives and dummy partners. Another Chinese businessman, a friend of Suharto's since the 1950s, Muhammad "Bob" Hasan, had extensive timber interests. Suharto called publicly for redistribution of Indonesian capital from Chinese to Indonesians but did not actually issue discriminatory decrees. Indonesia, thus, is more lenient toward its Chinese minority than is its next-door neighbor, Malaysia. In return for his indulgence, Suharto received fierce loyalty from the Chinese business community.

IRIAN JAYA AND EAST TIMOR

When he came to power, Suharto canceled Sukarno's unproductive confrontation with Malaysia and accepted the reality that Sarawak and Sabah—two large territories on the north coast of Borneo—were part of Malaya, but he did not renounce other parts of Sukarno's dream of a Greater Indonesia (Indonesia Raya). West New Guinea was taken over on May 1, 1963, and formally annexed in 1969 as Indonesia's twenty-sixth province, following an "act of free choice" of tribal leaders there. The province was renamed Irian Jaya in 1972. The Indonesian claim to the western half of this giant, jungled island could not be based on alleged racial, cultural, or linguistic similarities but had to rest on the fact that the territory had been occupied by the Dutch. Because Indonesia was the inheritor of all Dutch claims in the area, the argument went, Irian Jaya was Indonesian. Over Dutch protests, the UN acquiesced. Through the 1970s, Indonesian paratroopers battled ill-trained troops of a movement to free Papua, but Jakarta won this war.

The Indonesian claim to East Timor had no such legal justification, for that small territory had been a neglected backwater of the sleepy but amazingly long-lived Portuguese empire. In the 1970s, guerrilla movements triumphed in Portugal's African colonies, Angola and Mozambique, after the Portuguese Army and Navy finally threw in the towel. An armed forces movement, headed by left-wing army officers, seized power in Lisbon in April 1974 and announced that the people of East Timor could now freely decide whether to continue their association with Portugal, become independent, or join Indonesia.

Suharto's desire to round out Indonesia's borders by absorbing East Timor was augmented by his fear that a Marxist group, the Frente Revolucionária do Timor Leste Independente (Fretilin), might come to power in an independent People's Republic of East Timor. He had overseen the bloody demise of the PKI in 1965 and 1966 and was not prepared to tolerate communism now. Suharto calculated correctly that however much human rights groups might criticize an invasion and annexation, Western governments would accept a fait accompli.

Twenty thousand Indonesian Army troops invaded East Timor on December 7, 1975. They quickly set up a puppet government which petitioned for annexation by Indonesia. Suharto granted that wish on July 15, 1976, when East Timor became Timor Timur, Indonesia's twenty-seventh province. To the surprise of ABRI, the population of East Timor rallied behind Fretilin. Suharto's generals responded with bombing campaigns and food blockades against rebel zones, but these measures only inspired stubborn resistance.

On November 12, 1991, Indonesian troops opened fire on a group of peaceful demonstrators in Dili, the capital of East Timor. This time Suharto thought it politic to officially investigate the incident. The investigative report challenged the army's official account of events. In this instance, Suharto removed a number of senior commanders and issued an apology for the killings. In 1996, the Nobel Peace Prize was awarded to two East Timorese leaders, Catholic Bishop Carlos Ximenes Belo and exiled East Timor freedom fighter Jose Ramos Horta, for their "courageous" struggle against Indonesian intervention.

The Indonesian Army terrorized Timorese civilians for more than two decades. Tactics included mass arrests, forced resettlement in strategic hamlets, and suppression of Catholic religious practice. Torture was routine. Since 1975 more than 50,000 Timorese have died from Indonesian military activity and resulting famines. Although some observers claim that "the record of military and police behavior has steadily improved," Asia Watch reported in 1997 that Indonesian military officers were selling videotapes of torture sessions. A steady barrage of criticism from human rights groups made little impression on Suharto, who blandly described the Indonesian invasion as "a positive response to the people's movement in East Timor to set themselves free from the shackles of foreign colonialism."[20] After Suharto resigned in 1998, his successor agreed to an autonomy plan for East Timor.

Suharto's general foreign policy orientation is easily described: He was reliably pro-Western and tried to cooperate with all his Asian neighbors except for communist China, of which he was extremely wary. At the same time, Suharto cultivated relations with the Islamic world (for example, by providing money to build a mosque named after himself in Bosnia.)

The overriding political question for Indonesia in the 1990s was presidential succession. Suharto was especially sensitive to the popular appeal of Megawati Sukarnoputri, daughter of the man he overthrew. Therefore, in July 1996 Suharto asserted control of the opposition PDI by ordering his security forces to storm its headquarters. He forced the PDI to accept a different leader but then had to contend with angry outbursts all across the country. ABRI declared that rioters would be shot on sight. At least four people were killed, and many more were reported missing. In the 1997 parliamentary elections the PDI drew only 3 percent of the vote after Megawati called for a boycott of the PDI, led by Suharto's chosen opposition leader, Soerjadi. Megawati was the only opposition leader with charisma, and she benefited from a wave of nostalgia for her father, whose speeches were sold on tape cassettes at street corners, but she had virtually no experience in government. When Suharto was forced to resign in 1998, there was no one with the experience, stature, or popular acclaim to take his place.

A country can be depoliticized for some time—Suharto proved that—but politics cannot be abolished. Suharto said that his mission was "to engage in politics to suppress politics," but history shows it cannot last.[21] As elsewhere in Southeast Asia, a vigorous community of Indonesian nongovernmental organizations promoted democratic principles and advocated policy reforms in environmental matters and issues related to ethnic minorities, natural resources, youth, women, and cultural preservation.

THE DOWNFALL OF SUHARTO

The loss of his beloved wife, Siti Hartinah, in 1996 left a gap Suharto could not fill. Siti had exerted some control over the Suharto children, but the president himself seemed unable or unwilling to do so. So many different troubles broke out that nervous Javanese suggested that the *wahyu*, the gift of power, had left Suharto and was seeking a home elsewhere.

One million jobs were lost in Jakarta in the last half of 1997. The rupiah, which had traded at 2,500 to the dollar in September 1997, fell to 11,550 to the dollar by January 1998. Suharto's worried international patrons dispatched teams of financial experts to tell the president what he needed to do, but this had the effect of making him look helpless before powerful foreigners.

Newspapers suddenly dared to publish editorials suggesting that perhaps Suharto was showing his seventy-six years. Panic buying cleaned the shelves of grocery stores. The national railway started selling one-way tickets back to the provinces, at a 70 percent discount, to unemployed people in Jakarta. Ugly anti-Chinese riots broke out in East Java. A mob burned Liem Sioe Liong's house in Jakarta. Half a million people demonstrated in the streets of Yogyakarta. Students rioted in the capital on May 12; troops opened fire, killing six of them. More than 500 people died protesting the deaths of those six students. Suharto evacuated his grandchildren to England.

Suharto was abandoned by his own handpicked Parliament, the same people who had voted unanimously only two months earlier to give him a seventh five-year term. Finally General Wiranto, commander of the armed forces, called on Suharto. It was 10:35 P.M., May 20, 1998. Suharto resigned twelve hours later, asking forgiveness for "any mistakes and shortcomings" on his part. Suharto shook hands with his handpicked vice president and successor, B. J. Habibie, then turned and walked away without saying a word. In retirement Suharto found that few people called upon him. His only reminder of past glory was his trained parrot, which screeched "Good morning, Mr. President," whenever it saw him.[22]

PROBLEMS FACING INDONESIA IN THE POST-SUHARTO ERA

Well over half of Indonesia's 200 million citizens were born after Suharto took over and have never known another leader. Suharto's successor appears to be a weak man with few political skills, who is tolerated only because the alternative seems to be chaos.

Indonesian workers are becoming restive and less willing to accept the low wages with which Suharto attracted foreign investment. Just 3 percent of Indonesians own a majority of the nation's wealth, while some 22 million people languish in poverty. Wealth is so polarized that less than 10 percent of the population may be considered middle class. Workers know they are being exploited—as in 1997, when a fund that was supposed to protect laid-off workers was used to bribe parliamentarians to vote in favor of a bill to restrict labor rights.[23] The deputy governor of Indonesia's National Defense Institute called the urban poor "the single most important factor in future Indonesian politics. It's the urban poor who are the most politicized, the most deprived, and therefore the most volatile, and it's not difficult to incite them to violence."[24]

Ethnic tensions simmer beneath the surface. A single spark can set off a conflagration, as in 1997, when Makassarese burned hundreds of homes belonging to Chinese after a mentally ill Chinese man murdered a local girl. The post-Suharto era might see a repeat of anti-Chinese pogroms, this time sparked by resentment at the privileges they enjoyed under the New Order. Poor, rural ethnic Chinese would then become "scapegoats for both the rich Indonesian-Chinese and the government that abets them."[25] This explains the 1997 incident in Banjarmasin in which a mob of Muslims, angered by a Golkar election campaigner who disrupted services at a mosque, set fire to a shopping center, killing 124 people, then went on a rampage destroying Chinese-owned shops.[26]

There is a strong potential for religious conflict. A significant long-term development is the growing interest in strict Islam among the children of more relaxed *abangan* Muslims.

Indonesia's financial crisis appears to have no short-term solution. In November 1997 the IMF, the WB, the Asian Development Bank, and the U.S. government put together a $38 billion bailout package, but as of early 1999, almost no measures had halted Indonesia's economic decline.

Jakarta's family planning program has won widespread approval, but in spite of this the population of Indonesia will double to 400 million in forty years. The steady 7 percent annual economic growth rate of the Suharto years has been just sufficient to absorb the 2.5 million young men and women who enter the workforce every year.

Environmental problems can no longer be ignored. The next generation of Indonesians will be living in a tropical country that has cut down most of its forests. In the summer of 1997 smoke from forest fires—set to clear land for planting—caused respiratory problems for people all across the archipelago. This is a portent of much future misery. No progress can be made on environmental issues until the political system is cleaned up. The reforestation fund must be monitored. Loggers were supposed to pay money into it for every tree cut down, and the money was supposed to buy seedlings, but in fact the fund was used to build a pulp mill for one of Suharto's cronies.[27]

CONCLUSION

President Suharto liked to be called "Bapak Pembangunan," Father of Development. He made economic progress the centerpiece of his administration, no small achievement in a country that was overpoliticized and underdeveloped. Under his leadership, the percentage of Indonesians living in absolute poverty dropped from 70 percent in 1970 to less than 15 percent in 1996.[28] When Suharto took power in 1965 the economy was in chaos. Foreign investment had dried up, factories were closing, and the rate of inflation was more than 1,000 percent per year. Suharto surrounded himself with knowledgeable economists, many of whom held degrees from the University of California at Berkeley. Reversing Sukarno's strategy of import substitution, Suharto successfully pursued a strategy of export-oriented industrialization. The economic growth Indonesia enjoyed in the Suharto years was overwhelmingly positive for most citizens. High rates of growth, combined with a moderately successful family-planning program translated into rising living standards for all classes. Electrification reached many remote villages. New roads were constructed, new hospitals and schools built. Literacy and life expectancy increased.

Indonesia has probably reached the point at which further progress demands democratization. A modern free-enterprise system depends upon a free flow of information and a decentralized decisionmaking process. Suharto could not concede this.

NOTES

1. Soeharto, *Soeharto: My Thoughts, Words, and Deeds: An Autobiography* (Jakarta: Pt. Citra Lamtoro Gung Persada, 1991).

2. Jamie Mackie and Andrew MacIntyre, "Politics" in *Indonesia's New Order: The Dynamics of Socio-Economic Transformation*, ed. Hal Hill (Honolulu: University of Hawaii Press, 1994), p. 45.

3. Greg Sheridan, *Tigers: Leaders of the New Asia-Pacific* (St. Leonards, Australia: Allen and Unwin, 1997), p. 86.

4. William Lidsker, *Suharto Finds the Divine Vision: An Interpretive Biography* (Honolulu: Semangat Press, 1992), p. 5.

5. Harold Crouch, *The Army and Politics in Indonesia* (Ithaca, N.Y.: Cornell University Press, 1978), p. 124; and Daniel S. Lev and Ruth McVey, eds., *Making Indonesia: Essays on Modern Indonesia in Honor of George McT. Kahin* (Ithaca, N.Y.: Cornell University Studies on Southeast Asia, 1996), p. 115.

6. C. L. M. Penders, *The Life and Times of Sukarno* (London: Sidgwick & Jackson, 1974), p. 189.

7. Nawaz B. Mody, *Indonesia Under Suharto* (London: Oriental University Press, 1987), p. 31.

8. Suharto quoted March 12, 1996, in Paul F. Gardner, *Shared Hopes, Separate Fears: Fifty Years of U.S.-Indonesian Relations* (Boulder, Colo.: Westview Press, 1997), p. 240.

9. Gardner, *Shared Hopes, Separate Fears,* p. 241.

10. See William H. Frederick and Robert L. Worden, eds., *Indonesia: A Country Study* (Washington, D.C.: Library of Congress, 1992), pp. 212–13.

11. Frederick and Worden, *Indonesia,* p. 133.

12. See Mackie and MacIntyre, "Politics," p. 45.

13. Brian May, *The Indonesian Tragedy* (Singapore: Graham Brash, 1978), p. 158.

14. Robert Cribb, *Historical Dictionary of Indonesia* (Metuchen, N.J.: Scarecrow Press, 1992), p. 173.

15. Adam Schwarz, "Indonesia After Suharto," *Foreign Affairs* 76 (July–August 1997), p. 127.

16. Leo Suryadinata, "Democratization and Political Succession in Suharto's Indonesia," *Asian Survey* 38 (March 1997), p. 275.

17. Steven Erlanger, "For Suharto, His Heirs Are Key to Life After '93," *New York Times,* November 11, 1990, p. 12.

18. Jeffrey Winters, quoted in Adam Schwarz, *A Nation in Waiting: Indonesia in the 1990s* (Boulder, Colo.: Westview Press, 1994), p. 144.

19. *Christian Science Monitor,* July 21, 1998, p. 6.

20. John G. Taylor, *Indonesia's Forgotten War: The Hidden History of East Timor* (London: Zed Books, 1991), p. 207.

21. Frederick and Worden, *Indonesia,* p. 241.

22. *New York Times,* June 9, 1998, p. 1.

23. Jenny Grant, "Call to Repeal Labour Bill 'Illegally Subsidised' by Worker's Funds," *South China Morning Post Internet Edition,* November 21, 1997.

24. Schwarz, "Indonesia After Suharto," p. 125.

25. Schwarz, "Indonesia After Suharto," p. 129.

26. Susan Sim, "Suharto Asks Scholars to Study Reasons Behind Poll Violence," *The Straits Times* [Singapore], June 4, 1997, p. 14.

27. Sander Thoenes, "In Indonesia, A Year of Reforming Dangerously," *Christian Science Monitor,* December 16, 1997.

28. *U.S. News & World Report* (October 14, 1996), p. 53.

For Further Reading

Anderson, Benedict R. O'G. *Language and Power: Exploring Political Cultures in Indonesia*. Ithaca, N.Y.: Cornell University Press, 1990.

Bresnan, John. *Managing Indonesia: The Modern Political Economy*. New York: Columbia University Press, 1993.

Cribb, Robert. *Historical Dictionary of Indonesia*. Metuchen, N.J.: Scarecrow Press, 1992.

Crouch, Harold A. *The Army and Politics in Indonesia*. Rev. ed. Ithaca, N.Y.: Cornell University Press, 1988.

Dahm, Bernard. *Sukarno and the Struggle for Indonesian Independence*. Ithaca: Cornell University Press, 1969.

Drake, Christine. *National Integration in Indonesia: Patterns and Policies*. Honolulu: University of Hawaii Press, 1989.

Feith, Herbert. *The Decline of Constitutional Democracy in Indonesia*. Ithaca, N.Y.: Cornell University Press, 1962.

Frederick, William H. *Visions and Heat: The Making of the Indonesian Revolution*. Athens: Ohio University Press, 1989.

Frederick, William H., and Robert L. Worden, eds. *Indonesia: A Country Study*. Washington, D.C.: Library of Congress, 1993.

Gardner, Paul F. *Shared Hopes, Separate Fears: Fifty Years of U.S.-Indonesian Relations*. Boulder, Colo.: Westview Press, 1997.

Green, Marshall. *Indonesia: Crisis and Transformation, 1965–1968*. Washington, D.C.: Compass Press, 1990.

Hill, Hal, ed. *Indonesia's New Order: The Dynamics of Socio-Economic Transformation*. Honolulu: University of Hawaii Press, 1994.

Holt, Claire, ed. *Culture and Politics in Indonesia*. Ithaca, N.Y.: Cornell University Press, 1972.

Jackson, Karl D., and Lucian W. Pye. *Political Power and Communications in Indonesia*. Berkeley: University of California Press, 1978.

Jenkins, David. *Suharto and His Generals: Indonesian Military Politics 1975–1984*, Ithaca, N.Y.: Cornell University Modern Indonesia Project, 1984.

Kahin, Audrey R. *Regional Dynamics of the Indonesian Revolution: Unity from Diversity*. Honolulu: University of Hawaii Press, 1985.

Kahin, Audrey R., and George McT. Kahin. *Subversion As Foreign Policy: The Secret Eisenhower and Dulles Debacle in Indonesia*. New York: New Press, 1995.

Kahin, George McT. *Nationalism and Revolution in Indonesia*. Ithaca, N.Y.: Cornell University Press, 1952.

Legge, John D. *Sukarno: A Political Biography*. New York: Praeger, 1972.

Lidsker, William. *Suharto Finds the Divine Vision: An Interpretive Biography*. Honolulu: Semangat Press, 1992.

McDonald, Hamish. *Suharto's Indonesia*. Honolulu: University of Hawaii Press, 1981.

Mintz, Jeanne S. *Mohammed, Marx, and Marhaen, The Roots of Indonesian Socialism*. New York: Praeger, 1965.

Mody, Nawaz B. *Indonesia Under Suharto*. London: Oriental University Press, 1987.

Mortimer, Rex. *Indonesian Communism Under Sukarno: Ideology and Politics, 1959–63*. Ithaca, N.Y.: Cornell University Press, 1974.

Neill, Wilfred T. *Twentieth-Century Indonesia*. New York: Columbia University Press, 1973.

Osborne, Robin. *Indonesia's Secret War: The Guerrilla Struggle in Irian Jaya*. Sydney: Allen & Unwin, 1985.

Reeve, David. *Golkar of Indonesia: An Alternative to the Party System*. Singapore: Oxford University Press, 1985.

Ricklefs, M. C. *A History of Modern Indonesia Since c. 1300*. Stanford, Calif.: Stanford University Press, 1993.

Sato, Shigeru. *War, Nationalism and Peasants: Java Under the Japanese Occupation, 1994*. Armonk, N.Y.: M. E. Sharpe, 1994.

Schwarz, Adam. *A Nation in Waiting: Indonesia in the 1990s*. Boulder: Westview Press, 1994.

Sukarno. *Sukarno: An Autobiography (As Told to Cindy Adams)*. Hong Kong: Gunung Agung, 1965.

Taylor, John G. *Indonesia's Forgotten War: The Hidden History of East Timor*. London: Zed Books, 1991.

Vatikiotis, Michael R. J. *Indonesian Politics Under Suharto: Order, Development, and Pressure for Change*. London: Routledge, 1994.

Wild, Colin, and Peter B. R. Carey, eds. *Born in Fire: The Indonesian Struggle for Independence, An Anthology*. Athens: Ohio University Press, 1988.

Part V

India

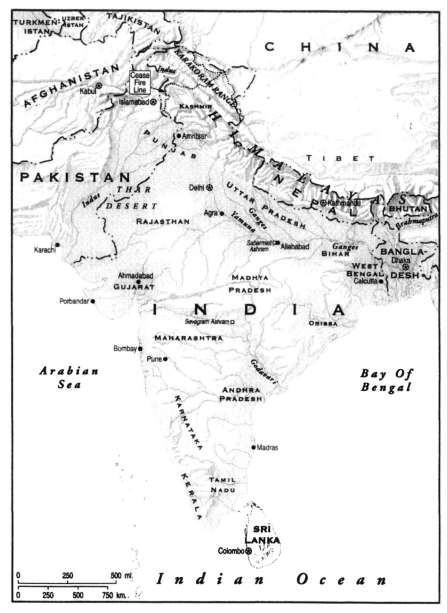

India

India Timeline

7000 B.C.	Agricultural revolution in Indus Valley; cereal crops, animals domesticated, first towns.
1750–1100 B.C.	Aryan migrations into India; Vedic culture begins.
c. 563 B.C.	Siddhartha Gautama (Buddha) born.
300–500	Golden age of Indian art, science, and literature.
1211	Muslims establish Delhi sultanate, which soon controls all of northern India.
1221	Mongols under Genghis Khan reach India.
1600	Queen Elizabeth I grants charter to East India Compan॒
1632	Construction of Taj Mahal begun (completed 1654).
1828	Lord William Betinck (governor-general) suggests demolishing the Taj Mahal and selling the marble.
1853	*Hindoo Patriot*, first nationalist newspaper, established.
1857	Sepoy Mutiny; rural uprisings across north India.
1869	Opening of Suez Canal galvanizes colonial economy.
1869 Oct 2	Mohandas Karamchand Gandhi born.
1885 Dec	Indian National Congress founded.
1888 Sep 4	Gandhi sails for England.
1893 May	Gandhi arrives in South Africa.
1910 May	Gandhi founds Tolstoy Farm near Johannesburg as an experiment in cooperative life and political noncooperation.
1919 Apr 13	Amritsar massacre.
1921 Dec	Mass civil disobedience campaign begins in India.
1922 Mar 10	Mohandas Gandhi and other nationalists arrested.
1930 Jan 26	Indian declaration of independence.
1930 Apr 6	Gandhi breaks Salt Law; inspires nationwide noncooperation; mass arrests.
1939–45	Indian troops fight on both fronts in World War II.
1940	Muslim League demands creation of Pakistan as a Musli state.

1946 Mar	British cabinet mission arrives in India to negotiate basis for Indian independence.
1946 Aug 15	"Great Calcutta Killing" (communal riots) claim 5,000 lives.
1947 Aug 15	Partition. British India divided into India and Pakistan.
1948 Jan 30	Mohandas Gandhi assassinated.
1962 Sep–Nov	Sino–Indian border war.
1965 Aug–Sep	India–Pakistan war over Kashmir.
1966	Indira Gandhi sworn in as prime minister.
1971 Mar	India supports Bangladesh independence from West Pakistan.
1974	India detonates atomic device in Rajasthan Desert.
1975–77	State of emergency declared; democracy suspended.
1984	Indira Gandhi assassinated.
1984–1991	Rajiv Gandhi era.
1985	South Asia's combined population reaches the 1 billion mark (22 percent of world total).
1986	Temple–mosque dispute at Ayodhya. Growth of Bharatiya Janata Party.
1987–90	Indian troops sent to Sri Lanka.
1991	Rajiv Gandhi assassinated.
1996 Oct	First McDonald's restaurant opens in New Delhi.
1998 May	Under newly elected Hindu nationalist government, India conducts a series of nuclear tests; Pakistan responds in kind.

The Indian Setting

India, the second most populous country in the world, is about the size of the United States east of the Missouri and Mississippi rivers. Its population of almost 1 billion constitutes one-sixth of the human race. More than a nation-state, India is a civilization of bewildering complexity with so many different races, religions, and castes that its future as a nation-state cannot be taken for granted. The subcontinent split along religious lines in 1947 when Pakistan was born; further division along linguistic lines is possible but by no means certain.

Contradictions abound in India. For one, a country founded on Gandhi's principle of nonviolence has built a nuclear arsenal. For another, India has an enduring caste system that condemns millions to untouchability, but its government is a functioning democracy. Another contradiction is that India's rich are exorbitantly wealthy, but the per capita gross national product (GNP) is less than $350 per year. Finally, India is a potential technological superpower, but in its villages life moves to a rhythm thousands of years old (about 40 percent of Indian men and 60 percent of the women are illiterate).

GEOGRAPHY

India is divided into three main geographical regions: (1) the Himalayan Mountains, which rise like a northern wall, effectively isolating India from the rest of Asia (ninety-two of the world's ninety-four highest peaks are found in the Himalayas; (2) the Indo-Gangetic plain, the world's largest and most densely populated alluvial plain, stretching 900 miles across northern India; and (3) peninsular, or southern, India, where the arid Deccan plateau is flanked by lush tropical lowlands to the east (the Coromandel Coast) and west (the Malabar Coast).

Rainfall increases as one moves from west to east across the flat northern Indian plain that is the country's agricultural and cultural heartland. In the Thar Desert only three inches of rain may fall in a year, while the hills of

Assam, in the far northeast, may receive 400 inches. India's climate is strongly monsoonal, with pronounced wet and dry seasons. Wheat and millet are the staple crops in the north and west, rice in the east and south. Sugar, jute, and cotton are the most important commercial crops. The agricultural sector is generally poor and backward, with worn-out soil and undernourished cattle. Deforestation, with its attendant soil erosion and flooding, is a major problem all over the subcontinent. India possesses coal and iron ore sufficient for its needs, but it is deficient in oil.

DEMOGRAPHY

Three Indian cities, New Delhi, Bombay, and Calcutta, have passed the 10-million mark as peasants migrate from the countryside hoping, often in vain, to find work. One out of four Indians lives in a city; that leaves about 750,000,000 people living in India's 550,000 villages. India's annual population increase of 1.9 percent yields a doubling time of thirty-seven years, and this figure is not likely to decline; thus most undergraduate students reading these words will live to see the population of India reach 2 billion.

Efforts to classify the races of India have been largely abandoned, as the categories formerly used have proven imprecise. Suffice it to say that today's Indians exhibit a wide variety of physiognomies and skin colors. Generally, those who live in the north are lighter skinned, while those in the south are darker. A more precise indication of the subcontinent's tumultuous history is the distribution of languages, eighteen of which are officially recognized: Assamese, Bengali, Gujarati, Hindi, Kannada, Kashmiri, Konkani, Malayalam, Manipuri, Marathi, Nepali, Oriya, Punjabi, Sanskrit, Sindhi, Tamil, Telugu, and Urdu. More than 300 minor languages have also been counted. The languages of northern India belong to the Indo-European language family; those in the south are in the Dravidian family. Hindi has been designated the national language but is understood by only about one-third of the population. English, the colonial language, remains the lingua franca of businessmen, educators, and government officials, much to the chagrin of Indian nationalists.

CULTURE

The two elemental features of Indian culture are religion and caste. Eighty percent of Indians are Hindu, and 12 percent are Muslim. The remainder are Sikhs, Christians, Jains, or followers of tribal religions. Polytheistic Hinduism is the most complex of the world's major religions, for its doctrines are eclectic and its practices infinitely varied. The labyrinthine pantheon in-

cludes innumerable local spirits but is dominated by three famous manifesta-
tions of God: Brahma, the creator; Vishnu, the preserver; and Shiva, the de-
stroyer. For Hindus, religion is not a distinct sphere of thought but a holistic
worldview that gives meaning to every act of daily life.

The term *caste*, by which Westerners attempt to make sense of the hierarchical Indian social order, comes from the Portuguese word *casta*, meaning
"breed." Indians themselves use the term *varna* (color) to distinguish the
four broad social ranks. Probably the caste system sprang from the contempt
Aryan invaders felt for the indigenes of the subcontinent they conquered.
The highest rank are Brahmans (scholars and priests, whose ritual sacrifices
preserve society). Next are the Kshatriyas (warriors and administrators).
Third are Vaisyas, the producers of wealth (farmers and merchants). Fourth
are the Shudras (manual laborers). So lowly are the Untouchables that they
are outside the caste system altogether (literally, outcastes). Their menial toil,
butchering animals for example, is ritually polluting. Caste Hindus may not
marry or accept food from Untouchables, and may even feel defiled by the
shadow of an Untouchable, but physical avoidance is obviously impractical
in modern cities. Less objectionable terms for this underclass include *harijans* ("children of God," a phrase coined by Mahatma Gandhi), *scheduled
castes* (a bureaucratic term), and *dalits* (the downtrodden) as they prefer to
call themselves. The above simplified schema hardly does justice to the intricacy of the caste system, for each occupation (*jati*) is a distinct, endogamous
group. It is impossible to say how many castes there are in total, but the
government of India officially identifies 405 kinds of "scheduled castes," or
Untouchables.

Indian society strongly favors males. Parents hope for male heirs to carry
on the family, and only men can perform certain essential Hindu religious
rituals. Women in the modern, urban, educated sector may pursue professional careers, but there are still cases in rural villages where women are
raped and killed for failure to provide a satisfactory dowry. Prime Minister
Indira Gandhi inherited power from her father and wielded it forcefully. She
was the strongest leader modern India has known, but she did not concern
herself particularly with women's issues.

HISTORICAL CONTEXT

Civilization began very early in the Indian subcontinent. Cereal crops were
first sown about 7000 B.C. in the valley of the Indus River (present-day Pakistan). True cities with forts and municipal sewage systems arose by 2000 B.C.
at Harappa and Mohenjodaro; these cities traded with Mesopotamia and Per-
sia. India subsequently evolved a distinctive and unique civilization that was
periodically enriched by discoveries and ideas from the Near East and

Greece. The Indus Valley civilization fell into decline by 1800 B.C. due to environmental change, defeat in battle, or both. Forceful Aryan tribes, the progenitors of modern northern Indians, filtered into the subcontinent from central Asia through the Khyber and Bolan passes, like so many invaders after them.

The Aryans' religious ideas shaped Indian culture. Their hymns were compiled into Vedas, or sacred texts. The Upanishads, subtle philosophical and spiritual poems and essays, were collected and written in Sanskrit by 500 B.C. A concern with caste purity and priestly ritual was already evident. Siddhartha Gautama, the Buddha (563–483 B.C.) rejected such fastidious rules as obstacles to achieving nirvana, or enlightenment, the only way to escape from endless cycles of suffering, death, and rebirth.

Under the Maurya dynasty (fourth century B.C.), technology in general, and metallurgy in particular, reached surprising levels of sophistication. Music and literature flourished. Two classics, the *Mahabharata*, at 100,000 stanzas the longest epic poem in the world, and the *Ramayana*, an entertaining tale of battles between gods and demons, reached their final form by about 400 B.C. Alexander the Great invaded India in 327 B.C. but found himself greatly overextended and did not linger. In the next century the great emperor Ashoka converted to Buddhism and dispatched missionaries to Macedonia, Egypt, Sri Lanka, and Southeast Asia. By the first century B.C. India was trading overland and by sea with the Roman Empire in the West and the Chinese Han dynasty to the east.

At no time was the entire subcontinent politically unified, for it was too vast and too varied. While empires rose and fell in the northern Ganges plain, other dynasties held sway in the Tamil-speaking south. The years from A.D. 300 to 500 are considered the golden age of classical India, before the Huns invaded, and in their turn Arabs, Afghans, Mongols, and Englishmen. All these intruders left their mark, and all but the last were assimilated racially and culturally.

Muslims from Central Asia established a sultanate at Delhi in 1211. The advent of Islam in northern India marked a radical break with the past and inaugurated a new age of achievement, for the Muslims had taken Greek mathematics and engineering to new heights. Hindu architecture had been constrained by ignorance of the arch and the dome; now Muslim Indians created masterpieces of architecture, such as the Taj Mahal. The Delhi sultans conquered parts of southern India before they were defeated by Mongols who sacked Delhi in 1398. With the decline of the Delhi sultanate, new Hindu states arose in the south. The Vijayanagara Empire, founded in 1336, despite its remote location on the Deccan plateau, was an entrepôt trading in luxury goods such as spices, pearls, and silk. Portuguese explorers described its capital as a grander city than Lisbon. Vijayanagara was defeated in battle in 1565 by a coalition of five petty sultanates, and its people were scattered. Today the visitor finds only sheep grazing amidst its granite ruins.

The first European colony in the subcontinent was established by the Portuguese at Goa on the Malabar Coast in 1510. All European powers were interested in "the Indies," of which they had only the vaguest knowledge. Trade was their main motive. Queen Elizabeth I of England granted a royal charter to the East India Company in 1600. British "factories" were established at Surat in 1612, at Madras in 1640, and at Hugli (near Calcutta) in 1651. By the third quarter of the seventeenth century there were British, French, Dutch, and Danish factories in Orissa and Bengal.

The Muslim Mughal dynasty, founded in 1526, built splendid palaces, tombs, and forts that stand today in Delhi, Agra, Jaipur, Lahore, and other cities of northern India. The first great Mughal emperor, Humayun, was temporarily defeated by Afghan invaders but retook Delhi in 1555, the year before his death. His tomb is laid out as a vast Persian-style garden. His son Akbar, who reigned for fifty years (1556–1605) expanded the empire to include all the territory between Kashmir, Gujarat, and Bengal, and built a magnificent new red sandstone capital for himself at Fatehpur Sikri, which, unfortunately, had to be abandoned for lack of a dependable water supply. Akbar was a broad-minded Muslim who married a Hindu princess; he was tolerant of Sikhs and of Christian missionaries.

The Mughals never worked out a peaceful means of succession, so the death of an emperor was usually followed by fratricide among his sons. Shah Jahan, who built the Taj Mahal as a memorial to his wife, was imprisoned for the rest of his life by his son Aurangzeb in the Agra Fort, from where he could look out at the Taj. The Mughal Empire declined rapidly in the 1700s, as the British brought more and more princely states under their sway. The decisive Battle of Plassey (1757) ensured British domination of Bengal. Lancaster cotton textiles now flooded the Indian market to the ruination of local producers. Despite periodic famines, the population of the subcontinent began the very rapid expansion that continues today.

British imperial arrogance infuriated Indians. One example was Governor-General William Bentinck's proposal to knock down the Taj Mahal and sell the marble in England. Wrecking cranes were moved into the garden, and the demolition crew was set to begin when word arrived from London that an initial auction of Indian marble from other sites had brought disappointing bids. Thus was the Taj Mahal spared.[1] Bentinck's prohibition of *sati* (widow immolation) was more progressive, but from the Indian point of view equally dismissive of their tradition.

In 1835 the Indian Civil Service was opened to Indians, and the next year English was made the official language of government. Native education was now encouraged in order to staff the bureaucracy. The first telegraph system was installed in India in 1850 and the first railway tracks laid in 1853. Universities were founded in Calcutta, Bombay, and Madras in 1857, the year of the Great Revolt (also known as the Sepoy Mutiny). The immediate spark was the spread of rumors that the bullets, which Indian soldiers had to bite before loading, were lubricated with cow fat. This is taboo to Hindus. As disturbances spread across northern India, it became clear that the rebels really wanted an end to British rule. The British suppressed the mutineers (blowing forty of them out of cannons in Peshawar as an example to others). Henceforth all political authority in India flowed directly from the British crown. The British Raj had begun, but the Indian desire for independence, once kindled, could never be extinguished. The man who channeled that elemental longing into nonviolent political action, Mohandas Gandhi, was born in Gujarat in October 1869.

NOTE

1. David Carroll, *The Taj Mahal* (New York: Newsweek, 1972), p. 133.

10

Mohandas Gandhi: The Spiritual Nationalist

A leader is one who, out of madness or goodness, volunteers to take upon himself the woe of a people.

John Updike

Mohandas Karamchand Gandhi never held any official title, yet he is considered a giant of the twentieth century. Indians call him the father of the nation, though Gandhi said he participated in politics only because politics encircled his people "like the coil of a snake."[1] He was first and foremost a religious figure, but his religion made him political. His close followers affectionately called him Bapu (Father); eventually the whole world knew him as the Mahatma (Great Soul).

Interpreting Gandhi would seem relatively easy; his ideas are recorded in far greater detail than those of any other Asian leader. Between 1958 and 1984 the government of India published his *Collected Works* in ninety thick volumes, and copies of 37,000 letters Gandhi wrote are preserved in a single library in India. Yet he remains enigmatic and elusive, not only because, as he admitted, "My language is aphoristic, it lacks precision." The deeper reason is that while pushing history forward, he yearned for a preindustrial Ramarajya (kingdom of God). Gandhi was fundamentally out of step with social and intellectual trends in Europe, as Fatima Meer has written: "At a time when Freud was liberating sex, Gandhi was reining it in; when Marx was pitting worker against capitalist, Gandhi was reconciling them; when dominant European thought had dropped God and soul out of social reckoning, he was centralizing society in God and soul."[2]

The India into which Mohandas Gandhi was born was in crisis. Its glorious Buddhist and Hindu empires were long gone; even the mighty Mughal dynasty had fallen into decrepitude. The English reigned supreme, or so they thought. Railroads were being built, which the British called the sinews of

Mohandas Gandhi (center), 1895

*Mohandas Gandhi with Herbert
Hoover, 1946*

empire, but in reality they were the sinews of nationhood. With the Sepoy Mutiny of 1857–58 suppressed and all political authority transferred from the East India Company to the Crown, the British had every reason to think their Raj would last forever. Natives were being educated for posts in the Indian Civil Service, but once they could read English, John Locke, Thomas Jefferson, and Karl Marx were open to them. Small-circulation vernacular newspapers appeared, and cotton plantations and jute mills created a new class of rural proletarians tied to the market economy.

FAMILY AND CHILDHOOD

India's emancipator was born on October 2, 1869, in Porbandar, a cosmopolitan seaside town in Gujarat, where Hindus lived along with Muslims, Sikhs, Zoroastrians, and Jains. Gandhi's father, Karamchand, was already in his late forties when Mohandas was born, the youngest child of four. The family was Vaishnava (Vishnu-worshipping), and they belonged to the Vaisya trading caste and the *modh bania* shopkeeper subcaste. Gandhi's ancestors were probably merchants (*gandhi* is the Gujarati word for "grocer"), but for three generations they had served as *dewans* (chief ministers) of small princely states. Karamchand was the *dewan* of Rajkot. Mohandas was profoundly influenced by his devout mother, Putlibai, who had been raised in a local Vaishnava sect that sought direct communion with God.[3] She fasted often; sometimes she increased or decreased her daily food intake as the moon waxed and waned. In some years, during the monsoon season, she fasted until she had seen the sun. Gandhi remembered her as "saintly," but to one Western biographer, "Putlibai's self-suffering had an important aggressive aspect: if she was for some reason dissatisfied with the behavior of another member of the family she would impose some penalty on herself so that, out of love for her, they would cease the activity."[4]

Gandhi entered primary school in Porbandar, but when he was seven his father was appointed *dewan* of Rajkot, a hundred miles inland. Here young Mohandas saw the sharp contrast between the dirty, crowded native city and the clean, spacious, geometrically ordered British cantonment. By his own account, Gandhi was a mediocre schoolboy: "My intellect must have been sluggish, and my memory raw," he wrote.[5] In 1880 he began high school in Rajkot. More vivid in his memory than anything inside the classroom were Christian missionaries, who "used to stand in a corner near the high school and hold forth, pouring abuse on Hindus and their gods. I could not endure this."[6]

ADOLESCENCE

In 1882 the thirteen-year-old Mohandas was married to a girl of the same age, Kasturbai Makanji, the daughter of a *modh bania* merchant. Gandhi's sister-in-law gave him hints about how to behave on his wedding night, but he later wrote that no instruction was necessary because he had remembered what to do from previous incarnations. For the first five years of the marriage Kasturbai spent about half her time at her parents' house, which is normal in Indian child marriages.

When he was about fifteen years old, Gandhi embarked on what he called his "experiments," or what we might now call an adolescent rebellion. A friend named Mehtab was his confederate. A Muslim, Mehtab ate meat. The Gandhis, of course, were strict vegetarians. Gujarati schoolboys sang a poem that piqued Gandhi's curiosity:

> Behold the mighty Englishman
> He rules the Indian small,
> Because being a meat-eater
> He is five cubits tall.

In his *Autobiography*, written forty years later, Gandhi recalled, "I wished to be strong and daring and wanted my countrymen also to be such, so that we might defeat the English and make India free."[7] One evening Mehtab took Mohandas down to the riverbank and fed him meat. That night Gandhi was haunted by a horrible nightmare: Every time he dropped off to sleep, he heard a live goat bleating inside him. Nevertheless he continued his meat-eating "experiments" for one year. Other experiments involved smoking cigarettes, and even stealing the money to buy them. Some biographers have inferred a period of agnosticism, or even atheism, but if the boy experienced doubts about metaphysics, his conscience compelled him to confess his furtive thefts to his father.

One day Mehtab made an appointment for Gandhi in a brothel and paid in advance. This experiment was a complete failure, for Gandhi was too nervous to do or say anything. The woman shouted insults out the door at him. This unpleasant incident paled beside a far worse experience in November 1885 that Gandhi never forgot. The sixteen-year-old Gandhi was nursing his mortally ill father. His duty was to massage his father's legs until the sixty-three-year-old man fell asleep. While rubbing his father's legs, Gandhi began thinking of rubbing the skin of his pregnant wife's, Kasturbai, and left his father to make love to her. A few minutes later, a servant knocked at the door to say that his father had died. When Kasturbai gave birth, the baby died after a few days. Gandhi ascribed this to divine retribution.[8] For the rest of his life he despised his own sexual drive, what he called his "animal passion."

In 1887 Gandhi took a college entrance examination in the large city of Ahmadabad. It was the first time he had ventured from the Kathiawar Peninsula, and he felt alone and frightened. He studied for a single semester at Samaldas College in Bhavnagar, but courses were taught in English, for which he showed no particular aptitude. Gandhi was homesick, and he experienced bouts of illness that may have been psychosomatic.

YEARS OF STUDY IN LONDON

British India was in ferment during Gandhi's youth. Indians were infuriated by symbolic humiliations, such as the whitewashing of the Red Fort at Delhi in 1876 for an official visit by the Prince of Wales. In that year, and for the next two, famine spread over much of India. In December 1885 the Indian National Congress (INC), the future organizational vehicle for Indian independence, was founded in Bombay. But the young Gandhi was uninterested in current events. He thought of becoming a doctor but was persuaded to follow the family tradition of government service. That meant studying law in London, but the *modh bania* caste prohibited ocean voyages, and caste elders tried to dissuade Gandhi from crossing the "black waters." When he decided to go anyway, they angrily pronounced him an outcaste. For the first time, Gandhi's legendary stubbornness showed itself; the order had no effect on him.[9] A final hurdle was overcome with the aid of a Jain monk who administered an oath in the presence of Gandhi's mother: While in England Gandhi would not touch meat, liquor, or women.

Gandhi, not yet nineteen, sailed from Bombay on September 4, 1888, aboard the *S.S. Clyde*. Not knowing how to use a knife and fork, he ate alone in his cabin. In London he was dreadfully homesick and clearly suffering from what is now known as culture shock. In his autobiography, he wrote: "At night the tears would stream down my cheeks. . . . Everything was strange—the people, their ways, and even their dwellings."[10] Despite his unhappiness, Gandhi tried hard to fit into English society. He spent a considerable sum of money on English clothes, dancing lessons, even a violin, but he hated the clothes and quickly concluded that he had no sense of rhythm. Two other initiatives, though, yielded lasting benefit: elocution lessons and a disciplined program of newspaper reading. On November 6 he enrolled as a law student at Inner Temple, London.

Food was a problem until Gandhi found a vegetarian restaurant. This opened whole new vistas, for English vegetarians tended to gravitate toward the experimental fringe of society. Gandhi read books making sweeping claims for vegetarianism. Henry Salt's *Plea for Vegetarianism* made an especially deep impression on him. Refusing meat was not merely healthy, it was economical, efficient, and humane. Vegetarianism would put the individual in spiritual harmony with nature and actually strengthen a nation's character. With a single stroke, many of Gandhi's psychological needs were fulfilled. He could keep his vow to his mother, stay within the Hindu tradition, and still be strong and progressive, healthier and holier than meat-eating Englishmen. He joined the London Vegetarian Society, founded a West London Food Reforms Society, and went door to door preaching vegetarianism and peace, showing Londoners how to prepare good vegetarian meals.[11]

Through his vegetarian friends, Gandhi gained exposure to various progressive causes such as pacifism and Fabian socialism. Here were Westerners who questioned industrial capitalism and advocated a return to nature. In November 1889 he met Helena P. Blavatsky and Annie Besant but declined to join their Theosophical Society. His thoughts began turning to religion. At the urging of a vegetarian friend he tried reading the Bible. The Old Testament put him to sleep, but he liked the New Testament, especially the Sermon on the Mount. Chagrined that his Theosophist friends knew more about the fine points of Hindu theology than he did, Gandhi read the *Bhagavad Gita* for the first time. This became the most important book in his life—again and again he turned to it for solace, reading verses from it every day.

Curious to see France, Gandhi went to the Paris Exhibition of 1890. He climbed the Eiffel Tower and ate lunch at its restaurant, but later called it a "toy" that only proved that "we are all children attracted by trinkets."[12] The cathedral of Notre Dame impressed him much more.

FIRST RETURN TO INDIA

Gandhi passed the bar examination on June 10, 1891, and sailed for Bombay two days later. He was met on the dock by his brother, who delivered the shocking announcement that their mother had died. The family had thought it best to withhold this bad news. (As Gandhi's wife, Kasturbai, was illiterate, they had not corresponded at all during their three years of separation.) Gandhi tried to regain his caste by pious acts, but with only partial success; some caste elders never forgave his previous defiance.

Gandhi still knew little about Indian law and was shocked to discover corruption in Indian courts, particularly that lawyers used touts to rope in customers, which he absolutely refused to do. He tried to start a legal practice in Bombay, yet his one and only courtroom appearance was a disaster: He stood up but could not utter a single word and just sank back into his seat. Gandhi refunded his client's money, and though he remained in Bombay six months longer, he failed to get another case. He returned to Rajkot, where he eked out a living drafting petitions, something he could have done without the years of study abroad. The only bright spot in this dismal period was the birth of his second son, Manilal, in spring 1892. Then came an offer of a one-year job as legal adviser to Dada Abdullah & Company, an enterprise in Natal, South Africa, owned by a Muslim from Porbandar.

THE SOUTH AFRICA YEARS

Gandhi arrived in South Africa in May 1893 and began his duties by attending court in Durban to observe how law was practiced in the British courts of Natal. Hats were prohibited in court, and the judge ordered Gandhi to remove his turban. To Gandhi, his turban was not a hat, so rather than comply, he left the courtroom.

Racial segregation in South Africa was unlike anything Gandhi had experienced in India or England. Indians, both Hindu and Muslim, had been brought to South Africa to work on sugar, tea, and coffee plantations, native Africans having shown themselves completely unwilling to perform such labor. Most of the Indians came under indenture and were treated almost as slaves. They were called "coolies" by their British masters. Soon free Indian immigrants followed: grocers, moneylenders, artisans, and professionals. These were "coolie merchants" or "coolie barristers" as the case might be. By 1893 there were almost as many Indians as Europeans in Natal, although both groups were greatly outnumbered by the black Africans. When considering the genesis of Gandhi's sense of Indian nationalism, it is important to note that in South Africa, all Indians were in the same boat. Regardless of caste, religion, or language—things that divided them at home—in South Africa all Indians were coolies.

The turning point in Gandhi's life, the moment when he clearly saw what he must do, came in June 1893. He was traveling by train to Pretoria in a first-class passenger car and refused the conductor's order to go to the car reserved for "Coloreds" at the back of the train. Consequently, he was ejected from the train at Pietermaritzburg and spent the night on the station platform, cold and alone. However, that wasn't the end of it. A later segment of his journey was by stagecoach. In this case, Indians were supposed to ride outside next to the driver if there were enough Europeans to fill the coach. Again, Gandhi refused. This time he was savagely beaten by the driver until the other passengers pleaded for mercy. He was never the same again. Gone was the shyness, the diffidence, the indecision. In their place was personal composure, quiet self-confidence—and a steely determination to prevail, no matter what the odds.[13]

Gandhi never did bring to trial the suit for which Dada Abdullah & Company had hired him because he managed to persuade the antagonists to reach a reasonable compromise settlement. Gandhi's entire approach to law was now incompatible with the English system; he thought lawyers should be mediators, not champions of one side. By the time he wrote *Hind Swaraj*, Gandhi's distaste for law had settled into bitter censure. Lawyers had "enslaved India," and the entire legal profession was teaching immorality.[14]

As he had in London, Gandhi turned seriously to religion, in an openminded quest for spiritual truth. He read the Bible, the Koran, and Leo Tolstoy's *The Kingdom of God Is Within You* (in which the great Russian philosopher rejects all forms of government). His contracted year nearing an end, Gandhi was ready to return to India in May 1894, when he learned of a proposed Franchise Amendment Bill under which Indians in Natal were going to be denied the right to vote. He immediately decided to stay on and by August had organized the Natal Indian Congress. In September he "pocketed the insult" of removing his turban in order to fight in the high courts of Natal and the Transvaal. Gandhi now divided his time three ways: fighting legal battles, organizing Indian workers and professionals, and exploring new dimensions of religion. In April 1895 he visited a Trappist monastery near Durban and was impressed by the monks' piety and self-sufficiency.

In June 1896 Gandhi returned to India to fetch the wife he had lived with for only five years of the fourteen they had been married. A second motive was to rally support at home for Indians in South Africa. He stayed in India for six months and returned to Durban in December. Gandhi's ship had departed Bombay during an outbreak of plague and thus was quarantined in Durban harbor for a month. During this time, in the minds of Durban whites, frightening rumors about the plague blended with intense hostility toward Gandhi, whom they knew to be an agitator. When Gandhi disembarked on January 13, 1897, he was attacked by a mob. They beat and kicked him so viciously that he fainted. When Gandhi was helped into a house, the crowd threatened to burn it down and sang chants about hanging him. They might have actually done so had Gandhi not been rescued by an Englishwoman, the wife of a police superintendent. So inflamed was the public that the police hid him inside the station house for three full days. Gandhi could identify some men in the mob but refused to press charges against them.

In October 1899 when the war broke out between the English and the Boers (white South African settlers of Dutch descent), Gandhi organized an Indian ambulance corps of 1,100 volunteers, arguing that if Indians wanted full rights within the British Empire, they had to be ready to defend it. The British initially refused but changed their minds when the war turned vicious.

Gandhi returned to India in October 1901, hoping to establish a law practice that would support his political activism. He spoke at a meeting of the INC in December, offering a resolution in support of Indians in South Africa. February 1902 found him in Calcutta, meeting with Gopal Krishna Gokhale (1866–1915), a nationalist who urged his compatriots to reform themselves before negotiating with the English for independence.[15] After a year in which he again failed to make a living as a lawyer, either in Rajkot or Bombay, Gandhi went back to South Africa at the request of Indians there who needed him to fight anti-Asiatic legislation in Transvaal.

In February 1903 Gandhi opened a law office in Johannesburg, and four months later he founded a journal called *Indian Opinion*. While advocating "home rule" for India (autonomy but not full independence), he was still ready to defend the empire by leading stretcher-bearers during the 1906 Zulu Rebellion in Natal. British officers were startled to find Gandhi nursing wounded Zulus with compassion equal to the compassion he extended toward wounded Englishmen.

In August 1906, the Boer-dominated Transvaal government published a draft Transvaal Asiatic Amendments Act that required fingerprinting and registration of all Indians in the province. As is common in such situations, symbolic humiliations mobilized previously indifferent people. At a meeting in a Johannesburg theater in September 1906, Gandhi presented his plan for a nonviolent campaign of mass civil disobedience. Indians would refuse to register and then calmly take whatever came. Gandhi called this strategy *satyagraha*, a neologism that can be translated as "truth power," "soul-force," or "love-force." Gandhi rejected the term *passive resistance* because there was nothing passive about conquering hatred. It was a mighty battle, fought within one's own soul.

Mohandas K. Gandhi was a famous man by October 1906 when he sailed to London to ask the newly elected Liberal government to protect the rights of Indians in South Africa. The man who had once found himself tongue-tied in a Bombay courtroom now addressed Parliament. There was little the British could do to eradicate race hatred from South Africa. In a campaign speech given while Gandhi was at sea, Boer leader Jan Christian Smuts proclaimed, "The Asiatic cancer, which has already eaten so deeply into the vitals of South Africa, ought to be resolutely eradicated."[16]

Britain granted the Boers "responsible government" in the Transvaal in January 1907. This meant that the Boer local legislatures could now write racially discriminatory laws. General Louis Botha promised "to drive the coolies out of the country within four years."[17] In July, the Registration Act took effect; a general strike followed by members of the Passive Resistance Association, an organization Gandhi had formed to lead a movement of civil disobedience. When Gandhi was arrested he conducted his own courtroom defense and was simply ordered to leave Transvaal. Re-arrested in January 1908, he was sentenced to two months in prison.

Gandhi's movement was a success, for very few Indians registered. General Smuts summoned Gandhi—his prisoner—and offered to compromise. The legal requirement that Indians must register would be lifted if Gandhi called an end to the *satyagraha* campaign and persuaded his volunteers to register of their own free will. Gandhi agreed, but it nearly cost him his life. On February 10 he was beaten unconscious by a giant Pathan named Mir Alam Khan, who had sworn to kill the first man who registered—Gandhi was that first man. Yet from his sickbed Gandhi forgave his assailant, who later publicly confessed that he had been completely in the wrong. When Smuts proved unable to deliver on his end of the bargain, Gandhi renewed the resistance campaign and orchestrated the public burning of thousands of registration certificates. Meanwhile, more trouble was brewing. The Boers passed a law prohibiting Indians from crossing the border from Natal to Transvaal. Gandhi was arrested leading many Indians across the border. He was given another two months' hard labor and used the time to study the *Bhagavad Gita* and books by Henry David Thoreau.[18]

PERSONAL LIFE IN SOUTH AFRICA

During Gandhi's twenty-one years in South Africa, his personal life evolved in a spiritual direction that, he insisted, was inseparable from political and social reform, the moral universe being indivisible. In the mid-1890s he was still wearing European clothing, including a necktie and polished shoes, and lived in an impressive European-style house in Durban. In May 1897 he assisted at the birth of his third son and three years later delivered his fourth son. His doubts about Western medicine were deepening along with his distrust of Western law.

In 1904, while on a long train ride, Gandhi read John Ruskin's *Unto This Last*, a sweeping critique of capitalism and a call for people to abandon the pursuit of wealth and power. Gandhi said that the book marked a turning point in his life.[19] Before the year was out he had established Phoenix Settlement, a self-sufficient community outside Durban where he and his followers (who by now were more like disciples) tried to live according to the religious and social principles of Tolstoy and Ruskin. This first of the four communities Gandhi founded became the model for the Indian ashrams of his later years.

Gandhi had long tried to master his so-called animal passions. Twice he had taken a vow of chastity, and twice failed. Now, in the summer of 1906, at age thirty-six, he renewed the pledge and remained celibate until his death by assassination at age seventy-eight. Kasturbai did not object. At first Gandhi was troubled by occasional nocturnal emissions, which he interpreted as a sign of lustful intent still lurking in his soul. Later in life, believing himself at last free even of carnal thoughts, he experimented on his own psyche by persuading young women to sleep naked with him, to be certain that he had really transcended animal passions. He had.

Gandhi had Quaker friends in Pretoria who encouraged his interest in Christianity. He was never going to restrict himself to a single faith, though, because he believed that all religions were true and that all ultimately merged into truth. By *truth* Gandhi meant something far more exalted than mere correspondence with facts. According to one keen interpreter of Gandhian thought, Gandhi believed that the notion of truth was similar to what Western philosophers meant by the term *natural law*.²⁰ In January and February 1907 Gandhi wrote a series of eight articles on Ethical Religion.

Gandhi carried on a fruitful correspondence with Count Leo Tolstoy. In 1910, when he founded a second model community on an 1,100-acre plot donated by a German–Jewish disciple named Herman Kallenbach, Gandhi called it Tolstoy Farm. Here people lived simply, growing their own food and making their own furniture. His followers included Hindus, Muslims, Parsis, and Christians.²¹ Their daily communal prayer meetings included readings, rituals, and hymns drawn from all these religions. Gandhi slept in the open on a thin cloth, and if he had to go into Johannesburg, he walked the forty-two miles round-trip. By 1912 he had given up European clothing in favor of a simple hand-spun *dhoti* and was experimenting with a pure fruit diet.

Political developments demanded Gandhi's attention, too. In 1909 he went to London to appeal for British support for his campaign against race discrimination in South Africa. He must have been thoroughly disgusted by what he found in England, for while aboard ship on his return voyage he wrote *Hind Swaraj*, a darkly pessimistic condemnation of every facet of industrial civilization. All of Gandhi's subsequent writing and action can be understood only in the light of this piece. Written in Gujarati and published in South Africa by the journal *Indian Opinion*, it was banned in India by the British colonial authorities. Gandhi translated it into English and sent a copy to Tolstoy.

Gandhi was emerging as an important figure in India as well as in South Africa. In October 1912 Gokhale visited South Africa, and Gandhi took him on a five-week tour. Upon his return to India, Gokhale said, "Gandhi has in him the marvelous spiritual power to turn ordinary men around him into heroes and martyrs."²²

Gandhi turned his *satyagraha* movement on and off depending on what concessions he could wring from the South African government. New insults were offered almost every year. For example, in 1913 the Supreme Court of Cape Province ruled that only Christian marriages were legal. This made the wives of all Indian Hindus and Muslims into concubines, and that is exactly how Gandhi pitched the issue. New nonviolent protests led to mass arrests. Gandhi's wife, Kasturbai, was given three months at hard labor in September. In November Gandhi led a protest march by striking coal miners, who were joined by sugar plantation workers. Colonial police fired on them. Gandhi was sentenced to nine months' hard labor (his fourth jailing in South Africa) but was released after one month because the political situation had become dangerous, with 50,000 Indian workers on strike and several thousand in jail. Upon his release, on December 18, 1913, Gandhi donned the clothes of an indentured laborer, and took only one meal a day until a settlement was reached between Smuts and himself. The *satyagraha* movement was suspended. Gandhi's work in South Africa was now done.

RETURN TO INDIA

Gandhi sailed from South Africa for the last time on July 18, 1914. He went to London to meet with Gokhale. World War I began while he was at sea. Gandhi set about organizing an ambulance corps of Indian students in London. Five years earlier he had written in *Hind Swaraj*, "I long for freedom from the English yoke. I would pay any price for it. I would accept chaos in exchange for it. For the English peace is the peace of the grave. Anything would be better than this living death of a whole people. This Satanic rule has well-nigh ruined [India] materially, morally and spiritually."[23] Now he admitted that the British Empire had certain ideals with which he had "fallen in love." When Gandhi returned to India in January 1915 he was awarded a medal for loyalty to the empire. This put him in an ambiguous position vis-à-vis other Indian nationalists, whose ranks were now swelling.

The political climate in India had changed during Gandhi's decades abroad. In the late 1890s plague and famine had spread across the land. The assassination of a British official in Pune (Poona) in 1897 signaled the beginning of a terrorist movement. Administrative partition of Bengal in May 1905—creating a Muslim-majority province in the east, today's Bangladesh—was a red flag to Indian nationalists. They retaliated with a Swadeshi (self-sufficiency) movement to use native products, not British imports. The INC, by now a force to be reckoned with, called for a complete boycott of English textiles. In December 1906 Congress declared *swaraj* (self-government), and nothing less, to be its goal. But the movement split on how to achieve that goal. Gandhi's mentor, Gokhale, was found among the moderates; a more extreme faction included Bal Gangadhar Tilak and Aurobindo Ghose.

In 1909 the so-called Morley–Minto reforms had provided for elections to provincial and legislative councils, with separate election rolls for Muslims. The British were always sympathetic to Indian Muslims' fears of being submerged in the Hindu majority. Still thinking that with adjustments their Raj could be prolonged indefinitely, the British transferred their seat of government to Delhi in 1912 and embarked on the grand project of laying out a New Delhi. The expansive broad avenues that we know today, and the monumental sandstone government buildings done in a hybrid Anglo-Indian style, were designed and built between 1913 and 1931 under the supervision of Edwin Lutyens and Herbert Baker.

Gandhi was reluctant to do anything that might embarrass the British while the war was on, so he threw his prodigious energy into his first model community in India, the Sabarmati Ashram, near Ahmadabad in his home province of Gujarat. In classical times an ashram had been a place of spiritual exertion. At Sabarmati, daily prayer was central. Meetings usually began with a Buddhist chant, then Hindu prayers, a few Arabic verses from the Koran, verses from Zoroastrian prayers, and Christian hymns. "Bapu," said a follower, "believed that praying and constantly repeating the name of God were the best ways to purify the mind of evil thoughts."[24]

Gandhi's utopian communities were created to serve as models for the larger society. At Sabarmati the farm chores were supplemented by daily sessions spinning homemade cloth (to substitute for imported British cloth) on tiny hand-wheels. It was a beautiful symbol of constructive noncooperation, and it became a virtual obsession with Gandhi, to the point that he claimed that the sound of the wheel as it turned healed the body. At Sabarmati, Gandhi lived in a room not much bigger than the prison cells in which he'd spent so much time. The ashram admitted an Untouchable family in September 1915, a clear challenge to defenders of Hindu tradition. Gandhi was now forty-six years old, and his complex philosophy had fully matured.

GANDHI'S PHILOSOPHY

By no means did the Mahatma reject everything from the West. His outlook was influenced by Ruskin, Salt, and Tolstoy, and especially by Henry David Thoreau (1817–62), the American writer and advocate of resistance to unjust laws. Thoreau's essay on civil disobedience, Gandhi said, "seemed to be so convincing and truthful" that he "felt the need of knowing more of Thoreau," so he quickly read whatever he could obtain, including *Walden*.[25] Louis Fischer points out an interesting circularity: "There was an Indian imprint on Thoreau; he and his friend Ralph Waldo Emerson had read the *Bhagavad Gita* and some of the sacred Hindu *Upanishads*."[26] Fundamental to comprehending Gandhian thought is recognizing that, much as we might like to separate his sublime ethics from his seemingly eccentric notions of hygiene and nutrition, Gandhi himself insisted that this could not be done. "I claim that human mind or human society is not divided into watertight compartments called social, political and religious. All act and react on one another."[27] His vision was holistic.

Western civilization must not be imitated by Indians, for it is "a disease" under which "the nations of Europe are becoming degraded and ruined day by day." His analysis of industrial society, shaped by Edward Carpenter's *Civilization: Its Cause and Cure*, is predicated on the belief that modern man is alienated from his true being: "Formerly, men worked in the open air only as much as they liked. Now thousands of workmen meet together and for the sake of maintenance work in factories or mines. Their condition is worse than that of beasts." Modern man is "enslaved by temptation of money and the luxuries that money can bring." Europeans "appear to be half mad." Like Karl Marx, Gandhi believed that "one has only to be patient and [industrial capitalism] will be self-destroyed."[28] At a time when other Asian nationalists were inspired by Japan's success in modernizing so rapidly, Gandhi wrote that the evil spirit of modern civilization was "blasting" Japan.[29] Japanese, like Europeans, would soon be worshipping the body more than the spirit, he predicted.

Gandhi expressed his abhorrence of industrial civilization clearly in a lecture he gave in Allahabad in December 1916:

> It is not possible to conceive gods inhabiting a land which is made hideous by the smoke and the din of mill chimneys and factories and whose roadways are traversed by rushing engines dragging numerous cars crowded with men mostly who know not what they are after, who are often absent-minded, and whose tempers do not improve by being uncomfortably packed like sardines in boxes.[30]

Gandhi's rejection of technology seems quaint, almost Luddite. Machinery "represents a great sin," and "is like a snake-hole which may contain from one to a hundred snakes." Railroads, in particular, drew his scorn. They "accentuate the evil nature of man" because they enable "bad men [to] fulfill their evil designs with greater rapidity." Railroads made it too easy to visit the holy cities of India and had thereby turned them into impious places, he believed. It was blasphemous to try to move so fast, because "God set a limit to man's locomotive ambition in the construction of his body."[31] Worst of all, the sheer scale of capitalist production had ruined the economy of village India. (This was undeniably true and applied equally to China.)

Whether Gandhi fully appreciated the irony, he would never have become famous without modern devices such as the printing press, camera, telegraph, and above all the microphone and loudspeaker. He was hardly a great orator. He spoke in a quiet, singsong voice, employing a conversational tone, but he could bring large crowds to order by raising one finger. He traveled across India by train, even as he blamed railways for spreading bubonic plague and causing famine by making it easier for commercial agriculture to replace subsistence agriculture.

To the obvious question, which he posed to himself in *Hind Swaraj*, "Is it good or bad that all you are saying will be printed through machinery?" he answered, "This is one of those instances which demonstrate that sometimes poison is used to kill poison." Despite all of this, there were two modern inventions that the Mahatma prized greatly, and never went without: eyeglasses and a watch.

Gandhi romanticized and misinterpreted Indian history. He thought that

Hindus and Muslims had lived together peacefully before the colonial era. He claimed that India had been "one nation" before the English came to India. He imagined that there was "no aloofness" between people from different parts of India, and that in traditional India there was "no system of life-corroding competition."[32] Ancient Indians could have invented machinery if they had wanted to, he asserted, but "our forefathers knew that, if we set our hearts after such things, we would become slaves and lose our moral fibre. They, therefore, after due deliberation decided that we should only do what we could with our hands and feet."[33] In the most glaring error of all, Gandhi wrote, "All scholars agree in testifying that the civilization of India is the same today as it was thousands of years ago."[34] Whatever Gandhi disliked about India must be new.

This is one form of nationalism. Gandhi extols Indian civilization, which "is not to be beaten in the world." It is better than Western civilization because "the latter is godless, the former is based on a belief in God." And "deportation for life to the Andamans is not expiation enough for the sin of encouraging European civilization."[35]

Gandhi was on firmer ground when he criticized the way history books are written—they are a record of kings and wars, he said, but real history is the story of cooperation: "The fact that there are so many men still alive in the world shows that it is based not on the force of arms but on the force of truth or love. . . . Little quarrels of millions of families in their daily lives disappear before the exercise of this force. Hundreds of nations live in peace."[36] By emphasizing the ubiquity of cooperation, not conflict, Gandhi directly contradicted Karl Marx and his followers.

Gandhi's ethical commandments are clear and simple. The first is *ahimsa* (translated as "nonviolence" or "love force"). It cannot be absolute: "Where there is only a choice between cowardice and violence I would advise violence. . . . I would rather have India resort to arms in order to defend her honour than that she should in a cowardly manner become or remain a helpless witness to her own dishonour."[37]

The second commandment is *brahmacharya* (celibacy, literally the realization of Brahma). Many Westerners regard celibacy as a harmful denial of natural instinct, but Gandhi characterized his years of study in England as "a long and healthy spell of separation" from Kasturbai. According to traditional Hindu belief, men should conserve their vital force. In a letter he wrote, "In the male the sexual act is a giving up of vital energy every time."[38] Therefore, celibacy must be the ideal, because a body that engages in sex can never be completely healthy.

In January 1931 Pope Pius XI issued an encyclical denouncing all forms of birth control. Gandhi agreed fully that the only acceptable reason for sexual intercourse was to maintain the species. In December 1935 Gandhi had an unintentionally hilarious non–meeting of the minds with Margaret Sanger,

founder of the American Birth Control League. She protested that denying
people a sexual outlet would cause nervous disorders and mental break-
downs. Gandhi replied that such people must be "imbeciles." Sanger asked
him, "Do you think it is possible for two people who are in love, who are
happy together, to regulate their sex act only once in two years, so that relationship would only take place when they wanted a child?" Gandhi replied,
"I had the honour of doing that very thing, and I am not the only one."[39]
Gandhi's ideal was that each person should exhibit both masculine and femi-
nine characteristics, as androgyny is a characteristic of some Hindu gods.

Gandhi believed in a connection between diet and morality and advised
his followers to avoid eating spices or drinking alcohol. He deliberately took
a very long time to chew and swallow. A disciple who lived at the Sevagram
Ashram remembered, "Bapu invariably asked them, 'Did you have a good
bowel movement this morning, sisters?' . . . He believed these bodily functions were as natural and sacred as eating."[40] To demonstrate the falsity of
Hindu ideas of ritual pollution, Gandhi amazed villagers by sweeping up
human excrement.

The only way to perfect a person—or a nation—was by self-denial. Every
Monday Gandhi remained silent; he regarded this as a religious duty. One
hears echoes of the Buddha in Gandhi's wish to become "absolutely pas-
sion-free in thought, speech, and action," and in his declaration, "What I
have been striving and pining to achieve these thirty years is self-realization,
to see God face to face, to attain *moksha*."[41] (In Buddhism, *moksha* means
"freedom from birth and death, release from the cycles of reincarnation.")
There seem to have been Christian elements in Gandhi's self-concept, too.
His daily massage of a leper at Sevagram recalls Jesus' washing of feet. Ved
Mehta states flatly that Gandhi "had come to believe that he was an instrument of God's will."[42]

Gandhi's program for social reform started with the principle of equality.
Men must not think themselves superior to women, and Hindus must abandon the whole idea of a social hierarchy. He coined a new term for Untouchables; they were *harijans* (children of God). One might think that Gandhi's
belief in human equality would lead him to champion political democracy,
but no: "It is a superstitious and ungodly thing to believe that an act of a
majority binds a minority."[43] The British "Mother of Parliaments is like a
sterile woman and a prostitute."[44] Gandhi was in fact quite naïve about the
dilemmas of political power, saying he did not know what democracy was
and that in his Ramarajya, "public opinion is the opinion of people who
practice penance and who have the good of the people at heart."[45] This is
exactly the elitist assumption that Marx and Lenin made, and which led all
Communist governments down the nightmare road to totalitarianism. Gandhi was naïve about fascists, too, professing to see no difference between
Nazi Germany and democratic England except that the Nazis were better

organized.[46] He advised a refugee from Nazi Germany to go back and organize nonviolent resistance there.[47]

In his Ramarajya, village government (the only government) would be in the hands of the traditional *panchayat*, five people elected by the villagers. The *panchayat* would have all power—legislative, executive, and judicial. Could he have been unaware that in practice village *panchayats* are inevitably dominated by the higher castes? It is unsettling to consider how easily Gandhi might have slipped into authoritarianism had he ever consented to hold political office. In the aforementioned dialogue with Margaret Sanger, Gandhi asked, "Why should people not be taught that it is immoral to have more than three or four children and that after they have had that number they should sleep separately? If they are taught this it would harden into custom. And if social reformers cannot impress this idea upon the people, why not a law?"[48]

Of course, Gandhi never sought state power. He distrusted all governments and advocated small-scale communes where all necessary business could be conducted face to face. Once national life becomes perfect, "each person will become his own ruler," and "there will be no political institution and therefore no political power."[49] If these passages sound unrealistic, the reader must remember that Gandhi was a shrewd, calculating political infighter, willing to compromise on everything but the basics. And he astutely recognized the contradictory nature of British imperialism: benevolent one day, repressive the next. His strategy was to provoke repression until popular resistance mounted and the oppressors grew ashamed of themselves.

One tactic Gandhi employed against the British was that which his mother had used to get her way inside the family—fasting. To Westerners it seemed coercive, a form of blackmail, but Gandhi saw it differently—he was taking others' sins upon himself. Gandhi's political tactics cannot be understood apart from his concept of how the universe works, namely, that human wickedness can provoke the gods. (For example, he attributed an earthquake in Bihar to mistreatment of Untouchables.) But atonement could set things right. When Gandhi made a pilgrimage to sacred Haridwar, where the river Ganges emerges onto the north Indian plain, he was appalled to see how filthy the town was, so "he resolved that thereafter he would restrict his diet in any given 24 hours to only five articles of food."[50]

GANDHI AND INDIAN INDEPENDENCE

In India dissatisfaction with the British mounted as World War I ground on. A great influenza epidemic in 1917 and 1918 further soured the public mood. Agitation for home rule was so widespread that Britain announced in August 1917 the gradual development of self-governing institutions in India. Concrete injustice, rather than the abstract goal of independence, spurred Gandhi to new activism. In February 1918 he led a *satyagraha* campaign on behalf of locked-out factory workers in Ahmedabad, forcing the mill owners to the bargaining table by fasting. The translator Gilbert Murray issued a prescient warning to British authorities in 1918:

> Persons in power should be very careful how they deal with a man who cares nothing for sensual pleasure, nothing for riches, nothing for comfort or praise, or promotion, but is simply determined to do what he believes is right. He is a dangerous and uncomfortable enemy, because his body which you can always conquer gives you so little purchase upon his soul.[51]

World War I ended on November 11, 1918. The hopes of colonized peoples focused on the Versailles Peace Conference because of President Woodrow Wilson's replacement of empires by a world of democratic republics. With incredibly poor timing, the British chose this juncture to pass the Rowlatt Bills, under which Indian newspapers were censored and Indian political agitators were jailed without trial. Gandhi immediately launched a new *satyagraha* campaign for self-rule. A nationwide *hartal* (general strike) to protest the Rowlatt Bills was called for April 6. Scattered violence broke out across India, and Gandhi immediately did penance for his own failure to gauge the political situation correctly.

In Amritsar, Brigadier General R. E. H. Dyer banned public gatherings and became furious when his order was ignored. On April 13, 1919, a crowd gathered in Jallianwala Bagh, a walled enclosure with no way for people to escape. Dyer moved his Gurkha and Baluchi troops up to the entrance and, giving no warning, ordered them to fire into the thickest part of the crowd. They did so for ten minutes. A court of inquiry later determined that 1,650 bullets had been fired, wounding 1,100 people and killing 400. General Dyer stated at his court-martial, "I thought I would be doing a jolly lot of good. There could be no question of undue severity," for "it was no longer a question of merely dispersing the crowd, but one of producing a sufficient moral effect not only on those who were present, but more especially throughout the Punjab."[52] Dyer was relieved of his command but was welcomed home by British Conservatives, who presented a jeweled sword to the "saviour of the Punjab."

The political atmosphere was now hopelessly poisoned. In the aftermath of the Amritsar massacre British aircraft bombed and strafed a rioting mob. Even more galling to Indians than the killings were symbolic humiliations such as the order that Indians in the Punjab must get down on all fours when an Englishman or Englishwoman walked by. Gandhi returned the medals he had been given for his help in the Boer War, the Zulu Rebellion, and World War I. Concentrating on ways to organize nonviolent resistance, he called for a boycott of the toothless legislative councils London had offered in place of home rule.

The INC had heretofore only a loose structure; now Gandhi turned it into a mass organization with local branches all across the nation. Foreign cloth was burned in Bengal and Punjab. Viceroy Lord Reading conferred with Gandhi in May 1921, but to no avail. On July 31 Gandhi personally presided over a bonfire in Bombay. In September he adopted the skimpy costume he wore for the rest of his life. In October he made a vow of daily spinning (also maintained for the rest of his life). Spinning had the practical effect of producing native cloth and acquired a higher significance in Gandhi's mind—it was a sacrament that turned the spinner's thoughts toward God.[53]

Gandhi and Congress raised the stakes, calling on Indians to quit the British Army. The British cracked down in December 1921, jailing 30,000 Congress followers. Gandhi struggled to keep the protests peaceful and fasted whenever violence broke out. Rioters killed twenty-two policemen in Uttar Pradesh in February 1922. Gandhi fasted for five days and suspended the civil disobedience campaign, incurring the scorn of Congress hotheads. London saw Gandhi's efforts to regulate the protests as the height of deceit. Pressure mounted to arrest him, and in March 1922 he was given six years in prison. He used the time to start writing *Satyagraha in South Africa*. Two years later, he was released after an emergency appendicitis operation, because the British feared what might happen if he died in their custody.

For the rest of the 1920s Gandhi concentrated on social reforms. He fasted for the abolition of restrictions on Untouchables and to promote Hindu–Muslim unity. His Sabarmati Ashram acquired an unusual convert in 1925 in Madeleine Slade, the daughter of a British admiral. Gandhi took a special interest in her and renamed her Mirabehn. That year he began the three-year task of writing his autobiography, *The Story of My Experiments with Truth*. As the decade ended, tension rose again. In 1927 the British appointed a commission, headed by Sir John Simon, to assess conditions in India and perhaps to recommend constitutional change. As the Simon Commission did not contain a single Indian member, Congress boycotted it.

On New Year's Day 1930 Gandhi unfurled the flag he had designed for Congress, with the spinning wheel in the center. (Today's Indian flag is a slight modification of Gandhi's design.) On January 26 Congress declared Indian independence from a draft written by Gandhi and gave the Mahatma authority to lead another civil disobedience campaign. This *satyagraha* was an act of political genius. Under the India Salt Act of 1882 the government maintained a legal monopoly on production of salt and levied a tax on its purchase, burdening the poorest people of India. But it was technically easy to break the law—all one had to do was to collect seawater and let the sun evaporate it. Gandhi conceived of a "Salt March" of 240 miles, from Sabarmati to the sea. He and his growing number of followers walked ten miles a day, preaching noncooperation to villagers at each stop. The Salt March assumed the character of a pilgrimage, and Gandhi wondered if he, like Jesus going to Jerusalem, might have to die. On April 6, 1930, he broke the law by making his own salt.

It was an irresistible story to the mass media, Indian and foreign. All across India, peasants made salt and went to jail. Muslims, who until then had not participated in Gandhi's campaigns, joined in. Riots broke out in the farthest corners of the country, Chittagong and Peshawar. Gandhi was arrested May 5 and jailed at Yeravda Prison in Pune. Eventually the British had to imprison 100,000 people. The Salt March was a brilliant success, for it mobilized Indians and shamed the English.

In the Great Depression, British imperial policy veered between repression and tolerance, out of fear that men more extreme than Gandhi might seize the initiative. Gandhi was released unconditionally in January 1931, and the British viceroy Lord Irwin began talks with him in February, much to the disgust of Winston Churchill who found it

> alarming, and also nauseating to see Mr. Gandhi, a seditious Middle Temple lawyer, now posing as a fakir of a type well-known in the East, striding half-naked up the steps of the Viceregal Palace, while he is still organizing and conducting a defiant campaign of civil disobedience, to parley on equal terms with the representative of the King-Emperor.[54]

Gandhi and Irwin signed an agreement under which Indians were allowed to make salt, and the *satyagraha* was called off. Gandhi was invited to attend a Round Table Conference in London. When his ship transited the Suez Canal, British police prevented Egyptians from seeing the man they had heard so much about. In London Gandhi stayed at a settlement house in the East End. By now he was world famous. He had been named *Time* magazine's "Man of the Year" for 1930. He met with George Bernard Shaw, Charlie Chaplin, and the archbishop of Canterbury (but not with Winston Churchill, who refused to see him). He visited workers at Lancaster cotton mills who would be thrown out of work by his cloth boycott, and gently explained why Indian hand-spinning must continue. He delivered talks at Eton and Oxford. In November he went to Buckingham Palace, clad in his loin cloth, and exchanged pleasantries with King George V and Queen Mary. When asked later if he had worn enough clothes for the occasion, he replied that the king had enough clothes for the two of them. Despite good humor all around, the Round Table Conference ended in failure. Gandhi held out for complete independence, but the British offered only limited autonomy. On his way back to India Gandhi wanted to meet the Pope, but Vatican officials refused to admit him without Western clothes.

In India Gandhi resumed civil disobedience, and British policy swung back toward its repressive pole. Congress was banned, and peaceful picket ing was outlawed. Gandhi was re-arrested on January 4, 1932, and put back in Yeravda Prison. Eighty thousand others were jailed in the spring of 1932. British strategy was to divide the opposition by playing on communal differences. To this end they proposed separate electorates (for legislative assemblies) for Muslims, Sikhs, Christians, and Untouchables. Gandhi pulled out all the stops and initiated a "fast unto death" against separate elections for Untouchables. This time he almost died before the British conceded enough to convince Gandhi to eat again.

Gandhi withdrew once more from politics, resigned from Congress, gave Sabarmati Ashram to Untouchables, and founded Sevagram Ashram near Wardha, in central India. He propounded a "Constructive Programme" of hand-spinning and rural education. Gandhi's ideas on the latter subject may by now be deduced. He dismissed as "false" and "rotten" Western education, sarcastically recalling that in his own high school he had been "taught all sorts of things except religion."[55] He praised India's ancient school system, where children were taught right conduct. Following John Ruskin, Gandhi declared the basis of education to be pure air, clean water, clean earth, gratitude, hope, and charity. His own children never forgave Gandhi for denying them the Western educations they ardently desired. Like China's Mao Zedong, Gandhi thought the masses were best fitted for manual training, not intellectualizing: "A peasant earns his bread honestly. He has ordinary knowledge of the world. . . . He understands and observes the rules of morality. But he cannot write his own name. What do you propose to do by giving him a knowledge of letters? Will you add an inch to his happiness? Do you wish to make him discontented with his cottage or his lot?"[56]

By the 1935 Government of India Act, Britain granted India a new constitution and established elective provincial legislatures but retained ultimate veto power. (This moderate concession angered Churchill, who snarled that "Gandhism and all it stands for must ultimately be grappled with and finally crushed.")[57] In the first elections, held in February 1937, Congress won majorities in seven of eleven provinces.

When war in Europe broke out in September 1939 Congress offered to support Britain in return for a promise of independence after the war was over, but London refused. In May 1940 Churchill became British prime minister. Jawaharlal Nehru, who had led Congress since Gandhi's resignation, was jailed. The British listened sympathetically to Indian Muslims' demand for a separate state (Pakistan), which was incompatible with Gandhi's dream of a united, independent India. Gandhi was now seventy years old and, by Robert Payne's account, on the verge of a nervous breakdown. On one occasion, he threatened to go on a fast because of a missing fountain pen.[58]

Congress leaders were released after Japan attacked Pearl Harbor. Singapore fell in February 1942 and then Rangoon. Indians were now offered dominion status (independence except in foreign affairs and defense) after the war, if they would support Britain. They refused. Gandhi, who had written an open letter to Hitler in December 1941, admonishing the Führer to cease his "monstrous" acts but assuring him that he did not really believe him to be a "monster," suggested that Congress pass a "Quit India" resolution, which it did on August 8, 1942. Gandhi was arrested (for the sixth time in India) the next day, and held in the Aga Khan Palace at Pune until the tide of war turned. Kasturbai was arrested, too; she died in prison on February 22, 1944. Gandhi was released on May 6 that year.

Lord Archibald Percival Wavell became the new viceroy of India. He hated Gandhi. "That old man," he confided to his diary, is "an unscrupulous old hypocrite." In another passage he described Gandhi as "an exceedingly shrewd, obstinate, domineering, double-tongued, single-minded politician."[59] Gandhi's worst fear was that Indian Muslims would break away and form their own state, but he could not dissuade Mohammed Ali Jinnah, the acknowledged Muslim leader, from following his own dream. In the summer of 1945, with the war's end in sight, the British released all Congress leaders and convened a conference of all interested political groups. Gandhi was there. The Simla conference achieved little, but in July the Labour Party came to power in Britain, and Clement Attlee replaced Winston Churchill as prime minister. Attlee pledged a transition to Indian independence, starting with local elections, which were held in the winter of 1945–46.

GANDHI'S BITTER LAST YEARS

The Mahatma was seventy-five years old when World War II ended. One would have expected him to condemn categorically the U.S. atomic bombing of Hiroshima and Nagasaki, but he said nothing about it for a year. This puzzling behavior is attributed by one scholar to Gandhi's political calculus that India needed President Harry Truman's support for independence.[60] It appears that Gandhi was plunging into despair because he could see freedom coming but that it would not be his kind of *swaraj*.

Gandhi now roamed restlessly around the giant nation in waiting, pleading for religious tolerance in Bengal and Assam, and for the abolition of untouchability in the south. He implored Tamils to embrace Hindi as their national tongue. Tempers were rising. The Royal Indian Navy was mutinied. British troops sprayed machine-gun fire on rioters in Bombay. Three-way negotiations between the British, Congress, and the Muslim League bogged down in recriminations. Jinnah asked for a "Day of Direct Action" and got the "Great Calcutta Killing":

At dawn on August 16 [1946], Moslem mobs howling in a quasi-religious fervor came bursting from their slums, waving clubs, iron bars, shovels, any instrument capable of smashing a human skull. . . . They savagely beat any Hindu in their path and left the bodies in the city's open gutters. The terrified police simply disappeared. . . . Later, the Hindu mobs came storming out of their neighborhoods, looking for defenseless Moslems to slaughter. . . . By the time the slaughter was over, Calcutta belonged to the vultures. In filthy gray packs they scudded across the sky, tumbling down to gorge themselves on the bodies of the city's six thousand dead.[61]

A similar slaughter took place in the remote town of Noakhali, on the southeast coast of Bengal, where Muslims had the advantage of numbers. They killed 5,000 Hindus, burned their houses, raped their women, mutilated their children. When news of this massacre reached the outside world, Hindus in Bihar, where they were the majority, took revenge on Bihari Muslims.

Gandhi hiked restlessly around East Bengal for four months (November 1946 to February 1947), going barefoot for greater penance, yet few people were now listening to him. He seemed to have lost his will to live.

Prime Minister Attlee announced that Britain would leave India and sent out a new viceroy, Lord Louis Mountbatten, to supervise the transition to independence. When Mountbatten arrived in India he called Gandhi to meet him in New Delhi, putting a plane at Gandhi's disposal. The Mahatma had never flown and did not intend to do so now. He went by third-class rail car.

In the end Jinnah refused all compromise, even Gandhi's desperate offer to form a Muslim government of all India. Partition was now certain. Mountbatten drew up a partition plan in June 1947, and Gandhi accepted the inevitable. The date was set for August 15. His Congress Party was jubilant at the thought of independence at last, but Gandhi was in mourning. He knew partition would bring terrible violence. He went to Calcutta, where he expected the situation to be worst, and stayed in a Muslim home as a tangible demonstration of brotherhood. A mob of angry Hindu teenagers threw bottles and stones at the Mahatma. At the stroke of midnight, August 15, 1947, India achieved *swaraj*. Gandhi would have less than six months to live.

In the greatest migration in human history, 14 million people left their homes. Columns of Muslims fleeing India and Hindus fleeing Pakistan passed each other going in opposite directions. Hindus and Muslims set about killing each other with grim resolution. No one knows how many were killed, perhaps 500,000. Gandhi performed his last services for his countrymen, fasting in October to bring peace to riot-torn Calcutta, then moving on to Delhi. His Delhi fast of January 13–18, 1948, restored peace to that city, saving thousands of lives, but it left Gandhi, now seventy-eight, very weak.

ASSASSINATION

On January 30, 1948, Gandhi spent some time studying Bengali, a language he thought he would need to spread his gospel in the troubled Ganges delta. While walking to his daily prayer meeting he was shot three times at point-blank range by Nathuram Vinayak Godse, a thirty-six-year-old Hindu fanatic. Godse and his co-conspirators hated Gandhi for his kindness to Muslims. Two oft-repeated reports of Gandhi's last day may be attributed to the sort of natural myth-building that occurs when a great soul is martyred, or perhaps they are really true. The first is that he had premonitions of his death and voiced them repeatedly. The second is that when he was shot, he died with the words "He Ram! He Ram! ("Oh God, Oh God") on his lips. In New York, the United Nations lowered its flag to half-mast.

The next day the Mahatma's body was brought to the cremation ground on an Indian Army weapons carrier. One million people attended the sacred Hindu ceremony on the banks of the Yamuna River. Gandhi's third son, Ramdas, lit the sandalwood pyre. The first son, Harilal, who had led a life of abject dissolution in rebellion against his father's saintliness, arrived late. Gandhi's ashes, mixed with those of the sandalwood funeral pyre, were sent all over India to be scattered in the nation's rivers.

News of Gandhi's death sparked riots in Bombay and other cities as mobs attacked offices of the Hindu Mahasabha, the extreme anti-Muslim organization to which Godse belonged. Nathuram Godse and Narayan Apte were executed on November 15, 1949. Three other conspirators were sentenced to life imprisonment.

By some unaccountable bureaucratic fluke, a portion of Gandhi's ashes ended up in a vault in the State Bank of India in Orissa Province, where they were forgotten until 1994. These were scattered on January 30, 1997, at the confluence of the sacred Ganges and Yamuna rivers. No national leaders of the Congress Party attended, but thousands of ordinary Indians cast flowers on the coffin carrying Gandhi's last ashes. A *New York Times* reporter wrote that a large crowd of pilgrims waded into the river and burst into a chant: "As long as the sun and moon rise," they cried, "so will your name live, Mahatma."[62]

NOTES

1. Raghavan Iyer, ed. *The Essential Writings of Mahatma Gandhi* (New Delhi: Oxford University Press, 1996), p. 45.

2. Fatima Meer, "The Making of the Mahatma: The South African Experience," in *Mahatma Gandhi: 125 Years*, ed. B. R. Nanda (New Delhi: Indian Council for Cultural Relations, 1995), p. 54.

3. Ved Mehta, *Mahatma Gandhi and His Apostles* (New Haven, Conn.: Yale University Press, 1993), p. 74.

4. E. Victor Wolfenstein, *The Revolutionary Personality: Lenin, Trotsky, Gandhi* (Princeton, N.J.: Princeton University Press, 1967), p. 76.

5. Mohandas K. Gandhi, *Autobiography: The Story of My Experiments with Truth* (New York: Dover, 1983), p. 3.

6. Gandhi, *Autobiography*, p. 30.

7. Gandhi, *Autobiography*, p. 18.

8. Gandhi, *Autobiography*, p. 27.

9. Gandhi, *Autobiography*, p. 37.

10. Gandhi, *Autobiography*, p. 40.

11. Mehta, *Mahatma Gandhi and His Apostles*, p. 89.

12. Gandhi, *Autobiography*, p. 69.

13. The reader will note an interesting parallel case, three years later in the United States, when a Louisiana man named Adolph Plessy, who was by race seven-eighths white and one-eighth black, was thrown off a passenger train for refusing to vacate a "Whites only" car. The resulting Supreme Court decision, which went against Plessy, laid the legal foundation for racial segregation in the United States until 1954.

14. M. K. Gandhi, *Hind Swaraj*, in *The Penguin Gandhi Reader*, ed. Rudrangshu Mukherjee (New York: Penguin, 1996), pp. 30, 31.

15. D. Mackenzie Brown, *The Nationalist Movement: Indian Political Thought from Ranade to Bhave* (Berkeley: University of California Press, 1970), pp. 59–61.

16. Louis Fischer, *Gandhi: His Life and Message for the World* (New York: New American Library, 1954), p. 25. Thirty-three years later, looking back, Smuts wrote, "It was my fate to be the antagonist of a man for whom even then I had the highest respect."

17. Fischer, *Gandhi*, p. 25.

18. B. R. Nanda, *Mahatma Gandhi: A Biography* (Delhi: Oxford University Press, 1996), p. 105.

19. Fischer, *Gandhi*, p. 30.

20. Unto Tähtinen, "Gandhi on Natural Law," in *Mahatma Gandhi: 125 Years*, pp. 198–205.

21. Nanda, *Mahatma Gandhi*, p. 108.

22. Fischer, *Gandhi*, p. 43.

23. Gandhi, *Hind Swaraj*, in *The Penguin Gandhi Reader*, p. 74.

24. Mehta, *Mahatma Gandhi and His Apostles*, p. 7.

25. Iyer, *The Essential Writings of Mahatma Gandhi*, p. 71.

26. Fischer, *Gandhi*, p. 38.

27. Shalu Bhalla, comp., *Quotes of Gandhi* (New Delhi: UBS Publishers, n.d.), p. 40.

28. All these quotes are from Gandhi's polemical tract *Hind Swaraj*, reprinted in *The Penguin Gandhi Reader*.

29. Iyer, *The Essential Writings of Mahatma Gandhi*, p. 89.

30. From a lecture entitled "Does Economic Progress Clash With Real Progress?" delivered to the Muir Central College Economic Society, Allahabad, India, on December 22, 1916. See also Iyer, *The Essential Writings of Mahatma Gandhi*, pp. 97–98.

31. These quotes are from Gandhi, *Hind Swaraj*, in *The Penguin Gandhi Reader*.

32. Gandhi, *Hind Swaraj*, in *The Penguin Gandhi Reader*, p. 35.

33. Gandhi, *Hind Swaraj*, p. 35.

34. Iyer, *The Essential Writings of Mahatma Gandhi*, p. 102.

35. The quotes in this paragraph are from Gandhi, *Hind Swaraj*, in *The Penguin Gandhi Reader*.

36. Gandhi, *Hind Swaraj*, p. 47.

37. Iyer, *The Essential Writings of Mahatma Gandhi*, p. 237.

38. Quoted in Joseph S. Alter, "Gandhi's Body, Gandhi's Truth: Nonviolence and the Biomoral Imperative of Public Health," *Journal of Asian Studies* 55 (May 1996), p. 308.

39. "Interview to Margaret Sanger [3/4 December 1935]," *The Penguin Gandhi Reader*, pp. 189–91.

40. Mehta, *Mahatma Gandhi and His Apostles*, pp. 13–14.

41. Gandhi, *Autobiography*, p. viii.

42. Mehta, *Mahatma Gandhi and His Apostles*, p. 114.

43. Gandhi, *Hind Swaraj*, p. 49.

44. Gandhi, *Hind Swaraj*, p. 13.

45. From Volume 35 of Gandhi's *Collected Works*, as quoted in *The Penguin Gandhi Reader*, p. xv.

46. Iyer, *The Essential Writings of Mahatma Gandhi*, p. 262.

47. Fischer, "Mahatma Gandhi—A Life for Nonviolence," in *Mahatma Gandhi: 125 Years*, p. 318.

48. "Interview to Margaret Sanger [3/4 December 1935]," *The Penguin Gandhi Reader*, p. 191.

49. From Volume 68 of Gandhi's *Collected Works*, as reprinted in *The Penguin Gandhi Reader*, p. xiv.

50. Mehta, *Mahatma Gandhi and His Apostles*, p. 133.

51. This oft-quoted admonition appeared in the *Hibbert Journal* in 1914. See Nanda, *Mahatma Gandhi*, p. 89.

52. Fischer, *Gandhi*, p. 67.

53. Fischer, *Gandhi*, p. 69.

54. Geoffrey Ashe, *Gandhi* (New York: Stein & Day, 1968), p. xi.

55. Gandhi, *Autobiography*, p. 28.

56. Gandhi, *Hind Swaraj*, p. 54.

57. Fischer, *Gandhi*, p. 135.

58. Robert Payne, *The Life and Death of Mahatma Gandhi* (New York: Smithmark, 1995), p. 489.

59. Quoted in Dennis Dalton, *Mahatma Gandhi: Nonviolent Power in Action* (New York: Columbia University Press, 1993), p. 65.

60. Dietmar Rothermund, "Gandhi's Concepts of Individual Conduct and Social Life," in *Mahatma Gandhi: 125 Years*, p. 183.

61. Larry Collins and Dominique Lapierre, *Freedom at Midnight* (New York: Simon & Schuster, 1975), p. 30.

62. John F. Burns, "Gandhi's Ashes Rest, But Not His Message," *New York Times*, January 31, 1997, p. 1.

11

Indira Nehru Gandhi: The Autocratic Democrat

How hard it is to keep from being king
When it is in you and in the situation.

Robert Frost

INDIRA'S ILLUSTRIOUS FOREBEARS

Four members of the Nehru–Gandhi dynasty personify modern Indian history. The extraordinary lives of Motilal Nehru (1861–1931), his son Jawaharlal 1889–1964), his granddaughter Indira (1917–84), and his great-grandson Rajiv (1944–91) embody all the turbulence of twentieth-century India.

Indira Nehru's illustrious grandfather Motilal Nehru was born May 6, 1861, into a prosperous Kashmiri Brahman family whose members had served the Mughal emperor in Delhi since the early 1700s. The family's fortunes had declined with succeeding generations—Motilal's father, Ganga Dhar, was merely a police officer at the Mughal court when the Sepoy Mutiny broke out in 1857. He fled to Agra to escape draconian British reprisals and died there three months before Motilal was born. Motilal was raised by his elder brother and given a very English education, earning the honorific title *pandit* (wise man, or teacher). Motilal was an agnostic with a scientific and secular outlook who respected and admired English civilization. He was an outstanding modernizer with a broad, international perspective.

People are frequently misled by Indira Nehru Gandhi's last name. She was not related to Mohandas K. Gandhi, the Mahatma, by birth or marriage but simply happened to marry a man with the same last name. Indira was the daughter of independent India's first prime minister, Jawaharlal Nehru. Her son, Rajiv Gandhi, served as prime minister after her assassination until he, too, was assassinated. To help avoid confusion, when Mohandas Gandhi is mentioned in this chapter, he is referred to with the respectful suffix *ji*: "Gandhiji." The reader should also remember that the Indian "Congress" is a political party not a legislature.

Indira Gandhi with Jawaharlal Nehru, 1938

Indira Gandhi with her son, Sanjay Gandhi, 1980

Motilal married a woman named Swarup Rani, and established a law practice in Allahabad, the north Indian sacred city located at the confluence of the Yamuna and Ganges rivers. He quickly grew very rich, which was a blessing when his elder brother died, leaving Motilal responsible for the brother's widow and seven children. Eighteen eighty-nine was an important year in Motilal's life: He joined the Indian Congress, a new reformist political club; he traveled to Europe and came back convinced that India must Westernize; and his son Jawaharlal was born on November 14.

Jawaharlal's childhood was lonely. There were few other children for him to play with, so he spent much time with his British governesses and his tutor, Ferdinand T. Brooks. Brooks taught Jawaharlal the English classics and modern science, and tried to influence him toward Theosophy, an American mystical movement loosely based on Hinduism. An Indian tutor was employed to teach the boy Hindi and Sanskrit. In 1900 Motilal moved the family into a forty-two-room mansion named Anand Bhavan (House of Happiness) in the new European section of Allahabad, away from the dirt and crowding of the old quarter. Anand Bhavan symbolized the bifurcated mentality of nineteenth-century Asian modernizers: The house was divided into a Western area (where Motilal ruled supreme) and an Indian area (where Swarup Rani was boss). Each side of the house had its own kitchen and served its own cuisine. Motilal decreed that only English was to be spoken in his part of the house.

The Nehru style can only be called grand. Anand Bhavan was the first home in Allahabad to be wired for electricity and to have piped, running water. There was a wine cellar, an indoor swimming pool with changing rooms for men and women, a grass tennis court, and a library with 6,000 books. There were Arabian riding horses for the adults and ponies for the children. More than fifty servants kept things running smoothly. Motilal's imported motor car created a local sensation. His frequent trips to Europe offended orthodox Hindus, for whom sea journeys were taboo, but cemented Motilal's already-close bonds with the British community of Allahabad.

In 1911 Motilal and Swarup Rani were invited to meet King George V during his royal visit to India. Motilal cabled Jawaharlal, then studying in London, to send specially made English clothes and shoes.[1] Apart from occasional attendance at Congress meetings, where he advocated gradual reform and close cooperation with the British, Motilal had little to do with politics until he reached middle age.

In 1905 Motilal took Jawaharlal to England and enrolled him in Harrow, a preparatory school. As an academic award, the boy was given a biography of the Italian patriot Giuseppe Garibaldi, which filled him with visions of similar deeds in India. During one summer vacation Jawaharlal traveled to Ireland, where nationalists agitated against British rule. The trip did not sit particularly well with his Anglophile father. In 1907 Jawaharlal graduated from Harrow and entered Trinity College at Cambridge where he studied natural science. Photographs show a handsome, serious young man whose bearing radiated confidence, but underneath he was lonely and moody. He graduated from Cambridge in 1910 and spent the next two years studying law at the Inner Temple in London. In 1912 he passed the bar examination and sailed home.

Jawaharlal opened a law practice in Allahabad, but working as a lawyer did not match his temperament. In 1916 he was married to Shrimati Kamala Kaul, an uneducated girl eleven years his junior. Motilal chartered a train to carry 500 guests to Delhi for weeklong wedding festivities. It was an arranged marriage and somewhat a poor choice, for Kamala did not speak English and could hardly compete for attention with Nehru's waspish sisters. Kamala might have gained acceptance if she had produced a male heir. When she gave birth on November 19, 1917, the Scottish doctor declared, "It's a bonny lassie." Swarup Rani blurted out, "Oh, but it should have been a boy."[2]

INDIRA'S HYPERPOLITICAL CHILDHOOD

Indira Nehru was an only child, a rarity in India. Jawaharlal, swept up in the nationalist movement, paid little attention to her, but Kamala taught her Hindu prayers—and resentment. In later life Indira told an interviewer that Kamala "considered the fact of being a woman a great disadvantage. . . . Hindu women had to go out in the *doli*, a kind of closed sedan chair like a catafalque. My mother always told me about these things with bitterness and rage."[3]

The Nehru family had begun to collaborate closely with Gandhiji and had forged a coalition between Congress and the Muslim League. The moderate Motilal was radicalized by the Amritsar massacre, and Jawaharlal encouraged his new anger. In December 1919 Motilal was elected president of the Indian National Congress (INC). Ready to follow the Mahatma into civil disobedience, Motilal felt it necessary to adopt a simpler lifestyle.

> The separate European kitchen in Anand Bhavan was closed down, and replenishments to the vast wine cellar were stopped. The stables were disbanded, and the large staff of servants drastically reduced. Exquisite crystal and china and costly drapes and furniture representing several exciting and extravagant shopping sprees in London and other European cities were given away.[4]

Motilal gave up his legal practice and sank much of his enormous fortune into the nationalist cause. In 1920 Motilal, Swarup Rani, and Jawaharlal toured peasant villages to see how most Indians really lived. Jawaharlal never accepted Marxism, advocating instead a democratic path to socialism. But at the same time he was a fiery patriot who wanted to confront the British directly. He was arrested for the first time on December 6, 1919. The next day Indira, sitting on her grandfather's lap, watched his trial at Allahabad's Naini Prison.

Now the previously shy and retiring Kamala convinced Motilal and Jawaharlal to make a great bonfire of their fine English suits. A few weeks later a visitor teased young Indira by saying that her doll had also been made in England. This disturbed the child greatly until she finally decided to burn the doll on the roof of Anand Bhavan. It must have seemed like a cremation. Years later she could not picture the doll but said, "I do remember how I felt. I felt as if I were murdering someone."[5]

Indira's childhood was saturated with politics. She literally sat on the laps of all the prominent Indian nationalists, including the Mahatma. Both her parents were repeatedly jailed. In 1921 Motilal and Jawaharlal were arrested and sentenced to six months in jail. Additionally, Motilal was fined 500 rupees. According to Gandhiji the laws under which they had been arrested were unjust, so the fine would not be paid. Thus, the police raided Anand Bhavan and carted off household furniture. The sight of strangers invading her living room sent young Indira into such a fury that she tried to chop off a policeman's thumb with a bread slicer.[6]

Gandhiji's civil disobedience campaign resulted in the jailing of 20,000 Indians in 1921. Forty years later Indira Gandhi recalled "the huge crowds of peasants and the shouting—the brutality—the searching of homes and persons—the arrests."[7] Even her grandmother was beaten in demonstrations. Indira's aunt recounts a "grave-faced little girl" saying politely to a visitor, "I'm sorry, but my grandfather, father and Mummy are all in prison."[8]

In 1922, while Motilal and Jawaharlal were in prison, the Nehru women made a pilgrimage to Gandhiji's ashram at Sabarmati. This was Indira's first encounter with the Mahatma. When her grandfather was released, he gave Indira a miniature *charkha*, the spinning wheel that symbolized Indians' determination to boycott British goods. Indira then taught other small children to spin.[9] The serious little girl delivered political speeches to her dolls and to the servants, many of whom remained on staff even after Motilal's alleged simplification of his life. Indira recalled, "I grew up like a boy, also because most of the children who came to our house were boys. With boys I climbed trees, ran races, and wrestled. I had no complexes of envy or inferiority toward boys. At the same time, however, I liked dolls. I had many dolls. And you know how I played with them? By performing insurrections, assemblies, scenes of arrest."[10]

Indira started kindergarten in Delhi, but in 1923, at Motilal's suggestion, she was enrolled in St. Cecilia's, a private school run by Englishwomen in

Allahabad. Jawaharlal objected so strongly that they had to call in Gandhiji to mediate the quarrel. The Mahatma sided with Jawaharlal, thus Indira was withdrawn from the school and given private tutors instead. This reinforced the deep loneliness that was becoming a defining theme of her girlhood.

In a material sense Indira lacked nothing. During the blindingly hot summers, when the very earth of north India seemed desiccated, the Nehru family retreated to Himalayan "hill stations" frequented by British civil servants. Indira was aware that her life was one of privilege: "My earliest memories are of a feeling that there was a debt I owed; I could never explain to whom or for what; but it was debt that I had to repay."[11] Indira's parents were so deeply involved in politics, and so frequently in jail, that she felt a deep, unfilled void. Her father became general secretary of the INC while Motilal launched the Swaraj Party with the goal of undermining the British Raj by electing candidates to new legislative councils. From 1924 to 1929 Motilal led the opposition in the Central Legislative Assembly.

In November 1924 Kamala, a frail woman with tuberculosis, gave birth prematurely to a son who died a few days later. Kamala's grief was compounded by her husband's neglect and by the continuing spiteful attitude of Indira's haughty aunt (Jawaharlal's sister) Vijayalakshmi. Indira's toughness can be traced to her witnessing the pain her mother endured: "I saw her [Kamala] being hurt and I was determined not to be hurt."[12] In March 1926 the family took Kamala to a Swiss sanatorium. Indira, only eight years old, became fluent in French while Jawaharlal and Motilal visited socialists in Brussels and observed the League of Nations in Geneva. Kamala's health continued its decline, so the family put her in a different sanitorium. Indira was now sent to board at L'Ecole Nouvelle at Bex, Switzerland, where she learned how to ski.

In the spring of 1927 Kamala's health improved, and the Nehrus traveled to Paris where they saw a stage performance of *St. Joan*. The play made a very deep impression on nine-year-old Indira, who later recalled that "[Joan of Arc] immediately took on a definite importance for me. I wanted to sacrifice my life for my country."[13] Indira also witnessed Charles Lindbergh's landing and met Albert Einstein. In the fall of that year Motilal and Jawaharlal went to Moscow for celebrations marking the tenth anniversary of the Bolshevik revolution.

Back in Allahabad, Indira entered a convent school. Her loneliness deepened, and she found a place to withdraw in the gardens around her school. Indira was closer to her indulgent grandfather than to her distracted father, but even Motilal was immersed in politics. In 1928 he wrote the "Nehru Report," which Congress adopted as a draft for a future Indian Constitution, based on dominion status for India. Jawaharlal led a Congress faction that advocated complete independence. Young Indira attended Congress sessions and watched Indian history being made by her father and grandfather. It is small wonder that she, too, chose a political path.

At the end of the decade Motilal was exhausted and discouraged, for the British were paying no attention to his proposals. He renamed his mansion Swaraj Bhavan (House of Independence) and donated it to the Congress Party. A new family house, only slightly less grand, was constructed on the grounds, and the name Anand Bhavan was transferred to it. Gandhiji presented Jawaharlal as his trusted lieutenant. Nehru's high-caste heritage and aristocratic outlook reassured wealthy Indian nationalists who would not have supported a radical party. On December 31, 1929, Jawaharlal was elected president of Congress. The increasingly willful Indira did not share her father's enchantment with Gandhiji: "He was always talking of religion. . . . He was convinced that he was right. . . . The fact is, we young people didn't agree with him on many things."[14]

THE 1930S

In January 1930 Gandhiji called for nonviolent disobedience to British laws. Motilal was one of the first to be imprisoned, and Anand Bhavan served as a twenty-four-bed hospital for those beaten by the police. Wanting desperately to be part of the grand struggle but too young for Congress membership, twelve-year-old "Indu" organized a children's unit she named Vanar Sena (Army of Monkeys) to run errands for the nonviolent freedom fighters. At this young age she showed extraordinary organizational ability, for the Army of Monkeys eventually included 5,000 children who performed office chores, served meals, and even memorized messages for congressmen in hiding.

The government salt monopoly had long been a burden on Indian peasants. Gandhiji made it a symbol of oppression and an opportunity for public, photogenic defiance. Anyone could make salt (and break the law) by simply collecting a pan of seawater and letting it dry in the sun. Jawaharlal was arrested on April 14, 1930, while making salt with Gandhiji. British police clubbed down demonstrators across the country, including Indira's sick mother, Kamala, her aunts Vijayalakshmi and Krishna, and even her grandmother Swarup Rani. Indira cut her hair and with her thin lanky body, the teenager was often mistaken for a boy. On her thirteenth birthday (November 19, 1930) Jawaharlal sent her from his prison cell the first of more than 200 learned essays that emphasized the grandeur and world significance of Indian history. He also sent her George Macaulay Trevelyan's life of Garibaldi, the same book that had inspired him twenty-five years earlier.

In January 1931, with his health failing, Motilal was released from prison. Gandhiji visited him frequently in the days before his death on February 6.

Motilal was cremated where the Ganges and Yamuna join, with his body wrapped in the Congress flag. Indira was devastated by her grandfather's death but found little consolation from her parents. Jawaharlal was freed but re-arrested in December. With Motilal gone, Indira's aunts dominated Anand Bhavan. One day Indira overheard her Aunt Vijayalakshmi call her "ugly" and "stupid." Indira's lifelong friend Pupul Jayakar thought that the incident marked a turning point. "Indira never forgave her aunt for those annihilating words. They blighted her youth. She was to refer to the remark with an intense passion throughout the years I knew her. Fifty-three years later, a fortnight before her death, the remark remained fresh in her memory."[15]

At Gandhiji's suggestion Indira was sent to Jehangir Vakil's "Pupil's Own School" in Pune, 700 miles from home, where she spent three unhappy years. She was the oldest girl in the school. In line with Gandhiji's philosophy, students cleaned their rooms and did their own laundry; however, Indira had never performed such chores before. Worse, she had to adjust to communal living after having enjoyed a degree of privacy almost unknown in India. She sometimes left the school grounds to visit the Mahatma, who was imprisoned nearby. Jawaharlal was jailed and released too frequently to recount. Indira sometimes cruelly refused to answer her imprisoned father's letters.

Sixteen-year-old Indira left Vakil's school in 1934 and was sent to yet another experimental school, this one in the forests of West Bengal. Shantiniketan, as it was named, was run by the nationalist poet Rabindranath Tagore who, like Gandhiji, abhorred urbanization. Classes were held in the open air. The living conditions were austere, too, but Indira learned to cook her own food. For the first time in her life she found friends her own age. A German boy named Frank Oberdorf taught her French and fell deeply in love with her, but Indira was afraid of his ardor. She appeared uninterested in another admirer, a boy named Feroze Gandhi (no relation to the Mahatma), whose relatives broached the subject of arranging a marriage. The families assumed the matter was over.

In 1935 Indira's mother needed an operation on her tubercular lung. Jawaharlal being in prison, Indira, now seventeen, withdrew from Shantiniketan to sail with Kamala to Europe. The operation took place on June 16. Kamala developed a postoperative fever and was sent to recuperate in the Bavarian Alps. Jawaharlal was released from jail on September 4 and flew to Germany. Indira now saw that her parents barely knew each other. Kamala had already decided to purify herself by renouncing sex. On February 28, 1936, Kamala Nehru died in a Swiss sanatorium.

Jawaharlal took Indira to England and enrolled her in the "progressive" Badminton School at Bristol. When the headmistress asked Indira why Indians came to England to be educated after everything the British had done,

Indira replied, "Because the better we know you the better we can fight you."[16]

At one political meeting in London, Indira tried to read a message from her father. Unaccustomed to public speaking, she mumbled. A wit in the audience shouted out, "She does not speak, she squeaks."[17] It is a measure of Indira's determination and self-discipline that she developed into a confident public debater.

Indira returned to India for a visit in 1937 but was appalled to find that her father had turned over Anand Bhavan to Vijayalakshmi. Worse, Jawaharlal had already fallen in love with another woman. In September Indira left again for England. For the first few days at sea she locked herself in her cabin and took her meals there. When she finally emerged, it was only to walk the decks alone. After the ship docked at Venice, Indira took a train to Paris where Feroze awaited her. They decided then to get married but kept it a secret.

In February 1938 Indira resumed her fragmented academic career at Somerville College, Oxford. She had traveled and met famous people but had never stayed in one school long enough to acquire knowledge in a systematic way. She did poorly in Latin and was eventually asked to leave Oxford, a shameful secret that was successfully covered up until after her death.

In 1938, as Europe slid toward war, Indira accompanied her father to Czechoslovakia and Hungary. On the trip, she caught cold, was diagnosed with pleurisy, and was hospitalized for three weeks before being transferred to Middlesex Hospital in England. By November she was well enough to sail for India with her father. It was then that she told him she had decided to marry Feroze. Jawaharlal, the modern liberal, could not have objected to his daughter's picking her own spouse, even one of a different religion (Feroze was a Parsee), but he must have been unenthusiastic, for Indira now used a tactic she ultimately raised to an art form: the stony silence. In this case she refused to speak to her father for the two weeks they were at sea, and then for the days it took them to go by train from Bombay to Allahabad.

Indira spent an unhappy five months in India. She could not abide Aunt Vijayalakshmi and repaired to a hill station. She joined the INC on her twenty-first birthday, November 19, 1938, but sailed for Europe again the following April for treatment for her pleurisy. She must have feared that it would develop into tuberculosis as had happened to her mother. Indira stayed in Switzerland for more than a year, journeying to London in November 1940 at the height of the blitzkrieg. This frail young woman helped fight fires in London, for which she was given an air-raid warden's helmet.

INDIRA RETURNS TO INDIA

In March 1941 Indira left England without a college degree but with a fiancé. Was she in love? She later said that her reason for getting married was "not to have a husband but to have children."[18] When the couple reached Bombay, Indira went to see Gandhiji at Sevagram. Probably her mission was to convince him to smooth the way for her planned marriage to Feroze. It was an unpleasant meeting, for the Mahatma reacted poorly to the fact that Indira was wearing lipstick. She left Sevagram angry and went straight to Dehra Dun in the north to visit her father who was in jail there. She informed him that she planned to marry, that she wanted children and a private life. In Jawaharlal's mind everything was now political. For a Nehru, the descendant of Kashmiri Brahmans, to marry outside her caste and outside her religion would have implications for the solidarity of the independence movement. Jawaharlal sent her to consult with Gandhiji again before he finally, reluctantly, consented to the marriage. This meeting did not go much better than the previous one, for Gandhiji asked her very personal questions about her relationship with Feroze. Gandhiji was now urging even newly married couples to abstain from sexual relations, but Indira told him bluntly that abstinence was pointless.

Indira married Feroze at Anand Bhavan on March 26, 1942. She was twenty-four, and he was five years older. At Gandhiji's insistence, the service was carefully choreographed in a way calculated to promote goodwill between Hindus and Parsees. Indira soon put Feroze on notice that the father-daughter bond would take precedence over the marriage.

Indira attended the historic Congress session in Bombay at which the "Quit India" resolution was passed. With the Japanese Army advancing on all fronts, the British were taking no chances. Soon Jawaharlal was re-arrested, and the Mahatma, too. It was a time of widespread street violence and harsh police repression. Feroze went into hiding but was eventually caught. Indira was arrested while speaking to a crowd in the old quarter of Allahabad. She later said that she was "glad to be arrested" because it had become a rite of passage into the nationalist movement.[19] The future prime minister was detained in Naini Jail from September 1942 until May 1943. It was cold in the brief winter and wretchedly hot in the long, dry summer, but the true ordeal was that she was imprisoned alongside Aunt Vijayalakshmi.

By the summer of 1943 Indira and Feroze had been released and were living at Anand Bhavan. Differences between the two had already begun to show, but their first son, Rajiv, was born on August 20, 1944, and Sanjay was born on December 14, 1946.

Meanwhile, India and Pakistan were hurtling toward independence. Jawaharlal was freed in June 1945. With Gandhiji's endorsement he became de facto prime minister of the government in waiting, and occupied an official house in New Delhi. Indira left Feroze to live with her father. Feroze moved to Lucknow to edit a newspaper and did not bother to conceal his pursuit of other women. For the next six years Indira and Feroze saw each other only intermittently.

Independence and partition arrived on August 15, 1947. Jawaharlal Nehru became prime minister of India, and Mohammed Ali Jinnah became prime minister of Pakistan. Indira was there when her father delivered his historic "Tryst With Destiny" speech. Savage fighting between Hindus, Muslims, and Sikhs ravaged the two new nations. Indira was on her way to the mountains with her young sons when she learned of the massacres. She immediately returned to New Delhi. When her train was stopped at one station, she saw Hindu rioters attack a Muslim. "I wrapped a towel around me, jumped out of the train and grabbed this person being attacked and took him into our compartment."[20] The mob turned elsewhere. For the rest of August and September Indira helped with relief work.

INDIRA'S APPRENTICESHIP (1950–64)

Prime Minister Nehru moved into Teen Murti Bhavan (Three Gods House), an estate in New Delhi with twenty-eight acres of gardens. As ever, Indira was living right in the heart of Indian politics. She and her three-year-old son Rajiv were among the last people to see the Mahatma alive, before he was assassinated by religious fanatics. Indira and Rajiv were both destined to meet the same fate.

Nehru traveled abroad frequently, and Indira usually accompanied him. Their visit to the United States in 1949 went poorly. Indira was shocked by the overabundance of food and material goods. To the aristocratic Nehrus, Americans seemed vulgar nouveau riches. In 1953 Indira visited the Soviet Union, where she was given a typical tour of model kindergartens and came away impressed. She went with her father to the 1954 Bandung Conference and met Indonesian president Sukarno. She visited China later the same year and in 1955 toured Soviet Central Asia. In 1956 it was Washington, D.C., in 1961 New York City, and 1963 Africa. In 1962 she entertained Jacqueline Kennedy at Teen Murti Bhavan. Mrs. Gandhi's wide acquaintance with foreign statesmen prepared her superbly to navigate the waters of international politics.

Nehru grew increasingly frustrated by Indian domestic politics but enjoyed international relations. The keystone of his foreign policy was neutralism. He insisted that the Third World must not be drawn into either cold war bloc. Along with Josip Broz Tito of Yugoslavia and Gamal Abdel Nasser of Egypt, he founded the so-called Nonaligned Movement. Indira's foreign-policy orientation did not differ noticeably from that of her father, except that events pushed her closer to Moscow.

As Jawaharlal was a widower, Indira became the official hostess at Teen Murti Bhavan, though she claims not to have liked it: "I hated the thought of housekeeping, and what I hated most was to be hostess at a party, as I always disliked parties and having to smile when one doesn't want to. But if one has to do a thing, one might as well do it well, so I grew into it."[21] Because Indira was always by Nehru's side, she was scarcely noticed and was thus able to listen while politicians from all across India struck their deals. She had an impressive memory, a politician's gift for names and faces, and filed everything away. While giving the appearance of being merely a traditional, self-effacing daughter, she was steadily accumulating the encyclopedic knowledge she would use to such devastating effect later. She began to serve as a go-between: Politicians would ask her to ask favors of her father. When he delivered, it was her I.O.U., too. This window on the seamy underside of Indian politics left her disdainful of the institutions of Indian democracy, especially Parliament.

India's new constitution, all 395 articles and eight schedules of it, entered into force on January 26, 1950. The first general elections with universal suffrage were held in 1952. As in many other newly independent countries, the party that had led the freedom struggle enjoyed such a decisive advantage in public opinion that it dominated politics for decades thereafter. The Congress Party named every prime minister of India for thirty years, although other parties sometimes governed the states of India's federal system. In such de facto one-party systems, political jockeying is channeled into factions inside the dominant party, and personal relations, not ideology, determine how alliances are formed and when they are broken. Congress spoke the language of socialism, but Congress politicians led a privileged existence. In the words of Indian political scientist Ramesh Thakur, Congress became "the party of patronage."[22]

During the seventeen years of his prime ministership (1947–64), Jawaharlal Nehru dispensed that patronage himself, and during the fourteen years of her prime ministership Indira Gandhi did the same; the difference was that while Jawaharlal allowed regional and local bosses their independence, Mrs. Gandhi was the great centralizer. Indira learned during her years of apprenticeship that "it was necessary to tolerate a certain amount of corruption."[23]

Feroze Gandhi decided to enter politics, too, and won election to the Lok Sabha (House of the People, or lower house) in the 1952 elections, representing Rae Bareli, a city in Uttar Pradesh located between Lucknow and Allahabad. He moved in with Indira at Teen Murti Bhavan in New Delhi, but this arrangement was intolerable because Indira, as Jawaharlal's daughter, ranked higher in the hierarchy of official protocol. Feroze ceased attending official functions and moved to the smaller bungalow to which he was entitled as a member of the Lok Sabha. Jawaharlal's distaste for his son-in-law could not be hidden. "Sometimes the two men would not speak to each other even when they were in the same room, and used Indira as the interlocutor."[24] Feroze enjoyed publicizing scandals in the Nehru government. He drank heavily and womanized openly. By 1958 he and Indira were on the verge of divorce.

In February 1955 Indira was elected to the Working Committee of Congress, and in September of that year to its Central Election Committee. In India's second election (1957), the woman who twenty years before had been unable to read a message in public hit the campaign trail for her father. By 1959 she had matured into a seasoned politician, though she soon found herself at odds with corrupt party bosses. These were men her father hesitated to antagonize, but his political style was more conciliatory than was hers. According to an observer of the Indian political scene, Mrs. Gandhi's actions as president of the Congress Party were

for Nehru as much a source of embarrassment as of pride. While in office, and particularly when bringing about the fall of the communist governments in Kerala, she betrayed a strong vein of ruthlessness and disregard for parliamentary traditions, and she was unscrupulously tenacious in pursuing her goals which were often narrowly conceived. [Nehru] was often put off, even hurt, by her assertiveness which she displayed just to prove that she could stand on her own feet.[25]

If Mrs. Gandhi's enhanced powers made her father uneasy, they drove her estranged husband wild. He tried unsuccessfully to dissuade her from toppling the Communist government in the southwestern coastal state of Kerala. There were hidden undercurrents in the family. Pupul Jayakar writes that Rajiv and Sanjay sided with their father, feeling that Indira had neglected him (as the young Indira had sided with her mother against her father for the very same reason). Feroze Gandhi died unexpectedly of a heart attack on September 8, 1960, and was cremated the next day on the Yamuna riverbank in New Delhi. Indira claims that despite their loveless marriage, "I was actually physically ill. It upset my whole being for years."[26] But she never kept a photograph of Feroze in her bedroom or study.

Mrs. Gandhi, though holding no formal government post, began to stake out independent positions and was able to influence many of her father's decisions. For example, when the Dalai Lama sought sanctuary in India after the 1959 Chinese crackdown in Tibet, Nehru worried about offending his friend Zhou Enlai, the Chinese foreign minister, but Indira convinced him to grant the Dalai Lama and other Tibetan refugees political asylum. Indira prevailed also on the division of Bombay State into Marathi- and Gujarati-speaking states, a move she favored because it undercut local politicians she disliked.

The great disaster of Jawaharlal Nehru's long prime ministership was the Sino-Indian border war of autumn 1962. India had inherited the McMahon Line, the northern border of the British Raj, which in most places ran along the crest of the Himalayas, except for a region north of Kashmir known as Aksai Chin, where the boundary line ran up and over the edge of the Tibetan plateau. Aksai Chin is so remote that when the Chinese brazenly built a military road right across the region in 1957, the Indians remained blissfully unaware. When they finally did discover this unpleasant fact, Nehru ordered aggressive military maneuvers. The Chinese hit back not in Aksai Chin but at a more favorable point along the disputed border, a thousand miles to the east in Assam, where they quickly humiliated the Indian Army. Jawaharlal was by this time a worn-down man, whereas Indira was coming into her own. She did not let her father stop her from visiting front-line troops, and she donated her gold jewelry to a national defense fund. The war ended with China in seemingly permanent occupation of Aksai Chin.

After this foreign policy disaster Nehru went into decline, withdrew from contact with most people, and became even more dependent on Indira. He suffered a stroke in 1963 and a second one in January 1964. Indira would relay messages and requests from politicians and ministers, and then she would deliver his answer. Jawaharlal Nehru died May 27, 1964, of a burst aorta. On the day of his cremation 1.5 million people stood by the roadside to pay their respects to the only prime minister they had ever known.

INDIRA IN THE SHASTRI CABINET (1964–66)

Indira Gandhi had developed a truly excellent sense of timing and decided that she was not ready to run for prime minister. She had many enemies and liked to keep them guessing. One biographer characterized her actions as "always carefully calibrated and designed, always designed, to further her own self-interest."[27] At this juncture an old antagonist, Morarji Desai, claimed senior status within the Congress Party, but regional party bosses preferred a milder man, and so Lal Bahadur Shastri was elected prime minister on June 1, 1964. Shastri wanted Indira in his cabinet; although she wished to be foreign minister, she settled for being named minister of information and broadcasting. She moved out of Teen Murti Bhavan, which was converted into a Nehru Memorial Museum, and into a more modest but still very comfortable official home. Here she began holding *durbars*, the public audiences at which anyone, no matter how modest his or her station in life, could petition a public official. Indian politicians commonly hold *durbars*, but it was unheard of for a bureaucrat to do so.

In August 1964 Mrs. Gandhi won her first elective office, to the upper house of Parliament, the Rajya Sabha (Council of States). Her debut as a lawmaker was shaky, and some members of Parliament (MPs) still underestimated her, even calling her a *gungi gudia* (dumb doll). Shastri and other politicians seriously misread Indira. When riots broke out in south India in 1965 over Tamil fears that Hindi, a north Indian language, would be declared official and imposed on them, Mrs. Gandhi (without consulting Shastri) flew to Madras and unilaterally promised Tamils that she would protect their language rights. She later told Inder Malhotra that she did not think of herself as a "mere Minister for Information and Broadcasting," adding, "Yes, I have jumped over the Prime Minister's head and I would do it again whenever the need arises."[28]

Even Mrs. Gandhi's enemies recognized her courage. In August 1965 India and Pakistan went to war over Kashmir, and Indira wanted to see the fighting for herself. When an air force officer told her it was far too dangerous, she climbed into a helicopter anyway and ordered the pilot to take her to the front. Then she flew back to Delhi to advise Prime Minister Shastri, far exceeding her authority as minister of information and broadcasting. The war ended with the Indian Army still in control of the vale of Kashmir but with Pakistani forces entrenched in mountains to the west. The Soviet Union brokered a peace treaty, which Prime Minister Shastri signed in Tashkent on January 10, 1966. He died unexpectedly a few hours later.

FIRST TERM AS PRIME MINISTER (1966–67)

The Congress was a decentralized political party, well suited to such an intricate society as India. It was dominated by the chief ministers of the various states. These local potentates feared Morarji Desai and hoped, despite abundant evidence to the contrary, that they could manipulate Indira Gandhi. On January 19, 1966, they elected her the leader of Congress—and thereby automatically the prime minister of India. Desai was beside himself. He and Mrs. Gandhi became lifetime enemies.

Indira Gandhi, at age forty-eight, had become leader of the world's largest democracy. At her first press conference she was asked the inevitable question: How did it feel to be the first woman prime minister of India? She answered, "I am just an Indian citizen and the first servant of my country."[29] She now despised the Indian Parliament, which she called a "zoo" and a "circus." Many MPs returned the hostility; within a month some presciently labeled her rule a constitutional dictatorship.

Indira Gandhi possessed a sense of entitlement, but she warned Congress that she did not see herself as "an imitation of Nehru." She could be imperious, even arrogant, telling one interviewer, "When one has had a life as difficult as mine, one doesn't worry about how others will react."[30] Problems quickly mounted. In February 1966 the United States resumed aid to Pakistan. In March Prime Minister Gandhi visited Washington, D.C. She was treated in a courtly manner by President Lyndon Johnson but felt deeply ashamed at having to ask for economic aid. On her way back to India she stopped in Moscow, where she felt patronized by Premier Alexsei Kosygin as well. It is a rare leader who truly can separate personal feelings from international politics. Prime Minister Gandhi publicly criticized the United States over the war in Vietnam, and President Johnson fumed about "ungrateful Indians." Then he began doling out food aid bit by bit.

Pressures on Prime Minister Gandhi mounted, and she began sleeping poorly. In June 1966 she devalued the rupee without warning. Parliamentary leaders were shocked that she would take such a serious step without even consulting them. Mrs. Gandhi had, in the words of one psychobiographer, a "determination to dominate, lest she be dominated."[31]

All Indian politicians must reckon with the fact that theirs is a very superstitious country. To many of Indira's countrymen, widows were considered inauspicious. Worse yet, during Mrs. Gandhi's first Independence Day address (August 15, 1966), which she delivered from the historic Diwan-e-Am (Hall of Public Audiences) inside Delhi's Red Fort, an earthquake struck during her speech.

Indira addressed India's communal problems with resolute determination. Yet it was ultimately to be her undoing. She decided in November 1966 to split the Punjab (or, more precisely, that part of the Punjab that remained in India at partition) into two states. The region immediately west of Delhi, where most people speak Hindi, became the new province of Haryana. What remained of Punjab now had a Sikh majority that felt it had been slighted in the internal partition.

SECOND TERM AS PRIME MINISTER (1967–71)

The fourth general election was held February 15–21, 1967. (Indian elections can never be held on a single day because of the logistical problem of organizing voting in hundreds of thousands of roadless villages.) In this campaign Mrs. Gandhi appealed directly to the poor with progressive rhetoric. She called for abolishing privileges of the well born and helping the poor. But voters were in an angry mood, and they punished her by reducing Congress to a bare majority in the Lok Sabha. One incident in the 1967 campaign shows what Indira Gandhi was capable of in her finest moments: She was speaking at a rally in Bhubaneshwar when someone in the crowd threw a stone that hit her in the face and broke her nose. Blood gushed forth, but she held it back with a corner of her sari and finished her speech.

The reelected prime minister decided to handle foreign affairs herself. The keystone of her policy was friendship with the Soviet bloc. She visited Poland, Bulgaria, Yugoslavia, and Romania in October 1967, and in November appeared in Moscow at the lavish celebrations marking the fiftieth anniversary of the Bolshevik revolution. In 1968 she addressed the United Nations

(UN) and toured Latin America. She presided over a military buildup that included the creation of an Indian submarine fleet. Mrs. Gandhi shored up India's northern defenses by visiting the Himalayan kingdoms of Bhutan and Sikkim and the northeast Indian state of Assam, where separatist tendencies run strong.

In 1969 Mrs. Gandhi transformed Indian politics by splitting the Congress Party—a bold, irreversible step her father never would have considered. The catalyst for this was a political battle precipitated by her abrupt nationalization of India's fourteen largest commercial banks. It was an act of populism that did not necessarily make economic sense, and she had consulted no one. Her finance minister resigned. Congress MPs were so furious that they expelled Mrs. Gandhi from the party. She responded by organizing spontaneous street demonstrations. Congress split between her supporters and her enemies. Until the next election, she governed through a parliamentary coalition that included the communists and some small regional parties. Few people realized it at the time, but Mrs. Gandhi's undermining of local politicians destroyed Congress's greatest virtue, which was that it was "an aggregative political force" containing disparate sectional interests "thereby reducing the risk of political fragmentation in the country."[32] When Mrs. Gandhi rearranged things so that all power flowed down from her office, she cut herself off from the political feedback she needed.

Prime Minister Gandhi began finding ways around the constitution. For example, to abolish the "princely purses" (an annual subsidy to faded Indian royalty), Mrs. Gandhi needed a constitutional amendment, but she lacked the necessary votes. Her solution was to convince India's figurehead president to accomplish the same end by issuing a proclamation.

Mrs. Gandhi consistently pursued the goal of making India a first-class world power. In 1970 she dedicated her country's first nuclear reactor. In that same year India began producing Russian-designed MiG jet fighter aircraft under license. Perhaps Mrs. Gandhi's great pride in these achievements went to her head, for her next surprise turned out to be a blunder of the first magnitude: She unilaterally decided that India did not need, and would not accept, any more food aid. Her pride was misplaced, however, for later in the decade India had to spend up to $2 billion per year for food imports, and self-sufficiency had to be abandoned.

THIRD TERM AS PRIME MINISTER (1971–75)

In 1971 Prime Minister Gandhi called a surprise general election a year before it was due. She threw herself passionately into electioneering, delivering more than 300 speeches. One observer commented that she had "her father's knack for appearing to be modest while saying consistently immodest things about herself."[33] When the votes were counted Mrs. Gandhi's "New Congress Party" had won a sweeping victory and enjoyed a two-thirds majority in the Lok Sabha.

While the Indian election was going on, Pakistan veered toward civil war. East Pakistan declared independence and renamed itself Bangladesh (Bengali Nation). The West Pakistani Army cracked down on March 25. There followed a gruesome reign of terror against the civilian population. Ten million refugees crossed into Indian West Bengal in the next six months. This tragedy acquired global significance when China announced its support for Pakistan and the Soviet Union championed India.

With another Indian–Pakistani war now almost inevitable, Mrs. Gandhi visited Moscow in September and Washington, D.C., in November. U.S. President Richard Nixon and National Security Adviser Henry Kissinger tilted toward Pakistan. They were secretly planning a rapprochement with China, using the Pakistanis as go-betweens. Nixon disliked Indians in general and Indira Gandhi in particular. In 1967, when he had visited New Delhi, she had treated him with bored indifference. In 1970, when she was in New York to address the UN, Nixon invited her to dinner but she turned him down. Now they resumed their feud, and Nixon delivered a very lengthy analysis of the situation. Prime Minister Gandhi listened angrily but said absolutely nothing. The next day Nixon "kept Indira waiting in the anteroom for 45 minutes before he appeared," and offered no apology.[34]

On December 3, 1971, Pakistan attacked nine Indian air bases, precisely what Mrs. Gandhi had been waiting for. She sent Indian troops across the border into East Bengal, and they quickly routed the demoralized Pakistani Army, which surrendered unconditionally on December 16. Indira Gandhi was at the high point of her career and her life. The press compared her to the Hindu warrior-goddess Durga, and a Gallup poll found her to be the most admired person in the world. But there is evidence that the strain—and perhaps the adulation—were warping Indira's reason, for she told a friend, "The color red suffused me throughout the war. On occasions I found myself speaking, saw things behind me which I could never have seen. The intensity disappeared immediately after the war ended and so have the experiences."[35]

Prime Minister Gandhi quickly capitalized on her victory by calling state elections (the first time they had ever been held separately from national elections). Her handpicked supporters now controlled most of the states of India, as well as the national Parliament. She shuffled and reshuffled cabinet members and party officers. What was the result of such a concentration of power? "More and more of the prime minister's time and energy had to be expended on dealing with [local] problems to the neglect of pressing national issues."[36]

Prime Minister Gandhi continued her assertive foreign and military policy, seizing Sikkim April 8, 1973, and annexing the once-independent kingdom two years later. India exploded a "peaceful nuclear device" in the Rajasthan Desert on May 18, 1974. Although this event represented the ultimate repudiation of everything the Mahatma had advocated, most Indians were jubilant. Mrs. Gandhi dismissed criticism from other nuclear powers as a form of apartheid. In 1975 India's first earth satellite was launched by the Soviet Union.

EMERGENCY (1975–77)

On June 12, 1975, the High Court of Allahabad ruled, in a suit challenging Mrs. Gandhi's campaign practices four years earlier, that she had violated the law by putting her campaign manager on the government payroll. The ruling surprised her—although this should not have been the case, for she had ordered the judge's phone to be tapped. The court barred her from holding public office for six years. Mrs. Gandhi used New Delhi's buses to bring thousands of supporters to her home for a show of support. Four hundred and fifty of her Congress MPs declared her continued leadership indispensable. On June 20 she addressed a crowd estimated at 1 million people. On June 26 she declared a State of Emergency, which was legal under Article 352 of the Indian Constitution.

Mrs. Gandhi ruled India for two years as a dictator. She claimed the country had become ungovernable by ordinary means and that the country needed her: "After my judgement in 1975, what could I have done except stay? You know the state the country was in. What would have happened if there had been nobody to lead it? I was the only person who could, you know. It was my duty to stay, though I didn't want to."[37]

Mrs. Gandhi must have laid her plans carefully, for the imposition of the Emergency went like clockwork. Certainly she had paid close attention to Philippine president Ferdinand Marcos's execution of a similar constitutional coup in 1972. Sanjay encouraged her bold action, but in the end the only convincing explanation for the Emergency is that it stemmed directly from Indira Gandhi's personality: She could not tolerate criticism or opposition and was becoming paranoiac. After the president of Bangladesh was assassinated in August 1975, she imagined that there was an international conspiracy and that her own life was in danger. But she was calm under pressure and boundlessly shrewd, as we might well expect of a woman called "cold-blooded" by Henry Kissinger.

Indira told a friend, "I feel that India is like a baby, and just as one should sometimes take a child and shake it, I feel we have to shake India."[38] Newspapers were censored and not even allowed to publish pages with blank spaces. Mrs. Gandhi told the Lok Sabha, "When there are no papers, there is no agitation."[39] Foreign journalists were deported. No one knew what to believe, and the whole country started operating on rumors. The prime minister's opponents were jailed (under reasonably comfortable conditions in the case of well-known men such as Jayaprakash Narayan and Morarji Desai). Twenty-six opposition parties were banned. Parliament was so intimidated that a constitutional amendment prohibiting legal challenges to the election of a prime minister passed in the Lok Rajya 336–0 and in the Lok Sabha 161–0.

The Supreme Court fell into line, even failing to object when Mrs. Gandhi decreed an end to freedom of speech, freedom of assembly, freedom of travel, freedom to join a labor union, and the right to own property. Habeus corpus was suspended. More than 100,000 people were imprisoned without trial under the 1971 Maintenance of Internal Security Act. Mrs. Gandhi followed the letter, but certainly not the spirit, of the law even as she rammed through a constitutional amendment making everything she did automatically legal.

A sudden dose of authoritarianism may yield benefits—at first. People can be shocked into observing traffic laws. Policemen become afraid to take bribes. A pattern repeats itself: When revolutionaries or strongmen deliver a major shock to a polity, corruption initially decreases—then, when the shock wears off, it dramatically increases.

India became overcentralized. Because Mrs. Gandhi handpicked the chief ministers of the states "her" party controlled, these men feared to make a decision without consulting her. For example, during his first 666 days in office, the chief minister of West Bengal spent 306 days in New Delhi, "mostly in Mrs. Gandhi's waiting room."[40]

Like most other authoritarian leaders, Indira Gandhi overreached, most clearly in July 1975 when she announced a twenty-point economic program to pull India out of poverty by imposing price controls and decreeing minimum agricultural wages. Such measures are not enforceable in any developing country, especially one with almost a billion citizens. But few dared to bring the prime minister bad news. Sycophants surrounded her.

The more distrustful she grew, the more Mrs. Gandhi relied on her son Sanjay. This twenty-eight-year-old man, holding no official position, began issuing orders to government ministers, who dared not defy him, even when he launched a birth control program that relied on forced sterilization. Few countries need family planning as badly as India, but peasant men saw no difference between a vasectomy and castration and hid in the fields when they saw government vehicles coming. Sanjay claimed to have achieved 6 million sterilizations, but the long-term effect was to set back the cause of family planning for decades. Mrs. Gandhi refused to countenance any criticism of Sanjay and explicitly denied that she was preparing him to assume power.

On January 18, 1977, Prime Minister Gandhi abruptly released imprisoned opposition leaders, lifted press censorship, and announced new elections for the Lok Sabha. Why did she take these steps? Probably because by now she was receiving only good news from toadies and thought she was still genuinely popular throughout the land. It was a great miscalculation. Campaign crowds were unenthusiastic. Mrs. Gandhi publicly apologized for the "inconvenience" of her two years of dictatorship. Her viperous Aunt Vijayalakshmi, now seventy-six years old, campaigned against her. The votes were cast between March 16 and 20. A makeshift opposition coalition called the Janata Party won 271 seats in the Lok Sabha to 153 for Indira's party. Mrs. Gandhi resigned March 22, saying that "the collective judgement of the people must be respected. My colleagues and I accept their verdict unreservedly in a spirit of humility."[41] Her political archenemy, Morarji Desai, an eighty-one-year-old ascetic who drank a glass of his own urine every morning, was sworn in as the new prime minister.[42]

OUT OF POWER (1977–80)

Mrs. Gandhi found herself with no official government home for the first time in almost thirty years. She felt disoriented, rejected, and betrayed. The Janata government appointed a commission to investigate the conduct of government during the Emergency. The Central Bureau of Investigation (CBI) called Sanjay in for questioning. Trying to renew her bond with the common people, Indira went to Bihar to console the Untouchable villagers whose relatives had been killed in communal violence. On another countryside tour, of Tamil Nadu, police fired into angry anti-Indira crowds.

Prime Minister Desai had been imprisoned by Indira Gandhi, and now he wanted revenge. On October 3, 1977, Mrs. Gandhi was arrested and charged with having granted an illegal government contract to a foreign oil company. Indira could be an inspired actress. When she grew angry her neck veins would bulge out and her eyebrow would twitch. She turned her arrest into a drama, keeping the CBI men waiting for an hour, then demanding that she be handcuffed.[43] She spent only one night in jail before a magistrate freed her for lack of evidence. She embarked on another hapless grassroots tour to the far south, where angry crowds stoned the train in which she rode.

Mrs. Gandhi split Congress once more, calling her loyalists Congress(I), with the "I" standing for Indira. Prime Minister Desai wanted to put her back in jail. In her first summons before the investigatory commission on January 9, 1978, she refused to acknowledge any wrongdoing, and at her second appearance on January 15 would not even sit down. The remainder of 1978 was spent in a cat-and-mouse game between Gandhi and Desai. She won election to the Lok Sabha, but he had her expelled. He also had her jailed again in December 1978 but she got out after a week. Then Sanjay was arrested and jailed. Indira observed nervously that former Pakistani prime minister Zulfikar Ali Bhutto was condemned for alleged corruption and hanged on April 4, 1979.

FOURTH TERM AS PRIME MINISTER (1980–84)

In 1979 Desai's quarrelsome Janata coalition came unglued. Congress(I) had become "a collection of sycophantic functionaries whose chief task was to perpetuate the rule of the Nehru–Gandhi dynasty," but Indian voters wanted a coherent government, and for this they returned Mrs. Gandhi to power in an electoral landslide in which Congress(I) again won a two-thirds majority in the Lok Sabha.[44] Sanjay also won a seat, and all charges pending against his mother and him were dismissed.

Mrs. Gandhi was sworn in as prime minister for the fourth time at age sixty-two on January 14, 1980, a date astrologers claimed was auspicious. They could not have been more wrong. On April 14 Indira survived a knife attack. Then on June 23 Sanjay died in a plane crash. A reckless amateur pilot, he may have been trying stunts over the capital. A strange scene took place at the hospital where Sanjay was declared dead: Indira began speaking about the political situation in Assam! This was probably a calculated display of fortitude, for in reality she was emotionally devastated by the tragedy. In the aftermath she parted ways with Sanjay's young widow, Maneka. The two women had never gotten along. Now Indira accused Maneka of plotting against her and threw her out of the house. Maneka retaliated by refusing to let Indira see her infant grandchild. Indira then drew close to her other daughter-in-law, Rajiv's Italian wife, Sonia, and began grooming Rajiv to take power one day. Maneka eventually organized an All-India Sanjay Party to pursue the feud.

The leitmotif of Mrs. Gandhi's final term as prime minister was spiraling sectarian violence. First, Sikhs in the Punjab were becoming agitated; some demanded an independent Sikh nation to be called Khalistan. Second, Tamils in south India were up in arms about the situation across the Palk Strait, where Buddhist Sinhalese discriminated against Sri Lankan Hindu Tamils. But as if in a Greek tragedy, Mrs. Gandhi furtively fanned the flames of communal strife in both situations. Angry Sikhs killed Indira in 1984, and angry Tamils killed Rajiv in 1991.

Violence between India's distinct religious communities was nothing new, but now it seemed to be occurring in all corners of the subcontinent at once. Hindu–Muslim friction exploded in massacres in villages across north India in the early 1980s. Hindus in Assam killed 5,000 Muslim immigrants from Bangladesh and left a quarter of a million people homeless. The most incendiary situation was in Indian Punjab, where 12 million Sikhs felt themselves oppressed by the Hindu-dominated government in New Delhi. Jawaharlal Nehru had always insisted that religion must not be the basis for territorial demarcation of states within India. Mrs. Gandhi imposed "presidential rule" to stem the violence, but at the same time her rhetoric began to include subtle references to Hinduism. She encouraged Sikh extremists in an effort to undermine the more moderate Alkali Dal Party, which opposed Congress(I) in Parliament. It was a fatal mistake.

On September 20, 1981, Sant Jarnail Singh Bhindranwale, a charismatic Sikh fundamentalist and former Indian Army general, was charged in the death of a newspaper editor. Nine days later Khalistanis hijacked an Indian Airlines passenger jet. Expatriate Sikhs in England and the United States donated money to buy arms for Bhindranwale's men. The Indian Army sent 20,000 paramilitary troops into Punjab in June 1983. In October Mrs. Gandhi dismissed the Punjab state government and assumed direct control over the strife-torn province. In December Bhindranwale moved his headquarters into a seventy-two-acre complex of religious buildings known as the Golden Temple, the holiest of shrines to Sikhs. That the Golden Temple was located in Amritsar, close to the border with Pakistan, lent superficial credibility to Mrs. Gandhi's accusation that Pakistani agents were stirring up the Sikhs.

The situation deteriorated. Sikh saboteurs derailed trains and burned railway stations. Gunmen shooting from inside the Golden Temple killed four policemen in February 1984. Terrorists assassinated a member of Parliament in April. The bodies of Sikhs killed in internecine factional struggles inside the by-now-fortified temple were dumped into its moat.

The Indian Army stormed the Golden Temple on June 6, 1984. Bhindranwale's men fought back with machine guns and mortars. The army used anti-tank rockets and a howitzer to kill the final holdouts, including Bhindranwale himself. Operation Blue Star, as it was called, took the lives of about 450 Sikhs. Disorders broke out in several Indian cities. Hundreds of Sikh troops deserted the Indian Army. Asked by a television reporter if she feared assassination, Prime Minister Gandhi answered, "I've lived a pretty full life. And it makes no difference if I die in bed or standing up."[45]

Mrs. Gandhi seemed to grow more religious as the danger mounted, performing mysterious purification rituals to protect herself. As a youth she had been exposed equally to her father's agnosticism and her mother's Hinduism. When first sworn in as prime minister in 1966 she had affirmed rather than sworn allegiance to the constitution. She had said that religion was a crutch she had no need for. But after Sanjay's death she started praying to a lithograph of the god Rama and finally fell under the spell of an unscrupulous swami named Dhirendra Brahmachari.

The prime minister's security men wanted to reassign all those among her bodyguards who were Sikhs, but Indira refused. On October 30, 1984, Mrs. Gandhi told a crowd, "If I die today, every drop of my blood will invigorate the nation." On the morning of October 31, while walking from her home to her office, the prime minister encountered Beant Singh, who had been a member of her guard detail for six years. As she politely greeted him with her hands folded in the Indian style, he shot her in the stomach. Immediately Satwant Singh, another Sikh bodyguard, opened fire with an automatic rifle and riddled Indira's body with at least a dozen more bullets. Other body-guards protected themselves by falling to the ground.

Although an ambulance was on duty twenty-four hours a day, the driver had gone for tea. Mrs. Gandhi was driven to the All-India Medical Center, in a passenger car that got stuck in traffic, and when they arrived they found the front gates locked. None of these frustrating delays made any difference, for Indira Gandhi was dead.[46] Her son Rajiv was sworn in as prime minister late that evening, saying, "She was mother not only to me, but to the whole nation." Indira Gandhi's body was cremated on November 3, 1984, on the banks of the Yamuna River in Delhi, near where Gandhiji, Jawaharlal Nehru, and Sanjay Gandhi had been cremated, and where Rajiv was to be cremated seven years later.

In the aftermath, Hindu mobs massacred some 5,000 Sikhs in New Delhi while police looked the other way (and in some cases may actually have directed the killers). H. K. L. Bhagat, Mrs. Gandhi's information minister, is widely thought to have instigated and led the 1984 killings. For all those revenge killings, only one man was ever convicted, fifteen years later.

RAJIV GANDHI

Rajiv Gandhi, a shy airline pilot, had harbored no political ambitions when his mother pushed him into the political arena after Sanjay's death. He was forty-eight years old when Indira was assassinated, and his term in office (1984–89) was widely considered disappointing. Rajiv had inherited his mother's enemies, and they included the Liberation Tigers of Tamil Eelam (LTTE), a Sri Lankan secessionist army known for cold-blooded brutality. The Liberation Tigers were supported by sympathizers in Tamil Nadu. Needing to appease Tamils for reasons of domestic politics, and savoring an opportunity to undermine Sri Lankan president Junius Jayewardene whom she had never forgiven for having called her "a cow," Indira had offered to mediate the conflict.[47] The vicious civil war in Sri Lanka escalated throughout the 1980s, and when Rajiv dispatched Indian peacekeeping troops in 1987, they quickly found themselves at war with the LTTE.

Rajiv was voted out of office in 1989 and was attempting a political comeback two years later when he was gruesomely murdered by a fearless young Tamil woman named Dhanu. On the night of May 21, 1991, as Rajiv walked into an election rally in the small town of Sriperumpudur, near Madras,

Dhanu bowed down before him with her hands pressed together. Then she pressed the detonator on a belt of shrapnel grenades concealed under her sari and blew to bits Rajiv, herself, and fifteen bystanders.

CONCLUSION

Indira Gandhi's life was filled with contradictions. She was a private, almost secretive woman who devoted her entire life to public service. She had a few close friends, but outside this small circle she trusted almost no one. "Her own shyness and stiff uncommunicativeness, often mistaken for hauteur, had never made friendship or closeness easy."[48] Mrs. Gandhi was a remarkable woman with serious limitations. The Italian journalist Oriana Fallaci wrote of Indira that "it was impossible to be a woman and not feel redeemed, vindicated, by her enormous success, which belied all banalities used to justify patriarchy in any society."[49] But her singular dominance left others with little to do. "There [was] no one left to share with her the blame of the regime's failings, no one of any stature to partake with her in the task of running her vast, benighted nation."[50]

Indira always subordinated her personal life to the needs of her country, but this left her with a trace of self-pity. She was uncommonly tenacious in pursuit of her goals—but to what end? She was a brilliant political tactician, but her talent was harnessed to no broad vision of what India could become. Although she was not intellectually lazy and had a lifelong passion for reading, Indira regarded Indian intellectuals with contempt. Her vague leftism gave way to pure pragmatism. She called herself a socialist but then defined socialism merely as the search for a better life. She was strongly patriotic and hardly exaggerated by referring to herself as a *desh sevika* (servant of the nation), but her nationalism was tinged with a sense of resentment that Indians were "always undervalued, underestimated, not believed."[51] She was sensitive to perceived slights from Westerners, and felt that U.S. diplomats were particularly condescending.

Mrs. Gandhi was shrewd. Her judgment of people was acute—except when it came to her own children. She could be disingenuous, never more so than when she claimed, "I don't enjoy what most people mean by politics—maneuvering and things like that, I simply can't stand it."[52] The pro-Moscow foreign policy she followed made sense, given the constellation of enemies India faced (China, plus a Pakistan allied with the United States), but her socialistic economic policies failed to lift Indians out of poverty and did not even redistribute the nation's wealth. Mrs. Gandhi carried on her father's policy of encouraging scientific and technological progress. In the military sphere she promoted India's assertion of regional supremacy and its entry into the nuclear club.

Elected democratically, she strangled civil liberties then restored them. She turned the Congress Party into an organization of yes-men. Indeed, she left Congress so bereft of ideas that in 1997 it inducted Sonia Maino Gandhi, Rajiv's widow, in the desperate hope that one of Indira's grandchildren might bring Congress back to power through the magic of the Gandhi name.

NOTES

1. Krishan Bhatia, *Indira: A Biography of Prime Minister Gandhi* (New York: Praeger, 1974), p. 19.

2. Bhatia, *Indira*, p. 5.

3. Oriana Fallaci, *Interview With History* (New York: Liveright, 1976), pp. 170–71.

4. Bhatia, *Indira*, p. 35.

5. Bhatia, *Indira*, pp. 44–45.

6. Zareer Masani, *Indira Gandhi: A Biography* (London: Hamish Hamilton, 1975), p. 18.

7. Arnold Michaelis, "An Interview With Indira Gandhi," *McCalls* 93 (April 1966), p. 105.

8. Krishna Nehru Hutheesing, *We Nehrus* (New York: Holt, Rinehart & Winston, 1967), p. 137.

9. Pupul Jayakar, *Indira Gandhi: A Biography* (New Delhi: Penguin Books India (P) Ltd., 1992), p. 17.

10. Fallaci, *Interview With History*, p. 172.

11. Jayakar, *Indira Gandhi*, p. xix.

12. Jayakar, *Indira Gandhi*, p. 55.

13. Fallaci, *Interview With History*, p. 172.

14. Fallaci, *Interview With History*, p. 174.

15. Jayakar, *Indira Gandhi*, pp. 44–45.

16. Masani, *Indira Gandhi*, p. 50.

17. Jayakar, *Indira Gandhi*, p. 95.

18. Fallaci, *Interview With History*, p. 174.

19. Michaelis, "An Interview With Indira Gandhi," p. 188.

20. Jayakar, *Indira Gandhi*, p. 139.

21. Masani, *Indira Gandhi*, p. 83.

22. Ramesh Thakur, *The Government and Politics of India* (New York: St. Martin's Press, 1995), p. 223.

23. Claire Sterling, "Ruler of 600 Million—And Alone," *New York Times Magazine*, August 10, 1975, p. 38.

24. Pranay Gupte, *Mother India: A Political Biography of Indira Gandhi* (New York: Scribner's, 1992), p. 220.

25. B. N. Pandey, *Nehru* (New York: Stein & Day, 1976), p. 397.

26. Masani, *Indira Gandhi*, p. 117.

27. Gupte, *Mother India*, p. 18.

28. Inder Malhotra, *Indira Gandhi: A Personal and Political Biography* (Boston: Northeastern University Press, 1989), p. 84.

29. Daniel Clifton, ed., *Chronicle of the Twentieth Century* (Liberty, Mo.: International Publishing, 1992), p. 944.

30. Fallaci, *Interview With History*, p. 158.

31. Henry C. Hart, "Indira Gandhi: Determined Not to Be Hurt," in *Indira Gandhi's India*, ed. Henry Hart (Boulder, Colo.: Westview Press, 1976), p. 266.

32. Thakur, *The Government and Politics of India*, p. 157.

33. Welles Hangen, *After Nehru, Who?* (London: Hart-Davis, 1963) p. 160.

34. Seymour M. Hersh, *The Price of Power: Kissinger in the Nixon White House* (New York: Summit Books, 1983), p. 456.

35. Jayakar, *Indira Gandhi*, p. 245.

36. Thakur, *The Government and Politics of India*, p. 229.

37. Dom Moraes, *Indira Gandhi* (Boston: Little, Brown, 1980), p. 220.

38. Jayakar, *Indira Gandhi*, p. 274.

39. Charles Monaghan, ed., *Facts on File Yearbook 1975: The Indexed Record of World Events*, vol. 35 (New York: Facts on File), p. 539.

40. Sterling, "Ruler of 600 Million—And Alone," p. 46.

41. Stephen Orlofsky, ed., *Facts on File Yearbook 1977: The Indexed Record of World Events*, vol. 37 (New York: Facts on File), p. 205.

42. According to Seymour Hersh, Desai was an informer for the Central Intelligence Agency who was paid $20,000 a year at least through 1971. See Hersh, *The Price of Power*, p. 450. Desai indignantly denied this and sued Hersh for libel. Henry Kissinger testified in favor of Desai, but the jury did not believe him and ruled in favor of Hersh. See David Margolick, "U.S. Journalist Cleared of Libel Charge by Indian," *New York Times*, October 7, 1989, p. 24.

43. Jayakar, *Indira Gandhi*, p. 342.

44. Thakur, *The Government and Politics of India*, p. 228.

45. Gupte, *Mother India*, pp. 104–05.

46. See Ritu Sarin, *The Assassination of Indira Gandhi* (New Delhi: Penguin Books India, 1990).

47. Gupte, *Mother India*, p. 5.

48. Nayantara Sahgal, "The Making of Mrs. Gandhi," *South Asian Review* 8 (April 1975), p. 196.

49. Fallaci, *Interview With History*, p. 153.

50. Sterling, "Ruler of 600 Million—And Alone," p. 52.

51. Fallaci, *Interview With History*, p. 169.

52. Masani, *Indira Gandhi*, p. 269.

The Nehru—Gandhi Dynasty

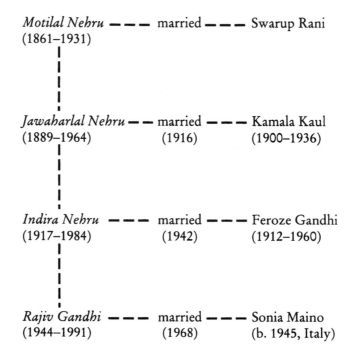

Motilal Nehru — — — married — — — Swarup Rani
(1861–1931)

Jawaharlal Nehru — — married — — — Kamala Kaul
(1889–1964)   (1916)   (1900–1936)

Indira Nehru — — — married — — — Feroze Gandhi
(1917–1984)   (1942)   (1912–1960)

Rajiv Gandhi — — — married — — — Sonia Maino
(1944–1991)   (1968)   (b. 1945, Italy)

For Further Reading

Ashe, Geoffrey. *Gandhi*. New York: Stein & Day, 1968.

Bhatia, Krishan. *Indira: A Biography of Prime Minister Gandhi*. New York: Praeger, 1974.

Borman, William. *Gandhi and Non-Violence*. Albany: State University of New York Press, 1986.

Brass, Paul. *The Politics of India Since Independence*. London: Cambridge University Press, 1990.

Brown, D. Mackenzie. *The Nationalist Movement: Indian Political Thought From Ranade to Bhave*. Berkeley: University of California Press, 1970.

Brown, Judith M. *Gandhi: A Prisoner of Hope*. New Haven, Conn.: Yale University Press, 1989.

———. *Gandhi and Civil Disobedience*. London: Cambridge University Press, 1977.

———. *Gandhi's Rise to Power*. London: Cambridge University Press, 1972.

Carras, Mary. *Indira Gandhi: A Political Biography*. Boston: Beacon Press, 1979.

Chatterjee, Margaret. *Gandhi's Religious Thought*. London: Thornton Butterworth, 1983.

Collins, Larry, and Dominique Lapierre. *Freedom at Midnight*. New York: Simon & Schuster, 1975.

Dalton, Dennis. *Mahatma Gandhi: Nonviolent Power in Action*. New York: Columbia University Press, 1993.

Datta, Dhirendra M. *The Philosophy of Mahatma Gandhi*. Madison: University of Wisconsin Press, 1972.

Dreiberg, Trevor. *Indira Gandhi*. New York: Drake Publishers, 1973.

Erikson, Erik. *Gandhi's Truth*. New York: W. W. Norton, 1969.

Fischer, Louis. *The Life of Mahatma Gandhi*. New York: Harper, 1950.

Green, Martin B. *Gandhi: Voice of a New Age Revolution*. New York: Continuum, 1993.

Gupte, Pranay. *Mother India: A Political Biography of Indira Gandhi*. New York: Scribner's, 1992.

Heitzman, James, and Robert L. Worden, eds. *India: A Country Study*. 5th ed. Washington, D.C.: U.S. Government Printing Office, 1996.

Iyer, Raghavan N. *The Moral and Political Thought of Mahatma Gandhi*. New York: Oxford University Press, 1973.

————. *The Essential Writings of Mahatma Gandhi.* New Delhi: Oxford University Press, 1996.

Jack, Homer A., ed. *The Gandhi Reader: A Sourcebook of His Life and Writings.* New York: Grove Press, 1994.

Jayakar, Pupul. *Indira Gandhi: A Biography.* New Delhi: Penguin Books India, 1972.

Johnson, Gordon. *Cultural Atlas of India.* New York: Facts on File, 1996.

Lazo, Caroline. *Mahatma Gandhi.* New York: Dillon Press, 1993.

Malhotra, Inder. *Indira Gandhi: A Personal and Political Biography.* Boston: Northeastern University Press, 1991.

Mehta, Ved. *Mahatma Gandhi and His Apostles.* New Haven, Conn.: Yale University Press, 1993.

Moraes, Dom F. *Indira Gandhi.* Boston: Little, Brown, 1980.

Mukherjee, Rudrangshu, ed. *The Penguin Gandhi Reader.* New York: Penguin, 1996.

Nanda, B. R. *Mahatma Gandhi: A Biography.* Delhi: Oxford University Press, 1996.

Rudolph, Lloyd, and Susanne Hoeber Rudolph. *Gandhi: The Traditional Roots of Charisma.* Chicago: University of Chicago Press, 1983.

Sharp, Gene. *Gandhi as a Political Strategist.* Boston: Porter Sargent, 1979.

Wolpert, Stanley. *A New History of India.* New York: Oxford University Press, 1989.

12

Conclusion

We have now surveyed the lives of ten Asian leaders and shall try in this chapter to answer the questions we posed in the Introduction. We also draw some conclusions about political leadership in each of the five countries reviewed, in Asia as a whole, and tentatively venture some hypotheses about political leadership in the Third World. We have identified five basic elements in political leadership:

1. *Leaders.* By definition all leaders bring their followers along, but in a unit as vast as a nation-state the political and psychological relationship is not simply between the leader and his followers, for there is a third element—the political organization or party; and once the leader has achieved power, there is a fourth element—the state.

The successful modern leader must communicate directly with the common people, speaking over the radio to peasants, most of whom will never see him in person. Of all our leaders, only one completely failed at this: Ngo Dinh Diem. His shortcoming proved fatal. Hugh Tinker concluded from his study of Asian and African nationalist leaders that a common feature was their "ability to express themselves with polish and with force in the language of the colonial power."[1] We find the same pattern. Ho Chi Minh, Diem, Norodom Sihanouk, and Pol Pot all were fluent in French and sometimes preferred that language to express political concepts and arguments. Mohandas Gandhi and Indira Gandhi spoke eloquently in English. Sukarno conducted his own legal defense in the Dutch language.

Must a successful leader be ruthless in eliminating rivals? The four communists (Mao, Deng, Ho, and Pol Pot) certainly were. Prince Sihanouk was almost irrationally suspicious of rivals and constantly plotted to turn them against each other. Diem had many rivals, but he regarded them with disdain and relied on his brother-in-law to neutralize them. Sukarno was content to be first among his nationalist peers and tolerated a broad range of dissent. Suharto tolerated no political opposition and squelched it for three decades. Indira Gandhi jailed her democratic opponents when she judged that the situation warranted it, but she ultimately returned India to the rule of law and accepted the verdict of the voters. Among our ten leaders, only Mohandas Gandhi could be said to have had no rivals and to have loved those who disagreed with him.

Our ten leaders were all tenacious. Every one struggled to victory, undiscouraged by setbacks. Mao Zedong's first effort at insurrection, the Autumn Harvest Uprising, was a fiasco. Deng Xiaoping survived numerous purges and never gave up. Ho Chi Minh experienced multiple imprisonments, decades in exile, and wars against France and the United States. Ngo Dinh Diem endured a decade of ignominious inactivity while waiting patiently for his moment to come. Norodom Sihanouk refused to accept his dethronement in 1970 and stubbornly persisted for the next twenty-eight years to restore Cambodia's traditional political system, as he himself had defined it. Pol Pot was willing to live in the jungle for many long years before and after his wild three and a half years of supreme state power. Sukarno did not abandon his dream of Indonesian independence despite long years of internal exile. Suharto patiently bided his time through many years of obscurity. Mohandas Gandhi welcomed adversity, which he thought necessary for moral, social, and political progress. Because he wanted nothing less than the reform of people's souls, he was destined always to be disappointed. Indira Gandhi fought to keep power, defying her enemies from her jail cell and returning to the prime ministership amid a wave of public admiration for her fighting spirit.

Not one of our ten leaders rose from the ranks of the Asian underclass—the squatters, the landless peasants, the urban coolies. Three were born into elite families (Diem, Sihanouk, and Indira Gandhi). Three were born into families positioned on the fringe of the traditional elite but without much money (Ho, Pol Pot, and Sukarno). Three came from families of relative prominence within a provincial town, but with no national reputation or outlook (Mao, Deng, and Mohandas Gandhi). Only one came from a completely obscure family (Suharto).

Two leaders studied in Paris: Deng Xiaoping and Pol Pot. A third, Ho Chi Minh, lived there and studied on his own. Mohandas Gandhi and Indira Gandhi both studied in England. The lives of these five leaders were profoundly altered by living and studying abroad, but it was exposure to a new culture, not formal learning, that changed them. Two leaders, Ngo Dinh Diem and Norodom Sihanouk, received excellent colonial educations that exposed them to Western learning but that also taught them their own traditions. Suharto attended only a military school. Mao was very well read, but as he was largely self-taught, his thinking lacked discipline.

Four leaders (Mao, Deng, Ho, and Pol Pot) led revolutionary armies despite their lack of formal military training or even experience in any nonrevolutionary army. They learned by doing, and each showed a flair for guerrilla strategy and tactics. Sukarno was the political leader of a revolutionary army but did not plan military strategy himself. Only one, Suharto, rose from the ranks of the uniformed military. Four (Diem, Sihanouk, Mohandas Gandhi, and Indira Gandhi) had no military experience.

2. *Ideas.* What universal values did our leaders proclaim, if any? Two of these nationalists propounded universal doctrines. Mohandas Gandhi's "experiments in truth" were not for Indians only but for all people. Mao sincerely believed that permanent revolution was desirable for all countries. The other eight made no such claims. Ho, Deng, and Pol Pot may have believed in the universal validity of Marxism, but they concerned themselves mainly with their own countries.

Eight of our ten leaders believed in human equality, at least in the abstract. Only two (Sihanouk and Diem) believed that society was inherently hierarchical. All the others espoused equality between the majority culture and minority ethnic groups, between social classes, and between the sexes. In Asian countries there is a wide gap between educated, wealthy city dwellers and uneducated peasants in the countryside. What did our leaders think and do about this? No pattern emerges. Four (Mao, Pol Pot, Sukarno, and Mohandas Gandhi) explicitly championed the interests of the peasants over those of the city dwellers. Four others (Deng, Diem, Sihanouk, and Suharto) pursued policies that favored city dwellers, usually without saying so. Two (Ho and Indira Gandhi) espoused and followed balanced policies.

3. *Organization.* Political action is group action. The leader must project an ideal, or at least much-improved, future but then must create and maintain an organization to achieve that vision. Of our ten leaders, four succeeded in this all too well, creating political organizations of frightening strength. Three of these four were communists (Mao, Ho, and Pol Pot). The fourth, Suharto, ran his political machine, Golkar, practically devoid of ideology or terror, but with plenty of corruption. Golkar is best understood as a variant of the sort of political machine built by Mayor Richard Daley of Chicago. Mohandas Gandhi and Indira Gandhi each led an organization, the Indian National Congress, that neither had created. Two of our leaders, Sukarno and Sihanouk, neglected the organizational details that might have prolonged their hold on power. Ngo Dinh Diem made a half-hearted effort to create a party, but to his Confucian way of thinking, popular consent was irrelevant. Only six of our leaders paid attention to organizational details (Deng, Ho, Pol Pot, Suharto, Mohandas Gandhi, and Indira Gandhi). The other four (Mao, Diem, Sihanouk, and Sukarno) developed an Olympian perspective and left organizational work to others.

4. *Followers.* We have not attempted a comparative analysis of the followers of our ten leaders. Social psychology and crowd behavior are subjects beyond the scope of this book. But we emphasize that leadership is not a one-way relationship, as Georg Simmel points out: "All leaders are also led; in innumerable cases the master is the slave of his slaves."[2]

5. *The situation.* Four of our ten leaders rose to power by leading movements of national independence. Mao triumphed in China, as did Ho Chi Minh in Vietnam, by blending patriotism and communism. Sukarno was clearly the popular choice to lead the Indonesian struggle for independence. Mohandas Gandhi so captured the imagination of the Indian people that leadership of the independence movement was conferred on him even when he did not seek it.

Two leaders achieved power without struggle. Norodom Sihanouk was picked by French colonial administrators to be king of Cambodia. Indira Gandhi was born and raised in the illustrious Nehru family. Two leaders rose to power by loyally serving, even while harboring deep reservations about the men who preceded them: Deng Xiaoping and Suharto.

This leaves one leader whose rise to power is harder to explain: Pol Pot. Various explanations have been offered. Pol Pot was eloquent, patient, and dedicated, but he would have remained the leader of a small, obscure revolutionary movement if the Vietnam War had not spilled over into Cambodia.

We find one similarity in all ten leaders: All sensed—and knew that their people sensed, too—that they were the inheritors of grand and ancient civilizations that had come to ruin, and they were willing to dedicate their entire lives to restoring lost national greatness.

COMPARISIONS WITHIN COUNTRIES

China

Mao Zedong and Deng Xiaoping were dedicated, lifelong communists and Chinese patriots. They shared a contempt for liberal democracy and a belief that politics was war by other means. Each was a gifted military strategist. But there the similarities end.

Mao was a utopian whereas Deng was a pragmatist. Mao spoke in oracular language; Deng was clear and specific. Mao was xenophobic, but Deng was eager to adopt Western innovations. Mao was a natural rebel; Deng rebelled because he thought China had no choice. Mao was incapable of normal family life whereas Deng was a devoted son, husband, and father. Mao was incapable of delegating authority, but China seemed to run on autopilot when Deng sank into his dotage.

Vietnam

Ho Chi Minh and Ngo Dinh Diem were both Vietnamese patriots who longed to free their country from the grip of French colonialism. Both were also bachelors who led austere personal lives. Both men were personally honest but could be coldly ruthless as well. Neither was concerned with civil liberties. Neither used flamboyant rhetoric to sway the masses, but both strove mightily to exhibit virtue, as a Confucian leader should. Ho's virtues were simplicity and self-denial; Diem's were filial piety and scholarship.

In other respects the two men differed sharply. Diem derived his identity from his family, whereas Ho was a loner. Ho was a man of quick wit; Diem was cold and humorless. Ho's simplicity was endearing, and it seemed natural for Vietnamese to call their leader who went about in rubber sandals "Uncle Ho." Diem, however, seemed like a Confucian father, always wearing impeccable Mandarin robes or white Western suits. Ho was a cheerful agnostic, whereas Diem was a pious Roman Catholic. In the end the essential distinction is that Ho, for all his Marxist modernism, remained in his heart a native Vietnamese; but Diem, for all his self-conscious traditionalism, was much too Westernized to win the loyalty of his people. Ho knew how to compromise when he had to, yet Diem was so rigid that he eventually broke.

Cambodia

Norodom Sihanouk and Pol Pot had no similarities other than a single-minded drive for political power and a morbid fear of Vietnamese domination.

Sihanouk was a prince with a populist streak. Pol Pot was the most frightening kind of elitist: a man convinced he possessed secret knowledge that would bring salvation to his country. Sihanouk was a lover of luxury, effete and pedantic. Pol Pot was more at home in a jungle camp than in any city. Sihanouk was easily seduced by flattery; Pol Pot assumed that any flatterer harbored an ulterior motive. Sihanouk surrendered to all the weaknesses of the flesh—he was a philanderer who fathered fourteen children. Pol Pot seems to have been faithful to his wife until she went insane, and he was affectionate toward his daughter by his second wife.

Their methods of exercising leadership were diametrically opposite. Sihanouk was a ham who starred in his own films. He wanted every Khmer to know and love him. Pol Pot was probably the most reclusive leader of the twentieth century.

Indonesia

Presidents Sukarno and Suharto were Indonesian nationalists. They played down their Javanese identities in favor of a pan-Indonesian identity, but each appealed to Javanese tradition to bolster his popularity. Both disdained Western-style democracy, and neither one made a pretense of being a serious philosopher.

Sukarno was flamboyant, Suharto taciturn and colorless. Sukarno was a womanizer, whereas Suharto was a devoted family man. Sukarno loved the emotion of wild speeches; Suharto was impassive at all times. Sukarno's populist "Marhaenism" was the direct opposite of Suharto's trickle-down economic theory. Sukarno sought a direct bond with the people and eschewed party organization; Suharto created a political machine that rolled inexorably on to one electoral victory after another. To sum up their differences, Sukarno was a revolutionary; Suharto wanted order above all else.

India

Mohandas Gandhi and Indira Gandhi both loved India more than their own lives, and both lost their lives at the hands of sectarian fanatics. Both were personally brave and legendarily stubborn, but capable of compromise at the last minute after having wrung the last concession from their opponents. Both Mohandas Gandhi and Indira Gandhi were mediocre students who learned more from foreign travel than from books, and the two were truly citizens of the world, although each perceived unique virtues in Indian civilization.

The Mahatma trusted in God to reward moral purity, but Indira Gandhi was willing to sacrifice principles if necessary. The Mahatma was a visionary, often quite out of touch with the real world, whereas Indira Gandhi was calculating and realistic. The Mahatma abhorred modern technology; Indira Gandhi set as a top national goal the rapid modernization of Indian science and technology. Both saw flaws in parliamentary democracy. Mohandas Gandhi, of course, never exercised supreme executive power, but one imagines that he would have been repelled by the sort of backroom arm-twisting that was Indira Gandhi's forte.

QUESTIONS ABOUT ASIAN LEADERSHIP

In the Introduction, we asked readers to keep in mind certain questions while reading the book. Here we venture our own conclusions, which the reader is invited to consider:

1. *Are there certain personality traits that all leaders possess?* An ideal leader would have these attributes: creativity, patience, a good sense of timing, courage, physical endurance, intelligence, emotional maturity, extroversion, sociability, and decisiveness. Indeed, most of our leaders possessed most of these traits. All ten were creative. But at least one exception may be found for each of the other ideal attributes. For example, Sukarno was impatient, Diem had a poor sense of timing, Sihanouk was not particularly courageous, Sihanouk and Sukarno both lacked emotional maturity, Diem and Pol

Pot were introverted, and Sihanouk's downfall was his indecision. It seems that all ten of our leaders were intelligent, but perhaps only Ho Chi Minh was brilliant.

2. *What personal satisfaction does the leader seek?* Of our ten leaders, only two—Mao Zedong and Indira Gandhi— clearly needed to rebel against their parents. There is no pattern of adolescent identity crises.

3. *Is there such a thing as "Asian leadership"?* We believe that the concept of political culture (the attitudes, beliefs, and values of a society toward political affairs) is valid and necessary, but that societies and cultures differ in ways that make generalization risky. There are, however, certain pan-Asian cultural similarities, including *(a)* group orientation over individualistic orientation; *(b)* strong family bonds; *(c)* vertically ordered hierarchical societies; and (d) a pervasive pattern of patron–client relations. Let us consider these Asian traits one by one:

    a. Group orientation. Five of our ten leaders (Mao, Deng, Ho, Diem, and Pol Pot) advocated personal sacrifice to achieve collective goals. Nine of our ten leaders explicitly rejected Western democracy as too individualistic. The only exception was Indira Gandhi.

    b. Family bonds. Some of our leaders tried to establish dynasties (Sihanouk, Suharto, and Indira Gandhi). Others were nepotistic (Mao, Deng, Diem, Sihanouk, Suharto, Indira Gandhi, and even Pol Pot). Only three leaders resisted such temptations (Ho, Sukarno, and Mohandas Gandhi). What is considered nepotistic or corrupt is culturally defined.

    c. Hierarchical societies. A basic aspect of modernization is the creation of equality. Five of our ten leaders wanted to destroy all hierarchy. Four of these five were communists (Mao, Deng, Ho, and Pol Pot), whereas the fifth thought in religious terms (Mohandas Gandhi). Four wanted to reform and modify the social and economic cleavages in their countries (Sihanouk, Sukarno, Suharto, and Indira Gandhi). Only one of our leaders (Diem) wished to preserve the traditional hierarchy, and he failed for precisely that reason.

    d. Patron–client relations. At least seven of our ten leaders dispensed favors to underlings in return for support, and three (Diem, Suharto, and Indira Gandhi) turned it into an art form. Three leaders insisted that their followers needed no material incentives (Mohandas Gandhi, Pol Pot, and Ho).

4. *Is there a distinct category of revolutionary leaders?* Mobilizing people to overthrow a regime is quite different from orchestrating their acquiescence to an established government. Because all five countries were formally or informally colonized, it is natural that national leaders were revolutionaries. Mohandas Gandhi and Indira Gandhi did not pick up the gun, but they went to jail for their peaceful protests. Only Diem and Sihanouk were never revolutionaries in any sense.

Eric Hoffer writes that the revolutionary leader "articulates and justifies the resentment dammed up in the souls of the frustrated. He kindles the vision of a breathtaking future so as to justify the sacrifice of a transitory present. He stages a world of make-believe so indispensable for the realization of self-sacrifice and united action."[3] This describes Mao, Deng, Ho, Pol Pot, Sukarno, and Mohandas Gandhi but not Diem, Sihanouk, Suharto, or Indira Gandhi. There is indeed a distinct category of revolutionary leadership. The problem comes after revolutionaries achieve power, for they find ordinary administration boring and may try to continue the revolution using state power. Revolutions cannot last forever, and sooner or later society will demand and get more ordinary leaders. Deng Xiaoping is a rare example of someone who proved equally adept at making revolution and creating political order.

5. *Are there particular characteristics of political leadership in developing countries?* There were fifty-one members of the United Nations in 1945 and 185 members by 1998. Typical characteristics of developing countries include poverty, overpopulation, high infant mortality, artificial borders drawn by Europeans, an economy dangerously dependent on the export of a few primary commodities, a capital city that dominates the countryside politically and socially, an overdeveloped executive branch, a weak legislative branch, and a captive judiciary. Can we make generalizations about the leadership of developing countries that are valid across cultures?

Having a "national" identity is a new thing for the citizens of many developing countries. It is likely that their grandparents identified psychologically with some group other than the nation, such as the clan, tribe, village, religious sect, caste, or language group. The individual can be conditioned to love the nation more easily if there is a father figure or mother figure who symbolizes and embodies the characteristics attributed to the nation. Hero-worship is a component of politics in newly created nations. Italy and Germany were newly created nations when Mussolini and Hitler rose to power.

Thus, we would expect the leaders of new nations to show through their speech, attire, and actions that they personify the new political order. All ten of our leaders did precisely that. Consider the matter of clothing: Our four communist leaders (Mao, Deng, Ho, and Pol Pot) wore a variation on the simple tunic favored by Josef Stalin. It symbolizes equality and simplicity—no fancy suits for these men—and it stands in sharp contrast to the flashy costumes of the old regime (the czar of Russia, the emperors of China and Vietnam, the king of Cambodia). Two of our leaders (Sihanouk and Diem) wore traditional finery on ceremonial occasions but preferred Western business suits at other times. Sukarno was a dandy who wore a traditional Muslim hat with a well-tailored army uniform. Suharto wore the same kind of hat but with a suit. Mohandas Gandhi always wore a homespun *dhoti* to symbolize India's past. He made no concession to modernity in his dress.

Indira Gandhi wore fine saris: It would have been unthinkable for her to wear Western clothing on any important occasion.

Leaders of developing countries typically try to establish a direct bond between themselves and the common people, because intermediary institutions such as political parties or legislatures may be embryonic or ineffective. They use the most basic technologies of mass communication: the printing press, the microphone, and the radio. Many citizens may not be able to read, so idealized portraits or airbrushed photographs of the leader are widely circulated. Of our ten leaders, nine made sure that their face would be instantly recognized by everyone in the country, and one (Mao) carried this to such an extreme that even rude peasant huts displayed a lithograph of the Great Helmsman. The only one of our leaders who completely eschewed a personality cult was Pol Pot, for he wanted people to obey him from fear, not from love.

This brings us to the intriguing but elusive concept of charisma. As the word was first used, it meant an extraordinary power given to a Christian by the Holy Spirit. In modern times the ultimate charismatic leader was Adolf Hitler, a man able to mesmerize large audiences. Charisma is a mysterious kind of personal magnetism. As defined by Ann Willner, the charismatic leader is perceived by his followers as somehow superhuman. They believe in him blindly, they love him, and they do whatever he commands.[4] Willner points out that since both Mohandas Gandhi and Hitler were called charismatic, charisma cannot reside in the personality of the leader, but must exist in the perceptions of the people. It seems that many people dearly want to surrender themselves to some leader who gives their lives meaning and who relieves them of the awful burden of choice. Of our ten leaders, five clearly had charisma: Mao, Ho, Sihanouk, Sukarno, and Mohandas Gandhi. It is not a coincidence that these five were in every case the earlier of the two leaders of each country. Note that their successors or rivals (Deng, Diem, Pol Pot, Suharto, and Indira Gandhi) lacked charisma. We conclude that a newly independent population needs to believe in a supremely wise leader more than the people of a country that is well established.

6. *Does leadership in communist systems differ fundamentally from leadership in noncommunist systems?* Totalitarian communist systems differ from "ordinary" dictatorships. Diem and Suharto might be considered ordinary dictators or authoritarians. They compelled obedience when they could, crushed dissent, and imprisoned political opponents. But communist regimes seek total control over society, and total control over the individual, so they are not content with mere obedience but demand enthusiastic obedience. They propagate an ideology for which claims of scientific correctness (absolute truth) are made, and so are driven to eliminate or severely restrict all organized religion. They believe that class struggle is "the locomotive of history," and that the state is an organ by which one class oppresses another.

In his classic work, *The Anatomy of a Revolution*, Crane Brinton writes that extremist leaders "combine, in varying degrees, very high ideals and a complete contempt for the inhibitions and principles which serve most other men as ideals. They present a strange variant of Plato's pleasant scheme: they are not philosopher-kings, but philosopher-killers."[5]

However, we can see from the example of Deng that communist regimes are capable of reform. Whether that will inevitably lead to the collapse of the Chinese and Vietnamese Communist Parties, as happened in the former Soviet Union, remains to be seen.

7. *Do leaders inevitably succumb to the "corruption of power"?* There are two kinds of corruption: The first, illegitimate self-enrichment, is not necessarily incompatible with freedom. The second, megalomania, is far more dangerous. At least four of our leaders grew corrupt in the sense that they craved luxury: Diem, Sihanouk, Sukarno, and Suharto. Two others tolerated corruption in their children: Deng Xiaoping and Indira Gandhi. Three others, all communists, became vain about their ideas, to the sorrow of their people: Mao, Ho, and Pol Pot. Only one, Mohandas Gandhi, was not corrupted, and he never exercised state power.

8. *Is nationalism such a dominant force in the present world that all leaders must be nationalists?* Modern nationalism is usually said to have begun with the French Revolution, although three peoples manifested proto-nationalist tendencies 2,000 years ago—the Jews, the Greeks, and the Vietnamese. In the present era, nationalists always seek a sovereign political unit—a state—to match their psychological identification with a nation. This Western idea has proven irresistible to Asians, but the nation-state model does not fit India very well, nor Indonesia. China, a former empire, is a nation-state today, even if certain minorities (Tibetans and Uighurs) would like to secede and form their own nation-states. In Cambodia and Vietnam, nationalism is so strong that it sweeps all before it.

The first countries where modern nationalism took root (France, Britain, and the United States) were generally successful and satisfied powers. The prime ingredient in their nationalism was pride. In Germany and Russia, by contrast, nationalism assumed a sullen, resentful tone. Grievances were carefully nurtured. Defeats and humiliations were recounted over and over. Most of the Third World, including all five countries we have studied in this book, has adopted a type of embittered nationalism. This is a tragedy, for as the Polish journalist Ryszard Kapuscinski has written, "Nationalism cannot exist in a conflict-free condition; it cannot exist as a thing devoid of grudges and claims. Wherever the nationalism of one group rears its head, immediately, as if from beneath the ground, this group's enemies will spring up."[6]

Great minds in the West hoped that nationalism would prove only a passing phenomenon. Albert Einstein called it "an infantile disease . . . the measles of mankind," and Franz Kafka called it "a defensive movement against the crude encroachments of civilization."[7] The end of nationalism has been proclaimed many times, by Woodrow Wilson, by Vladimir Lenin, by free traders. We do not agree. Where communists repudiated nationalism they were defeated (India and Indonesia), but where they embraced nationalism they triumphed (China, Vietnam, and Cambodia).

9. *Does leadership inevitably become oligarchic or can a single dictator maintain control indefinitely?* Sociologist Robert Michels proposed in his book *Political Parties* (1911) an "iron law of oligarchy," according to which mass democracy was impossible, because power would inevitably gravitate to bureaucratic oligarchies. Others, reviewing the Soviet and Chinese experiences, have argued that a single dictator cannot hold all the reins of power indefinitely, for industrialization generates diverse interests in society. We think that China after Mao and Vietnam after Ho illustrate the difficulty or even impossibility of power remaining centralized forever.

Many African and Asian leaders have disputed a fundamental premise of Western political philosophy, that a plurality of interests is inevitable. They imagined that they could create, if not unanimity, then at least a general consensus that would eliminate the need for opposition political parties and an adversarial legislature. In every case this proved a chimera. We are confident that some form of pluralism will come to China, Vietnam, Cambodia, and Indonesia. It has always been present in India. The jury is still out on whether mass democracy will work in those countries.

10. *Do the masses actually want to participate in politics or would they rather be led?* Eric Hoffer defined a leader as one who tries to turn his followers into children, and that well describes nine of our ten leaders. Mao turned his into frenzied children. Indira Gandhi ("Mother India") tried to make hers obedient. Ngo Dinh Diem exhorted Vietnamese to act like dutiful children. Ho wanted his children to be fulfilled. Sukarno tried to amuse his child-citizens, and so did Prince Sihanouk. Suharto and Deng Xiaoping treated their citizens like adolescents, to be indulged but also disciplined. Pol Pot preferred to abuse and terrify his children. Only Mohandas Gandhi treated his followers as adults with moral reasoning. Asian autocrats such as Lee Kuan Yew have argued that democracy is incompatible with "Asian values." We reject that argument and refer our readers to a rejoinder by Korean prime minister Kim Dae Jung, who wrote, "Asia should lose no time in firmly establishing democracy and strengthening human rights. The biggest obstacle is not its cultural heritage but the resistance of authoritarian leaders and their apologists."[8]

The fine dreams of most of our leaders were dashed. Mao Zedong, Pol Pot, and Mohandas Gandhi dreamed of autarky (radical economic self-reliance), but today their countries are fully integrated into the world trading system. Ngo Dinh Diem's wish for an independent South Vietnam turned out to be a pipe dream. Norodom Sihanouk's desire to preserve Cambodia as an island of peace amidst the wars of Indochina was most cruelly denied by fate—and by presidents, generals, and revolutionaries. Mohandas Gandhi dreamed of an undivided India stretching from Afghanistan to Burma, a country of Hindu–Muslim brotherhood, but was bitterly disappointed by the bloody partition of 1947. Pol Pot achieved temporarily his demented dream of asserting total control over society but died a broken man.

Other dreams were realized, at least partially. All ten of our leaders thirsted for national independence, and all five countries have taken their rightful places in the family of independent and sovereign nations. These nationalist leaders dreamt of regained national self-respect, of being taken seriously by Westerners, of being treated as international equals. It has happened, in no small part, due to their own efforts. They dreamt of national unity. It was achieved and maintained by China, Vietnam, Cambodia, and Indonesia. India was partitioned, but the slightly smaller India that emerged has held together for a half century despite its potential for disintegration. These leaders dreamt of national prosperity, and that appears within reach if the urgent problem of too-rapid population growth is solved. They dreamt, most of them, of equality. There is a long way to go, but progress is undeniable. The caste system endures in India as it has for thousands of years, but in 1997 K. R. Narayan, an Untouchable, rode to his inauguration as president of India in a gilded carriage once used by Britain's viceroys.

NOTES

1. Hugh Tinker, *Men Who Overturned Empires: Fighters, Dreamers, and Schemers* (Madison: University of Wisconsin Press, 1987), p. 238.

2. Georg Simmel, *The Philosophy of Georg Simmel*, ed. and trans. Kurt H. Wolff (Glencoe, Ill.: Free Press, 1950), p. 185.

3. Eugene E. Brussell, ed., *Webster's New World Dictionary of Quotable Definitions* (Englewood Cliffs, N.J.: Prentice-Hall, 1988), p. 317.

4. Ann Ruth Willner, *The Spellbinders: Charismatic Political Leadership* (New Haven, Conn.: Yale University Press, 1984), p. 8.

5. Crane Brinton, *Anatomy of a Revolution* (New York: Vintage, 1952), p. 165.

6. Ryszard Kapuscinski, *Imperium* (New York: Vintage, 1995), p. 167.

7. Brussell, *Webster's New World Dictionary of Quotable Definitions*, p. 387.

8. Kim Dae Jung, "Is Culture Destiny? The Myth of Asia's Anti-Democratic Values," *Foreign Affairs* 73 (November–December 1994), p. 194.

Glossary

ABRI: (Indonesia) Angkatan Bersenjata Republik Indonesia (Armed Forces of the Republic of Indonesia).

ahimsa: (India) Nonviolence and noninjury to living things.

All-India Sanjay Party: (India) Political party organized by Sanjay Gandhi's wife, Maneka, to compete against Indira Gandhi.

amok: Malay word for irrational behavior.

Angka: (Cambodia) "Organization." Secretive ruling group led by Pol Pot.

Angkor: (Cambodia) Center of Khmer Empire, ninth through thirteenth centuries.

ARVN: (Vietnam) Army of the Republic of Vietnam (South Vietnam).

ASEAN: Association of Southeast Asian Nations.

Bandung Conference: Meeting of African and Asian leaders in Indonesia in 1955.

bapakisme: (Indonesia) "Fatherism," or patron–client ties.

Bapu: (India) "Father." Nickname given to Gandhi by his followers.

Bhinneka tunggal Ika: (Indonesia) "Unity in Diversity," national motto.

Boxer Rebellion: (China) Anti-foreign uprising, 1900.

brahmacharya: (India) Gandhi's term for celibacy.

Brahmans: (India) Highest caste, includes scholars and priests.

CCP: Chinese Communist Party.

CGDK: (Cambodia) Coalition Government of Democratic Kampuchea. Front for alliance of Khmer Rouge, Son Sann, and Prince Sihanouk, which opposed Vietnamese-installed government of Hun Sen and Heng Samrin, 1982–90.

CPK: (Cambodia) Communist Party of Kampuchea.

DK: (Cambodia) Democratic Kampuchea, official name of Khmer Rouge state.

doi moi: (Vietnam) "Renewal." Term describing market reforms.

DPR: (Indonesia) Dewan Perwakilan Rakjat (People's Representative Council).

DRV: (Vietnam) Democratic Republic of Vietnam (North Vietnam).

dwi fungsi: (Indonesia) "Dual function"; doctrine authorizing civilian development tasks assigned to the army.

Four Modernizations: (China) Development program championed by Deng Xiaoping, emphasizing agriculture, industry, science and technology, and national defense.

FUNCINPEC: (Cambodia) French acronym for National United Front for an Independent, Neutral, Peaceful, and Cooperative Cambodia. Political party led by Norodom Ranariddh, Sihanouk's son.

Geneva Conference: International conference that established agreements ending the First Indochina War.

gotong royong: (Indonesia) Mutual benefit.

Great Leap Forward: (China) Mao Zedong's campaign to modernize China extremely rapidly, 1958–59.

haj: Muslim pilgrimage to Mecca.

halus: (Indonesia) Refined and passive.

Khmer Issarak: (Cambodia) "Free Khmer." Independence movement established 1940.

KMT: (China) Kuomintang (also spelled Guomindang). Chinese Nationalist Party led by Chiang Kai-shek.

Lok Sabha: (India) India's lower house of Parliament.

Mahayana Buddhism: A branch of Buddhism followed by many Vietnamese.

mandate of heaven: (China) Divine authority to rule.

mufakat: (Indonesia) Unanimous agreement by a group.

musyawarah: (Indonesia) Consultation and discussion.

Nahdatul Ulama: (Indonesia) Islamic organization founded 1926.

NASAKOM: (Indonesia) A slogan denoting nationalism, religion, and communism.

NLF: (Vietnam) National Liberation Front, also called "Vietcong."

Pantja Sila: (Indonesia) The five principles of Indonesia's state philosophy: nationalism, humanitarianism, popular sovereignty, social justice, and belief in one god.

PLA: (China) People's Liberation Army.

PNI: (Indonesia) Nationalist Party of Indonesia.

PRC: People's Republic of China.

priyayi: (Indonesia) Javanese aristocratic class.

PRK: (Cambodia) People's Republic of Kampuchea (pro-Vietnamese).

Sangkum Reastr Niyum: (Cambodia) Prince Sihanouk's political party in 1950s.

Sarekat Islam: (Indonesia) Islamic Union.

UNTAC: (Cambodia) United Nations Transitional Authority in Cambodia.

Viet Minh: (Vietnam) Vietnam Independence League.

Appendix:
Populations and Economies

Country	Population Mid-1998	Annual Increase (%)	Doubling Time (years)	Per Capita GNP (US$)
India	988,700,000	1.9	37	380
China	1,242,500,000	1.0	69	750
Vietnam	78,500,000	1.2	57	290
Cambodia	10,800,000	2.4	29	300
Indonesia	207,400,000	1.5	45	1,080

Note: Per capita Gross National Product figures do not reflect the consequences of the Asian financial crisis of 1998.

Source: Population Reference Bureau, *1998 World Population Data Sheet* (Washington, D.C.: PRB, May 1998).

Index

Abangan Muslims, 211, 248
ABRI. *See* Angkatan Bersenjata Republik Indonesia
Aceh, 208, 214
Acton, John E., 6
Agriculture: in Cambodia, 143, 189; in China, 40–41, 61–62; in India, 266; in Vietnam, 80, 108, 131
ahimsa, definition of, 339
Aidit, Dipi Nusantara, 226, 233–34, 244
Akbar, 269
Aksai Chin, 310
Alexander the Great, 268
Alienation, Gandhi on, 283–84
All-India Sanjay Party, 318; definition of, 339
Allman, T. D., 197
American Friends of Vietnam (AFV), 121–22
amok, definition of, 339
Amritsar massacre, 288, 300
Anarchism, Mao and, 35
Ancient Mystical Order of Rosicrucians, 231
Angka, 184, 187, 189–90; definition of, 339
Angkatan Bersenjata Republik Indonesia (ABRI), 242–43, 248–49
Angkor, 144–48, 153; definition of, 339
Angkor Wat, 145–46, 159, 161–62, 187, 190
Angola, 253
Animism, 211
Apte, Narayan, 294
Aquino, Benigno, 4
Aquino, Corazon, 4
ARVN. *See also* South Vietnam, army of; definition of, 339
Aryans, 268
ASEAN, definition of, 339
ashimsa, 285
Asia: culture of, 333; currency crisis in, 250, 255; current state of, 4; leadership in, 9, 332–38
Asian Development Bank, 256

Asia Watch, 254
Assam, 313
Ataturk, Kemal, 219, 229
Atomic weapons: Gandhi on, 292; use in Japan, 101–2
Attlee, Clement, 292–93
Aung San Suu Kyi, 4
Aurangzeb, 269
Autumn Harvest Uprising, 29, 328

Baker, Herbert, 282
Bali, 208, 214
Bandung Conference, 158, 230, 307; definition of, 339
Bao Dai, emperor of Vietnam, 92, 101–2, 105–6, 119–22, 124–25
bapakisme, definition of, 339
Bapu, definition of, 339
Bayh, Birch, 233
Becker, Elizabeth, 184, 186, 192, 197–98
Belo, Carlos Ximenes, 254
Bentinck, William, 269
Besant, Annie, 276
Bhagat, H. K. L., 320
Bhindranwale, Sant Jarnail Singh, 319
Bhinneka tunggal Ika, definition of, 339
Bhutan, 313
Bhutto, Benazir, 4
Bhutto, Zulfikar Ali, 4, 317
Binh Xuyen, 124
Biography: approaches to, 2; subjective natu of, 9–10
Blavatsky, Madame, 276
Blum, Léon, 98
Boer War, 278
Bolsheviks, 28, 94
Borodin, Mikhail, 96
Botha, Louis, 279
Boxer Rebellion, 23, 50; definition of, 339
brahmacharaya, definition of, 339

Brahmachari, Dhirendra, 319
brahmacharya, 285
Brahmans, definition of, 339
Brink, Francis, 105
Brinton, Crane, 336
Britain: and China, 22; Gandhi and, 275–76, 279, 282, 290; Ho Chi Minh in, 92; and India, 269–73, 287–91; and Indonesia, 225; and Islam, 282; in Malaya, 131; and Malaysia, 232; and Vietnam, 101, 103
Brooks, Ferdinand T., 299
Broz, Josip (Tito), 158, 179, 307
Brzezinski, Zbigniew, 194
Buddha, 268
Buddhism, 20, 268, 286; in Cambodia, 144–45, 147, 178; Deng and, 49; Gandhi and, 283; in Indonesia, 209–10; and killing fields, 197; Mahayana, 81, 340; Ngo Dinh Diem and, 132; Pol Pot and, 184, 190; Theravada, 81, 124, 144, 147
Budi Utomo, 214, 219
Bui Tin, 107, 110
Burma, 250
Bush, George, 64
Buttinger, Joseph, 99, 122
Byrd, Richard E., 122

Caldwell, Malcolm, 193
Cambodia: background on, 143–50; bombing of, 85–86, 111, 148, 162–63, 166, 183; and China, 149, 158–59, 169; civil war in, 183–86; culture of, 144–45, 184; geography of, 143–44; history of, 145–49; independence in, 157–63; and killing fields, 197; leadership in, 331; map of, 140; population of, 341; under Sihanouk, 151–74; timeline of, 141–42; Vietnam War and, 160–62; women in, 145
Camus, Albert, 47
Cao Dai, 124
Capitalism: Gandhi on, 284; in Vietnam, 99
Carlyle, Thomas, 2–3
Carpenter, Edward, 283
Carter, Jimmy, 66, 194, 197
Caste system, 265–67; Gandhi on, 286
Castro, Fidel, 33
Catholicism: in East Timor, 209, 254; Gandhi and, 285; Ngo Dinh Diem and, 117–18, 121–22, 125–26, 129, 132; Pol Pot and, 190; in Vietnam, 81, 91, 107, 121, 123–24, 126
CCP. *See* Chinese Communist Party
Ceausescu, Nicolae, 107
Central Intelligence Agency (CIA), United States, 101, 123, 133, 160, 165, 188, 234, 244; and Suharto, 252

CGDK. *See* Coalition Government of Democratic Kampuchea
Chandler, David, 178, 183, 186, 197–98
Chang Fa-kwei, 100
Chaplin, Charlie, 290
Charisma, 229–30, 335
Chen Duxiu, 28
Chen Yun, 56
Chiang Ching-huo, 50
Chiang Kai-shek, 23, 29–31, 38, 51–53, 96, 101, 103
China: background on, 19–23; and Cambodia, 149, 158–59, 169; culture of, 20–21; under Deng Xiaoping, 47–69; geography of, 19–20; history of, 21–23; Ho Chi Minh in, 96; and India, 309–10; and Khmer Rouge, 185; leadership in, 330; under Mao Zedong, 25–46; map of, 14; nuclear capability of, 110; and Pol Pot, 182, 188–89, 193; population of, 341; and Sihanouk, 165, 167, 170, 172; timeline of, 15–17; and United States, 184; and Vietnam, 80, 82–83, 91, 103, 105–6, 108–10, 193; women in, 3, 21, 37, 39
Chinese Communist Party (CCP), 23, 27, 31, 37, 43, 47, 52, 96; Deng and, 68; founding of, 29
Chinese, in Indonesia, 207, 213, 234, 243, 245, 247, 252–53, 256
Chinese Socialist Youth League, 50
Chinese thought, Mao and, 35–36
Christianity, Gandhi and, 280–81, 283, 286
Churchill, Winston, 101, 290–92
CIA. *See* Central Intelligence Agency
Civil disobedience, 279, 283, 289–91, 301, 303
Class: in China, 22–23; Khmer Rouge and, 189–90; and leadership, 328
Clinton, Bill, 86
Clothing, 334–35; of Gandhi, 278, 280–81; of Ho Chi Minh, 95, 107; of Mao, 38; of Ngo Dinh Diem, 117
Coalition Government of Democratic Kampuchea (CGDK), 171, 193–94
Coedès, George, 154
Colonialism, 5
Commercial Import Program (CIP), 125
Communications media: Gandhi and, 284; and leadership, 6, 327, 335; Mao and, 32, 44; Sukarno and, 224, 226, 232
Communism: in Cambodia, 156, 158–59, 167, 171; in China, 53–54; and Democratic Kampuchea, 187; in East Timor, 253; Ho Chi Minh and, 95–98; ideology in, 98; Indira Gandhi and, 309; in Indonesia, 226, 230, 233–34, 247; and killing fields, 197; leadership in, 335–36; Mao and, 28, 33–34, 36–37; Ngo Dinh Diem and, 118–19; Pol

Pot and, 179, 181; in South Vietnam, 134; Sukarno and, 221; in Vietnam, 99–100, 107
Communist Party of Kampuchea (CPK), 161, 182
Conein, Lucien, 133–34
Confucianism, 20–21; and democracy, 129; Deng and, 49; and emperor, 122; Mao and, 25; in Vietnam, 80–81, 91
Congress Party, 308, 311; Indira Gandhi and, 313, 316
Corruption, 336; in China, 67; in India, 308, 316; in Indonesia, 250–53; in Vietnam, 124, 132
CPK. *See* Communist Party of Kampuchea
Cultivation System, 213–14
Cuong De, 121

Dada Abdullah & Company, 276–77
Dalai Lama, 41, 309
Daoism, 20, 49
d'Argenlieu, Thierry, 103–5
de Gaulle, Charles, 101, 107, 161
Dekker, Eduard Douwes, 213–14
Democracy: in China, 63–64, 67; Gandhi on, 286; guided, 231; in Indonesia, 227–28; Ngo Dinh Diem and, 129; Suharto and, 248–50
Democratic centralism, 231
Democratic Kampuchea (DK), 168, 186–93; economic organization, 189; forced labor in, 190; ideology of, 188–89; political organization of, 187–88; social organization of, 189–90
Democratic Party, Cambodia, 155–57
Democratic Republic of Vietnam (DRV), 102, 106–10, 180. *See also* North Vietnam
Deng Dan, 49
Deng Liqun, 67
Deng Pufang, 56, 58, 67–68
Deng Shuping, 55, 58
Deng Wenming, 49, 53
Deng Xiaoping, 7, 47–69; in Cultural Revolution, 57–58; and democracy, 63–64; early socialization of, 47–49; early years in power, 55–57; education of, 49–51; family of, 55–56; foreign policy of, 65–67; in France, 28, 49–51; later years in power, 60–61; leadership style of, 61, 328–30, 332–38; marriages of, 51–53, 55–56; photographs of, 48; political style of, 54–55; reforms of, 61–63; rehabilitation of, 58–60; rise to power of, 44, 51–54; and Tiananmen Square massacre, 55, 64–65; and Vietnam, 193
Deng Zhifang, 56, 68
Denver, John, 66
Desai, Morarji, 310–11, 316–18

Deuch, 191
deva raja, 144, 156–58
Developing nations, leadership in, 334–35
Development Unity Party (DPP), 249
Devillers, Philippe, 115
Dewan Perwakilan Rakjat (People's Representative Council; DPR), 232, 249
Dhanu, 320–21
Diah, B. M., 245
Dictatorship: Indira Gandhi and, 315–17; Mao and, 25; versus oligarchy, 337; Suharto and, 247–48
Dien Bien Phu, battle of, 84, 106, 122
Diet, Gandhi on, 275–76, 286
Ding Peng, 68
Diponegoro, 213
Djojobojo, 223
DK. *See* Democratic Kampuchea
doi moi, 86; definition of, 339
Domino theory, 85, 122, 227
Donovan, William J., 121
Dooley, Thomas A., 123
Douglas, William O., 121
DPR. *See* Dewan Perwakilan Rakjat
DRV. *See* Democratic Republic of Vietnam
Dudman, Richard, 192
Duke, Angier Biddle, 122
Dulles, John Foster, 106, 124, 130, 156, 158, 230
Duong Van "Big" Minh, 133–34
Dutch: and Indonesia, 213, 215, 225–27, 232; and Suharto, 243; and Sukarno, 221–22, 224, 230; in World War II, 223
Dutch East India Company, 213
dwi fungsi, definition of, 339
Dyer, R. E. H., 288

East India Company, 269, 273
East Timor, 8, 209, 247, 250, 253–55
Economic development: Deng and, 61–62; Mao and, 36–37; Suharto and, 241, 250–51
Education: in Cambodia, 144; Cultural Revolution and, 62; Gandhi on, 291; in India, 269–70; and leadership, 328; Pol Pot and, 190; in Vietnam, 84
Einstein, Albert, 302, 336
Eisenhower, Dwight, 106, 122, 126, 158, 230
Emerson, Ralph Waldo, 89, 283
Engels, Friedrich, 33
etak-etak, 212

Factory workers, in Marxism, 98
Fall, Bernard, 89, 106
Fallaci, Oriana, 151, 167, 321
Family: in Asian culture, 333; Pol Pot and, 190; in Vietnam, 80–81
Family planning, in India, 316

Fang Lizhi, 63–64
Fasting, Gandhi and, 287–88, 291, 293
Fatmawati, 223, 225, 228
Feng Yuxiang, 50–51
Fischer, Louis, 283
Fishel, Wesley, 121–22
FitzGerald, Frances, 128
Followers, and leadership, 329
Four Modernizations, 61–63; definition of, 339
Four Noble Truths, 81
France: and Cambodia, 147–49, 153, 161–62, 178; Deng in, 28, 49–51; and First Indochina War, 104–6; Ho Chi Minh and, 92–93, 97, 99; Ngo Dinh Diem and, 118, 123–24; Pol Pot and, 178–79, 181; and Sihanouk, 153–57, 165, 170; United States and, 101; and Vietnam, 83–84, 91, 96, 101–3, 105, 119–20, 122; in World War II, 98
French Communist Party, 95
French Embassy, Phnom Penh, 186
Frente Revolucionária do Timor Leste Independente (Fretilin), 253–54
Frost, Robert, 297
FUNCINPEC, 170, 172–73; definition of, 339

Gajah Mada, 210
Gama, Vasco da, 213
Gandhi, Feroze, 304–6, 308–9
Gandhi, Indira Nehru, 4, 8–9, 297–324; apprenticeship of, 307–10; assassination of, 318–20; character of, 308; childhood of, 300–303; education of, 301–2, 304–5; family of, 297–300; foreign policy of, 314–15; leadership style of, 327–30, 332–38; marriage of, 305–6, 308–9; photographs of, 298; political style of, 309; as prime minister, 311–15, 318–20; return to India, 305–7; in Shastri cabinet, 310–11; and women's issues, 267; years out of power, 316–17
Gandhi, Karamchand, 273–74
Gandhi, Kasturbai Makanji, 273–74, 276, 278, 280–81, 285, 292
Gandhi, Manilal, 276
Gandhi, Mohandas, 8, 271–96; adolescence of, 273–75; assassination of, 294, 307; in Britain, 275–76, 279, 290; and celibacy, 285–86, 306; character of, 271; education of, 273–76; family and childhood of, 273; first return to India, 276; Ho Chi Minh and, 95, 104; and Indian independence, 287–92; and Indira Gandhi, 300–304, 306; last years of, 292–93; leadership style of, 327–30, 332–38; marriage of, 273–74; personal life of, 280–82; philosophy of, 283–87; photographs of, 272; Pol Pot and, 178; religion of, 276–78, 280; in South Africa, 277–82
Gandhi, Putlibai, 273
Gandhi, Rajiv, 306, 309, 318, 320–21
Gandhi, Sanjay, 298, 306, 309, 315–18
Gandhi, Sonia Maino, 318, 322
Gang of Four, 43–44, 58–60
Garibaldi, Guiseppe, 299, 303
Garnisih, Inggit, 219–20, 223
Gautier, Georges, 154
Geertz, Clifford, 239
Geneva Conference, 85, 106, 122, 157; definition of, 340
George III, king of Great Britain, 21
George V, king of Great Britain, 290, 299
Germany, 59, 101, 223, 286–87
Ghose, Aurobindo, 282
Gia Long, 83
Giap, Vo Nguyen, 84, 92, 99–100, 105–7
Godse, Nathuram Vinayak, 294
Gokhale, Gopal Krishna, 278, 281–82
Golden Temple, 319
Golkar, 248–49, 252
Gorbachev, Mikhail, 64, 68
gotong royong, 212, 231; definition of, 340
Gracey, Douglas, 103
Great Calcutta Killing, 292–93
Great Depression, 97, 119, 290
Greater East Asia Co-Prosperity Sphere, 98, 223
Great Leap Forward, 40–41, 56–57; definition of, 340
Great Man theory of history, 2–3
Great Proletarian Cultural Revolution, 35–37, 41–43, 49, 55–58, 62, 182
Green, Marshall, 233, 245
Greene, Graham, 123
Group orientation, in Asian culture, 333

Habibie, B. J., 255–56
haj, 211; definition of, 340
halus, 212, 248; definition of, 340
Hariati, 228
Harjojudanto, Sigit, 252
Harkins, Paul, 133
Hartinah, Siti, 242, 251, 255
Hartini, 228, 235
Hasan, Muhammad (Bob), 252
Hatta, Mohammad, 221–25, 228
Heng Samrin, 169–71, 192–93
Henru, Jawaharlal, 291
He Ping, 56
He Zizhen, 29–30, 42
Hierarchical societies, in Asian culture, 333
Hind Swaraj, 281–82, 284

Hinduism, 299; in Cambodia, 146–47; Gandhi and, 281, 283, 285; in India, 266–67, 320; in Indonesia, 208; and Islam, 292–94, 307, 318

Hitler, Adolf, 31–33, 128, 223, 292, 335

Hoa Hao, 124

Ho Chi Minh, 7, 81–82, 84–86, 89–113; and Cambodia, 156; character of, 89–91, 103–4, 107; and Democratic Republic of Vietnam, 107–10; early socialization of, 92; education of, 92; and First Indochina War, 104–7; leadership style of, 327–38; marriage of, 99; and Ngo Dinh Diem, 120, 133; photographs of, 90; time abroad, 92–98; and Vietnamese independence, 98–104; and Vietnam War, 110–11

Hoffer, Eric, 115, 333–34, 337

Hong Kong, 61, 97, 102

Horta, Jose Ramos, 254

Hou Youn, 157, 179–80

Hua Gofeng, 44, 60

Huai-Hai campaign, 53–55

Human rights: in East Timor, 254; in Indonesia, 250–51; in Vietnam, 86

Humayun, 269

Humpuss Group, 250–51

Hundred Flowers campaign, 34, 40, 56

Hu Nim, 157, 180, 182

Hun Sen, 169–73, 193–95

Huxley, Thomas, 22

Hu Yaobang, 52, 64

ICP. *See* Indochinese Communist Party

Ida Njoman Rai, 217

Ideology, and leadership, 329

Ieng Sary, 156–57, 167, 171–72, 178, 180–82, 193–95

INC. *See* Indian National Congress

Increased intracranial pressure, 180

Independence movements, and leadership, 330

India: background on, 265–70; and China, 309–10; Civil Service, 269, 273; constitution of, 302, 308, 313; culture of, 266–67; demography of, 266; geography of, 265–66; history of, 267–70; independence of, 287–92; under Indira Gandhi, 297–324; and Indonesia, 210, 218; leadership in, 332; map of, 262; in Mohandas Gandhi's era, 271–96; nuclear capability of, 313, 315; and Pakistan, 311, 314; partition of, 293, 307; population of, 341; self-sufficiency movement in, 282; timeline of, 263–64; women in, 3, 265, 267

Indian Congress, 299–300

Indian National Congress (INC), 218, 275, 278, 289, 300

India Salt Act, 289

Indische Partij, 219

Indochina War: First, 104–7, 121; Second. *See* Vietnam War

Indochinese Communist Party (ICP), 97–98, 100–101, 103, 156

Indonesia: army of, 209, 227, 230, 233–34; background on, 207–14; constitution of, 225, 227–28, 231; culture of, 209–12; demography of, 207–9; extremism in, 233–34; geography of, 207; guided democracy in, 231–33; history of, 209–14; independence in, 227–28; leadership in, 331–32; map of, 204; National Defense Institute, 256; nationalism in, 218–23; New Order in, 246–48; population of, 256, 341; resources of, 223; revolution in, 225–27; society in, 211–12; under Suharto, 239–58; after Suharto, 256–57; under Sukarno, 215–37; timeline of, 205–6; women in, 212; World War II and, 223–25

Indonesian Communist Party, 214

Indonesian Nationalist Union, 214, 221

Indravarman I, king of Angkor, 146

Industry: in Cambodia, 189; in China, 62; Gandhi on, 281; in Vietnam, 108–9

Intellectuals, Mao and, 27–28

International Monetary Fund (IMF), 4, 246, 256

Irian Jaya, 209, 253–55

Islam: Gandhi and, 281, 283, 285, 290; and Hinduism, 292–94, 307, 318; in India, 266–67, 291–92; in Indonesia, 208, 210–11, 226, 228, 230, 247, 256; Japanese and, 223; pillars of, 211; Suharto and, 248, 254; Sukarno and, 229, 234

Jackson, Karl, 197

Jamieson, Neil, 125

Japan: atomic weapons and, 101–2; and Cambodia, 148–49, 154–55, 177; and China, 28, 31, 53; Ho Chi Minh and, 99; and India, 291–92; and Indonesia, 214, 224–25, 249; industrialization of, 219, 284; and Sukarno, 223–24; and Vietnam, 84, 91–92, 98, 101, 119–20; in World War II, 223

Jarai tribe, 183, 191

Java, 208. *See also* Indonesia; culture of, 241–42, 247; mythology of, 229

Jayakar, Pupul, 9, 304

Jayavarman II, king of Angkor, 146

Jayavarman VII, king of Angkor, 161

Jayewardene, Junius, 320

Jefferson, Thomas, 102

Jiang Qing, 30–31, 42–44, 54, 57–58, 60

Jiang Zemin, 68

Jinnah, Mohammed Ali, 292–93, 307

Jin Weiying, 52
Johnson, Lyndon B., 7, 132, 134, 233, 311
Jones, Howard, 233
Judd, Walter, 121
Juliana, queen of the Netherlands, 227

Kafka, Franz, 336–37
Kalimantan, 208
Kallenbach, Herman, 281
Kang Sheng, 60
Kapuscinski, Ryszard, 336
Karnow, Stanley, 119
kasar, 212
Kaul, Shrimati Kamala, 300, 302–4
Kebatinan, 248
Keng Vannsak, 178–79
Kennedy, Jacqueline, 162, 307
Kennedy, John F., 41, 85, 110, 121, 126, 131–34, 233; assassination of, 134, 160
Kertosudiro, 241–42
keterbukaan, 250
Khalistan, 318–19
Khan, Mir Alam, 279
Khieu Ponnary, 179–80, 184, 194
Khieu Samphan, 156, 167, 171, 177, 185, 188, 194–95; beating of, 159, 181
Khmer Issarak, 155, 177; definition of, 340
Khmer Loeu, 144
Khmer People's National Liberation Front (KPNLF), 170
Khmer People's Revolutionary Party (KPRP), 156
Khmer Rouge, 8, 86, 144, 149, 166, 171; China and, 185; effects of, 167; and evacuation of Phnom Penh, 186–87; and forced labor, 190; and killing fields, 190; and liberated zones, 184; Mao and, 45; and North Vietnam, 182; under Pol Pot, 175–200; Sihanouk and, 151–53, 158, 165, 167–72
Khmers, 143
Khrushchev, Nikita, 40, 56–57, 85, 109–10; photographs of, 90
Khum Meak, 177
Kia Motors, 250
Kierkegaard, Søren, 1
Kiernan, Ben, 181, 191, 197–98
Killing fields, 168, 190–91; explanations of, 196–98
Kim Il Sung, 57, 107, 168, 171, 190
Kingship: in Cambodia, 144, 156–58; in Indonesia, 210, 219, 223, 229
Kissinger, Henry, 43, 59, 148, 162, 314–15
KMT. *See also* Kuomintang; definition of, 340
Komando Cadangan Strategis Angkatan Darat (Kostrad), 243
Kontrontasi, 232–33
Korean War, 39, 105

Kossamak, queen of Cambodia, 153, 160, 165, 168
Kosygin, Alexsei, 165, 312
Krom Pracheachon, 159
Kuomintang (KMT), 23, 29–31, 51–54, 96, 101, 103

Land reform: in Cambodia, 184, 189; in China, 39, 61–62; Ngo Dinh Diem and, 126–27; in Vietnam, 108
Lan Ping. *See* Jiang Qing
Lansdale, Edward G., 123–24, 126–27
Lawyers, Gandhi on, 277
Leadership, 1, 327–29, 332–33; Asian, 9, 332–38; in communist societies, 335–36; in developing nations, 334–35; in Indonesia, 211–12; sex and, 3–4
Legge, John, 229
Le Loi, 83
Lenin, Vladimir, 29, 95–96, 231, 337
Leninism, 197; Deng and, 61, 63; Ho Chi Minh and, 95, 108; Mao and, 28, 33; Sukarno and, 229; in Vietnam, 81–82
Liberation Tigers of Tamil Eelam (LTTE), 320
Li Dazhao, 28
Liem Sioe Liong, 252, 255
Li Lisan, 52–53
Lin Biao, 34, 41–43, 57–58
Lindbergh, Charles, 302
Linggajati Agreement, 226
Li Peng, 64, 68
Liu Binyan, 63
Liu Bocheng, 51, 53, 55
Liu Huaqing, 68
Liu Shaoqi, 42–43, 51, 56–58, 110
Li Zhisui, 33
Lodge, Henry Cabot, 116, 133–34
Lok Sabha, definition of, 340
Long March, 30, 52
Lon Nol, 148–49, 161, 164–66, 169, 177, 181–83, 186, 197
Lon Non, 177
Luce, Henry, 121, 232
Lu Han, 103
Luytens, Edwin, 282
Ly, 125

MAAG. *See* United States, Military Assistance Advisory Group
MacLaine, Shirley, 66
Magsaysay, Ramon, 123
Mahapahit empire, 210
Mahayana Buddhism, 81; definition of, 340
Majelis Permusyawaratan Rakyat (MPR), 249
Malaka, Tan, 221, 226
Malaysia: Suharto and, 253; Sukarno and, 220, 232–33

Malhotra, Inder, 311
Malik, Adam, 234
Malthus, Thomas, 36
Maluku (The Moluccas), 209
Mandate of heaven, 81; definition of, 340; and
   Ho Chi Minh, 92, 102; and Ngo Dinh
   Diem, 125, 134
Mansfield, Mike, 121, 132
Mao Zedong, 6–7, 25–46, 182; and Deng, 47,
   51–52, 54–59; as dictator, 25; early social-
   ization, 25–28; early years in power,
   39–40; education of, 27; foreign policy of,
   41; and Ho Chi Minh, 98; ideology of,
   31–38; later years in power, 40–44; leader-
   ship style of, 107, 327–30, 332–38; mar-
   riages of, 27–31; personal life of, 41–42;
   photographs of, 26, 48, 90; political style
   of, 38; rise to power of, 28–31
Marcos, Ferdinand, 246, 250, 315
Marhaenism, 221
Maritain, Jacques, 129
Marx, Karl, 32–33
Marxism, 197; in China, 23; Deng and, 63; in
   East Timor, 253; factory workers in, 98;
   on history, 3; Ho Chi Minh and, 91–92,
   95; Mao and, 32–34; and nationalism, 7;
   Sukarno and, 221, 234; in Vietnam, 81–82
Masyumi, 228, 230
Masyumi Party, 231
May Fourth Movement, 28, 49
McClintock, Robert, 159
McMahon Line, 309–10
McNamara, Robert, 115
Meer, Fatima, 271
Megalomania, 336; Ho Chi Minh and, 108;
   Mao and, 37–38; Sihanouk and, 151; Su-
   karno and, 233
Merlin, Martial-Henri, 96
Michels, Robert, 337
Michigan State University, 121, 126
Military experience, and leadership, 328–29
Military strategy, Mao and, 37
Ming dynasty, 83
Mody, Nawaz, 245
Mohammed, 210–11
moksha, 286
Monivong, king of Cambodia, 153, 177
Mounier, Emmanuel, 129
Mountbatten, Louis, 293
Mozambique, 253
mufakat, 212, 231, 247; definition of, 340
Mughal dynasty, 269
Murray, Gilbert, 288
Mus, Paul, 105
musyawarah, 212, 231, 247; definition of, 340
Muslim League, 300
Mussolini, Benito, 33

Nahdatul Ulama, 228, 230; definition of, 340
Narayan, Jayaprakash, 316
NASAKOM, 231; definition of, 340
Nasser, Gamal Abdel, 158, 230, 307
Nasution, 234, 243–44, 250
Natal Indian Congress, 278
Nationalism, 1–2; Gandhi and, 285; in Indo-
   nesia, 214, 218–23; and leadership, 336;
   Mao and, 32–33; Marxism and, 7; Pol Pot
   and, 181; in Vietnam, 82–83, 91
Nationalist Extremist Movement, Vietnam,
   121
National Liberation Front (NLF; Vietcong),
   85, 109, 127, 134; and Ngo Dinh Diem,
   130–31
Navarre, Henri, 106
Naxalites, 45
Nehru, Jawaharlal, 4, 158, 208, 230, 297–307
Nehru, Motilal, 297, 299–304
Nehru, Rajiv, 297
Nehru, Vijayalakshmi, 302–6, 317
Nepotism: Ngo Dinh Diem and, 128; Suharto
   and, 250–53
Ngo Ding Can, 129, 134
Ngo Ding Luyen, 129
Ngo Dinh Can, 118–19
Ngo Dinh Diem, 7, 85, 115–36; assassination
   of, 134, 160; in bureaucratic service,
   118–19; and Catholicism, 81; celibacy of,
   118; character of, 115–17; decline of,
   125–32; downfall of, 132–34; family and
   childhood of, 117–18; and First Indochina
   War, 121; ideology of, 129; leadership
   style of, 327–38; opposition to, 129; pho-
   tographs of, 116; as prime minister,
   122–25; reasons for decline of, 127–32; re-
   ligion of, 118; years of political inactivity,
   119–22
Ngo Dinh Kha, 92, 117–18
Ngo Dinh Khoi, 117, 120
Ngo Dinh Luyen, 118
Ngo Dinh Nhu, 118, 128, 132–34
Ngo Dinh Thuc, Monsignor (Pierre Martin),
   117, 129, 132, 134
Ngo Quyen, 83
Nguyen Huu Bai, 118
Nguyen Thi Minh Khai, 99
Nguyen Van Thieu, 166
Nhek Bun Chhay, 195
Nhu, Madame, 128–29, 132–34
Nietzsche, Friedrich, 3
Nixon, Richard, 66, 85–86, 106, 314; and
   Cambodia, 85, 111, 148, 162–63, 166, 183,
   197
NLF. *See also* National Liberation Front;
   definition of, 340
Nolting, Frederick E., 130, 133

Nonaligned Movement, 307
Noncooperation: Gandhi and, 283; Sukarno and, 221–22
Norodom, king of Cambodia, 153
North Korea: and Cambodia, 167–68, 171; and Pol Pot, 189; and Sihanouk, 172
North Vietnam. *See also* Democratic Republic of Vietnam; army of, 131, 183; and Cambodia, 184; history of, 84–86; Khmer Rouge and, 182; and Pol Pot, 183; Sihanouk and, 160–62, 165
Nuon Chea, 181, 188, 191

Oberdorf, Frank, 304
Office of Strategic Services, United States, 101, 121
Oligarchy, versus dictatorship, 337
Opium Wars, 22
Organization, and leadership, 329
Osborne, Milton, 161

Pakistan, 291–93, 306–7, 311, 314
Pantja Sila (Five Principles), 212, 224; definition of, 340
Parsis, Gandhi and, 281
Partai Demokasi Indonesia (PDI), 249, 254
Partai Indonesia, 222
Partai Komunis Indonesia (PKI), 220, 226, 228, 230, 233–34, 243–44
Partai Nasional Indonesia (PNI), 221–22, 228, 230
Partai Persatuan, 249
Partai Sosialis Indonesia (PSI), 223
Passive resistance. *See* Satyagraha
Patron-client relations: in Asian culture, 333; in Cambodia, 146; in Indonesia, 211; Sukarno and, 219; in Vietnam, 81
Payne, Robert, 291
Peasants: in China, 23, 62; Gandhi on, 291; and history, 2–3; Ho Chi Minh and, 96, 98, 108; and killing fields, 198; leadership and, 335; Mao and, 33–34, 38, 40; Ngo Dinh Diem and, 122, 127, 131; and politics, 337; Pol Pot and, 183–84; and show trials, 39; Sihanouk and, 159, 162–63; Sukarno and, 215, 217, 230
Pembela Tanah Air (Peta), 224, 242
Pemudas, 224–25
Peng Zhen, 54, 58
Pen Saloth, 175
People's Liberation Army (PLA), 31, 35, 37, 59, 64–65, 68
People's Republic of China (PRC), 19–20, 31, 54–55
People's Republic of Kampuchea (PRK), 171, 193
Personalism, 129

Pétain, Philippe, 98
Peterson, Douglas, 86
Pham Hong Thai, 96
Pham Ngoc Thao, 131
Pham Van Dong, 92, 96, 99, 107, 183
Phan Boi Chau, 84, 92, 96, 117–19
Philippines, 218–19, 231, 250, 315
Phnom Penh: evacuation of, 186; Pol Pot in, 180–81
Phoenix Settlement, 280
Phouk Chhay, 182
Pius XI, pope, 285
PKI. *See* Partai Komunis Indonesia
PLA. *See* People's Liberation Army
Plassey, battle of, 269
PNI. *See* Partai Nasional Indonesia
Police state tactics, Ngo Dinh Diem and, 129–30
Polo, Marco, 19
Pol Pot, 8, 86, 144, 148–49, 166, 169–70, 175–200; and Cambodian civil war, 183–86; character of, 175, 178, 181; decline and fall of, 195–96; and Democratic Kampuchea, 186–93; in eastern Cambodia, 179–80; education of, 177–79; evil of, explanations for, 196–98; family and background of, 175–77; and guerilla warfare, 193–95; ideology of, 188–89; in jungle, 181–83; and Khmer Rouge, 171; and KPRP, 156; leadership style of, 327–38; marriages of, 180, 194; in Phnom Penh, 180–81; photographs of, 176; private life of, 191–92; and Sihanouk, 151, 157, 169–70; and war with Vietnam, 192–93; and Zhou Enlai, 168
Ponchaud, François, 186–87, 197
Pope, Allen, 231
Populism: Mao and, 34; Sukarno and, 221
Portuguese, 253; in India, 268–69; in Indonesia, 213
Prawiranegara, Sjafruddim, 231
PRC. *See* People's Republic of China
priyayi, 213, 218–19; definition of, 340
PRK. *See* People's Republic of Kampuchea
Probosutedjo, 252
Punjab, 312, 318
Pusat Tenega Rakyat, 224
Putra, Hutomo Mandala (Tommy), 250–51
Pye, Lucian, 19, 60–61

Qin Shihuang, 21
Quakers, 280
Quinn-Judge, Sophie, 98

Racism: and killing fields, 197–98; in South Africa, 277–80
Raden Sukemi, 217, 219
Radford, Arthur, 106

Ranariddh, prince of Cambodia, 172–73, 194
Rani, Swarup, 299–301, 303
Ratna Dewi, 228
ratu adil, 219, 223
Reagan, Ronald, 194, 197
Red Guards, 42–43, 52, 57–58, 63
Religion: Chinese, 20, 49; Gandhi and, 276–78, 280; in India, 266–67; in Indonesia, 207–8, 210–11; Pol Pot and, 190; in Vietnam, 81, 117, 124
Republican Youth Movement, 128
Revolutionary leaders, 333–34
Revolutionary Youth Association, 118
Revolutionary Youth League, 96–97
Revolution, Mao on, 33
Rizal, Jose, 218–19
Rolling Thunder bombing campaign, 111
Roosevelt, Franklin D., 101, 103
Rotary Club, 231
Royal Dutch Shell Company, 208, 214
Royal Netherlands Indies Army, 242
Roy, M. N., 96
Rukmana, Siti Hardijanti Jastuti (Tutut), 252
Rusk, Dean, 233
Ruskin, John, 280, 283, 291
Russia. *See also* Soviet Union; Japan and, 219; revolution in, 28, 94

Sabarmati Ashram, 283, 289, 291, 301
Sailendra empire, 210
Sainteny, Jean, 103–4
Saleh, Chaerul, 224
Salisbury, Harrison, 55
Saloth Nhep, 177, 196
Saloth Roeung, 177, 197
Saloth Sar. *See* Pol Pot
Saloth Seng, 175–77, 192
Saloth Suong, 180
Salt, Henry, 275, 283
Salt March, 289–90, 303
Samlaut Rebellion, 162, 183
Sanger, Margaret, 285–86
Sanger, Yurike, 228
Sangkum Reastr Niyum, 157, 161, 180; definition of, 340
Santri Muslims, 211
Sarekat Islam, 214, 219–20
Sarit Thannarat, 160
sati, 269
Satyagraha, 279, 281–82, 288–90
Schmidt, Helmut, 59
Schoenbrun, David, 104
Science, in China, 62
Seekins, Donald, 218
Self-denial, Gandhi on, 286
Sendero Luminoso, 45
Sepoy Mutiny, 270, 273

Sevagram Ashram, 286, 291, 306
Sex, and leadership, 3–4
Shah Jahan, 269
Shaplen, Robert, 115
Shastri, Lal Bahadur, 310–11
Shaw, George Bernard, 290, 302
Shawcross, William, 162
Sheehan, Neil, 122
Shoup, David M., 110
Siam. *See also* Thailand; and Cambodia, 147, 177
Siddharta Gautama (Buddha), 268
Sieu Heng, 181
Sihanouk, Monique, 163, 165, 168–69
Sihanouk, Norodom, 7–8, 144, 147–49, 151–74, 230; background of, 153; and bombing of Cambodia, 162–63; character of, 151–53; childhood of, 153–54; downfall of, 163–66; education of, 153–54; exiles of, 166–68, 170–71; family of, 153, 168–69; and Ieng Sary, 195; and Khmer Rouge, 185, 188; and killing fields, 196–97; as king under French, 154–57; as leader of independent Cambodia, 157–63; leadership style of, 164, 327–38; photographs of, 152; and Pol Pot, 177–79, 194; as prisoner of Khmer Rouge, 168–70; return to power, 172–73; and women, 153
Sikhs, 266, 307, 318–20
Sikkim, 313
Simmel, Georg, 329
Simon, John, 289
Singh, Beant, 320
Singh, Satwant, 320
Sino-Indian War, 309–10
Sino-Vietnamese War, 67
Sirik Matak, 164–66
Sisowath, king of Cambodia, 147–48, 153
Slade, Madeleine, 289
Slavery, in Cambodia, 146–47
Smuts, Jan Christian, 279, 282
Snow, Edgar, 33, 38, 53
Social Darwinism, 22, 32
Socialism: Mao and, 34; Marx on, 33
Socialist Republic of Vietnam (SRV), 79
Soetomo, 215
Sok Nem, 175
Son Ngoc Thanh, 154–58, 160, 163, 177–79
Son Sann, 170
Son Sen, 179, 191, 194–95; and KPRP, 156
South Africa, Gandhi in, 277–82
South Korea, 250
South Vietnam: army of, 86, 130–31, 169; and Cambodia, 160–61, 165, 169, 183; constitution of, 126; history of, 84–86; and Indonesia, 231; Parliament of, 129
Soviet Union. *See also* Russia; and Cambodia,

149, 159; and China, 39–40, 43, 56–57, 64, 66–67; Deng in, 50; Ho Chi Minh and, 95–97; and India, 311–14; Indira Gandhi in, 307; Sihanouk and, 165; Sino-American alliance against, 184; and Vietnam, 85–86, 96–97, 108–10, 192; and Yugoslavia, 179
Spellman, Francis, 121
Spencer, Herbert, 3
Spice trade, 212–14
Spinning: Indira Gandhi and, 301; Mohandas Gandhi and, 283, 289–90
Sri Lanka, 320
Stalin, Josef, 31–32, 39, 56, 97–98, 101, 184, 221, 334; leadership style of, 107
Stalina, Nadezhda Alliluyeva, 184
Sudharmono, 250
Sudwikatmono, 252
Sufi Islam, 248
Suharto, 8, 239–58; character of, 239–41; childhood and background of, 241–42; as dictator, 247–48; downfall of, 255; and East Timor and Irian Jaya, 253–55; economic policy of, 241, 250–51; education of, 242; and facade of democracy, 248–50; leadership style of, 328–38; marriage of, 242; and military, 241–43, 248–49; New Order of, 246–48; opposition to, 249–50; and overthrow of Sukarno, 234, 243–45; photographs of, 240; in power, 245–46; religion of, 248; rise to power of, 235; succession to, 254; and Sukarno, 242–43
Sukarno, 8, 158, 214–37; character of, 215–17, 228–29; charisma of, 229–30; education of, 218–20; family and background of, 217–18; and guided democracy, 231–33; ideology of, 221, 230; and independence, 227–28; and Indonesian nationalism, 219–23; and Indonesian revolution, 225–27; last years of, 235; leadership style of, 328–38; marriages of, 219–20, 223, 228, 235; overthrow of, 234–35, 243–45; personal life of, 228–29; photographs of, 216; supernatural claims of, 218, 228; trial of, 221–22; and women, 215, 228; World War II and, 223–25
Sukarnoputri, Megawati, 4, 212, 250, 254–55
Sukirah, 241–42
Sulawesi (Celebes), 208–9
Sumatra, 208
Sun Tzu, 37
Sun Yat-sen, 23, 27, 29, 51
Supersemar decree, 245–46
Surabaya, Battle of, 225
Suramarit, prince of Cambodia, 153, 157, 159
Suryavarman II, king of Angkor, 146
Suryavarman I, king of Angkor, 146
Syahrir, Sutan, 221–24, 226–28

Tagore, Rabindranath, 304
Taiping Rebellion, 23
Taiwan, 31
Taj Mahal, 268–69
Tamils, 318, 320
Ta Mok, 194
Tanaka, Kakuei, 249
Technology: in China, 62; Gandhi on, 284
Tenacity, and leadership, 328
Tenpin theory, 122
tertutup, 239
Thailand: and Cambodia, 143, 149; and Indonesia, 231; and Pol Pot, 193; United States and, 160
Thakur, Ramesh, 308
Thanh Thai, emperor of Vietnam, 117–18
Thayer, Nate, 195–96
Theosophical Society, 276
Theosophy, 299
Theravada Buddhism, 81, 124, 144, 147
Thich Quang Duc, 132
Thion, Serge, 146, 189, 192
Thiounn Prasith, 194
Thomas, Norman, 122
Thoreau, Henry David, 280, 283
Thorez, Maurice, 105
Tiananmen Square massacre, 55, 64–65, 68
Tibet, 41, 309
Tilak, Bal Gangadhar, 282
Timor, 209
Timor (automobile), 250
Tinker, Hugh, 327
Tjokroaminoto, Omar Said, 215, 219–20
Tolstoy, Leo, 277–78, 280–81, 283
Tolstoy Farm, 281
Total, 250
Totalitarianism, versus Suharto's New Order, 247
Tou Samouth, 180–81
Tran Van Don, 133–34
Trevelyan, George Macaulay, 303
Trihatmodio, Bambang, 252
Trinh Minh, 124
Trotsky, Leon, 50
Truman, Harry S, 101, 103, 105, 226–27, 292
Trung sisters, 82–83, 128
Truong Chinh, 99, 108
Tuol Sleng Prison, 191, 195
Turkey, 219

United Issarak Front (UIF), 155, 179
United Nations: and Cambodia, 168, 171; China and, 59; and Gandhi, 294; India and, 312–14; and Indonesia, 227, 232, 234; and Pol Pot, 194; Transitional Authority in Cambodia (UNTAC), 171, 194
United States: and Cambodia, 148–49, 162–

63, 165–66, 170, 183, 185–86; and China, 31, 43, 59, 66, 184; and First Indochina War, 104–7; and France, 122; and Ho Chi Minh, 92, 101; and Indira Gandhi, 311–12, 314, 321; and Indonesia, 226–27, 231, 256; and killing fields, 197; Military Assistance Advisory Group (MAAG), 125–26, 130; Nehru in, 307; and Ngo Dinh Diem, 121, 124, 130–33; and Pakistan, 311; and Philippines, 250; and Pol Pot, 193–94; Sihanouk and, 156–60, 162–64, 169–70; and South Vietnam, 125–26, 131–32, 160; and Suharto, 244, 250; and Sukarno, 232–34; and Vietnam, 79, 85–86, 91, 101–3, 123; and Vietnam War, 110–11; in World War II, 98

Unocal, 250

UNTAC, 171, 194; definition of, 340

Untouchables, 266, 291

U Nu, 158

Updike, John, 271

Utari, Sitti, 219, 222

Utopianism, Mao and, 36

Vakil, Jehangir, 304

Valluy, Jean, 105

Vanar Sena, 303

van den Bosch, Johannes, 213

Vegetarianism, Gandhi and, 275–76

Versailles Peace Conference, 288

Vietcong. *See* National Liberation Front

Viet Minh (Vietnam Doc Lap Dong Minh Hoi), 98–104, 120, 122, 124, 127; definition of, 340; in First Indochina War, 105–7; and Ngo Dinh Diem, 121

Vietnam. *See also* North Vietnam; South Vietnam; background on, 79–87; and Cambodia, 143, 147, 149, 164–66, 184, 193; and China, 66–67, 80, 82–83, 91, 103, 105–6, 108–10, 193; culture of, 80–82; geography of, 79–80; history of, 82–86; under Ho Chi Minh, 89–113; independence movement in, 98–104, 120; leadership in, 330–31; map of, 74; under Ngo Dinh Diem, 115–36; partition of, 106–7, 122; Pol Pot and, 192–93; population of, 341; timeline of, 75–77; women in, 3, 82

Vietnam Communist Party, 97

Vietnam War, 41, 79, 85–86, 107, 109–11, 160–62, 181–82

Vijayanagara Empire, 268–69

Voitinsky, Gregory, 29

Wang Hongwen, 43, 59–60

Wavell, Archibald Percival, 292

wayang kulit, 218, 241, 245

Wei Jingsheng, 63

Western Europe: and China, 19; Gandhi on, 284; imperialism of, 2

West New Guinea, 232

Willner, Ann, 335

Wilson, Woodrow, 93, 288, 337

Wiranto, 255

Wolfowitz, Paul, 250

Women: in Cambodia, 145; in China, 3, 21, 37, 39; Gandhi on, 286; Hinduism and, 300; Ho Chi Minh and, 107; in India, 3, 265, 267; in Indonesia, 212; and leadership, 3–4; Mao and, 41–42; Sihanouk and, 153; Sukarno and, 215, 228; in Vietnam, 3, 82

Women's Solidarity Movement, 128–29

World Bank, 4, 246, 256

World War I, 282, 287–88

World War II, 305; Ho Chi Minh in, 100–102; and India, 291–92; in Indonesia, 223–25; and nationalism, 2; and Pol Pot, 177; and Vietnam, 98

Wu, Lily, 30

Xia Bogen, 55

Xie Fuchi, 60

Yang Kaihui, 28–30

Yang Kaiwei, 42

Yang Shangkun, 68

Yao Wenyuan, 60

Ye Jianying, 59

Youth: Mao and, 42–43, 57–58; Pol Pot and, 149, 166, 186, 191

Yuan Shikai, 27

Yufeng, Zhang, 43

Yugoslavia, Pol Pot in, 179

Zhang Qianyuan, 50–51

Zhao Chunqiao, 60

Zhao Ziyang, 52, 64

Zhou Enlai, 28, 44, 56–57, 61, 106, 230, 309; and Deng, 50–51, 54–55, 58–59; and Mao, 39, 43; and Pol Pot, 168; and Sihanouk, 158–59, 165, 167

Zhu De, 30, 37, 56, 59

Zhuo Lin, 53, 55–56, 58

Zoroastrianism, Gandhi and, 283

Zulu Rebellion, 279

About the Authors

Ross Marlay is professor of political science at Arkansas State University.

Clark Neher is professor of political science at Northern Illinois University.

CPSIA information can be obtained
at www.ICGtesting.com
Printed in the USA
LVOW08s1353170117

521247LV00001B/36/P